MANAGERIAL MARKETING
Policies, strategies, and decisions

MANAGERIAL MARKETING

Policies, strategies, and decisions

EUGENE J. KELLEY, Ph. D.
Research Professor of Business Administration
The Pennsylvania State University

WILLIAM LAZER, Ph. D.
Professor of Marketing
Graduate School of Business Administration
Michigan State University

 1973

RICHARD D. IRWIN, INC.   Homewood, Illinois   60430
IRWIN-DORSEY INTERNATIONAL   London, England   WC2H 9NJ
IRWIN-DORSEY LIMITED   Georgetown, Ontario   L7G 4B3

First Printing, April 1973

ISBN 0-256-00270-3
Library of Congress Catalog Card No. 72–92418
Printed in the United States of America

To Dorothy and Joyce

PREFACE

MARKETING is an evolving discipline subject to continued reassessment, redirection, and restructuring. During the 1950s and 1960s, marketing thought underwent a major conceptual revision. A managerial orientation emerged; the marketing management concept with its emphasis on policies, analyses, strategies, and planning was well received in both marketing education and practice. The influence of this period has had an enduring effect evidenced by an internalization of the marketing concept and the managerial approach to marketing in literature and business practice.

New theories and approaches to marketing thought are emerging in the 1970s. Social marketing and related developments have attracted considerable attention from every sector of the economy. Once again some of the fundamental concepts and dimensions of marketing are being challenged, resulting in a further reorientation of marketing thought.

The companion volumes, *Managerial Marketing: Policies, Strategies, and Decisions* and *Social Marketing: Perspectives and Viewpoints*, are designed to reflect these changes. Both books provide a realistic and comprehensive orientation to the study, analysis, and management of change in marketing. Both managerial marketing and social marketing are necessary complements to an understanding of business in contemporary society. The volume, *Managerial Marketing: Policies, Strategies, and Decisions*, is designed to present the most current perspectives on marketing management while highlighting the changing environmental forces influencing and shaping marketing policy and strategy. The companion volume, *Social Marketing: Perspectives and Viewpoints*, treats the evolving societal approach to marketing. The marketing management and social marketing volumes, however, are complete and self-sufficient. They are designed for use as independent learning units or as an integrated package at both undergraduate and graduate levels. When read together, they provide an integrated overview of both social and managerial focuses. Moreover, the contents and material in both volumes have been carefully selected and coordinated to reflect an integrated overview and learning approach to contemporary marketing.

The articles included in *Managerial Marketing: Policies, Strategies, and Decisions* and *Social Marketing: Perspectives and Viewpoints* were selected for their fundamental contributions, forward-looking insights, and effectiveness in stimulating marketing thought and understanding. Several manuscripts were developed especially for these volumes by leading marketing authorities. The coverage of these volumes has been extended to give more emphasis to emerging marketing topics.

Both volumes evolved from previous editions of *Managerial Marketing: Perspectives and Viewpoints*. The first edition, published in 1958, reflected the new managerial directions of that time. The readings in that volume emphasized problem solving and decision making, a managerial focus, and an interdisciplinary approach. Readings in theory were included to challenge, extend, and perhaps excite some students. The materials on managerial marketing and marketing theory emphasized the need of making the innovations and adjustments necessary to adapt the firm to a continuously changing environment.

The second edition of *Managerial Marketing: Perspectives and Viewpoints*, published in 1962, focused on the basic elements of managerial marketing. It included, in addition, an emphasis on quantitative methods and models, consideration of behavioral science-based marketing contributions, attention to the impact of systems thinking on marketing thought and practice, the development of the managerial functions of marketing, and greater stress on the marketing consequences of innovation and change. The majority of the articles appearing in this second edition did not appear in the first edition. Several manuscripts were developed or reworked specifically for the second edition.

Published in 1967, the third edition of *Managerial Marketing: Perspectives and Viewpoints* likewise featured the managerial approach to the study of marketing. The majority of the articles in this edition were also new to the book. Four major topics received greater coverage in this edition. First, the systems approach to the study of marketing was featured. The systems approach was identified as a promising area in the first edition. At the time of the third edition, the systems approach was receiving increasing emphasis. Second, the international dimension of marketing was considered in a separate section containing coverage of both its impact on the multinational firm and its contribution to economic development. Third, greater emphasis was given to the decision-making developments—including mathematical models and computers—and the new technology that were shaping marketing strategy. Fourth, attention was directed to the societal dimensions of marketing— the area of marketing beyond the profit motive. At the time it was stated that the public policy area would be receiving increasing attention by marketing scholars and practitioners. We are now devoting an entire volume to the developing area of social marketing.

We are grateful that the three previous editions were well received and used widely as teaching vehicles in marketing management courses, seminars, and executive development programs. We owe a deep debt of thanks to the teachers and students who used the three editions and whose acceptance made these new volumes possible.

Four major topics are presented in the first new volume, *Managerial Marketing: Policies, Strategies, and Decisions.* First, a systems-oriented conceptual framework for managerial marketing is developed. Second, the expanding area of consumer behavior is appraised in terms of the changing demographics and life styles and values of the consumer market. Third, the systems approach is focused on marketing management activities, both domestic and international. Fourth, the book closes with a series of articles on various elements of the marketing mix, i.e., products and services, distribution and communications.

The managerial orientation of this volume extends and clarifies, rather than alters, the fundamental focus and objectives of previous editions of *Managerial Marketing: Perspectives and Viewpoints.* The selections emphasize the dynamic aspects of marketing management, including developments in marketing theory that underlie and ultimately influence the practice of marketing. Consideration of the behavioral sciences, quantitative-based marketing contributions and the interdisciplinary focus are featured.

Currently, a new stream of marketing thought and action which is characterized by the term "social marketing" is evolving. Social marketing is concerned with the application of marketing knowledge, concepts, and techniques to enhance social as well as economic ends. It is also concerned with analysis of the social consequence of marketing policies, decisions, and activities.

The second new volume, *Social Marketing: Perspectives and Viewpoints,* considers this "new marketing" in its initial stages of development. The articles presented in this volume reflect the newness of the concept. However, this very newness provides an opportunity to students and scholars to develop in these areas. The definitive statement of social marketing is yet to be written. This volume, however, does attempt to position the subject in marketing thought at this point in time.

First, a conceptual framework for social marketing is presented and marketing's social role is appraised. Second, consumers, consumerism, and marketing are discussed from a social perspective. Next, specific marketing activities are appraised from the viewpoints of social responsibility, the quality of life issue, and governmental and business impact on the marketplace. The volume closes with a section illustrating the social interfaces of the marketing mix.

The selections in both volumes are intended to be used in educating students and administrators to analyze problems in an environment of increasing business and social change. The thrust of the selections is toward the frontiers of marketing knowledge. Many of the selections in the books invite careful study and rigorous analysis. However, understanding a discipline which proposes to explain and predict human action in the modern marketplace requires substantial intellectual effort. It requires a desire and capacity to continue learning. It is to those with such desire and capacity that these books are addressed.

It is hoped that students and managers of marketing will form their own framework and priorities concerning the societal implications and responsibilities of marketing. In this way, present and future marketing people can reflect this thinking in those decisions which concern each firms' market opportunities, plans, programs, organizations, and control.

We are greatly indebted to several groups of people in preparing these volumes. We wish to thank the authors and publishers who gave us permission to reproduce their articles and the authors who prepared original contributions for these volumes. Without their cooperation these books would not have been possible. These companion volumes have become a reality because of the complete cooperation of contributors and publishers.

We are grateful to our wives for their encouragement and assistance during the preparation of these volumes. We also wish to acknowledge the assistance of several graduate students for their valuable aid in the technical preparation of the manuscripts. Those graduate students to whom we are particularly indebted include: John Antil, Philip Cooper, Rebecca Gould, James Harvey, Priscilla LaBarbera, Lawrence Lepisto, Scott Luley, Fernando Robles, Ronald Socha, Lewis Tucker, and Richard Whiteley. We also wish to thank Mrs. Brenda N. Grenoble for her many secretarial contributions to the development of the manuscripts.

We shall feel well rewarded if these companion volumes bring further clarity to the marketing management approach and to the study of social marketing, and if they can convey some of the challenge and excitement of marketing to the university classroom and to executive development programs.

April 1973   Eugene J. Kelley
                                                William Lazer

CONTENTS

1 MANAGERIAL MARKETING: A CONCEPTUAL FRAMEWORK

a.

Managerial approach to marketing

MARKETING has undergone continued introspection and change ever since it was recognized as a field central to the study of business administration. The "new marketing" is not yet to the point where it can be readily defined. However, two major themes are seen as predominately influencing contemporary marketing literature, education, and practice. The first of these themes concerns the managerial approach to marketing, while the second is concerned with the social aspect of marketing. Both were described in the January 1973 issue of the *Journal of Marketing*. The managerial theme is described as involving:

. . . the increased sophistication and application of quantitative tools and behavioral theories to marketing problems. Linking behavioral and quantitative approaches provides marketing with potentially rich opportunities for theory development and empirical research. Improved analytical tools and more accurate and current information in greater quantity and quality offer the promise of dramatically improved executive decision making. Continuing innovations in information technology, computer technology, and intelligence systems have permitted the marketing decision-maker to profitably adapt these techniques to the dynamic and competitive business environment of which he is a part. Computerized intelligence systems have also permitted corporate information flows to keep pace with the fast-changing business conditions.

Rapid developments in computers and the techniques of quantitative and behavioral analyses have been fundamental forces for change in marketing. The use of multivariate methods, simulation, and on-line, real-time information systems in marketing continues to grow, changing marketing from a field based on intuition and experience to one firmly grounded on principles, theory, and rigorous scientific approaches.[1]

---

[1] From the Editor, *Journal of Marketing* (January, 1973), p. 2.

The marketing concept underlies the managerial approach. The marketing concept is a customer-oriented philosophy of business which directs corporate resources to profitably meet customer satisfactions. The customer-oriented philosophy of business was first recognized as coming into existence during the 1930s. While it is continually being investigated and refined, it is basically concerned with the knowledge of who buys a company's product, for what reason, and where and how it is purchased.

The social aspect of marketing is another contemporary theme in debate. The new needs and aspirations of increasingly concerned and educated publics challenge marketing to incorporate the dimensions of social values and social responsibilities in marketing theory and practice. These publics' growing concern with social values and social responsibilities has added a more distinct societal dimension to the marketing concept. The need for a societal orientation in the solution of marketing problems is a direct result of a recognized need for developing a feeling of social sensitivity that is, and was seen as, lacking in many managerial decisions.

Marketing is becoming more involved with social and environmental issues. Marketing emphasis is no longer solely on the corporate enterprise; issues of consumerism, government regulation, and ethics have become very relevant to all concerned with marketing. Scholars and practitioners alike consider social marketing as an area relevant to their current professional development.
. . . The force of social value changes may be the most powerful contemporary influence on marketing and the management of change in marketing. In essence, marketing is being challenged to apply its "new technology" to issues of interest to society. . . .[2]

The development of social concerns in the marketing concept is one of the dimensions of broader applications in marketing. Scholars and marketers are now extending their considerations beyond business to nonbusiness applications. Marketing is evolving beyond its traditional environment and is now in the process of entering a new and expanded one. Thus, the dimensions and concept of marketing are becoming deeper and broader than ever before.

Both managerial and social marketing are subparts of the total marketing concept. Together, managerial and social marketing principles function to assist marketers with the implementation of the marketing concept and the fundamentals of marketing decisions. The present volume, *Managerial Marketing: Policies, Strategies, and Decisions* provides the reader with a comprehensive, systematic collection of readings organized around the managerial theme. Its companion volume, *Social Marketing: Perspectives and Viewpoints,* is designed to fulfill a similar objective, with readings organized around the social theme. Both volumes, then, reflect the meaning of contemporary marketing.

Both managerial and social marketing are interrelated; there is a need for the intermeshing of the micro and macro dimensions of marketing.

---

[2] From the Editor, *Journal of Marketing* (January 1973), p. 2.

Formulation of marketing policies, plans, programs, and decisions cannot be accomplished without consideration of the external, the macro, and the micro point of view.

The overall theme of the following discussion is that profitable solutions to marketing problems can be found only if the significance of environmental change on the firm and its customer is accepted as the foundation for planning. This volume is designed to assist readers to achieve a deeper understanding of how change influences marketing management decision making.

This chapter discusses the essential elements of the managerial approach to marketing, the marketing concept, and the marketing mix. Throughout the discussion, a systems approach to the management of change is utilized, and emphasis is placed on the interrelationships among the variables that confront the marketing manager.

Marketers and the management of change

An accelerating rate of change is a dominant characteristic of the environment in which marketing management operates. Peter Drucker has pointed out that today's society is characterized by "discontinuities," or breaks with the past, which are changing the structure and meaning of economics, politics, and technology.[3] Today, changes in consumer attitudes, values, and needs are providing new marketing challenges and opportunities. To make progress, marketing managers must learn from the past. "Yet as we learn from and progress beyond the past, we run the risk of employing obsolete dogmas for new times. The issue is not whether knowledge and know-how are transferable. It is whether they are applicable."[4]

The effect of this reflection of a dynamic business and social environment is the creation of a variety of problems requiring decisions involving a high degree of uncertainty and risk. Successful operation under these conditions necessitates that the marketing manager assume a position of dual responsibility. This duality can be defined as involving:

1. Monitoring, anticipating, and adapting to environmental change that affects the short-run viability of the existing product mix.
2. Anticipation, implementation, and capitalization of opportunities to develop products and services that have a potential value in the future environment.

Even when marketing management has successfully recognized change, adaptation to change is not a simple task. The large scale and complexity of most corporate systems restrict their flexibility and often hinder adjust-

---

[3] Peter F. Drucker, *The Age of Discontinuity: Guidelines to Our Changing Society* (New York: Harper & Row, 1968), p. 394.

[4] T. Levitt, "The New Markets—Think Before You Leap," *Harvard Business Review* (May–June 1969), p. 67.

ment efforts. However, the way in which firms adapt to environmental change is now of crucial importance. In marketing " . . . meeting competition has long been the primary yardstick which we have used for measuring our performance. But today, *how* we meet competition is under the careful scrutiny of many people. . . ." [5]

Corporate management's most basic function is to strive for balance between the enterprise system and its external environment. This interface encompasses product and service offerings on the one hand, purchase and use on the other. The interaction between the firm and consumers (all public, not just customers) is a process that must be delicately maintained in order that both sectors can keep as close to equilibrium as possible.

In total, then, the firm must come face to face with its environment, recognizing the need to be flexible enough to overcome a multitude of problems and take advantage of evolving opportunities.

Contemporary marketing

Contemporary marketing not only encompasses, but also integrates the managerial orientation and social orientation to marketing thought and practice. Figures 1A–1 to 1A–4 illustrate the multiple elements the business firm must contend with; they also reflect the meaning of contemporary marketing. These illustrations provide a basis for various areas of discussion throughout both volumes. Figure 1A–1 illustrates the interaction of the managerial marketing dimension and the social marketing dimension as both influence the decision-making process in marketing.

The many forces of the external environment that confront a business enterprise are listed in Figure 1A–2.

The two major contemporary approaches to marketing, the managerial and social orientations, are presented in Figure 1A–3. The shaded area indicates the aspects of the managerial orientation discussed in this volume.

The mutually interdependent relationship between the marketing concept, the profit concept, and the system concept is indicated in Figure 1A–4. Notic that it is not until all three elements. are combined that the managerial approach is operational.

THE MARKETING CONCEPT: HISTORICAL AND CONCEPTUAL BASES

A consumer orientation is the central core of the marketing concept. Only since the 1950s has the marketing concept received widespread atten-

---

[5] E. B. Weiss, "Pious Posturing—Marketing's Most Dangerous Posture," *Advertising Age* (May 29, 1967), p. 78.

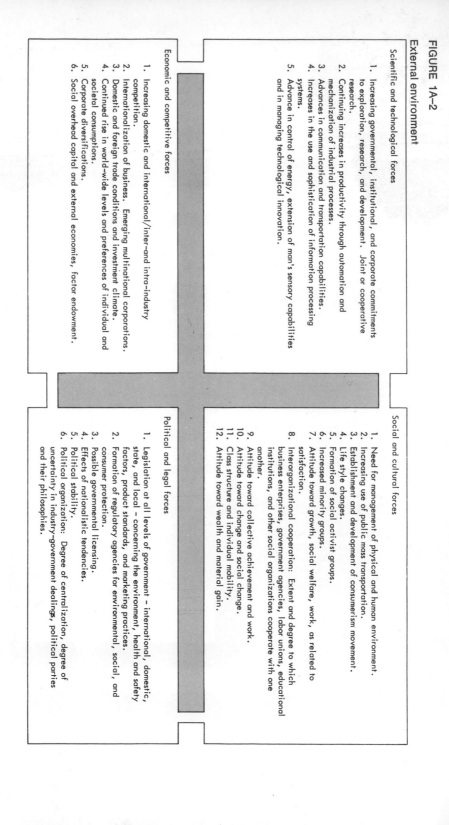

Scientific and technological forces

1. Increasing governmental, institutional, and corporate commitments to exploration, research, and development. Joint or cooperative research.

2. Continuing increases in productivity through automation and mechanization of industrial processes.

3. Advances in communication and transportation capabilities.

4. Increases in the use and sophistication of information processing systems.

5. Advance in control of energy, extension of man's sensory capabilities and in managing technological innovation.

Economic and competitive forces

1. Increasing domestic and international/inter-and intra-industry competition.

2. Internationalization of business. Emerging multinational corporations.

3. Domestic and foreign trade conditions and investment climate.

4. Continued rise in world-wide levels and preferences of individual and societal consumptions.

5. Corporate diversifications.

6. Social overhead capital and external economies, factor endowment.

Social and cultural forces

1. Need for management of physical and human environment.

2. Increasing use of public mass transportation.

3. Establishment and development of consumerism movement.

4. Life style changes.

5. Formation of social activist groups.

6. Increased minority groups.

7. Attitude toward growth, social welfare, work, as related to satisfaction.

8. Interorganizational cooperation: Extent and degree to which business enterprises, government agencies, labor unions, educational institutions, and other social organizations cooperate with one another.

9. Attitude toward collective achievement and work.

10. Attitude toward change and social change.

11. Class structure and individual mobility.

12. Attitude toward wealth and material gain.

Political and legal forces

1. Legislation at all levels of government – international, domestic, state, and local – concerning the environment, health and safety factors, product standards, and marketing practices.

2. Formation of regulatory agencies for environmental, social, and consumer protection.

3. Possible governmental licensing.

4. Effects of nationalistic tendencies.

5. Political stability.

6. Political organization: Degree of centralization, degree of uncertainty in industry–government dealings, political parties and their philosophies.

FIGURE 1A–3

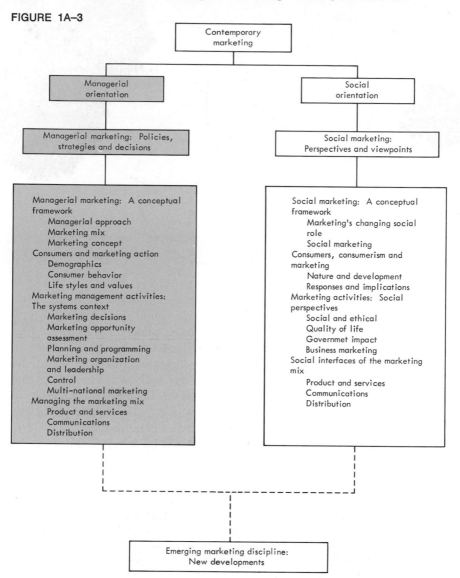

tion in marketing literature.[6] However, despite its recent popularity, implementation of the marketing concept is often incomplete or nonexistent in many business firms.

---

[6] F. J. Borch, "The Marketing Philosophy as a Way of Business Life" in *Marketing Series No. 99* (New York: American Management Association, 1957), pp. 193–95; J. B. McKitterick, "What is the Marketing Management Concept?" in *The Frontiers of Marketing Thought and Science*, F. M. Bass (ed.) (Chicago, Ill.: American Marketing Association, Winter, 1957).

FIGURE 1A–4

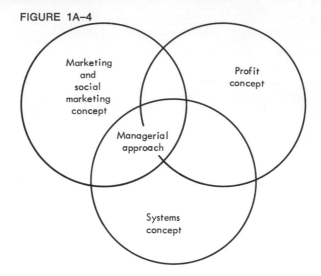

Authors have redefined the marketing concept,[7] broadened it,[8] and even labeled it differently.[9] There have been philosophical as well as operational definitions of the term. Indeed, there is no accepted definition. However, "Common to all views is this important thought: while the movement toward the new theory or concept will be a function of the type of industry, the character and vision of top management, the nature of the product, and other factors—the movement is inevitable. Marketing with its many ramifications must start with the consumer." [10]

The centrality of the consumer was discussed by Adam Smith when he wrote:

Consumption is the sole end and purpose of all production; and the interest of the producer ought to be attended to, only so far as it may be necessary for promoting that of the consumer. The maxim is so perfectly self-evident, that it would be absurd to attempt to prove it. But in the mercantile system, the interest of the consumer is almost constantly sacrificed to that of the producer; and it seems to consider production, and not consumption, as the ultimate end and object of all industry and commerce.[11]

[7] M. I. Bell and C. W. Emory, "The Faultering Marketing Concept," *Journal of Marketing* (October 1971), pp. 37–42.

[8] P. Kotler and S. J. Levy, "Broadening the Concept of Marketing," *Journal of Marketing* (January 1969), pp. 10–15.

[9] L. M. Dawson, "The Human Concept: New Philosophy for Business," *Business Horizons* (December 1969), pp. 29–38.

[10] J. Douglas, "A Comparison of Management Theory Y with the Marketing Concept," in J. B. Kernan and M. S. Sommers, *Perspectives in Marketing Theory* (New York: Appleton-Century-Crofts, 1968), p. 256.

[11] Adam Smith, An Inquiry into the Nature and Causes of the Wealth of Nations, 1776 (New York: Modern Library, 1937).

Much can be gained in developing an understanding and appreciation of contemporary marketing by taking a historical perspective of the development of marketing thought. During the 1930s, the sales orientation emerged. The earlier emphasis on production shifted to distribution, although much importance was still placed on the production system. Nonetheless, marketing was viewed only as a selling function. The channels of distribution were recognized as being key elements in selling the company's products. Personal selling and advertising were also viewed as other important activities.

In the last two decades, the consumer orientation of marketing has become the central core of the marketing concept. This consumer orientation has been recognized as an important influence on product design, development, and production. Thus, its influence began to direct corporate activity. The consumer orientation was supported by the control function in marketing, which systematically integrates the marketing concept with the effort of the firm. Such a managerial-systems approach to marketing has been utilized in policy making and operations and used to define the total corporate activities from a marketing perspective. This thereby allowed an integration of the marketing, profit, and systems concepts in the implementation of decisions.

In the 1970s, a further development of the marketing concept has been taking place. This involves a social orientation to marketing. Under such an orientation, the primary problem of business becomes the extension of the customer-satisfaction philosophy to more aggregate and abstract levels of social and environmental needs. The environment will be viewed in terms of social systems. Furthermore, a new emphasis on cultural, social, and human values by both business and consumers will alter the relationship between business and the consumer. Production design, promotion, and distribution will also be considered under the constraints of social dimensions. All these changes will place a greater responsibility on both producers and consumers. Thus, marketers become obliged to design safer and more useful products, while consumers will have the responsibility of carefully assessing products that fail to benefit the long run welfare of society.

Thus, as time passes, the definition, roles, and functions of marketing evolve.

Figure 1A–5 depicts the development of the marketing concept over time; that is, firms, even today, tend to go through these various stages of marketing development. At any given time, a firm should be able to locate its position on this continuum and should be continually concerned with the attainment of the next stage. The successful firm of tomorrow will be operating at the societal orientation level; firms at lower levels will experience societal pressures which may jeopardize their existence.

Adherence to the marketing concept can often cause very dramatic internal changes within a company. In response to consumer wants and

FIGURE 1A–5

Development of the marketing concept

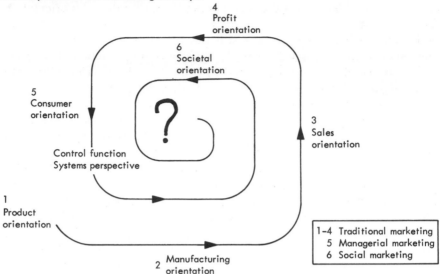

needs, not only are products and entire product lines changed, but the corporate mission and objectives are frequently modified. One example is characterized by Black and Decker, a manufacturer of portable tools, who, in the late 1950s, decided to redefine its corporate mission to be a manufacturer of labor-saving devices. "Every time the cost of labor is increased, the base of the power-tool market is broadened." [12] This redefinition of the company's product line has made Black and Decker a most successful corporation today.

Planned innovation, which involves adjusting to the new tactics of competitors and providing creative counterinnovations, is basic to the modern marketing concept. It has become a necessary part of corporate survival and growth. Innovation through programmed research and development is now a standard competitive weapon.

MARKETING CONCEPT BROADENED

One of the most important current questions in marketing concerns the extent to which marketing principles can be applied to nonbusiness activities. Kotler and Levy [13] believe that the marketing concept can be applied to many nonbusiness organizations and activities. These authors feel that nonbusiness organizations have customers and products just as business

---

[12] "At the Top and Busy Climbing," *Business Week* (November 21, 1964), p. 96.

[13] P. Kotler and S. J. Levy, "Broadening the Concept of Marketing," *Journal of Marketing* (January 1969), pp. 10–15.

organizations do; however, they are more generically defined. For this reason, the marketing concept may be applied to such nonbusiness organizations in much the same way as currently applied to business organizations. Marketing in this sense may be viewed as "consumer satisfaction engineering."

Kotler and Levy define outputs as physical products, services, persons, organizations, and ideas. This generic definition permits the product to take many forms. If our objective, as marketers, is to satisfy consumer needs, why must the products which satisfy those needs be limited to commercial goods and services only? An expanded definition of "product" should enable marketers, both in business and outside, to better satisfy a wide and expanding range of consumer needs. "The choice facing those who manage nonbusiness organizations is not whether to market or not to market, for no organization can avoid marketing. The choice is whether to do it well or poorly, and on this necessity the case for organizational marketing is basically founded." [14]

Lazer believes that "what is required is a broader perception and definition of marketing than has hitherto been the case—one that recognizes marketing's societal dimensions and perceives of marketing as more than just a technology of the firm. . . . For marketing cannot insulate itself from societal responsibilities and problems that do not bear immediately on profit." [15]

Kotler and Levy first advanced the proposal that marketing is relevant to all organizations having customer groups in the January 1969 issue of the *Journal of Marketing*. That article stimulated considerable discussion about the role of marketing. In another article published in 1972, they extended their analysis. They stated that their original broadening proposal should be broadened still further to include the transactions between an organization and *all* of its publics. This important article is included in this book. It offers the broadest view of marketing yet advanced—that of generic marketing—in which marketing is viewed in terms of function rather than structure; and it posits that marketing takes place in a great number of situations, including political campaigning, church membership drives, and lobbying.

How far can the marketing concept be broadened? The answer is necessarily general. "Generic marketing is a philosophy available to all organizations facing problems of market response." [16] Limits to the application of the marketing concept to nonbusiness organizations will be recognized only as these applications are made, fail, and are reported in the literature. Business and academic efforts of the future will enable realization of the full potential of a broadened marketing concept.

---

[14] Ibid., p. 15.

[15] W. Lazer, "Marketing's Changing Social Relationships," *Journal of Marketing* (January 1969), p. 5–9.

[16] P. Kotler, "A Generic Concept of Marketing," *Journal of Marketing* (April 1972), pp. 46–64.

The Social-marketing concept

A companion volume, *Social Marketing: Perspectives and Viewpoints,* covers the development of the social marketing concept. Similar to the managerial marketing concept, social marketing deals with the achievement of a higher level of consumer welfare. At the macro level, consumers express collective needs implicitly or explicitly that are important to society as a whole. The corporate enterprise system has an added responsibility, *and opportunity,* to satisfy these higher levels of need, as expressed by the collective membership of consumer-citizens. The trend towards the broadening of the (managerial) marketing concept to include social marketing, deserves thorough consideration by marketing decision makers.

Adherence to the social marketing approach suggests that it is *not* sufficient merely to satisfy personal consumer needs, especially if the particular product is detrimental to societal or environmental well-being. Corporate management must seriously consider the effects of its product offerings on society. This responsibility can be used to advantage in exploring and capitalizing on new and profitable market opportunities. The trend toward a sociomarketing orientation has already created new market opportunities in such areas as the alleviation of air, water, and noise pollution.

Though this new view of marketing is just beginning to take form, the following six major elements provide a conceptual framework for viewing this merging concept.[17]

1. *The mission of the business is defined in social system terms of long-run profitable service to the consumer-citizen.* Sociomarketing issues are seen as critical and urgent, impacting not only on profits but also being relevant to the survival of the enterprise in society.

2. *The firm recognizes that service to the consumer-citizen requires fulfilling societal and environmental concerns as well as the satisfaction of traditional economic goods and services.* Therefore, sociomarketing programs are evaluated and tested in terms of societal impact as well as traditional balance sheets and profit-and-loss statements.

3. *Products are defined as social outputs, as well as economic goods.* Analysis of sociomarketing product policies considers the social effects— on the individuals within the corporate system, on larger systems within which the firm operates, and on customers. The firm is aware of its role as a molder of social values for both employees and consumer-citizens.

4. *Profit and cost concepts are recognized in their full social as well as economic complexity.* Sociomarketing firms are concerned with redefining profit and costs to reflect contemporary values and needs. For example, the concept of "social profit" might provide for more efficient resource

---

[17] Eugene J. Kelley, Socio-Marketing and Marketing Education, *Southern Journal of Business,* Vol. 7 (May 1972), pp. 11–19.

management and rehabilitation over the long run, instead of simply being a monetary sum or accounting figure accumulated during the fiscal year.

5. *Organizational commitment to sociomarketing is reflected in prioritized action programs in each area of sociomarketing performance.* A company cannot do everything at once and still stay in business. Priorities are required.

6. *The firm acknowledges that its sociomarketing performance is now, or will be, evaluated by external groups.* Examples include Nader, the Council on Economic Priorities, student groups, and governmental agencies. Sociomarketing firms are auditing their societal as well as economic performance, partly in anticipation of the time when such audits may be legislatively mandated.

b.

Implementing the marketing concept*

Eugene J. Kelley † and Edward J. Kane ‡

THE PRACTICAL ASPECTS of implementing the marketing concept are emphasized in this section. A framework is provided for managing the marketing concept in business organizations. The marketing concept is treated as the key to disciplined planning and the management of change in today's increasingly competitive environment.

The marketing concept is a customer-oriented philosophy of business which focuses all corporate resources on the profitable production of customer satisfactions. Companies operating under the marketing concept focus marketing resources and effort and other major corporate departments on objectives of market and consumer satisfaction. The marketing concept is simple in principle but complex in implementation. The conceptual and philosophical bases of the marketing concept are often misunderstood by management; however, implementing the concept through the marketing management approach into corporate decision making is a basic problem of corporate management.

The starting point for an organization operating under the marketing concept is to define its corporate mission in terms of customer satisfaction and of the marketplace. Satisfaction of consumer needs and excellence of service hold a top-priority position in such a company. Taking advantage of its natural or developed capabilities, the organization operating under the marketing concept anticipates change and disciplines itself to the management of that change.

* Commissioned contribution.
† Pennsylvania State University.
‡ International Business Machines Corporation.

16

The marketing concept is not new to business, as the experience of Sears, Roebuck suggests:

Sears, Roebuck and Company has excelled in the management of change in distribution methods in the United States. It pioneered the idea of mass merchandising by mail, then successfully developed itself as a large chain store operation. It was one of the first companies to locate its retail stores in suburban areas. The giant retailer is continuing to manage change by altering its image from a seller of private brands to a merchandiser of name brands, for example, DieHard batteries and Steel-Belted Radial tires. Sears recognized the consumer's desire for name-brand merchandise, and adapted its own wide distribution network to take advantage of TV advertising on their name-brand products.

All successful businesses follow the path of customer orientation to some extent. The new element is the integrated application of the marketing concept in companies that have grown in size beyond the point where the decision makers can achieve first-hand knowledge of consumer needs. This application is also new in companies whose traditional products no longer fulfill marketing needs and who define the business in market-relevant terms of customer needs and satisfactions, rather than in product or industry terms; for example, entertainment, not movies; transportation, not railroads; problem solving, not computers. No successful company can continue to be successful if it does not meet the needs of its customers nor be aware of changes in the marketplace.

Marketing management

A system is needed to effect this new emphasis in corporate decision making. Conscious corporate effort is required to translate the theory into practice. Implementation may be complex enough to incorporate a market research department with the services of a battery of consultants and service companies. Or, it may be as simple as the combination of a marketing manager with vision and a staff with authority to manage the changes that are occurring. This is the essence of marketing management; it requires new thinking, new skills, and often new organization to perform the activities identified in Figure 1B–1.

Figure 1B–1 identifies typical marketing management activities, grouped by the functions of planning, direction, and control.

Executives employing the marketing concept are environmentalists. They are dedicated first to identifying the role of the organization in the environment and then to identifying the specific customer set. These tasks lead to setting goals about the relationships that will be established between the organization and its customers. Of particular importance is the conscious selection of customer needs to be fulfilled by the organization. The services and support to be provided, and the policies and practices to be established, are key decisions which must be made by marketing executives early in the product design and development process.

FIGURE 1B–1

Marketing management activities

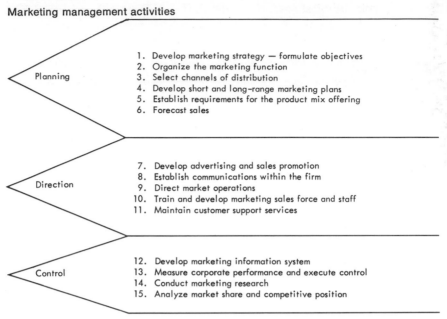

The customer orientation must be supported by a total marketing effort. This is generated with the objective of maximizing customer satisfactions within the profit objectives established for the company. In this way, company objectives are coordinated with the marketing concept philosophy.

Magic Chef, Incorporated, a manufacturer of stores and home appliances, is a small firm operating against giant companies in a highly competitive industry. This manufacturer is almost insignificant when compared with a company such as General Electric; however, Magic Chef has shown skill in taking advantage of market opportunities. The company has 35 percent of the market for mobile home stoves, and in the last 10 years its revenue has grown fivefold. Even more importantly, earnings have increased geometrically. Success in Magic Chef's case has been a matter of sound management decisions, enabling the company to capitalize on profitable market opportunities.

Social responsibility of marketing management

The solution of certain societal problems may constitute a key objective for the organization operating under the marketing concept. This objective does not arise from basic altruism, although some companies may strongly hold that objective, but because many companies understand that serving their customers' needs not only as individuals, or firms, but as consumer-citizens, will ultimately serve the corporation's best interests. Social responsibility should be particularly evident in large companies that have a broad base of users and enough resources to make a major impact on social problems. Marketing management in companies operating under the marketing concept must integrate three areas of organizational concern:

1. Customer satisfaction.
2. Company profit.
3. Social responsibility.

The marketing concept, therefore, may be defined as a customer-focused orientation that guides all business functions within the organization toward the profitable achievement of corporate objectives through satisfaction of the economic and social needs of the consumer-citizen.

THE MARKETING CONCEPT CYCLE

Management of change

If the activities identified in Figure 1B–1 are to be meaningful, the company must be:

1. Environmentally oriented.
2. An anticipator of future trends and changes.
3. Organizationally flexible enough to change.
4. A critical and systematical auditor of all policies and practices relating to the consumer.

Today, proper implementation of the marketing concept remains more of a goal than a reality. For this reason, the key question becomes: How can the marketing concept be applied? In other words, how can marketing management more effectively achieve the consumer-satisfaction objectives of the firm?

Market-related activities of management must be accompanied by an attitude which is continuously aware of change and the opportunity it creates. For example, many companies today envision a requirement for change which has led companies to product-line diversification of a general and dramatic nature. The R. J. Reynolds Company and other tobacco companies have diversified into the food industry. These activities, along with the entry of Magnavox into furniture and cable television (CATV), are examples of diversification into nontraditional lines. Depending on many of their existing capabilities, these companies continue to use their established channels of distribution. Kimberly Clark's entry into disposable diapers and paper towels was accompanied by a move out of several traditional areas, such as the shutdown of their "slick" paper (magazine) operations.

Changes occur primarily in two ways: environmentally and technically. The company employing the marketing concept is characterized by a conscious effort to recognize and capitalize on *both* types of change. Anticipating the direction and timing of these changes provides the corporation with a valuable competitive edge in the marketplace. Imbued with this attitude, the organization may apply the marketing concept in many different ways; however, some activities should be common to all applications. Figure 1B–2 graphically shows the eight stages of activities, action programs, and methods that are part of any marketing concept implementation program.

Critical aspects of implementing the marketing concept in an organization are discussed below.

1. *Focus on the marketplace environment.* The company operating under the marketing concept must focus on the environment in which it operates, for this is where the opportunities for consumer satisfaction are found. Before establishing its major objectives, the company must carefully evaluate the economic condition of the world, the country, and its own industry. Basic strategies must be determined and objectives set for the planned period. Objectives and strategies are used to establish a standard against which marketing results may be evaluated. This actual-versus-expected comparison may suggest modifications in the current corporate strategy.

Then, general economic indicators may be used to shape the boundaries of strategy and determine rough target objectives. These targets must be sharpened and modified through many iterations. Modifiers include: competitive analysis, evaluation of existing product lines, an audit of support services, and the identification of customer needs. Analytic tools are also a necessity. They may include everything from a corporate economics department and its computer models to a subscription to the most prominent industry trade papers. The essential point is that these factors be evaluated in a comprehensive approach aimed at identifying corporate opportunities. Only then can realistic objectives be set.

2. *Determine the nature of the company's business.* Little needs to be said about the realities of marketing myopia, that is, about the many companies that have failed to realize what business they were in. The task here is essentially the setting of corporate strategic objectives and the challenge of achieving them. These strategic objectives must be based on realistic information about the product and marketplace. Whatever method is used, the result should be a documented, long-range strategy that clearly communicates the agreed-upon corporate objectives. Successful implementation of the marketing concept demands commitment, and good management requires documentation. The strategic plan must be comprehensive and explicity expressed in writing to ensure that:

FIGURE 1B–2

Applying the marketing concept

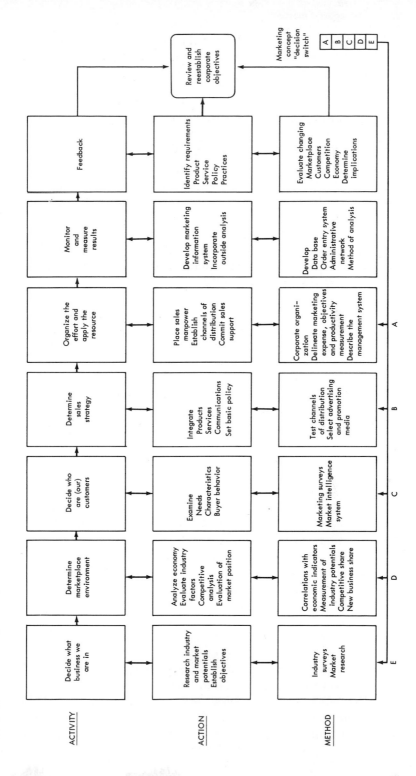

1. The plan has been clearly and thoroughly thought out and analyzed.
2. The plan becomes a working document that has been developed and agreed upon by those who will implement it.

For the larger company, support for the long-range strategy must be found in both external and internal industry surveys and market research reports.

3. *Identify the customer set.*   The third phase of activity in the application of the marketing concept is closely allied to the first two. In studying the marketplace environment, an attempt was made to identify basic customer needs. In defining the company's business, the customer set was further narrowed. Now, the task is to identify the product line to be developed or modified. Determination of the action to be taken will demand a detailed examination of the characteristics, needs, and buyer behavior of the selected customer set. Definition of the consumer set must be very current; therefore, this phase of the marketing concept cycle must be reviewed periodically.

There are many influences on the customer. He is not only a customer for our company's product but also for those of our competitors and for other product lines. He is influenced by socioeconomic forces and changes in life style. Modern market research must assist us in identifying these dynamic trends. An aware, well-disciplined sales force will also be of assistance in identifying customer requirements. The area that requires the greatest effort is that of anticipating new consumer needs and innovating the products to satisfy them. As stated before, change occurs through technological discovery and social or environmental change. For this reason, a market intelligence system must account for both these forces. The company operating under the marketing concept must be very sensitive to the marketplace in order to detect changing attitudes and new demands. This feedback process should be the primary basis on which new products and services are developed. The organization must also recognize that some wants and desires may not manifest themselves until new products or technologies are made available. For example, it is questionable whether the need for vast amounts of additional information was recognized prior to the invention of the electronic computer.

It is important to search for new opportunities from advanced technological efforts and from changing social values of the marketplace. A market intelligence system for any given company will vary in structure and complexity. However, most will combine marketplace requirements by integrating the output from development research for the introduction of new products and the modification of existing ones.

4. *Determine product, sales, and distribution strategy.*   Entry into phase four marks the mainstream of the marketing concept cycle. Each planning period will necessitate an in-depth analysis of company plans, strategies, and objectives. Depending on where in the cycle the organiza-

tion finds itself, it may be introducing new products and/or modifying existing ones. Long-range strategies and plans should be updated frequently and periodically. Marketing plans should specify sales by territory and reflect the expectations from promotional efforts and sales campaigns.

Specific elements of the product, sales, and distribution strategy which relate to the achievement of marketing objectives are:

1. Basic policy and practices—terms and conditions, accounts receivable.
2. Product line—test marketing new products.
3. Channels of distribution—dealers, wholesalers.
4. Anticipated competitive actions and counterstrategies.
5. Inventory management.
6. Pricing strategy.
7. Promotion and advertising.
8. Maintenance and service.

5. *Organize the effort and apply resources.* This fifth phase is vital to the achievement of marketing objectives. It incorporates research, planning, organization, and the strengths and weaknesses of personnel in determining the structure and function of the organization.

Good management principles must be applied in directing the marketing organization. Once the product line has been established along with the marketing plan, much needs to be done to direct the sales force toward achieving the objectives. The sales force must be recruited, selected, trained, and organized for maximum field coverage, in order to realize territory potential and achieve revenue and profit objectives.

A highly motivated field force is needed to achieve the optimistic results for which the executive employing the marketing concept strives. Depending on the company and the industry, salesmen will come from varied backgrounds, will have different amounts of experience, and will have responsibility for many different job duties. Such a situation makes it difficult to generalize exactly what constitutes prime sales motivation. There are, however, three important motivating factors for most sales jobs: money, recognition, and advancement. The manager operating under the marketing concept must use all of them.

Historically, money has been recognized as the key motivating factor for salesmen. Incentive compensation plans have been popular for just this reason; however, they require frequent evaluation to keep them consistent with company objectives. This is particularly true in a company which operates in fast-changing market environments, such as those for technological instruments and data processing equipment. In these cases, there may be many incentive plans within each individual sales force.

Recognition of the individual is a powerful motivating force and should not be underestimated by the executive using the marketing concept. Top-flight salesmen are often the aggressive individual performers who need and want to be recognized as leaders.

Advancement may or may not be a prime motivator, depending on the company's hiring policy and career-planning program. The IBM Corporation, for example, has tried in the past to hire computer salesmen whose primary interest was to become top executives. The salesmen are encouraged to think in terms of advancement and to strive for promotion out of the sales ranks as quickly as possible. Companies that are expanding less rapidly may have a different hiring policy. Such a company may wish to hire men who are interested in selling as a career. In each case, the company policy toward hiring should directly reflect the corporate objectives.

Employee motivation is an important key to success and should, therefore, occupy a good part of an effective manager's time. The use of management specialists can be very helpful in developing the basic plan and in providing maximum experience within a short time.

6. *Monitor and measure the results.*   The effective marketing manager must periodically evaluate the progress his organization is making toward the achievement of its objectives. He must have relevant information about his operations—too much data can be confusing and stifling, and incomplete data can be deceiving. Both situations result in poor decision making. A marketing manager needs information that is timely, allowing him to identify the problem, formulate corrective alternatives, and choose a course of action.

Control can be achieved through data-processing techniques. Display terminals may be installed to provide spontaneous information about orders and inventories. The question the marketing manager must answer is, "How much sophistication is needed?" An answer to this question requires considerable knowledge about the company's operations and market. This information must be timely enough to enable the marketing manager to take corrective action.

The marketing manager must be involved in the development of the system, so that the results can be measured against planned objectives on a periodic basis. Data sources, such as order entry, administrative reporting, and inventory analysis, must be identified and integrated into the system to insure complete analysis of the various markets. Techniques of communicating the information must be developed. A simple form letter or handwritten report will serve to inform the marketing manager about what product, what territory, or what class of customer is involved in his problem. Again, his purpose is to identify problem areas and take corrective action.

Some marketing functions are not easily measured. Promotional and market development may well require marketing research to provide adequate analysis. If the marketing manager's system is sophisticated, he may utilize a model with which to simulate alternatives, thereby determining their impact before he commits himself and his company resources. In any case, effective marketing management must incorporate a control system capable of monitoring the achieved results and measuring them against those forecast. This process allows the marketing manager to concentrate his attention and effort on the exceptions, which are usually problem areas.

7. *Establish feedback system.* The final test for an organization using the marketing concept is to determine how well its products and services have been accepted in the marketplace, and whether it has achieved its corporate objectives. The organization must depend on its marketing intelligence system to provide information on changes in the marketplace and on the acceptance of its products by customers within each of the various markets. These data are necessary to properly evaluate changes in the needs and wants of customers. Corporate management must evaluate how these needs translate into product requirements by analyzing competitive actions and reactions and interpreting their impact on the company's marketing strategy. Sales force feedback, customer panels, market surveys, and advertising tests must all be used to obtain the information needed to modify mathematical models of the business system. Only in this way can the organization remain consistent with the environment, yet sensitive to changes in it. However used, and through whatever vehicles, a system of feedback and forecast must be established as an integral part of the marketing concept cycle.

Summary

The key point to remember in applying the marketing concept is that the activities are cyclical and that the organization cannot afford to be static. The corporation must be dynamic, continually updating and reevaluating its position in relation to the industry, the economy, and its customers. The marketing manager must, therefore, be dedicated to the management of change and must adapt accordingly. A system must be developed which helps the marketing manager incorporate the marketing concept into his job today and assists him in predicting tomorrow's changes.

IMPLICATIONS

For the marketing concept company, the implications of the preceding discussion may be summarized as follows:

1. *Acceptance of change and environmental orientation.* Organization personnel must be trained and motivated to manage change in order to adjust to the accelerating rate of environmental change being imposed on all organizations. Every organization has traditions and policies that have stood through the years. The marketing concept, with its focus on

changing environmental conditions, customer needs, and competitive strategies, mandates that all processes and activities of the company be subject to systematic analysis and reexamination.

2. *The company determines its survival potential through focusing on consumer needs.* The focus on consumer needs is central to all marketing decisions in particular and to all business functions in general. Demographic, sociographic, and psychographic analysis of both present and potential customers is necessary if the company is to be responsive to consumer demands.

3. *The importance of disciplined planning.* Not only must marketing activity be planned, but the plan must be integrated and updated with the execution of marketing functions. The plan must be an active description of the marketing action that is taking place.

4. *Use of a market intelligence system.* A marketing intelligence system must provide current customer and competitive information that the company can use in planning its effort to satisfy marketplace requirements.

5. *Product planning and development.* Data from the marketing intelligence system is integrated with internal information inputs, such as product and technological developments, and serves to modify the basic strategy. In this way, the company manages internal, as well as environmental change.

6. *Control.* It is essential that an effective control system be designed and established to monitor and measure the progress that the organization is making toward achievement of its objectives. It must focus attention on problem exceptions, rather than on corporate activity that is effectively achieving the objectives as planned.

7. *Social responsibility.* The organization operating under the marketing concept must recognize that service to its customers involves a much broader objective than merely satisfying economic desires. The corporation has a responsibility to satisfy the social needs of all consumers, not just their own customers. Marketing objectives should be established with consideration for their impact on social problems. Objectives and programs designed under a marketing concept orientation must satisfy consumer needs, while remaining consistent with the long-run profit objectives of the firm.

C.

The concept of the marketing mix*

William Lazer †, James D. Culley †, and Thomas A. Staudt ‡

UTILIZING the systems perspective, the authors discuss a logical framework for understanding the character and role of the firm's marketing mix. They offer an orientation, a description, and guidelines for developing an effective mix. The elements of a firm's marketing mix are identified and synthesized into a perspective helpful for today's marketing executive.

The creation of market offerings, a key responsibility of marketing executives, involves both the formulation and the implementation of basic marketing strategies. Marketing executives, in developing market offerings, focus upon two types of variables which affect marketing success—those controlled by the firm and those outside the firm's influence. The meaningful organization of the controllable variables which directly influence customer and consumer transactions is generally called the firm's marketing mix. Success as a marketer depends heavily on an understanding of the forces of the marketplace and skill in devising a marketing mix that adjusts profitably to them.

ORIGIN OF THE MARKETING MIX

The origination of the term *marketing mix* is associated with Professors James W. Culliton and Neil H. Borden. In a 1948 Harvard research bulletin, Professor Culliton described the business executive as: "A 'decider,'

---

* Commissioned contribution.
† Both of Michigan State University.
‡ General Motors Corporation.

an 'artist'—a 'mixer of ingredients' who sometimes follows a recipe prepared by others, sometimes prepares his own recipe as he goes along,
sometimes adapts a recipe to the ingredients immediately available, and
sometimes experiments with or develops ingredients no one else has yet
tried." [1] This description of a marketing executive as a "mixer of ingredients" appealed to Professor Borden, who soon began to use the term
"marketing mix" to describe the results.[2]

There is greater significance to the idea of a marketing mix, however,
than the fact that it is of relatively recent origin. In a competitive environment, management is constantly faced with the problem of effectively integrating and coordinating all of the parts of the enterprise into a total
system of actions in order to maximize profits. It is the performance of the
firm as a whole which is of singular importance. Components of the firm
only exist and find justification to the extent that they enhance total system performance. In such an environment, the marketing mix acts as a
framework for coordinating and integrating in a meaningful and logical
manner all of the marketing variables controlled by the firm.

DEVELOPING THE MARKETING MIX

What are the market forces marketing executives must understand and
consider in developing an optimal marketing mix? What elements should
be included in the firm's marketing mix? In what proportions should these
elements be combined so that together they will have maximum impact on
the desired markets? These are perplexing questions to handle.

To answer them the marketing executive should first know: (1) the specific target markets he wants to appeal to, (2) the response function of the
target markets to different levels of expenditures for each of the relevant
marketing mix variables, and (3) the response function of the firm's target
markets to different levels of expenditures for all of the marketing mix
variables taken together. This information is difficult if not impossible to
obtain. Moreover, it changes from market to market and in the same
market over time. Yet, regardless of such variations, it is possible to list
some generally useful guidelines in developing a marketing mix.

STEPS IN DEVELOPING A MARKETING MIX

Step 1: Determine the needs of the target market

The wants and needs of a target virtually determine the nature of the
firm's marketing mix. Thus, the initial step in developing the firm's marketing mix is concerned with delineating homogeneous sets of potential cus-

---

[1] James W. Culliton, *The Management of Marketing Costs* (Boston, Mass.: Division
of Research, Graduate School of Business Administration, Harvard University, 1948),
p. 6.

[2] Neil H. Borden, "The Concept of the Marketing Mix," in George Schwartz (ed.),
Science in Marketing (New York: John Wiley & Sons, Inc., 1965), pp. 386–97.

tomers whose needs can be satisfied profitably by the firm. The ultimate market success of a firm will rest eventually on its ability to adapt its resources and marketing activities to the wants and needs of potential customers.

Step 2: Formulate the components of the marketing mix

The components of the marketing mix are portrayed in Figure 1C–1. The marketing mix comprises three submixes: the product and service mix, the distribution mix, and the communication mix. The product and service mix is concerned with all the elements and ingredients that make up the actual product offered for sale by the company. They should be integrated to complement one another. Included are such factors as the number of product lines carried, as well as the product planning, product development, size, color, price, packaging, warranties and guarantees, branding, labeling, and servicing of each individual product. The product and service mix is the actual offering that a company makes to the marketplace as perceived by customers.

FIGURE 1C–1

The marketing mix

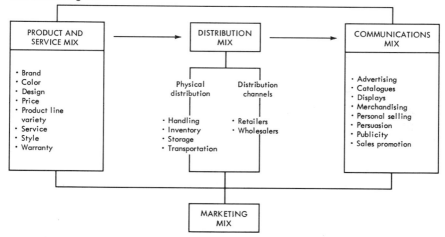

Source: William Lazer, *Marketing Management: A Systems Perspective* (New York: John Wiley & Sons, Inc., 1971), p. 17.

The distribution mix comprises two components: the channels of distribution and the activities of physical distribution. Channels of distribution are the chains of institutions used by a company in transporting products and titles to markets. Physical distribution activities are concerned with the physical flow of goods to market. Thus, the distribution mix deals with such factors as inventories, materials handling systems, storage facilities, modes of transporation, distribution centers, and related areas involved in the firm's distribution strategy.

The communications mix pertains to the strategic combination of advertising, personal selling, sales promotion, and other promotional tools used in communicating with the marketplace. This mix serves three basic management purposes. First, it bridges information gaps existing among manufacturers, middlemen, and customers. Second, it helps coordinate the promotional activities of the marketing system. Third, it helps adjust the marketing mix to customer needs.

The degree of control that management enjoys over the three submixes varies by industry, product type, and market conditions. Every product has some restrictions placed upon it. A wool garment must bear a label as to the authenticity of the virgin fiber. Aspirin must pass the requirements of the U.S. Food, Drug, and Cosmetic Act as to purity. Automobiles must possess minimum safety and pollution standards. Dangerous or toxic products must bear clear labels and can be transported only under specified conditions. Packaging must assure reasonable protection from performance failures. Licensing is required for alcoholic beverages, food, and beauty establishments, among others, to assure quality control. Even the prices charged by the firm are restricted by the prices set by the firm's competition or by the rate-setting powers of government commissions.

All three submixes are interdependent—decisions in one mix area affect mixes in other areas. Coordination, therefore, becomes critical. The marketing executive must recognize the need for subsystem concessions. For example, although manufacturers, wholesalers, and retailers comprise the institutions in a distribution system, their objectives to an extent may be in conflict. Nevertheless, it is the extent to which objectives are held in common and to which cooperation is gained that lends cohesiveness to the business system components.

Step 3: Blend the components into a marketing mix

The coordination of the component mixes into an overall marketing mix is the third step in the marketing mix process. Such coordination is necessary in order to attain optimum system performance. "Tradeoffs" must be made to create the best overall impact on the selected target market segments. The larger number of possible mixes coupled with a market in continual change makes the achievement of a truly optimum marketing mix virtually impossible. However, there are many combinations that can succeed, and it is the task of the marketing executive to try to find them.

Step 4: Monitor and control the firm's market offering

It is not enough for marketing executives to formulate market offerings. The decisions made must be implemented, and the offerings must be revised as changing conditions dictate. The fourth step in the marketing mix development process emphasizes that marketing executives should continually monitor market offerings and make the necessary changes in them over time.

The market environment contains forces which can greatly influence the success of the firm's marketing mix. Figure 1C–2 depicts the relationship between the internal and external aspects of the marketing mix. It indicates that internal company resources and objectives are linked to the external agencies through which the firm receives its supplies and delivers its market offering to the final customer. The chart shows that the firm-market interface occurs in an external environment over which the firm has little, if any, direct control.

The internal dimensions portrayed in Figure 1C–2 focus on the adjustment of the firm's corporate resources to customer needs and wants. The base of this internal dimension represents the human, financial, and physical resources of the firm. The marketing mix is rooted in and supported by these forces, and acts as the link between the internal aspects of the firm and its markets.

The external dimensions portrayed in Figure 1C–2 can be viewed as consisting of two levels. The uppermost level represents the broad scientific and technological; ethical, legal, and social; economic and political; and life style and life space setting. It establishes a backdrop against which the determinants of customer purchase behavior operate. Management skill in meeting and adjusting to these forces is a significant determinant of the firm's profitability and growth.

The next level represents the competitive business structure, the available business agencies and channels, and the government. These institutions more specifically and directly establish the business climate in which consumption occurs by a society in motion.

VARIATIONS IN THE MARKETING MIX

Many checklists and guides featuring different elements of the marketing mix have been proposed since the concept first came into being. Some systems, such as those of Kelley and Lazer,[3] McCarthy,[4] Lipson and Darling,[5] and Stanton,[6] are convenient because they are easily memorized and can be systematically diagrammed. Other systems, such as the checklist

---

[3] Eugene J. Kelley and William Lazer, *Managerial Marketing: Perspectives and Viewpoints* (3d ed.; Homewood, Ill.: Richard D. Irwin, Inc., 1967), pp. 415–573.

[4] E. Jerome McCarthy, *Basic Marketing: A Managerial Approach* (4th ed.; Homewood, Ill.: Richard D. Irwin, Inc., 1971), pp. 44–46.

[5] Harry A. Lipson and John R. Darling, *Introduction to Marketing: An Administrative Approach* (New York: John Wiley & Sons, Inc., 1971), pp. 585–619.

[6] William J. Stanton, *Fundamentals of Marketing* (3d ed.; New York: McGraw-Hill Book Co., 1971), pp. 29–30.

FIGURE 1C-2

Marketing action system

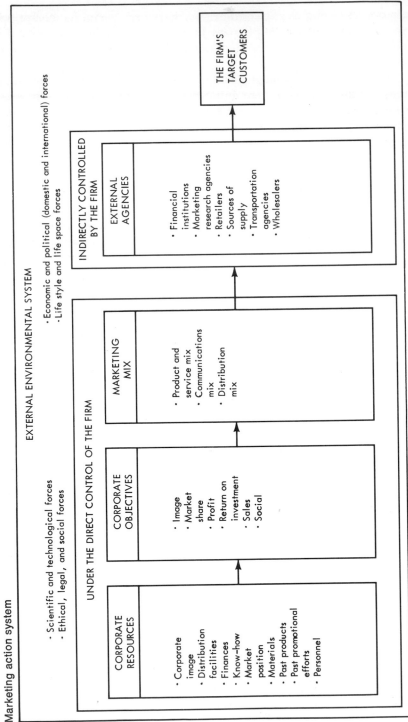

approaches of Neil Borden [7] and Albert Frey,[8] are useful for getting a feel for the many factors that the marketing executive must consider. They provide a handy device for understanding the complex and interrelated nature of the firm's marketing activities.

Unfortunately no system gives a full discussion of what is involved in implementing the marketing mix concept in a real business setting—nor can such a system be expected. The fact that firms deal with dynamic and complex objects makes it impossible to construct deterministic models for analysis. The marketing concept is just too broad to be reduced to a series of steps that anyone can follow in any situation to achieve a desired market effect.

The great varieties in the makeup of company marketing mixes are reflected in the firm's operating statement. Even among businesses operating in the same "industry" there is little uniformity. Such diversity is accounted for largely by the fact that products, sales volumes, and target markets for businesses tend to be unique and constantly changing. For instance, the advertising expense figure, which reflects the percentage of the marketing mix expenditures going to advertising, will often vary dramatically. One study showed that, in 1970, drug and cosmetic manufacturers spent on the average from 3 to 36 percent of their total sales dollars on advertising. At the other extreme, automobile and tire manufacturers, oil companies, the major airlines, and telephone service and equipment companies spent 2 percent or less of their total sales dollars on advertising.[9] Similarly, the percentage of the marketing mix expenditures devoted to personal selling will cover a wide range among different types of industries and firms.

The variety and flexibility of the distribution components of the marketing mix can be illustrated by considering the institutional arrangements in the food industry alone. Many manufacturers and processors of food products sell through food brokers who are familiar with market conditions and can offer their services to the manufacturer at a relatively low fee. Manufacturers of packaged goods such as milk and bread often sell direct to retailers using their own salesmen and delivery fleet. For other food products, the vending machine is an important part of the firm's marketing mix. For example, in the United States in 1970, $2.1 billion in cigarettes, $1.5 billion in soft drinks, and $671 million in candy bars were sold through vending machines.[10] Some food manufacturers and processors use "manufacturers agents" to sell and deliver their products to retail establishments, while they provide advertising and promotional aids.

---

[7] Neil H. Borden, *Note on Concept of the Marketing Mix* (Boston, Mass.: Intercollegiate Case Clearing House, Harvard University, 1957).
[8] Albert W. Frey, *The Effective Marketing Mix* (Hanover, N.H.: Amos Tuck School, Dartmouth College, 1956).
[9] *Advertising Age* (August 30, 1971), p. 22.
[10] "Census of the Industry—1971," *Vend* (May 1971), pp. 34–64.

A relatively new institution in the food wholesaling area is the rack job-ber. These wholesalers frequently specialize in such products as house-wares, hardware items, and health and beauty aids. The items are dis-played on the wire racks the jobbers provide. Canned goods are often sold by merchant wholesalers who take title and assume ownership for the goods they handle. Many food retailers do not deal with independent wholesalers at all but band together in cooperative chains to set up their own wholesaling organization in order to achieve the economies of scale in distribution enjoyed by corporate chains.

Wide variations are also likely to be found in the pricing components and price policies of the marketing mix of even the same firm in different markets or over time. Terms of trade such as F.O.B. pricing; quantity, seasonal, and cash discounts; advertising allowances; and trading stamps all become a part of the final price the firm will charge any given customer at any particular time. The complexities of the price variable are easily seen in the following description of the $4.60 "price tag" on a ton of iron ore:

. . . not merely $4.60 a ton but $4.60 per gross long ton of 2,240 pounds of Mesaba Bessemer ore containing exactly 51.5 percent of iron and 0.045 percent of phosphorous, with specified premiums for ore with a higher iron content or a lower phosphorous content and with specified discounts [too complicated to include here] for ore with a lower iron content or a higher phosphorous content; samples to be drawn and analyzed on a dry basis by a specified chemist at Cleveland, and cost being divided equally between seller and buyer; 48,000 tons to be delivered at the rate of approximately 8,000 tons per month during April-September, inclusive, on board freight cars of the New York Central Rail-road at Cleveland, Ohio; the purchaser to pay all charges involved in moving ore from the rail of the lake steamer to the freight car and other port charges, such as unloading, dockage, storage, reloading, switching and handling; ore to be weighed on railroad scale weights at Cleveland; payment to be made in legal tender or bank checks of the buyer to the Cleveland agent of the mining com-pany on the 15th of each month for all ore received during the preceding month.[11]

In short, marketing executives can combine the elements of a firm's marketing program in many ways. Even within the same market, it is likely that businesses will change their marketing mix in order to adjust to changing market forces. For the marketing executive, therefore, the search is to find the marketing mix best suited to achieving the firm's objectives in each of the firm's target markets. He must juggle the marketing mix components with a keen eye on the resources he has. And he must judge the impact of consumers, competition, and the environment in the light of his position and the influence he can expect to exert on the market.

---

[11] Reavis Cox, "Nonprice Competition and the Measurement of Prices," *Journal of Marketing*, Vol. 10, No. 4 (April 1946).

LIMITATIONS AND IMPLICATIONS OF THE MARKETING MIX CONCEPT

Simple as the marketing mix framework may appear, its application in actual decision making is not easy. For one thing, there is a lack of information necessary for effective implementation. Not only are initial pieces of data on the firm's own resources and objectives difficult to obtain but the available data are often not in the form users require. On the cost side, data generally are reported by natural expense categories, such as salaries, taxes, supplies, and advertising; whereas the costs relevant for strategic decision making are the functional expenses associated with the various marketing activities. On the demand side, the principal problems are due to a lack of sales data by *relevant* consumer classifications and uncertainty about the size and stability of the firm's revenue possibilities. Informational problems such as these severely limit the ease with which marketing mix decisions can be made on a routine basis. More significant limitations exist, however, which are summarized below.

The determination of relevant needs

The heart of the marketing mix, as we have seen, rests on knowledge of the firm's target markets and of the unsatisfied needs and wants in this market. However, little agreement exists as to what these needs and wants are. Behavioral research findings indicate that potential customers are subjected to various stimuli, and based on these stimuli as well as on certain internalized factors, they may or may not take a course of action. No one simple explanation exists of how individuals behave. Thus, in developing the firm's marketing mix, marketing executives still must rely in many cases on estimates and guesses in addition to marketing research.

Multiple goals and interaction among decision variables

The objectives and goals of the firm—what they are and what they should be—are the subject of much current research. Even if long-run profit maximization is acknowledged as the most general of managerial objectives, this single goal becomes qualified and fragmented in the context of specific marketing management decisions. Any marketing mix decision built upon such multiple objectives is subject to severe limitations. For example, it seems logical to search for the profit-maximizing price for a particular product under particular distribution and communication conditions. It also seems logical to try to develop the best communication strategy, or the best method of distribution, for a particular product with a particular price. But the optimal marketing mix, the overall "best decision" for the firm, the one that the marketing executive really is trying to develop, may conflict with the decisions in each of these submix areas.

Spatial, temporal and product interaction

The marketing period of any given product stretches out far beyond the occurrence of the financial outlays. The exact impact of this "carry-over effect" is hard, if not impossible, to determine. It presents a problem in the optimal timing of the marketing mix throughout the planning horizon. Furthermore, the firm typically sells a number of different products, in many territories and to various target markets. Thus, the question of spatial and product interaction plagues many firms. Marketing mix strategies cannot be developed for each separate market without considering their effect on the sales of the rest of the business. Unless the marketing executive grapples with this problem he can never hope to approach optimal results.

CONTRIBUTIONS OF THE CONCEPT

Although these limitations are very real, marketing managers using the concept of the marketing mix can achieve a high degree of integration and develop a coordinated marketing thrust that should lead to a substantial improvement in market performance. The marketing mix as an organizational framework contributes to an understanding of the complex and interrelated nature of the firm's marketing activities. It furnishes a conceptual plan upon which management can approach marketing problems and opportunities. It is the logical basis for developing marketing strategies that meet the needs of specific target markets.

To summarize, the marketing mix provides a basis for a logical, coherent, and orderly analysis of the activities which bear upon the marketing operations of a firm. It is a systems concept aimed at integrated effort for achieving the firm's objectives. The concept focuses attention on broader issues than those contained in any one marketing activity. Furthermore, it stresses adaptive change and adjustment by emphasizing the dynamic impact of the market environment.

The marketing mix concept has added to the understanding of the marketing process in several areas. One of its major contributions is that it has helped change the concentration of marketing scholars and practitioners from a predominant concentration on the marketing variables themselves to a concentration on the results of such operations.

The marketing mix concept also allows for heterogeneity in the market. By recognizing that separate market offerings are needed to appeal to different target markets, the marketing executive places a new emphasis on the realities of competition not found in the classical writings on the subject.

Now more than ever, marketing executives are under pressure to produce the best total mix of ingredients to meet the demands of both the marketplace and the firm. An understanding of the forces that constrain and influence marketing effort, as well as an awareness of the impact the interaction of various marketing mix ingredients may have, is a necessity in such an environment.

d.

A systems perspective

MARKETING INSTITUTIONS and operations can be perceived as complex, large-scale systems. Any group of marketing elements and activities that can be physically or conceptually delineated is a marketing system. A system is a collection of entities such as manufacturers, wholesalers, or retailers that can be understood as forming a coherent group. The fact that the entities can be defined as a coherent group is what differentiates a system from a meaningless collection of parts.[1]

Marketing systems may be of two types—conceptual or physical. Most marketing systems are approached conceptually. Some systems, such as physical distribution systems, are physical entities. The parts of a marketing system may be within or outside the formal boundaries of the firm.

Furthermore, marketing systems may be perceived of as small systems, middle-range systems, and large systems.[2] The large system, such as the macro marketing system, is concerned with marketing's linkages among industries or to the environment. The "macro" perspective has a metacorporate scope that is beyond or outside the corporation and broader than the traditional marketing concepts involved at the "micro" level. As viewed from the social/environmental system by the aggregated mass of consumers, the macro concept includes: the sociomarketing concept, the socioprofit concept, and the sociosystems concept. Marketing systems, therefore, include the following components:

---

[1] Stafford Beer, "What Has Cybernetics to Do with Operational Research?" *Operational Research Quarterly*, Vol. 10, No. 1 (March 1959), p. 3.

[2] Wroe Alderson, *Dynamic Marketing Behavior* (Homewood, Ill.: Richard D. Irwin, Inc., 1965), chap. 1.

1. A set of functionally interdependent marketing relationships among people and institutions in the system—manufacturers, wholesalers, retailers, facilitating agencies, consumers, and other public institutions.
2. Interaction between individuals and firms to maintain relationships, and facilitate adjustment to change, innovation, cooperation, and competition.
3. Establishment of objectives, goals, targets, beliefs, symbols, and sentiments that evolve from and reinforce the interaction, thus producing realistic marketing objectives and plans, and creating favorable images, attitudes, and opinions.
4. A consumer- and/or social-oriented environment in which interactions take place; subject to the constraints of a competitive market economy, the legal and socio-economic environment, and the evolving relationships and methods of marketing entities.
5. Technology of marketing, including communications media, credit facilities, standardization and grading, marketing research and physical distribution.

To form a complete large-scale system, both managerial and social approaches to marketing may be integrated. Naturally conflicts may arise. Subsystem concessions must be made. This broader macro perspective is highlighted in the companion volume to this book: *Social Marketing: Perspectives and Viewpoints.*

Small systems (or micro marketing systems) are mainly concerned with marketing within the firm. They include the middle-range systems concerned with marketing's linkage to other functional activities such as finance and production. This book has adapted the managerial approach— the viewpoint of the firm—in evaluating contemporary marketing problems and policies. This approach is directly related to the micro systems approach in marketing.

A marketing system is an assemblage or combination of activities, institutions, and operations composed of subsystems. Any marketing component can be explained in terms of various systems. Hierarchies of subsystems exist and vary with each company. Marketing systems are linked to form larger formal systems. For example, the advertising department can be viewed as a system, as can the marketing department, the total complex of one business enterprise, or the totality of a number of business enterprises such as manufacturers, governmental agencies, or consumers.

In marketing systems, there are flows of products, services, money, equipment, and information. Marketing activities themselves are subdivided into three component subsystems—products and services, distribution, and communications. The analysis of flows and communications within and outside the firm is greatly emphasized in the marketing systems approach. The three mixes are integrated into a coordinated marketing system that stresses the development of communication systems for transmitting information about changing market environments and subsequent adjustments of marketing policies and strategies. "A central-systems problem of marketing management is to combine all the marketing elements and resources into a marketing mix (product and services, distribution, communication) that will insure the achievement of such corporate goals as profit, volume, image, reputation, and return on investment by satisfying consumers wants and needs." [3] Thus, what is required is a total, integrative, systems approach.

THE SYSTEMS APPROACH

The systems approach provides a master model for marketing activity. Like other models, it is imperfect. It has the advantage of focusing attention on issues broader than those usually contained in any single aspect of marketing. It places emphasis on the inputs to the system and the outputs produced. It greatly aids in the formulation of overall marketing and corporate objectives, and the development of marketing programs and the total marketing mix. However, the systems model of marketing activity makes no attempt to predict or understand human behavior. It focuses on the components of the marketing systems in terms of performance rather than understanding.[4]

CHART 1

Kinds of systems

Systems variable	Mechanical systems	Hydraulic systems	Electrical systems	Traffic systems	Marketing systems
Propensity . . . . . Velocity		Pressure	Voltage	Density	Cost or price per unit of marketing effort
Flow . . . . Force		Flow rate	Current	Current	Sales or profit per unit

What are the benefits of adopting a systems perspective? First, it provides a good basis for the logical, orderly, and coherent analysis of marketing activity. This viewpoint stresses marketing linkages inside and outside the firm. It emphasizes inputs and relates them to outputs. Systems thinking furnishes information about adaptations of systems, emphasizes changing environments, and provides a conceptual framework for control.

To a large extent, the effectiveness of marketing systems depends on having and using the right information. Markets can be understood only

---

[3] William Lazer, *Marketing Management: A Systems Perspective* (New York: John Wiley & Sons, 1971), p. 16.

[4] W. M. A. Brooker, "The Total Systems Myth," *Systems and Procedures Journal* (July–August 1965), p. 29.

through the study of information—communications and messages. Systems must be adjusted to markets. Thus, the information base of a system is critical to its survival and effectiveness.

SYSTEMS AND MARKETING MANAGEMENT

The marketing management concept, with its emphasis on integration, implies a systems approach to the management of marketing effort. Marketing management includes a recognition of the interrelation and interconnection between marketing and other business elements. It adopts a systems approach as the basis for the solution of marketing problems; it is concerned with integrated and coordinated use of marketing resources to achieve predetermined and realistic objectives in an effective manner.

In accepting total responsibility for all marketing activities, and in striving for the effective use of total resources, the marketing manager must be able to see the interrelationships between various parts of the system. This perspective is suggested by Forrester. In referring to the systems view of perceiving the firm as a dynamic whole, he states, "The company will come to be recognized not as a collection of separate functions, but as a system in which the flows of information, materials, manpower, capital equipment, and money set up forces that determine the basic tendencies toward growth, fluctuation, and decline." [5]

SYSTEMS CONCEPT

Four groups of concepts in general systems theory have significance for marketing systems: descriptive factors, regulation and maintenance factors, factors concerning dynamics and change, and factors related to the decline and breakdown of systems.[6]

Descriptive factors are those concepts that make important distinctions in the classification of systems, structures, elements, and processes. For example, there are open and closed systems, input-output systems, boundaries and environments, orders of interaction, interdependence and independence.

Regulation and maintenance concepts deal with the control, stabilization, and regulation of systems. They are concerned with systems stability, systems equilibrium, systems feedback, homeostasis and regulation, steady-state maintenance, and communication.

Dynamics and change are internally generated factors that deal with the response of systems to environmental conditions. They include such

---

[5] Jay W. Forrester, "Industrial Dynamics," *Harvard Business Review*, Vol. 36, No. 4 (July–August 1958), p. 52.

[6] O. R. Young, "A Survey of General Systems Theory," *General Systems*, Vol. 9 (1964), pp. 61–62.

concepts as adaptation of a system, plasticity and elasticity of systems, learning and growth, change, dynamism and dynamics.

Decline and breakdown concepts are concerned with the disruption or breakdown of a system. Included are such factors as overload, stress, disturbance, decay, and decline.

If the integration of marketing activities is not recognized organizationally, a marketing system is not complete. However, the system need not be rigidly controlled from a central point. The components of the system can be guided by common purpose and policy without rigid control.

Two concepts are important in understanding the integrated character of the systems approach. First is the concept of synthesizing the elements and subsystems into a whole. It is concerned with integrating the abovementioned component parts into a system. Second is the concept of linkages. Linkages are the paths of connection that integrate two or more separate and distinct major or minor subsystems; each of which can function independently, to create a higher order system.

Application of the systems approach requires analysis of the elements and their functions and interactions from the point of view of individual contributions to the total system. It reflects the philosophy of the operations researcher and his perception of business as a total system of action.

CONFLICTING GOAL ORIENTATION

To function effectively as a system, a marketing organization should be goal directed. Unfortunately, however, the goals or objectives of marketing systems and subsystems are not always clearly specified or even compatible. It is difficult for the marketing manager to precisely define the objectives of his particular unit. To the extent that a marketing organization does not clearly specify its objectives, and is not able to coordinate various marketing subsystems to achieve goal-directed action, a complete systems approach has not been achieved.

In trying to achieve common goals, every business system operates through subsystems that have their own respective goals. As a result, there are usually conflicts in any business system, and a goal tradeoff between subsystems becomes important in order to achieve greater efficiency of the overall system. Given existing or likely marketing constraints, determination of the one marketing program that promises an optimal total marketing position becomes the major objective of a systems approach to marketing. Intrasystem concessions must occur if major marketing and corporate goals are to be achieved.

SYSTEMS AND GOAL MODELS

There is a basic difference between systems and goal models—largely a difference of focus and emphasis. The goal model starts with a task to be achieved and focuses directly on the use of company resources to achieve it. It implies that output is directly related to input. Doubling resources is usually equated with doubling output. The goal model, therefore, may lead to segmented perspectives and may not be the most effective model of total marketing operations.

Two inherent dangers must be recognized in using a goal model. (1) The danger that in solving problems management will adopt the perspective of one subgroup in the organization. This is especially true when pressure exists from action-oriented marketing groups. For example, marketing managers are likely to be sales-oriented, since most marketing goals are achieved through sales. (2) The administrative, facilitating, and control functions of the marketing system may be neglected. Management must allocate resources and perform functions necessary for the maintenance of the marketing system itself.

The systems model is based on the assumption that all marketing system elements function together to achieve the objectives of the overall system, rather than the objectives of a subsystem. The starting point in the systems model is not a goal but the model of the total functioning unit. A systems model is a more realistic representation of an ongoing marketing entity capable of achieving multiple goals. The systems model recognizes the multifunctional and multidimensional units involved in reaching marketing goals. It emphasizes that some resources must be allocated to nongoal-directed effort. Resources are allocated to functions involved in maintaining the marketing organization itself. These functions include supporting marketing services and action that permits the use of effective marketing striking power. Such functions are not always directly goal-oriented.

SCOPE AND COMPLEXITY OF MARKETING SYSTEMS

Marketing systems are often large and complex. For example, consider the dollar and physical volume of goods handled, the number of people employed, the number and variety of components of an advertising campaign, or the components of a sales promotion campaign in any major business concern today. Other additional considerations include the alternative methods of selling, distribution, or advertising, the number and types of functions performed, the possible combination of marketing inputs, and the dimensions of absolute marketing costs and revenue.

Marketing systems contain a wide variety of components, elements, and interrelationships that have infinite gradations. In addition, there is incomplete information concerning each element, thus forcing marketing management to always deal with systems under conditions of uncertainty. The complexity of the marketing decision problem is compounded by the large number of variables that are generated by the dynamic nature of the marketing process.

Large and complex marketing systems contain not only harmonious but also discordant or dysfunctional elements. For example, tension, strains, and conflict are intrinsic to marketing systems when one considers what is best for the wholesaler versus the retailer versus the manufacturer in a total system. The best course of action for the wholesaler may be the worst for the manufacturer.

OPEN SYSTEMS

Conceptually, marketing systems may be either open or closed; however, most marketing systems are open. An automatic vending machine is an example of a closed system. Known inputs (money) are put into the machine, and known outputs are obtained from it (provided the machine is working properly). Thus, the vending machine represents a highly predictable, deterministic system.

Uncertainty plays an important role in most marketing decisions. Results vary from those predicted because of changes in inputs and unpredicted variances in the states of the environment. Such systems are indeterminate and are frequently referred to as probabilistic systems. They present a more difficult planning and operating environment than does a closed system.

INTELLIGENCE NETWORKS AND SYSTEM ADJUSTMENT

An important characteristic of a marketing system is the existence of complex intelligence networks. The intelligence network includes multiple feedback and forecast loops. Normally, marketing management feedback loops are thought of in terms of various marketing research, sales management, and distribution cost accounting activities; which provide management with information about events that have already occurred. Forecast loops may be viewed as providing future information derived through predictive processes, such as sales forecasting and simulations. The availability of pertinent past and future information is essential to system control and integration.

Despite the existence of complex intelligence networks, marketing systems do not automatically adjust to changing market conditions. Information systems are necessary for recognition of new developments and management of marketing change. The use of existing automatic control systems will not insure automatic adjustment of the marketing system. The present state of the art in information management has not produced a device similar to the servomechanism, which has widespread application in engineering.

Automatic control mechanisms cannot be instituted in most areas of marketing, although it is sometimes possible to set up an automatic control system for certain routine inventory decisions. Marketing activity is at a stage of development where human beings are involved in controlling the direction of company activity to a considerable extent.

Continuing advances in electronic data processing technology and in systems and procedures applications will improve marketing intelligence. Marketing managers will be provided with more timely, pertinent, dependable information on which to base decisions. Marketing activities generate huge quantities of data, from which essential information can probably be best assembled and communicated through computer processing. Improved control and more rapid adjustment of marketing systems should result from new and increased computer applications to marketing problems. For example, market simulation computer problems now provide strategic information that is not available through any other means.

COMPETITION AND CHANGE

A characteristic of most marketing systems in free enterprise and mixed economies is that they are competitive. Each competitor faces opponents who constantly seek to promote their individual advantages. Competitors can be expected to react to offensive strategies with either a defensive strategy or a new offensive effort. Thus, marketing managers are faced with the problem of evaluating the probable effects of not only their own decisions but also their competitors' reactions. Maintenance of market position and growth of the firm require a willingness and ability to change.

The marketing system is characterized as a system constantly adjusting its elements and focus. The interaction of changing technology, research and development, shifting consumer attitudes and opinions, together with competition, necessitate continuous system adjustment. The marketing manager must plan for change and accept it as an integral part of the systems approach to marketing.

Bibliography

A. THE MARKETING MANAGEMENT APPROACH

ANSHEN, M.   "The Management of Ideas," *Harvard Business Review,* July-August 1969, pp. 99–107.

DRUCKER, P. F.   *The Age of Discontinuity.* New York: Harper & Row, 1968.

GALBRAITH, J. K.   *The New Industrial State.* Boston: Houghton-Mifflin, 1967.

GELLNER, E.   *Thought and Change.* Chicago: University of Chicago Press, 1965.

SCHOEN, D. R.   "Managing Technological Innovation," *Harvard Business Review,* May-June 1969, pp. 156–67.

LAWRENCE, P. R.   "How to Deal with Resistance to Change," *Harvard Business Review,* January-February 1969, pp. 4–176.

MACHLUP, F.   *The Production and Distribution of Knowledge in the United States.* Princeton, New Jersey: Princeton University Press, 1962.

McHALE, J.   *The Future of the Future.* New York: George Braziller, 1969.

REICH, C.   *The Greening of America.* New York: Random House, 1971.

SCHAN, D. A.   *Technology and Change.* New York: Dell, 1967.

KAHN, H. AND WIENER, A. J.   *The Year 2000.* New York: The Macmillan Company, 1967.

SERVAN-SCHREIBER, J.   *The American Challenge.* New York: Avon, 1967.

TOFFLER, A.   *Future Shock.* New York: Random House, 1970.

B. THE MARKETING CONCEPT: HISTORICAL AND CONCEPTUAL BASES

ANDERSON, W. T. AND SHARPE, L. K.   "New Marketplace: Life Style in Revolution," *Business Horizons,* Vol. 14, August 1971, pp. 43–50.

BARKSDALE, H. C. AND DARDEN, B.   "Marketer's Attitudes Toward the Marketing Concept," *Journal of Marketing,* Vol. 35, No. 4, October 1971, pp. 29–36.

BECKMAN, T. N., DAVIDSON, M. R. AND ENGEL, J. F.   *Marketing.* 8th ed. New York: The Ronald Press Co., 1967, pp. 40–44.

BELL, M. L. AND EMORY, C. W.   "The Faultering Marketing Concept," *Journal of Marketing,* Vol. 35, No. 4, October 1971, pp. 29–36.

BROFFMAN, M. H.   "Is Consumerism Merely Another Marketing Concept?" *MSU Business Topics,* Winter 1971, pp. 15–21.

Cook, C. W. "Social Values of Marketing," *The Conference Board Record*, Vol. 4, February 1967, pp. 32–37.

Haley, R. I. and Gatty, R. "Monitor Your Market Continuously," *Harvard Business Review*, May-June 1968, pp. 65–69.

Hise, R. T. "Have Manufacturing Firms Adopted the Marketing Concept?" *Journal of Marketing*, July 1965, p. 9.

Kaplan, R. M., ed. *The Marketing Concept in Action*. Chicago: American Marketing Association, 1964.

King, Robert L. "The Marketing Concept," *Science in Marketing*. New York: John Wiley & Sons, Inc., 1965, pp. 70–98.

LaLonde, B. J. and Morrison, E. J. "Marketing Management Concepts Yesterday and Today," *Journal of Marketing*, January 1967, p. 9.

McNamara, C. P. "The Present Status of the Marketing Concept," *Journal of Marketing*, January 1972, Vol. 36, No. 1, pp. 50–57.

Muse, W. V. and Kegerreis, R. J. "Technological Innovation and Marketing Management: Implications for Corporate Policy," *Journal of Marketing*, Vol. 33, October 1969, pp. 3–9.

Serchuk, A. "How Do You Know When to Make What?" *Electronic News*, Vol. 13, January 29, 1968, p. 39.

Weiss, E. B. "Products with Shorter Life-Span Will Make It in Anti-Materialistic Society," *Advertising Age*, Vol. 42, September 27, 1971, p. 73.

C. THE PROFIT CONCEPT

Fahlenberg, J. F. "Profitability Analysis: A Marketing Tool," *Journal of Commercial Bank Lending*, Vol. 52, February-March 1970, pp. 2–16.

Fiedler, E. R. "Structure of Profits," *Conference Board Research*, Vol. 7, March 1970, p. 10–15.

Konopa, K. J. "Is Profit a Dirty Word?" *Banking*, Vol. 56, April 1964, p. 112+.

Renner, R. R. "Profit Control: Back to the Basics," *Management Review*, Vol. 57, October 1968, pp. 2–9.

Schreiber, W. "Social Functions of Profits," *Management International Review*, Vol. 9, No. 2–3, 1969, pp. 63–76.

Wilkinson, J. D. "Profit Performance Concepts and the Product Manager," *Management Service*, Vol. 5, July 1968, pp. 17–25.

D. THE SYSTEMS APPROACH

Ackoff, Russell L. "Management Misinformation Systems," *Management Science Journal*, Vol. 14, No. 4, December 1967, pp. B147–B156.

Amstutz, Arnold E. *Computer Simulation of Competitive Market Response*. Cambridge, Mass.: The MIT Press, 1967.

Amstutz, Arnold E. "Market-Oriented Management Systems: The Current Status," *Journal of Marketing Research*, Vol. VI, November 1969, pp. 481–96.

Berenson, Conrad. "Marketing Information Systems," *Journal of Marketing*, Vol. 33, No. 4, October 1969, pp. 16–23.

BOULDEN, JAMES B., AND BUFFA, ELWOOD S. "Corporate Models: On-line, Real-time Systems," *Harvard Business Review,* Vol. 48, July-August 1970, pp. 65–83.

CHURCHMAN, E. WEST. *The Systems Approach.* New York: Delta Publishing Co., Inc., 1968.

COX, DONALD F., AND GOOD, ROBERT E. "How to Build a Marketing Information System," *Harvard Business Review,* May-June 1967.

FERGUSON, ROBERT L., AND JONES, CURTIS H. "A Computer Aided Decision System," *Management Science,* Application Series, Vol. 15, June 1969, B550–B561.

JONES, CURTIS H. "At Last: Real Computer Power for Decision Makers," *Harvard Business Review,* Vol. 48, September-October 1970, pp. 75–90.

KELLEY, EUGENE J. "Business Marketing's New Technology in an Information Society," an unpublished address to the 1970 Advertising to Business Workshop, March 24, 1970.

KOTLER, PHILIP. "Corporate Models: Better Marketing Plans," *Harvard Business Review,* Vol. 48, July-August 1970, pp. 135–49.

KOTLER, PHILIP. "The Future of the Computer in Marketing," *Journal of Marketing,* Vol. 34, January 1970, pp. 11–14.

MARTIN, E. W., JR. "The Systems Concept," *Business Horizons,* Spring 1966.

MASSEY, WILLIAM F. "Information and the Marketing Manager: A Systems Analysis," *Computer Operations Journal,* Vol. 2, No. 4, October 1968, pp. 6–18.

MONTGOMERY, DAVID B., AND URBAN, GLEN L. *Management Science in Marketing.* Englewood Cliffs, N. J.: Prentice-Hall, Inc., 1969, pp. 7–94 and 293–369.

SMITH, SAMUEL V.; BRIEN, RICHARD H.; AND STAFFORD, JAMES E. *Readings in Marketing Information Systems.* Boston: Houghton Mifflin Co., 1968.

STASCH, STANLEY F. *Systems Analysis for Marketing Planning and Control.* Glenview, Illinois: Scott Foresman and Company, 1972.

UHL, KENNETH P., AND SCHONER, BERTRAM. *Marketing Research–Information Systems and Decision Making.* New York: John Wiley & Sons, Inc., 1969.

WEITZ, HAROLD. "The Promise of Simulation in Marketing," *Journal of Marketing,* Vol. 31, July 1967, pp. 28–33.

ZANI, WILLIAM M. "Real-Time Information Systems: A Comparative Economic Analysis," *Management Science,* Application Series, Vol. VI, February 1970, B350–B356.

E. IMPLEMENTING THE MARKETING CONCEPT

BELL, MARTIN L., AND EMORY, C. WILLIAM. "The Faltering Marketing Concept," *Journal of Marketing,* Vol. 35, No. 4, October 1971, pp. 37–42.

KELLEY, EUGENE J. *Marketing Planning and Competitive Strategy.* Englewood Cliffs, N. J.: Prentice Hall, Inc., 1972.

KOTLER, PHILIP. *Marketing Management: Analysis, Planning and Control.* 2d ed. Englewood Cliffs, N. J.: Prentice Hall, Inc., 1972.

LAZER, WILLIAM.   *Marketing Management: A Systems Perspective.* New York: John Wiley & Sons, Inc., 1971.

MCNAMARA, CARLTON P.   "The Present Status of the Marketing Concept," *Journal of Marketing,* Vol. 36, No. 1, January 1972, pp. 50–57.

F. THE CONCEPT OF THE MARKETING MIX

BORDEN, NEIL H.   "The Concept of the Marketing Mix," *Science in Marketing.* George Schwartz, ed. New York: John Wiley & Sons, Inc., 1965, pp. 386–97.

KOTLER, PHILIP.   *Marketing Management: Analysis, Planning and Control.* 2d ed. Englewood Cliffs, N. J.: Prentice Hall, Inc., 1972.

LAZER, WILLIAM.   *Marketing Management: A Systems Perspective.* New York: John Wiley & Sons, Inc., 1971.

STAUDT, THOMAS A., AND TAYLOR, DONALD A.   *A Managerial Introduction to Marketing.* 2d ed. Englewood Cliffs, N. J.: Prentice-Hall, Inc., 1970.

2 CONSUMERS AND MARKETING ACTION

UNDERSTANDING the consumer is essential to marketing planning and action. The marketer's main concern is satisfying consumers' wants. He must be sensitive to shifts in characteristics, values, and attitudes of precisely defined market segments if he is to meet corporate goals.

Interest in human behavior is not new, but the *systematic* exploration of behavioral phenomena by marketers did not begin until recently with an increased interest in the "behavioral sciences." Psychology, sociology, cultural anthropology, political science, and other social sciences provide insights into consumer behavior. In addition to the knowledge provided by the behavioral sciences for understanding human behavior. Demography and economics are among other disciplines that have also contributed to the understanding of consumer behavior.

Significant advances have been made in the development of the behavioral and policy analysis sciences. The use of quantitative techniques have been instrumental in the construction and testing of behavioral theories and models. Additionally, more sophisticated sources of information are emerging from independent professional research organizations and are available on a "subscription" as well as a "project" basis. This information covers such items as lifestyle trends, social indicators, and corporate and government goals, in addition to traditional data such as market share, sales potential, and the like.

As the contemporary marketing-oriented firm attempts to satisfy more unfulfilled wants, it will increasingly rely upon behavioral models previously considered too theoretical for practical application. Management has the difficult task of understanding and utilizing behavioral literature while at the same time appreciating its limitations and applicability in achieving corporate goals.

a.

Demographics

STUDYING the vital marketing statistics or the demographic measures of the market is just one way of classifying consumers. Age, population patterns, leisure time and disposable income, family size, education, and work patterns are but some of the demographics helpful in understanding and segmenting the market.

However, the main benefit of demographics comes from projecting these measures to predict the composition of future markets. Any advance knowledge of markets offers a competitive advantage to the marketer. Information about potential markets and demographic trends permit marketing managers to adjust product orientation and marketing effort to coincide with the new environment.

Therefore, the alert marketing manager must anticipate, evaluate, and react to present and future demographic structures. In addition, he must build flexibility into his marketing projections by setting up alternative courses of action. Having done this and given the actual or most probable market outcome, the marketing manager can choose that alternative which seems to be of the greatest value to the firm in terms of the market.

In the first article, Smallwood and others project demographic indices into the next decade. Brown then explores future potential demographic changes in the country. In the last article, Kelley and Harvey discuss the changing effects of time and convenience on buyer behavior.

Marketers are interested in the evaluation and analysis of market demographics and potential demographic changes.

They are particularly concerned with how changes in market demographics affect potential opportunities and influence marketing strategies. Thus, the demographics of future markets are important to managers attempting to keep pace with changing markets. The present article presents some projected demographic changes that would have a significant impact on the structure of the future marketing environment.

---

1. DEMOGRAPHICS OF THE SEVENTIES *

John Smallwood, William Lazer, William Henry, Dennis Knight, Lee Rainwater, and George Stolnitz †

POPULATION TRENDS

During the 1970s population growth will increase significantly. The addition to our population will be about 25 million. The result will be the addition of a population base greater than that of Canada. The total 1980 population is expected to be approximately 230 million. This represents a growth rate in the decade of about 12%.

The most important aspect of population growth through the 1970s is the large variation in both the magnitude and direction of growth rates of different parts of the age spectrum. The U.S. is currently at a low point with respect to the relative size of the adult population: 60% of the 1970 population is 20 and over, but by 1980 the percentage will be 65-70%.

A comparison of population growth by age groups is given in Table 1. The figures are rounded in millions.

The main labor force entry and household formation age groups (20-34), will realize a marked growth in the 1970s. The most striking demographic fact is the spectacular growth in the 25-34 age group—a 46% growth over the 1970-80 decade. This is a fourfold increase over the gain of the 1960s. By 1980 one in every six of our population will be in this age bracket. These are the prime years for family formations. . . .

More than one half of the expected total population increase between

---

* Reprinted from John Smallwood, William Lazer, William Henry, Dennis Knight, Lee Rainwater, and George Stolnitz, *CELS–80: A Report on Consumer Environments and Life Styles of the Seventies* (Benton Harbor, Mich.: Whirlpool Corporation, 1971), pp. 8–17.

† The authors are from these respective institutions: Whirlpool Corporation, Michigan State University, University of Chicago, University of Wyoming, Harvard University, and Indiana University.

TABLE 1

Population shifts 1960–70–80 (in millions of resident population and ten-year changes)

Age	Population			Percent change	
	1960	1970	1980	1960–70	1970–80
0–19	70	78	77	+12%	– 1%
20–24	11	17	21	+55	+22
25–34	23	25	37	+11	+46
35–44	24	23	26	– 5	+11
45–54	21	24	22	+14	– 5
55–64	16	18	21	+13	+17
65 and over	16	20	24	+25	+20
Totals	181	205	228		

1970 and 1980 will be in the 25–34-year age group. The 35–44-year-old age group, after declining by 5% in the 1960s, will grow by 11% in the 1970s. An additional 28 million people (about the population of West Germany) will be in their 20s, 30s and early 40s. Thus the next 10 years may well be titled the age of the young married.

In the other age categories, the under-19 group will actually decrease both absolutely and relatively, while the 20–24-year-old age group will grow, but less proportionately than they did between 1960–70. The 65-and-over group will show a substantial 20% increase.

Estimates of fertility rates, which are quite variable, can have a significant effect on population projections. From 1966 through 1969 there has been a large drop in the fertility rate. The degree to which this will continue is debatable. About 2.5 children per family seems likely. . . .

Life expectancy will continue to increase for both males and females. It is rising from the 1967 level of 67 years for males to 69 years and from 74+ to 75+ years for females in the 1980s.

PRODUCTIVITY

The projection of productivity figures for the 1970s has important implications for growth, inflation, real income, cost and profit expectations. Studies of the sources of productivity reveal that the most important productivity gains, after those from capital applications, are attributed to improvements in the quality of the labor force (education, skills, research, etc.), improved technology, more effective organization and management. These factors are tempered somewhat by increases in the relative importance of the service sector which characteristically has realized lower growth rates.

Productivity figures are published on a regular basis by the Bureau of Labor Statistics and The Conference Board. The customary measure of productivity is output per man-hour. . . . the relationship of economic outputs to man-hour inputs for both the manufacturing and non-manufacturing sectors. From 1947 through 1969 productivity rose at an annual average rate of 3.2%. The annual average rate over these 22 years varied from 2.4% to 4.0% with the output per man-hour rising at a fairly steady rate. This increase in productivity has been the most important single determinant of the growth in economic output accounting for over 80% of the rise in our total output since 1947.

In the 1970s several changes will occur in the labor force that are expected to affect productivity favorably. The proportion of the population in the work force will increase from 40.1% to 44.3%. The average age of the work force will fall strikingly by almost three years. The average number of hours worked will show only the most modest decline. Automation will be more extensive and productivity will be bolstered by the fruits of substantial expenditures on research and development during the 1960s. The educational levels and skills of the labor force will increase particularly among the underprivileged. A larger proportion of women will be in the labor force. Increases in the significance of the service sector will not completely offset such favorable forces. Projected average annual productivity gains by major sectors of the private economy based on Bureau of Labor Statistics data are given in Table 2. An expected average annual increase in productivity across all sectors, private and public, of about 3.0% over the decade of the 1970s, seems to be a reasonable projection.

INCOME AND EXPENDITURES

Individual and family real income will continue to increase steadily and dramatically through the 1970s. Some relative comparisons will help establish a framework for a discussion of income statistics. In the 17-year period from 1968 to 1985, median real income will increase as much as it has over the previous 50 years. By 1985 one half of the U.S. population is expected to enjoy a level of living that characterized only the top 3% of the population in 1947, or the top 15% of the population in 1968. The large bundle of goods and services represented by this mass abundance can be expected to affect and be affected by the emerging life styles of the 1970s.

An annual growth rate of over 4½% in real income between 1970 and 1980 is projected. This is a higher rate of income growth than the 3¾% that occurred between 1950 and 1965. By 1980 real gross national income is expected to be approximately $1.5 trillion.

There will be a significant rise in expenditures during the 1970s. Predictions are that total expenditures on services—government and others—

TABLE 2

Projected productivity, by major sector, private economy, 1968–80

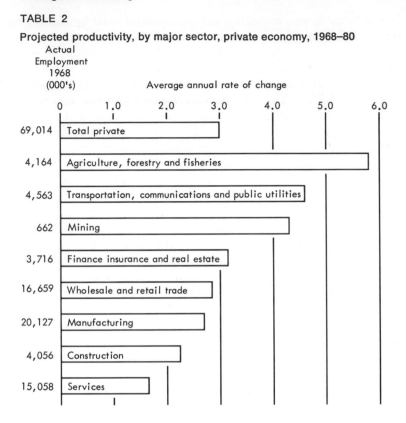

will exceed expenditures on goods by 1980. There will be considerable disparity, in growth rates of various goods sectors. For example, agriculture and mining in the aggregate are expected to grow at a slower rate than the national average. Manufacturing components are expected to show wide variations. Projected growth pattern for consumer goods industries, between 1968 and 1980, and the average annual expected growth rates are as shown in Table 3.

FAMILIES AND HOUSEHOLDS

A striking characteristic of demographic projections of the 1970s is that of the total growth of household formations and families, coupled with variations among different age groups. During the 1970s, 14 million net new households, an increase of over 20%, is anticipated. Currently, estimates of total numbers of households vary from 63–65 millions. By 1980 they will be approximately 78 million.

A parallel rate of growth is expected in the number of families. For example, in 1970 there were an estimated 2,146,000 marriages. This is

TABLE 3

Growth pattern for consumer goods industries

Industry classification	Expected annual rate of growth
1. Radio, T.V., records	8.1%
2. Toiletries	6.7%
3. Foreign travel	6.5%
4. Automobiles	6.4%
5. Higher education	6.0%
6. Drugs	5.8%
7. Gas, electricity	5.7%
8. Medical services	5.5%
9. Appliances	5.5%
10. Shelter	5.4%

Source: *The Consumer of The Seventies*, The Conference Board, p 67.

50% above the 1960 level and the rates are expected to increase during the decade. An expected growth in families of 10 millions in the 1970s seems to be conservative. To accommodate them and other households the addition of an average 2 million new dwelling units per year is required of the housing industry each year of this coming decade.

Family income will increase significantly. In 1970 approximately 15 million families had real incomes (in 1970 dollars) greater than $10,000. By 1980 over 31 million families will have total real incomes greater than $10,000. Mean family incomes in 1970 prices will rise from approximately $11,100 in 1970 to approximately $15,400 in 1980.

There will be a shift in the age of heads of households in the 1970s. The previously mentioned 46% increase in the 24–35-year-old age group will be reflected. Families with household heads between 24 and 35 years of age, which now buy approximately 35% of all houses sold, will buy about 45% in 1980. The phenomenal bourgeoning of the 24–35 age group will result in the growth of more settled household and housing demands. . . .

The distribution of families by both age of head of household and income reveals important shifts. The dramatic rise in the 25–44 age groups and $10,000 and over income groups (in 1970 dollars) is striking. By 1980 they will account for 34% of the families and 40% of the total purchasing power. Data for 1970 and 1980 comparisons are given in Table 4. The data show that the under-25 group will remain between 5–10%, the 45–54 group will decline relatively as will the 55-and-over category despite their rise in absolute numbers.

Husband-wife households now account for the major part of the rise in household formations. They will continue to do so. However, this dominance should not obscure the continuing sharp uptrends in households headed by individuals, singles, widows, and widowers. The increase will range between 33⅓% and 40% in the 1970s.

TABLE 4

Distribution of families by age of head and income (all income in 1970 dollars)

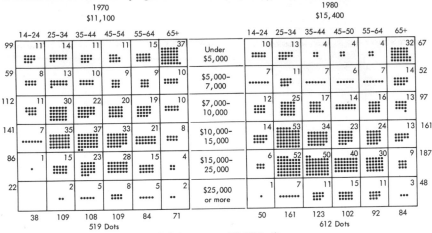

1970 $11,100							1980 $15,400					
14-24	25-34	35-44	45-54	55-64	65+		14-24	25-34	35-44	45-50	55-64	65+
99 11	14	11	11	15	37	Under $5,000	10	13	4	4	4	32 67
59 8	13	10	9	9	10	$5,000–7,000	7	11	7	6	7	14 52
112 11	30	22	20	19	10	$7,000–10,000	12	25	17	14	16	13 97
141 7	35	37	33	21	8	$10,000–15,000	14	53	34	23	24	13 161
86 1	15	23	28	15	4	$15,000–25,000	6	52	50	40	30	9 187
22	2	5	8	5	2	$25,000 or more	1	7	11	15	11	3 48
38	109	108	109	84	71		50	161	123	102	92	84

519 Dots   612 Dots

Each dot represents 100,000 families

WORK FORCE

The total labor force in 1970 is estimated to be approximately 83 million. By 1980 it is expected to reach 100 million experiencing a 2% average annual growth rate over the decade. These predictions reflect the very moderate rise in the under 20 group to 1975 and the decline in the 1980s, the leveling off of the 20–25 age group, and the phenomenal jump of the 25–34 age group in the 1970s. There will be a 60% increase in the number of workers in this latter group. By 1980 one out of every four workers will be in the 25–34 age group compared with one in five in 1968. The proportion of the population in the work force will increase from 40% in 1970 to over 44% in 1980. Table 5 highlights these data.

The net result of the variations by age group is that the average age of the work force is expected to fall strikingly by approximately 3 years in the coming decade to a 35-year average by 1980. This means that the proportion of the labor force in the most productive years is increasing. It may be well to recall that the upsurging 25–34 group, about to become such a large part of our labor supply, will be a product of the new educational approaches and life styles of the 1960s exhibiting greater imagination, flexibility, social concern and a tendency to protest and action.

The origins of the working woman is depicted by a consideration of 1969 data. These show first that the proportion of women working increases directly with total family income until family income reaches $25,000 and then drops sharply. Second, the higher the proportion of college graduates and postgraduates, the higher the proportion of work-

TABLE 5

Population and work force

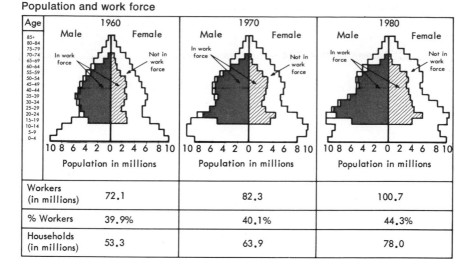

	1960	1970	1980
Workers (in millions)	72.1	82.3	100.7
% Workers	39.9%	40.1%	44.3%
Households (in millions)	53.3	63.9	78.0

ing women. Third, the percentage of women working increases as children reach school age and leave home. Rising income and education trends of the 1970s will be coupled with the fact that families will tend to have their children in a shorter span of time and the "empty nest" family period will expand. Data on women in the labor force is highlighted in Table 5. . . .

By 1980 a larger proportion of wives will be wage earners. In 1970 approximately 16 million wives worked and the figure will be increased to about 20 million by 1980. Over 40% of married women will be working in 1980 with a greater proportion holding professional level jobs. Working wives will be a major reason for the marked increase in real family income. This pattern is evident in the 1969 data.

In the decade of the 70s a larger proportion of women of working age are expected to be members of the work force. This may be partially attributed to the increase in the proportion of working wives, the relative growth of the 25–54-year-old age group, the increasing proportion of women college graduates, and the recently emerged sense of greater personal worth for women as vocalized by the Woman's Lib movement and others.

EDUCATION

Education of the labor force is changing most dramatically among the minority groups. For nonwhite males in the 1970s, years of schooling are expected to rise by over 10%. For nonwhite females they will increase by

over 5%. By 1980 our population will have 74 million high school graduates, 18 million more than the previous decade. Also 18 million people
will have a college degree, which is an increase of 6.5 millions over 1970.
The proportion of the population with an elementary education only will
drop from approximately 23% to 10% in the decade while the proportion with high school only will increase from 47% to 65%. These developments are significant because of the direct contributions of education to
productivity which are well substantiated.

---

*Will George Orwell's 1984 become a reality confronting fu-
ture marketing managers? Even though the Bureau of the
Census is capable of calculating the evolving demographic
trends, the uncertainty of the future and the unpredicta-
bility of the human element over time can both influence
and alter seemingly projectable trends. The author analyzes
and integrates demographic trends and their implications
for life styles and changing social values.*

---

2. PATTERNS OF CHANGE IN THE UNITED STATES—THE FUTURE*

George Hay Brown †

In a talk several months ago I referred to George Orwell and the views
of the future which he expounded in the widely read book *1984*. Orwell
died some 20 years ago, shortly after the book was published, but his
work is still discussed, largely because he predicted a continuing drift
into a totalitarian state.

Perhaps he did not really believe it. It may be that he meant only to
warn of the fate which could befall us if we grow careless of our liberties.

Orwell's preoccupation with the future provides a good framework for
an explanation of what the Census Bureau does because that topic—the
future—is a large part of my job.

Everyone knows that the bureau spends most of its time in learning
where we are, how many of us, how we live, our ages, and the state of

---

* Commissioned contribution.
† Director of the Bureau of the Census.

our prosperity. It is from that knowledge of our present condition, however, that we derive a pretty accurate picture of what we can expect in the future.

Orwell concerned himself with abstractions, ideas, and philosophies for the things he foresaw in *1984,* whereas the Census Bureau deals in facts —precise numbers of people, their ages, sex, incomes, and the exact physical boundaries within which they live.

Because of this, the bureau is highly accountable. In announcing figures about a city, a state, or the entire nation we are not dealing with philosophies or with abstract notions. We are held accountable and even challenged, as was done after publication of some of the city and state totals from the 1970 census.

To predict what is ahead for us in the middle of the next decade is a major undertaking. It requires a lot of hard work by a lot of people; a lot of facts and figures recorded and examined. Above all, it represents a team effort that addresses itself to the condition of the nation, not in terms of philosophies but in the facts which can be derived from the statistics painstakingly acquired from the census.

A study of those facts convinces me that George Orwell was wrong. Everything I see indicates we are headed toward 1985 with a country still characterized by strong individualism, a free market, and a democratic society beset, as always, by many problems but continuing to solve them without loss of liberty and dignity.

Any projection as to the state of our people in the next decade must start with population probabilities. Back in 1967, the bureau made some population projections based on four possible fertility ranges.

The first, Series A, assumed a fertility rate of 3.35 children per woman, the rate of the 1950s. That means, simply, that at the end of their childbearing years, 1,000 women would have produced 3,350 children. Series B, based on expectations data, assumed a rate of 3.10 children. Series C assumed a birth rate of 2.78, the rate of the early 1960s, and Series D assumed a rate of 2.45 children, the rate of the late 1960s.

Changing fertility trends, however, led to a revision. We decided to drop the Series A based on 3.35 children because it no longer seems a reasonable possibility for the 1980s. Between 1940 and 1957, average age at marriage declined; the proportion of women who were married increased; birth intervals became shorter, and fertility rose sharply, especially during the postwar years. As a result, population growth between 1947 and 1957 averaged 1.7 percent per year, a very high rate for an industrial nation. Since 1957, however, age at marriage and the spacing of births have increased slightly and fertility dropped sharply. The current level of fertility is at Series D, approximately 2.5 children per woman.

As a result of that change we have added a Series E, based on 2.11 children, which in time, except for immigration, would result in a stationary population.

The fertility decline of recent years means that young women are now having fewer children than women in the same age groups had in the 1950s and 1960s. Surveys show that most women in those brackets say they want an average of three children. The fact that the present birth rate is below the expressed desire may mean that many of them are only postponing childbirth, but many demographers believe that postponement will actually result in a reduction of completed fertility. That is a factor which cannot be predicted with any accuracy.

The indications now are that the population of the country in 1985 will be between 240 and 250 million people, an increase of 35–45 million above the present level of about 204 million. This will occur because of the sharp gain in the absolute number of young adults in the next 10 to 15 years. The number of births will probably be between 3.5 and 4.5 million a year, and the rate of population increase should be from 1.1 to 1.4 percent per year, assuming a continuation of current levels of fertility. However, the level could well drop in view of easing of restrictions on abortion laws and the growing concern with the effect of population increase on the environment. If many states remove restrictions on abortion, it is considered likely that a further reduction in fertility would follow. Nations in which abortions have been legalized have noted that effect.

The United States gets about 400,000 persons a year now through immigration and that figure is not likely to change soon. The current law established a ceiling of 270,000 on alien immigration, but refugees and other special classes are admitted, bringing the total to 400,000. At that rate, by 1985 there would be about 6 million persons who had entered the country after 1970 and they would have had about 1.5 million children. An interesting paradox is that immigrants contribute more than their share of births in this country although age-by-age their fertility rates are less than that of the native population. The reason is that a high proportion of immigrants are in the prime childbearing age ranges.

If fertility rates drop as projected by Series E, immigration will contribute about a fourth of the total population growth from 1970 to 2000. Without any immigration, the replacement fertility assumption of Series E would eventually produce a stationary population. The population would level out at 275 million around the year 2037. With continued immigration, a stationary population level could only be obtained if fertility rates were to drop below the replacement level.

Even with a low fertility rate, the population growth will increase during the next decade because the proportion of women in childbearing ages will increase. On the information available, however, the growth rate might well return to its present level in the 80s or even drop below it.

A slower rate of growth would make it easier to cope with some of the domestic problems attributed to a booming population, according to some interested persons. Others contend that a stationary population would mean only that the population would be considerably older than at present. It would have an equal number of people under 15 and over 60 as compared with today when we have twice as many under 15 as over 60. The median age would be 37 as compared with 28 today. Concern has been expressed by some that an older, stationary population would be more resistant to change. The results of either growth or stabilization are debatable and outside the realm of the Census Bureau.

The expected changes in geographic distribution between now and 1985 constitute another important factor in projecting our future. The most significant geographic shifts in population we have seen are those which have occurred and are expected to continue in the central cities and suburbs of metropolitan areas. It is well known that people throughout the world have a preference for city life. The question of advantages versus disadvantages is open to discussion but that again is outside our field.

In the United States, two out of every three people now live in metropolitan areas. In 1900 only about 42 percent of our population lived in metropolitan areas. Between 1950 and 1960, when the nation as a whole grew by about 19 percent, the metropolitan areas grew by 27 percent. In the period since 1960, when the national growth was about 12 percent, that of the metropolitan areas was about 15 percent. The significance of those figures is obvious. They indicate that, although metropolitan areas are still growing more rapidly than the rest of the country, the differential is narrowing. If the trends of the past decade continue, the result could be that the proportion of the population living in metropolitan areas would increase by one percentage point during the ten-year span between 1965 and 1975—compared with an increase of four percentage points between 1940 and 1950 and an additional four percentage points between 1950 and 1960.

Our experts have made another interesting observation. We know that nonmetropolitan counties as a whole in the United States are growing below the national average. However, those nonmetropolitan counties crossed by a freeway and having a moderately sized urban center—between 25,000 and 50,000 people—are growing more rapidly than others. These counties, since 1960, grew at the same rate as the national average. The growth in these counties contradicts the popular notion that our nation's population is on the high road to engulfing itself in a number of big, densely packed urban centers.

We are now in the era of the suburbs. In recent years, practically all of the growth in metropolitan areas was in the suburban rings. Since 1960, central cities as a whole grew only about 1 percent. The suburban rings soared in population by 28 percent. And the balance between central cities and suburban rings has clearly shifted since 1960. At that time, suburban areas had slightly fewer people than the central cities. Since then, more than half the people in our metropolitan areas live outside central cities and every indication is this fraction will grow.

The black population is now more heavily concentrated in the central cities than the white population. About three fourths of the growth in the black population since 1960 has occurred in central cities of metropolitan areas. Although central cities gained only three quarters of a million persons between 1960 and 1969, this net change was the result of an increase of 2.7 million in the black population and a decline of 2.1 million in the white population.

Looking 15 years ahead, some of our experts at the Bureau of the Census say that in 1985, if past trends continue, nearly half of our national population will be living in the suburban parts of our metropolitan areas and only one fourth will be living in central cities. Virtually all of the white growth has occurred in the suburban ring. The nonwhite growth has taken place primarily in the central cities. Unless there is a sharp change in the trends we observed in the decades 1950–60 and 1960–70, one third of central city residents would be black in 1985 compared to one fifth at present.

In discussing growth, we must consider individual states and the factors contributing to their population changes. Population growth in most places is affected more by the excess of births over deaths than by migration. Obviously, therefore, the greatest absolute growth now and in the future is expected in the most populous states. But if we examine gains due to net migration, we find that now and in the future the following states will attract the greatest number of migrants: California and Arizona in the West, Florida and Maryland in the South, and New Jersey and Connecticut in the Northeast. Census experts believe that most of the north central states can expect continued out-migration of their population to other areas of the country.

It is important to realize that many areas of the nation are losing people and have been losing them for a long time. There has been an absolute decline in population in almost 44 percent of our counties between 1960 and 1970, particularly those in the central and southern areas where agriculture has been the dominant occupation. About 75 percent of all counties had more out-migrants than in-migrants. The following areas lost population between 1950 and 1960 and again between 1960 and 1970: a band of counties in the Middle West from the Dakotas and Minnesota to Texas and Louisiana and across the South to Georgia and South Carolina. In addition, there are areas in South Appalachia and in the sections adjoining the northern Great Lakes which have a long history of population decline.

A report of the National Goals research staff says this: "A deliberate policy of encouraging growth in alternate growth centers away from large urban masses—coupled with a complementary effort of the use of new towns—is a viable option that warrants consideration." Alternative growth centers are defined as "middle size communities"—usually upwards of 50,000 but as small as 25,000—which are growing or have the potential for self-sustained growth."

Much remains to be done to determine the reasons for exceptional growth and the probable future for each area. Work has been started on assembling data from our economic census to serve as a base for evaluating possibilities for private enterprise in each potential growth center. We hope to be able to identify those kinds of business which tend to be associated with areas of unusual growth.

Another significant trend is the expanding metropolis. Eighteen new metropolitan areas have been added to the census rolls since 1960. The land area of several other metropolitan areas also has expanded considerably since that time. The size of metropolitan areas (defined as a central city of 50,000 or more plus adjacent counties socially and economically integrated with that city) will grow as technology improves and as new highways and other transportation systems are built. These make it possible for people in outlying areas to travel to nearby large cities for work, entertainment, and culture. This expansion in the size of the metropolitan areas is expected to result in a continued decrease in population density.

Our demographers have made computations showing population densities for major urbanized areas (100,000 persons or more) from 1920 to the year 1960. These areas generally represented either a zone of continuous urban counties clustered around one major metropolitan area, or separate metropolitan areas that were not adjacent to other metropolitan areas. These data show the following: population per square mile in these urbanized areas declined from 6,580 in 1920 to 4,230 in 1960. By the year 2000—when it's estimated that 70 percent of the U.S. population will be living in these areas—the population per square mile is expected to decline still more—to 3,732.

The reason for this seeming paradox is that despite more people in metropolitan areas, there has been a lesser concentration of population density within these areas. This is because of expanded utilization of the land area in suburban rings by an increase in the number of people living in these outlying areas. This flight to suburbia has been made possible through advances in technology. Cars and trucks, new highways, electric power, the telephone—all these have allowed people to move farther and farther away from central cities without inconvenience including, in many cases, any major barrier in commuting. As a matter of fact, one of our studies shows that only about one fifth of all commuters spend more than a half hour getting to work.

Here's a look at 1985 from still another important angle: There will be a dramatic rise in the number of younger adults from now to 1985. One third of the expected total population increase will be in the 25 to 34 year group. Altogether, we expect to have an additional 28 million people who will be in their 20s, 30s, and early 40s. On the other hand, there will be virtually no change in the number of people between 45 and 64. Most of the remaining 16 million persons, who are expected to be added to segments of the population in the next 15 years, will be:

—Pre-schoolers (8 million).
—Persons over 65 (6 million).
—School age children from 5 to 15 years old (2 million).

The most significant fact about the expected change in age composition is the very sharp increase in the number of persons in their 20s and early 30s. The meaning is clear: The next 15 years is the era of the young married.

Therefore, we anticipate a rapid rate of household formation and relatively large numbers of births. During the past few years there has been an average of nearly two million marriages per year, up from 1 million in the early 1930s. Census experts believe this will continue for the next 15 years, reaching a peak of about 2.5 million by 1985. They also see it as creating a mixed pattern of housing for the next 10 years. For one thing there may be a short-term decline in home ownership as the heavy crop of young marrieds start their wedded life in apartments since in many cases both husband and wife are likely to work and to postpone family increase for a time. However, as they begin to acquire a savings account and as children are born, the majority will probably buy a home in the suburbs.

Home ownership is a continuing part of the American tradition. The figures from the 1970 census show that 62.9 percent of all households owned their own homes. This is up from 61.9 percent as recorded in the 1960 census. The percentage, of course, varied according to the age of the household's head. Under 25 years, the percentage was 20.3, but it rose steadily to a peak of 74.5 percent in the 45 to 54 age bracket. After that it declined to 70.4 for those 65 and older. Those who spent childhood years in a house rather than an apartment are likely to have a feeling of nostalgia for the qualities of a house.

There is reason to believe that the houses which these young people buy are increasingly likely to be row houses or, as the real estate developers now call them, town houses. With 70 percent of our population already living in metropolitan areas, the supply of land within 30 minutes driving time to the central city is steadily diminishing and will be even more scarce by 1980.

To a large degree this underlying trend will surface in the form of cluster housing—groups of three to six town houses with possibly each unit sold as a condominium. These clusters will not have all the features of detached houses. They will have a little land around them but not enough to let each husband spend his weekends with a lawnmower.

The increasing shift to the suburbs will not be limited to white families. As minority people become more affluent, some of them will leave the central cities. This in turn will bring about a change in the inner city dwellings.

All of us are familiar with the residential pattern so common to the older eastern cities—four- to six-story structures stretching block after block with no open areas except the streets. Before the days of the automobile this was an efficient way to live, with school, church, work, and shopping all within walking distance or easily reached by public transportation. With the changing times, this particular type of city dwelling is increasingly less satisfactory. Many of these buildings will be pulled down in the years to come and most of them are apt to be replaced by high-rise apartments with surrounding green areas.

Although much will be done to correct the current ills of the inner cities, it seems very doubtful that anything will reverse the exodus to the suburbs. Our experts say that if the past is any indication of the future, nearly half of our population will be living in the suburbs in the 1980s while only a fourth will be in the central cities.

We have already considered some of the major trends in age distribution—foreseeing the accent on young adults. These trends will have an important impact in the next 15 years on school enrollments. The number of elementary school pupils will probably drop slightly in the next few years, return to its present level by 1980, and then rise somewhat by 1985. High school enrollment is expected to change relatively little in the next 15 years. However, the number of college students is expected to rise by more than 50 percent from its present level of 7.5 million to about 11.5 million in 1985. About half the expected rise in college enrollment is due to population increase; an equal amount is due to the proportion of young people attending college. It is obvious that, if our society is to have the ability to handle the numbers of young people who expect to attend college, we not only need more facilities and faculties and college presidents, but farsighted vision and understanding on the part of the public if we are to plan adequately for the next 15 years.

There is still another way of looking at our coming age distribution:

1. Rapid growth among young adults between 20 and 34.
2. Lack of growth in the 45 to 64 year age group.

Some say such an age ratio could mean the following: There may be a shortage of experienced older men for positions of leadership in government, industrial management, and politics. There could be pressure on some older men to postpone retirement. In any event, by 1985 we may expect to see more young leaders in government, private industry, and politics than ever before.

Census experts believe American families will have far greater incomes in 1985 than they have today. All we need to do is assume that the level of income will continue to rise at the same rate it has for the past decade and that the cumulative percent distribution of families and of income will be constant for each age group. Overall, the U.S. growth rate in constant dollars has been a little more than 3 percent per year.

Based on these assumptions, real incomes would grow by more than 100 percent during the next 15 years. In 1968, family money income totaled $500 billion. By 1985, it is expected to exceed $1 trillion in 1968 dollars. Average family income is expected to rise from the $8,600 of 1968 to $15,000 in 1985, measured in dollars of constant purchasing power. It is estimated that median family income was about $10,000 in 1970. About one third of total income in 1968 was received by families with income over $15,000. By 1985, over half of family income will be in the hands of families whose income was over $15,000. Moreover, because of the combined impact of both income and population growth, the number of dollars in constant-purchasing-power at this upper income level will be about five times as great as it was in 1968.

About half of the added purchasing power will be in hands of the 25–44 age group by 1985. At present, about 42 percent of all purchasing power is represented in the 25–44 age category.

We are heading into a society of an affluent majority. This statement has tremendous economic, social, moral, political, and other major implications. It is here, perhaps, that a man like George Orwell is needed. For it is here that the role of statistician stops. Could it be that the danger to society lies not with our political and personal freedom, but with our new-found affluence—not in far away places, but inside America?

Is our national inheritance of such riches going to bring about the following: greater pollution of our air and water, more consumption of each natural resource, more goods and services, gadgetry gone wild, more crime, more narcotics . . . more and more and more?

Or will we use our increase in affluence to pay for pollution-free cars and planes; for cleaned-up rivers and lakes; for better schools; for updating of penal systems and institutions—a gamut of public services and needs?

We must begin a new search—not for more quantity in life, but for balanced and purposeful growth. This search will be conducted in an environment where we will see continued expansion of suburbs, but, at the same time, new growth centers. No big need to build more elementary and high schools for a while, but the necessity to prepare for greatly expanding college enrollment, the so-called population bomb being defused; But for the present there will be a sizable increase among newlyweds in the 1980s. Our population is expected to be somewhere between 240 and 250 million Americans by 1985, but the nation will have far more affluence than any society has ever seen.

This is an exciting time to be alive. This is an important time to be alive. Each and everyone of us is inescapably involved in the problems the next 15 years will bring.

Buyer behavior is influenced by both product and convenience costs. A trend, which offers a key to the future under-

*standing of buyer behavior, is evolving. Consumers are plac-
ing an increasing importance on time and other convenience
forms. The present article discusses consumer valuation of
several forms of convenience, with special attention devoted
to time and place convenience.*

---

3. THE POVERTY OF TIME, SPATIAL CONSIDERATIONS, AND BUYER BEHAVIOR *

Eugene J. Kelley † and James W. Harvey ‡

Forecasts of social and economic trends for the 1970s indicate that:

1. Urbanization with its problems of urban congestion and decay will continue.
2. Individualism and personal goal fulfillment will be increasingly important.
3. The desire for mobility—geographic, occupational, and social—will increase.
4. Affluence will increase dramatically.[1]
5. The "psychology of affluence" will become increasingly important.
6. The reaction against complexity in our lives will gain momentum.[2]
7. The concern with quality of life issues will increase.

These and other factors will contribute to a phenomenon which will continue to profoundly influence buyer behavior: the poverty of time. Poverty of time is a phenomenon that reverses the major constraint on consumption from money to time. This important trend was described in the Whirlpool study as "A New Poverty of Time." Time will become a more significant factor in product/service selection and use. Furthermore, the marketing paradox of the 1970s may be that increasing affluence will result in less rather than more free time because the alternatives competing for the consumers' time will increase significantly.

As urban congestion continues, the desire for mobility and self-expression increases, and consumers attach new importance to time considera-

---

* A 1973 revision of "The Importance of Convenience in Consumer Purchasing,"
Journal of Marketing, Vol. 23, No. 1 (July 1958), pp. 32–38.
† Pennsylvania State University.
‡ Pennsylvania State University.
[1] CELS—Whirlpool Research Report.
[2] Yankelovich Monitor, p. 13 ff.

tions; the marketer needs to take a new look at the commodity and convenience costs which comprise his product/service market offer. Commodity costs are defined as the monetary price paid to the seller to obtain possession of goods and services. Convenience costs are incurred through the expenditure of time, physical and nervous energy, the money required to overcome the frictions of space and time, and the effort required to obtain possession of goods and services.

The dimensions of conflicting social values which comprise the poverty of time are growing exponentially. Many situations exemplify the growing antagonism between the limited environmental resources and the rush for more personalized lifestyles. During the mid-60s, for example, general aviation units numbered 95,000 in the United States and were growing at a rate twice that forecast by the Federal Aviation Agency.[3] The FAA warned at that time consumption may have to be significantly curtailed in the 70s due to inadequate supporting facilities. Likewise, the National Association of Engine and Boat Manufacturers reported 7.8 million recreational boats in service during the same period with only 5,400 marinas, boat yards, and yacht clubs to serve them.[4] During the 100th anniversary of the National Parks System in 1972, the secretary of the interior announced that parts of selected national parks would no longer be freely accessible. For a period of time, certain wilderness areas will only be open on an application basis controlled by the Park Service. Similar fears and solutions are being expressed about Honolulu, Hawaii, and Waikiki Beach [5] as well as every other major metropolitan area.

Other trends, the new affluence—emphasizing increased purchasing power, the desire for personal fulfillment, and a shortened work week all contribute to the strain on our limited living space. Illustrating this new affluence, income projections indicate that over the 17 years from 1968 to 1985 the median real income will increase as much as it has over the previous 50 years.[6] By 1985, 50 percent of the population will enjoy the same level of living characterized by the top 15 percent of the population in 1968.[7] The median family income in 1980 will be $15,400 compared to a 1970 figure of $11,400, in constant 1970 dollars.[8]

The desire for personal fulfillment reflects itself in the "psychology of affluence" and anticomplexity trends which constitute a new awareness and desire for personal satisfaction.[9] These trends manifest themselves in the former with a new focus on the quality of living, physical self-enhancement, physical fitness and well-being, and personal creativity. A "return to nature," the desire for life simplification, and the regaining of

---

[3] "Bugs in the Leisure Boom," *Printer's Ink* (July 22, 1966), p. 3.
[4] Ibid.
[5] *Wall Street Journal* (April 5, 1972), p. 1.
[6] CELS—Whirlpool Research Report, p. 11.
[7] CELS—Whirlpool Research Report, p. 11.
[8] CELS—Whirlpool Research Report, p. 45.
[9] Yankelovich Monitor, p. 13 ff.

a sense of control over one's destiny emerge in trends centered on personal satisfaction.

The final strain on living space—a shortened work week—is already becoming a reality. A significant number of firms are on the four-day work week already. The six-month work year [10] and the three-day work week "are being seriously proposed." [11] However, real leisure time may not increase for some time. This is due to the inefficiencies and demand for labor in our distribution and services sectors of the economy.[12] Furthermore, the rise in affluence will mean a rise in accumulated possessions. It will take time and money to support this new wealth. It has been estimated that by 1980 the typical middle-income family will be spending 15 percent of its income for servicing its possessions.[13] This difficulty in dealing with acquired technology appears to be a significant block to real leisure time.[14] Also, there is evidence that as the work period shrinks, the demand for a second job increases.[15] Furthermore, an empirical study indicated leisure time has not changed from the 1930s: approximately five hours per day.[16]

As these measures of conflicting social values come into greater focus, the illusion of leisure time becomes increasingly apparent and the legitimacy of the poverty of time is underscored. Consistent with the prediction of the new poverty of time, consumers are likely to place higher value on products and services which minimize time expenditures. This new evaluative dimension has important implications for marketing policy makers responsible for developing product, promotion, and distribution strategies. Perhaps the most readily apparent implication is that marketing executives will need to augment their decision-making guidelines to include this new consumer awareness of multidimensional product costs. The task confronting the decision maker is to implement creative strategies which will better balance consumer commodity costs with convenience costs. Including these new convenience cost criteria in decision models may very well be the key to differential advantage in the face of an increasingly hostile marketplace.

There appear to be ten major dimensions of convenience costs which need to be considered. While time and place appear to have the most significant impact on consumer decision making, others deserve brief con-

---

[10] "A 6-Month 'Work Year' Is Called a Possibility," *Wall Street Journal* (March 29, 1972), p. 1.

[11] *Sales Management* (April 1, 1970), pp. 37–39.

[12] "There'll Be Less Leisure Than You Think," *Fortune* (March 1970), pp. 86 ff.

[13] E. B. Weiss, "Inconvenience and Expense of Home Appliance, Servicing Grow," *Advertising Age* (March 13, 1972), p. 47.

[14] Kenneth Boulding, "Time as a Commodity," *New Republic* (February 21, 1970), pp. 27, 28; "The Myth of Milady's Leisure," *Printer's Ink* (April 22, 1966), p. 35; Edwin Blakelock, "A Look at the New Leisure," *Administrative Science Quarterly* (March 1960), pp. 446–67.

[15] *Monthly Labor Review* (September 1967), pp. 21, 22.

[16] *Time* (September 8, 1967), p. 61.

sideration. A closer examination of some of the specific factors contributing to the proverty of time will underscore the significance of this trend.

SHOPPING COSTS AND THE POVERTY OF TIME

The question of consumer time expenditures for shopping is an interesting one. It has been estimated that there is a minimum of five billion adult leisure hours each week in the United States. This reflects in part a population concensus to accept a substantial share of the benefits of the production and marketing revolutions in increased leisure. Paradoxically, the increase in leisure time has been accompanied by a reaction against spending much of that leisure shopping. The modern family is confronted with too many more attractive possible uses of time.

Many forces favor higher consumer valuations of leisure and other convenience considerations. The suburban population movement with its living habit changes and broader family interests is one such force. In urban areas also, fundamental social forces are operating which have resulted in families functioning more as a group than as individuals in certain activities, even to the extent of buying together. Such forces favoring higher convenience cost valuations include the large numbers of working housewives, the age group imbalance within the population, and higher educational levels.

Consumer estimates of purchasing costs are determined by their evaluations of alternative trading and social opportunities. Purchase decisions are made at the point where the total of commodity and convenience costs are considered minimal.

On the supply side, sellers are operating in what seems to be an increasingly standardized production and legal matrix which is tending to limit price competition. The relatively narrow price spread among most retailers carrying identical nationally advertised merchandise suggests a new importance for convenience costs in the strategy determination of sellers. It appears reasonable to speculate that the range of competitive advantage based on commodity costs will narrow. In this setting, it is probable that convenience considerations will assume more importance as determinants of purchase behavior and seller strategy, and that more of the competition of the future will focus on convenience considerations.

Ten convenience forms

The importance of convenience as a determinant of consumer acceptance of products and services can be observed in an increasingly wide range of convenience features built into new products and in new convenience forms appearing in the marketing system. Charles G. Mortimer, President of the General Foods Corporation, has described ten forms of convenience which the American consumer now expects almost as a matter of course.[17]

1. *Form convenience*—cigarettes in various sizes and tips, and vest-pocket radios.
2. *Time convenience*—typified by evening hours, and fresh fruits and vegetables out of season.
3. *Place convenience*—life insurance in airline terminals, drive-it-yourself automobile rental services; and the planned shopping center.
4. *Quantity or unit convenience*—aspirin in tins of 12, or bottles of 500; and smaller pianos for the smaller home.
5. *Packaging convenience*—disposable and utility packages; and the packaged vacation plan. The packaged home is already on the market.
6. *Readiness convenience*—instant coffee; precooked foods; and *The Reader's Digest.*
7. *Combination convenience*—do-it-yourself kits; and combination and matched sets.
8. *Automatic operations convenience*—automatic kitchen equipment; power steering and brakes on automobiles; and automation in many fields.
9. *Selection convenience*—the new variety of dairy products; and automobile color combinations.
10. *Credit convenience*—cars; homes; vacation cruises; and education on credit.

Four aspects of place convenience

Sellers should study all ten convenience forms to find areas in which consumer convenience costs may be reduced. This article is concerned specifically with place convenience. In maximizing place convenience advantages, sellers have related decisions at four levels to make about the spatial positions that products ideally should occupy in the market.

1. The geographic area or areas in which the goods or services are to be offered must be selected. In these areas or markets are found the consumers of the goods. This seller decision usually is not of concern to the shopper who may choose from the offerings of many sellers of substitute products.

The shopping mobility of consumers has tended to be limited to one metropolitan area, but this may not be the case in the future. Perhaps some larger scale retailers may become concerned about competition between metropolitan areas as well as with competition within a metropolitan area. For instance, it may represent the same expenditure of

---

[17] Charles J. Mortimer, *Two Keys to Modern Marketing* (Scarsdale, N.Y.: The Updegraff Press, Ltd., 1955), pp. 7–17.

convenience costs for a West Hartford resident to order by mail from Hartford, or even to make the trip to downtown Hartford. Conceivably, a Hartford department store could become concerned about the drawing power of New York, Boston, and Providence department stores, as well as competition from suburban Hartford stores.

On the other hand, as metropolitan areas grow together to form urban regions, the primate cities of New York, Chicago, and Los Angeles are likely to lose some of their retail leadership to burgeoning regional and provincial metropolitan areas. This may occur in the same fashion, and for much the same reasons, that the central business district has lost ground to suburban elements in the retail structure.

2. The most satisfactory positions within the market must be selected from those offered by distributors and retailers selling space in the market. Channel-of-distribution decisions are involved. The one-stop shopping tendency of consumers has made channel selection more difficult for sellers in today's fluid market.

3. Choices must be made among competing retail and wholesale institutions offering access to the customer. Should a full service wholesaler be utilized, or would a limited function wholesaler represent a better channel choice? Are urban or suburban positions preferred? What is the role of the shopping center?

The planned shopping center movement can be rationalized with some justification in terms of consumer convenience. At the same time, planned centers are more than devices for convenient shopping or mechanisms for retail sales expansion in suburban areas. Planned shopping centers are a basic part of the restructuring of metropolitan communities. Their long-term importance to the economy is based on a continuing reassessment by consumers of shopping and social activities. Consumer convenience is still probably the basis of the shopping center movement. But the social, economic, and architectural concepts underlying planned centers are geared to a new kind of social pattern and to what may be an eruption into a new American social dimension in which consumer desires will require new patterns of marketing.

4. Problems of positioning of goods within outlets must be settled. Display and layout decisions are involved at this level. An experiment by Alfred Politz suggests the importance of convenience within the store. In studying the anatomy of the sale, he purchased and operated a large hardware store in Tampa, Florida. He found that if a product is sufficiently well known to get consumer acceptance and is conveniently located, the consumer will buy it in preference to a better known product. While the customer will not select a product he has not heard about, "the least little bit of inconvenience wipes out the impressiveness of even the best known brands." [18]

---

[18] Alfred Politz, "Politz Studies Store Customers," *Tide*, Vol. 21 (September 28, 1956), pp. 20–21, from p. 21.

Conflicting cost considerations

A dominant characteristic of consumer goods marketing at present is the state of flux of consumer valuations of commodity and convenience costs. While such developments as the discount house reflect strong consumer interest in the reduction of commodity costs, it is quite possible that convenience costs will increase in importance as patronage determinants for more low dollar value items. This will pose anew one of the most challenging problems facing retailers in our complex distribution system: offering the right mix of convenience and economy to customers. Rich rewards may go to merchants able to do this successfully. A wedding of the shopping center concept and the discount house idea represents one promising approach.

Convenience cost pressures are likely to affect more marketing agencies in the future. Some of the possible impacts on planned shopping centers and established business districts are suggested below.

CONVENIENCE FORCES AND THE RETAIL STRUCTURE

Planned center increase

The shopping center movement is so new that currently two thirds of existing centers are less than ten years old. This fact, together with the predicted center expansion, indicates that the full impact of the movement has yet to be felt. A fundamental change in the retail structure of metropolitan communities seems certain, as a result of shopping center growth. Over 13,000 planned shopping centers are now in operation. Estimates have been made that by 1980, 21,000 of them will be operating. This means a planned shopping center for each 10,700 of a projected 1980 population of 225 million. This expansion is not expected to be uninterrupted. Many poorly planned intermediate centers are particularly vulnerable to new competition.

Individual stores and shopping centers are tending to be larger. Department store branches of 300,000 square feet, and supermarkets of 50,000 square feet have already appeared. A minimum site for regional centers used to be considered 50 acres. Regional center developers are now thinking in terms of 100 acres as a minimum site. Tracts of this size are extremely expensive, especially if they are in or near large cities. The increasing size of regional centers may mean that in the future such centers will be located farther from large population concentrations, and nearer the suburban periphery.

Consumer convenience considerations also set a limit to the growth of individual stores and centers. For instance, it is generally agreed that shoppers resist walking more than 600 feet from their parked cars to the nearest center store. With planned centers, this suggests a limit for the maximum parking distance that can be used before the planned center loses its advantages over unplanned shopping districts.

The distance concept and convenience

The distance concept involves time-cost elements rather than a purely spatial one. High-speed roads enabling consumers to travel farther from home on shopping trips are changing consumer views on distance. In our society of automobile-borne suburbanites, distance between metropolitan points will increasingly be judged on a time basis, not a mileage basis. The impact of this on established retail patterns is already evident. Downtown retailers have had to compete aggressively for suburban business in order to hold a satisfactory market position. Effective downtown competition for suburban trade is still possible. Indeed, a pattern for the rehabilitation of central business districts has developed. It includes improving access, traffic, and parking conditions; modernizing physical facilities; conducting imaginative promotions; and strengthening mass transportation. In short, it means restoring some of the lost convenience aspects to central business district shopping.

Changing functions in the metropolitan retail structure

The central business district and suburban shopping center provide essential but different services to the community.[19] Retail functions within the central business district and the other elements of the metropolitan retail structure are being modified. Store locations are shifting in the inner core, inner belt, and outer belt of the central business district and main business thoroughfares. Similarly, retailers in planned and unplanned secondary commercial sub-districts, neighborhood business streets, small store clusters, and planned regional shopping centers are modifying functions to adapt to the needs of consumers living and shopping over a wider area. The downtown area may respond by becoming more of a business, service, and recreational center and less of a mercantile one. Opinions on this vary widely. Frank Lloyd Wright visualized the city of the future without a central shopping district. Others anticipate a downtown renaissance stimulated in part by shopping center competition, which will force more downtown property owners and merchants into rehabilitation and redesign programs.

Other dimensions of convenience

In addition to spatial and temporal aspects, convenience has social and esthetic dimensions. This is one reason shopping centers are likely to play

---

[19] Eugene J. Kelley, "Retail Structure of Urban Economy," *Traffic Quarterly*, Vol. 9, No. 3 (July 1955), pp. 411–30, from p. 411.

an increasingly important role in community social life. All shopping centers are likely to benefit by following a policy of community identification, although the benefits are particularly apparent with the larger community and regional centers. Auditoriums, meeting rooms, restaurants, and other facilities making shopping more convenient are found in more planned centers. As more planned centers include such amenities, shopping centers may come to resemble earlier marketplaces, which served social as well as trading functions.

Consumers favor centers in which merchandise is presented conveniently, informally, and interestingly. Shopping-center planning, therefore, extends logically to promotions and events calculated to restore some of the excitement and pleasure to shopping. The modified bazaar concept of the center is likely to gain favor as weather-controlled centers without window displays and partitions come into being. For instance, Southdale, the new regional center outside Minneapolis, has a glass enclosed mall connecting the various stores in the center.

Convenience and new retail types

New store types are likely to appear in planned centers. Since shopping centers are located on choice, relatively low-cost land compared with downtown stores, one-floor retailing operations are possible to an extent not practical downtown. This may mean a reduction in handling costs and in the number of people needed to conduct and supervise operations. Some specialty stores in planned centers should be in a position to offer more variety in prices and styles than downtown specialty stores operating in less space.

Convenience pressures may provide a stimulus for other retailing developments offering lower convenience costs to consumers. Among these may be increased direct-to-consumer selling, catalogue and telephone selling, perhaps a combination of television and telephone selling, and automatic vending machines. Improved vending equipment selling an increasingly broad variety of merchandise could turn some planned centers and store clusters into round-the-clock merchandising machines.

Implications for decision making

The success of convenience-based innovations, such as planned shopping centers, raises questions about the role of spatial and other convenience considerations in marketing. The shopping center movement is distinguished by its spatial differentiation from other elements in the metropolitan retail structure. Essentially, consumers have attempted to overcome friction of space; and sellers have responded by offering a spatially or convenience-differentiated product. The results have been outstanding. Yet many sellers have ignored the lessons implicit in shopping center success. In most retailing operations the major concentration of managerial attention is still focused on the product and the promotion of the product, while the convenience conditions surrounding the sale of the product receive little study. But the retailing process exists in space over time; and retailers are concerned with the creation of place and time as well as possession utilities. Indeed, the very art of marketing is based on the skillful manipulation of spatial, temporal, and ownership forces in the market to achieve that objective.

Understanding of the current state of the art requires acceptance of change itself as the dominant characteristic of marketing. If understanding of the process of market change, the forces producing change, and, therefore, ability to develop policies under accelerated change conditions is to be increased, more attention to the convenience aspects of marketing seems justified.

More goods and services will be distributed at the price in convenience and commodity costs that consumers are willing to pay, as more sellers develop convenience-based policies. It seems probable that sellers reacting ponderously to the new consumer assessment of convenience costs will suffer. On the other hand, sellers creatively alert to the importance of convenience costs to contemporary consumers, and who adjust strategy accordingly, should strengthen their market position. These sellers will also contribute to producing the volume of transactions necessary to maintain and expand the American economy.

b.

Consumer behavior models and theories

CONSUMER BEHAVIOR and buyer behavior (a subset of consumer behavior) are two of the most critical dimensions in the field of marketing left unsolved. They remain mysterious to the marketing planner with all their complexities, uncertainties, and seemingly irrationalities being controlled and hidden within the traditional psychological "black box."

By examining the behavior of consumers, marketers can at least move one step closer to understanding the processes the consumer goes through in making purchase decisions. However, the marketing strategy should recognize the potential in the understanding of the interrelationship between behavior and the psychological process of consumer decision-making.

Behavioral science concepts and theories can be used to provide a fresh appreciation of the causes of many aspects of consumer behavior and thereby allow the marketer to better design, modify, and refine his product and market activities. In addition, linking behavioral science research findings with the firm's own research findings would provide a greater understanding of the firm's market segments.

There is often a tendency to concentrate on the behavior of individual consumers; however, people are social animals and their behavior is directly or indirectly influenced by others. Marketing has benefited greatly from the use of sociological and social-psychological concepts and approaches in studying mass behavior, small group behavior, and generally group versus individual interaction influence and behavior. Furthermore, one's knowledge of how people are influenced, and under what conditions, also has an important application in the development of the promotional and various other marketing areas of activity of the firm. In total, then, the behavioral sciences have a great deal to contribute to the area of marketing, but this should not free marketing researchers from their own research responsibilities.

In the first article, Maslow presents his well-known theory of motivation. Lazer then examines this theory from a marketing viewpoint. Coleman uses a sociological base for market segmentation in the third article. In the next selection Grubb and Grathwohl explore the relationship between a person's self-concept and the symbolic value of the goods he buys. Then Kotler presents the main types of behavioral models used in studying consumer behavior. Finally, the last article, by Lazer, provides an overview to a comprehensive model of buyer behavior.

Sound marketing decisions are based on a knowledge of consumer motivations. Man is characterized as a wanting animal with a hierarchy of needs. Behavior should be viewed as a channel through which multiple needs are expressed and satisfied. These aspects are considered in the present article.

4. A THEORY OF HUMAN MOTIVATION *

A. H. Maslow †

INTRODUCTION

In a previous paper various propositions were presented which would have to be included in any theory of human motivation that could lay claim to being definitive. These conclusions may be briefly summarized as follows:

* Reprinted from "A Theory of Human Motivation," *Psychological Review*, Vol. 50, No. 4 (July 1943), pp. 370–96. For a later, comprehensive treatment of human motivation, see A. H. Maslow, *Motivation and Personality* (New York: Harper & Row, Publishers, 1954), pp. 80–160. For a discussion of psychological theories and their relevance to the study of consumer behavior, see James A. Bayton, "Motivation, Cognition, Learning—Basic Factors in Consumer Behavior," *Journal of Marketing*, (January 1958), pp. 282–89.

† Brandeis University.

1. The integrated wholeness of the organism must be one of the foundation stones of motivation theory.

2. The hunger drive (or any other physiological drive) was rejected as a centering point or model for a definitive theory of motivation. Any drive that is somatically based and localizable was shown to be atypical rather than typical in human motivation.

3. Such a theory should stress and center itself upon ultimate or basic goals rather than partial or superficial ones, upon ends rather than means to these ends. Such a stress would imply a more central place for unconscious than for conscious motivations.

4. There are usually available various cultural paths to the same goal. Therefore conscious, specific, local-cultural desires are not as fundamental in motivation theory as the more basic, unconscious goals.

5. Any motivated behavior, either preparatory or consummatory, must be understood to be a channel through which many basic needs may be simultaneously expressed or satisfied. Typically an act has *more* than one motivation.

6. Practically all organismic states are to be understood as motivated and as motivating.

7. Human needs arrange themselves in hierarchies of prepotency. That is to say, the appearance of one need usually rests on the prior satisfaction of another, more prepotent need. Man is a perpetually wanting animal. Also no need or drive can be treated as if it were isolated or discrete; every drive is related to the state of satisfaction or dissatisfaction of other drives.

8. *Lists* of drives will get us nowhere for various theoretical and practical reasons. Furthermore, any classification of motivations must deal with the problems of levels of specificity or generalization of the motives to be classified.

9. Classifications of motivations must be based upon goals rather than upon instigating drives or motivated behavior.

10. Motivation theory should be human-centered rather than animal-centered.

11. The situation or the field in which the organism reacts must be taken into account, but the field alone can rarely serve as an exclusive explanation for behavior. Furthermore, the field itself must be interpreted in terms of the organism. Field theory cannot be a substitute for motivation theory.

12. Not only the integration of the organism must be taken into account, but also the possibility of isolated, specific, partial or segmental reactions.

It has since become necessary to add to these another affirmation.

13. Motivation theory is not synonymous with behavior theory. The

motivations are only one class of determinants of behavior. While behavior is almost always motivated, it is also almost always biologically, culturally and situationally determined as well. . . .

SUMMARY

1. There are at least five sets of goals, which we may call basic needs. These are briefly physiological, safety, love, esteem, and self-actualization. In addition, we are motivated by the desire to achieve or maintain the various conditions upon which these basic satisfactions rest and by certain more intellectual desires.

2. These basic goals are related to each other, being arranged in a hierarchy of prepotency. This means that the most prepotent goal will monopolize consciousness and will tend of itself to organize the recruitment of the various capacities of the organism. The less prepotent needs are minimized, even forgotten or denied. But when a need is fairly well satisfied, the next prepotent ("higher") need emerges, in turn to dominate the conscious life and to serve as the center of organization of behavior, since gratified needs are not active motivators.

Thus man is a perpetually wanting animal. Ordinarily the satisfaction of these wants is not altogether mutually exclusive, but only tends to be. The average member of our society is most often partially satisfied and partially unsatisfied in all of his wants. The hierarchy principle is usually empirically observed in terms of increasing percentages of nonsatisfaction as we go up the hierarchy. Reversals of the average order of the hierarchy are sometimes observed. Also it has been observed that an individual may permanently lose the higher wants in the hierarchy under special conditions. There are not only ordinarily multiple motivations for usual behavior, but in addition many determinants other than motives.

3. Any thwarting or possibility of thwarting of these basic human goals, or danger to the defenses which protect them, or to the conditions upon which they rest, is considered to be a psychological threat. With a few exceptions, all psychopathology may be partially traced to such threats. A basically thwarted man may actually be defined as a "sick" man, if we wish.

4. It is such basic threats which bring about the general emergency reactions.

5. Certain other basic problems have not been dealt with because of limitations of space. Among these are (a) the problem of values in any definitive motivation theory, (b) the relation between appetites, desires, needs and what is "good" for the organism, (c) the etiology of the basic needs and their possible derivation in early childhood, (d) redefinition of motivational concepts, i.e., drive, desire, wish, need, goal, (e) implication of our theory for hedonistic theory, (f) the nature of the uncompleted act, of success and failure, and of aspiration-level, (g) the role of association, habit and conditioning, (h) relation to the theory of interpersonal

relations, (*i*) implications for psychotherapy, (*j*) implication for theory of society, (*k*) the theory of selfishness, (*l*) the relation between needs and cultural patterns, (*m*) the relation between this theory and Allport's theory of functional autonomy. These as well as certain other less important questions must be considered as motivation theory attempts to become definitive.

What motivates customers? Maslow's hierarchy provides a framework to study behavioral dimensions of consumption and buying. Marketing strategies and management are and will be influenced by this theory. This article provides a marketing-oriented interpretation of the hierarchy of motives.

---

5. A NOTE ON MASLOW'S THEORY OF MOTIVATION *

William Lazer †

For marketing purposes, of the theories of motivation that have been advanced by different writers, and of the lists of drives, needs, motives, wants, and desires, Maslow's hierarchy of motives presents a conceptual framework as concise, direct, and logical as any.[1] It seems to offer a good perspective for better understanding of purchase and consumption behavior.

What motivates customers? Maslow states that "the study of motivation must be in part the study of ultimate human goals, desires, or needs."[2] He distinguishes five basic needs, goals behind which we cannot go, as we analyze consumer behavior. These needs stem from a multiplicity of conscious desires that seem to be ends in themselves that apparently do not need further justification or demonstration. This is shown in Chart 1.

The hierarchy of motives is a positive theory of motivation. Gratification becomes as important in the hierarchy as deprivation is to motivation theory. Gratification releases the person from the domination of certain needs and permits the emergence of others.

---

* Reprinted from William Lazer, *Marketing Management: A Systems Perspective* (New York: John Wiley & Sons, Inc., 1971), pp. 463–65.

† Michigan State University.

[1] A. H. Maslow, *Motivation and Personality* (New York: Harper & Row Publishers, 1954), pp. 66–92.

[2] Ibid., p. 66.

CHART 1

Hierarchy of motives

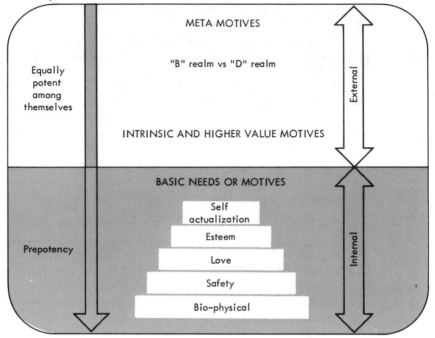

Physiological needs are considered the most prepotent of all. For instance, people who are hungry will be dominated by physiological needs and will not be concerned with other needs. All other needs are either pushed into the background or become nonexistent. When, however, the physiological needs are satisfied, other higher needs emerge and start to dominate the organism. When these are satisfied, newer and still higher needs keep emerging, and so on.

After seeking physiological satisfaction, the buyer becomes a safety-seeking mechanism. Our society makes people feel secure from criminals, assault, tyranny, fire, and animals. We satisfy safety needs through such devices as savings accounts, insurance of various types, pension plans, healthful foods, proper refrigeration, automobile accessories, and packaging.

When the physiological and safety needs are well gratified, the love needs, including affection and belongingness, emerge. These needs will be keenly felt as never before. People will hunger for affectionate relations with other people—for a place in various societal groups. As a result, different status groups and symbols emerge as a means of satisfying such needs.

Next in the hierarchy of human motivations is esteem. People desire self-esteem or self-respect, and prize a high evaluation of themselves by

others. Esteem needs are classified into two sets: (1) the desire for sufficient mastery and competence to achieve confidence, independence, and
freedom; (2) the desire for reputation, prestige, status, dominance, recognition, attention, and appreciation. Satisfaction of the self-esteem need
leads to feelings of strength, adequacy, usefulness, capability, and self-
confidence. "The most stable and, therefore, most healthy self-esteem is
based on *deserved* respect from others rather than on external fame or
celebrity and unwarranted adulation." [3]

The fifth and last basic need is self-actualization. "What a man *can*
become he *must*. This need we may call self-actualization." [4] It refers
to man's desire for self-fulfillment, the tendency to develop to the fullest.

Maslow's theory, therefore, is based on the following propositions.
There are at least five goals, which are termed basic needs. These are
the physiological, safety, love, esteem, and self-actualization needs. People
are motivated to achieve various conditions through which satisfaction
of these basic needs will be realized. These needs are related in a hier-
archial order of prepotency, which means that the most powerful one
will monopolize the consciousness. It will tend to recruit various capacities of the person, denying or minimizing the less prepotent needs. When
a need is satisfied, however, the next prepotent need emerges to dominate
the conscious reactions and serve as the focus of organization of human
behavior.

Buyers are perpetually in want. The average buyer is only partially
satisfied with respect to his vast and continuous array of needs. Usually
multiple motivations exist for behavior, and the satisfaction of one need
to the exclusion of others is the exceptional situation. In an economy of
abundance, furthermore, other determinants besides motives influence
behavior.

What happens when the stage of self-actualization is reached? What
happens after the accumulation of prestige, recognition, and symbols
such as the yacht, several homes, and travel? Maslow has postulated a
theory of meta motives. It states that self-actualizing people, having
gratified their basic needs, are motivated in other ways. They become
devoted to tasks "outside themselves," to tasks that embody intrinsic
values. At this level the self is enlarged to include other aspects of the
world; "pay" requires a higher level of definition, and inner requiredness
corresponds with external requiredness.

Maslow in his theory differentiates between the B realm—the realm
of being or the eternal—and the D realm—the realm of deficiencies or
the practical. Meta needs refer to the B realm, the intrinsic values. "The
hierarchy of basic needs is prepotent to the meta needs, but the meta
needs are equally potent among themselves." [5]

---

[3] Ibid., p. 91.
[4] Ibid., p. 92.
[5] This is shown in Chart 1 based on Abraham Maslow, "A Theory of Metamotiva-
tions," *The Humanist* (May–June 1967), p. 83.

Social class frequently exerts a significant influence on consumer purchasing behavior. Differences as well as similarities exist within each social class. The concept of under- and overprivileged families is introduced as an example of an intraclass difference. However, some situations, social class, like income, may not be a relevant factor in explaining market behavior.

6. THE SIGNIFICANCE OF SOCIAL STRATIFICATION IN SELLING*

Richard P. Coleman †

Dating back to the late 1940s, advertisers and marketers have alternately flirted with and cooled on the notion that W. Lloyd Warner's social class concept [1] is an important analytic tool for their profession. The Warnerian idea that six social classes constitute the basic division of American Society has offered many attractions to marketing analysts when they have grown dissatisfied with simple income categories or census-type occupational categories and felt a need for more meaningful classifications, for categorizations of the citizenry which could prove more relevant to advertising and marketing problems. However, in the course of their attempts to apply the class concept, marketers have not always found it immediately and obviously relevant. Sometimes it has seemed to shed light on advertising and merchandising problems and at other times it hasn't—with the result that many analysts have gone away disenchanted, deciding that social classes are not much more useful than income categories and procedurally far more difficult to employ.

It is the thesis of this writer that the role of social class has too often been misunderstood or oversimplified, and that if the concept is applied in a more sophisticated and realistic fashion, it will shed light on a great many problems to which, at first glance, it has not seemed particularly relevant. What we propose to do here, then, is discuss and illustrate a few of these more subtle, more refined and (it must be acknowledged) more complicated ways of applying social class analyses to marketing and advertising problems. In other words, the purpose of this paper is to

---

* Reprinted from "The Significance of Social Stratification in Selling," *Proceedings of the Winter Conference of the American Marketing Association*, 1960, pp. 171–84.
  † Social Research, Inc.
  [1] See W. Lloyd Warner, Marchia Meeker, and Kenneth Eells, *Social Class in America* (Chicago: Science Research Associates, 1949).

clarify *when* and *in what ways* social class concepts are significant in selling, and to suggest when they might not be as significant as other concepts, or at least need to be used in concert with other analytic categories.

THE WARNERIAN SOCIAL CLASSES

The six social classes which are referred to in this paper are those which W. Lloyd Warner and his associates have observed in their analyses of such diverse communities as Newburyport, Massachusetts,[2] Natchez, Mississippi,[3] Morris, Illinois,[4] Kansas City, Missouri,[5] and Chicago. These social classes are groups of people who are more or less equal to one another in prestige and community status; they are people who readily and regularly interact among themselves in both formal and informal ways; they form a "class" also to the extent that they share the same goals and ways of looking at life. It is this latter fact about social classes which makes them significant to marketers and advertisers.

Briefly characterized, the six classes are as follows, starting from the highest one and going down.[6]

1. The Upper-Upper or "Social Register" Class is composed of locally prominent families, usually with at least second- or third- generation wealth. Almost inevitably, this is the smallest of the six classes—with probably no more than one-half of 1 per cent of the population able to claim membership in this class. The basic values of these people might be summarized in these phrases: living graciously, upholding the family reputation, reflecting the excellence of one's breeding, and displaying a sense of community responsibility.

2. The Lower-Upper or "Nouveau Riche" Class is made up of the more recently arrived and never-quite-accepted wealthy families. Included in this class are members of each city's "executive elite," as well as founders of large businesses and the newly well-to-do doctors and lawyers. At best only 1½ percent of Americans rank at this level—so that all told, no more than 2 percent of the population can be counted as belonging to one layer or the other of our Upper Class. The goals of people at this particular level are a blend of the Upper-Upper pursuit of gracious living and the Upper-Middle Class's drive for success.

---

[2] See W. Lloyd Warner and Paul Lunt, *The Social Life of a Modern Community* (New Haven: Yale University Press, 1941).

[3] See Allison Davis, Burleigh B. Gardner and Mary R. Gardner, *Deep South* (Chicago: University of Chicago Press, 1941).

[4] See W. Lloyd Warner and Associates, *Democracy in Jonesville* (New York: Harper & Bros., 1949).

[5] The writer's observation on the Kansas City social class system will be included in a forthcoming volume on middle age in Kansas City, currently being prepared for publication by the Committee on Human Development of the University of Chicago.

[6] Some of the phrases and ideas in this characterization have been borrowed from Joseph A. Kahl's excellent synthesizing textbook, *The American Class Structure* (New York: Rinehart & Co., Inc., 1957).

3. In the Upper-Middle Class are moderately successful professional men and women, owners of medium-sized businesses and "organization men" at the managerial level; also included are those younger people in their 20s or very early 30s who are expected to arrive at this occupational status level—and possibly higher—by their middle or late 30s (that is, they are today's "junior executives" and "apprentice professionals" who grew up in such families and/or went to the "better" colleges). Ten percent of Americans are part of this social class and the great majority of them are college educated. . . .

4. At the top of the "Average Man World" is the Lower-Middle Class. Approximately 30 percent or 35 percent of our citizenry can be considered members of this social class. For the most part they are drawn from the ranks of non-managerial office workers, small business owners, and those highly paid blue-collar families who are concerned with being accepted and respected in white-collar dominated clubs, churches, and neighborhoods. The key word in understanding the motivations and goals of this class is Respectability, and a second important word is Striving. The men of this class are continually striving, within their limitations, to "do a good job" at their work, and both men and women are determined to be judged "respectable" in their personal behavior by their fellow citizens. Being "respectable" means that they live in well-maintained homes, neatly furnished, in neighborhoods which are more-or-less on the "right side of town." It also means that they will clothe themselves in coats, suits, and dresses from "nice stores" and save for a college education for their children.

5. At the lower half of the "Average Man World" is the Upper-Lower Class, sometimes referred to as "The Ordinary Working Class." Nearly 40 percent of all Americans are in this class, making it the biggest. The proto-typical member of this class is a semiskilled worker on one of the nation's assembly lines. Many of these "Ordinary Working Class" people make very good money, but do not bother with using it to become "respectable" in a middle-class way. Whether they just "get by" at work, or moonlight to make extra money, Upper-Lowers are oriented more toward enjoying life and living well from day to day than saving for the future or caring what the middle-class world thinks of them. They try to "keep in step with the times" (indeed, one might say the "times" are more important than the "Joneses" to this class,) because they want to be at least Modern, if not Middle Class. That is, they try to take advantage of progress to live more comfortably and they work hard enough to keep themselves safely away from a slum level of existence.

6. The Lower-Lower Class of unskilled workers, unassimilated ethnics, and the sporadically employed comprises about 15 percent of the population, but this class has less than 7 to 8 percent of the purchasing power, and will not concern us further here. Apathy, fatalism, and a point of view which justifies "getting your kicks whenever you can"

characterize the approach toward life, and toward spending money, found among the people of this class.

Now, we do not mean to imply by these characterizations that the members of each class are always homogeneous in behavior. To suggest such would be to exaggerate greatly the meaning of social classes. To properly understand them, it must be recognized that there is a considerable variation in the way individual members of a class realize these class goals and express these values. . . .

SOCIAL CLASS VERSUS INCOME

Let us proceed now to stating the basic significance of this class concept for people in the selling field. In the first place, it explains why income categories or divisions of Americans are quite often irrelevant in analyzing product markets, consumers' shopping habits and store preferences, and media consumption. For example, if you take three families, all earning around $8,000 a year, but each from a different social class, a radical difference in their ways of spending money will be observed.

An Upper-Middle Class family in this income bracket, which in this case might be a young lawyer and his wife or perhaps a college professor, is apt to be found spending a relatively large share of its resources on housing (in a "prestige" neighborhood), on rather expensive pieces of furniture, on clothing from quality stores, and on cultural amusements or club memberships. Meanwhile, the Lower-Middle Class family— headed, we will say, by an insurance salesman or a fairly successful grocery store owner, perhaps even a diesel engineer—probably has a better house, but in not so fancy a neighborhood; it is apt to have as full a wardrobe though not so expensive, and probably more furniture though none by name designers. These people almost certainly have a much bigger savings account in the bank.

Finally, the Working Class family—with a cross-country truck driver or a highly paid welder as its chief wage earner—is apt to have less house and less neighborhood than the Lower-Middle or Upper-Middle family; but it will have a bigger, later model car, plus more expensive appliances in its kitchen and a bigger TV set in its living room. This family will spend less on clothing and furniture, but more on food if the number of children is greater, as is likely. One further difference: The man of the house probably spends much more on sports, attending baseball games (for example), going hunting and bowling, and perhaps owning a boat of some description.

The wives in these three families will be quite noticeably different in the kind of department stores they patronize, in the magazines they read, and in the advertising to which they pay attention. The clothing and furniture they select for themselves and their families will differ accordingly, and also because they are seeking quite different goals. This has become very clear in studies Social Research, Inc., has done for the *Chicago Tribune* on the clothing tastes of Chicagoland women, for the Kroehler Company on the place of furniture in American homes, and for MacFadden Publications on the purchasing patterns and motivations of their romance magazines' Working Class readers.[7] (These have been contrasted in turn with the motivations of Middle Class women who read service magazines.) . . .

Up to now, we've been talking about product areas—clothing, furniture, and residential neighborhoods—where the relationship between social class and quality of goods purchased is highest. In these things the so-called "Quality Market" and the Upper-Middle (and higher) markets coincide. That is, the purchasers of highest quality clothing and highest quality furniture are more nearly from the Upper-Middle and Upper social classes than from the highest income categories, and so on it goes down the hierarchy. The correlation between price of goods purchased and social class is relatively quite high in these product areas while the correlation between price paid and annual income is lower than one might expect. . . .

Two important elements in the study of consumer behavior are the individual's self-concept and its relationship to the symbolic value of the product. These dimensions are examined for their potential value in predicting consumer behavior. A theoretical model is presented to clarify these relationships.

---

7. CONSUMER SELF-CONCEPT, SYMBOLISM, AND MARKET BEHAVIOR: A THEORETICAL APPROACH *

Edward L. Grubb † and Harrison L. Grathwohl ‡

Efforts to understand the totality of consumer behavior have taken researchers into related fields, with some of the most fruitful results in terms of both theory and practice coming from the behavioral sciences.

---

[7] This study has been published under the name *Workingman's Wife* (New York: Oceana Press, 1959) by Lee Rainwater, Richard P. Coleman, and Gerald Handel.

* Reprinted from the *Journal of Marketing*, national quarterly publication of the American Marketing Association, Vol. 31, No. 4 (October 1967), pp. 22–27.

† Portland State College.

‡ University of Washington.

Two conceptual areas within the behavioral sciences which promise to yield meaningful information about consumer behavior are self-theory and symbolism. A substantial amount of work has been done in these areas, primarily by psychologists, but marketing researchers and theorists do not seem to have developed the marketing potential of the available theory and sustance.[1] Some products, brands, and stores have long been recognized as having psychic values to certain market segments, but little has been done to fabricate formal theories useful in predicting consumer behavior.

This article is an effort to develop a partial theory of consumer behavior by linking the psychological construct of an individual's self-concept with the symbolic value of goods purchased in the marketplace. The authors briefly examine previous research and lay theoretical footings from which a set of hypotheses and a qualitative model of consumer behavior are promulgated. . . .

SELF-THEORY

. . . Self-theory has been the subject of much psychological and sociological theorizing and empirical research with the accompanying development of a rather large body of assumptions and empirical data.[2] The available knowledge strongly supports the role of the self-concept as a partial determinant of human behavior and, therefore, represents a promising area for marketing research.

Current theory and research places emphasis on the concept of the self as an object which is perceived by the individual. The self is what one is aware of, one's attitudes, feelings, perceptions, and evaluations of oneself as an object.[3] The self represents a totality which becomes a principal value around which life revolves, something to be safeguarded and, if possible, to be made still more valuable.[4] An individual's evaluation of himself will greatly influence his behavior, and thus, the more valued the self, the more organized and consistent becomes his behavior.

THE SELF AND THE INTERACTION PROCESS

The self develops not as a personal, individual process, but it evolves through the process of social experience. From the reactions of others, man develops his self-perception. According to Rogers:

---

[1] George A. Field, John Douglas, and Lawrence X. Tarpey, *Marketing Management: A Behavioral Systems Approach* (Columbus, Ohio: Charles E. Merrill Books, 1966), p. 106.

[2] See, for example, Ruth Wylie, *The Self-Concept* (Lincoln, Nebr.: University of Nebraska Press, 1961).

[3] Calvin S. Hall and Gardener Lindsay, *Theories of Personality* (New York: John Wiley & Sons, Inc., 1957), pp. 469–75, or David Krech, Richard S. Crutchfield, and Egerton L. Ballachey, *Individual in Society* (New York: McGraw-Hill Book Co., 1962), pp. 495–96.

[4] Theodore M. Newcomb, *Social Psychology* (New York: Dryden Press, 1956), p. 319.

A portion of the total perceptual field gradually becomes differentiated as the self . . . as a result of the interaction with the environment, and particularly as a result of evaluational interactions with others, the structure of the self is formed—an organized, fluid, but consistent conceptual pattern of perceptions of characteristics and relationships of the "I" or the "me" together with values attached to these concepts.[5]

Since the self-concept grows out of the reactions of parents, peers, teachers, and significant others, self-enhancement will depend upon the reactions of those people. Recognition and reinforcing reactions from these persons will further strengthen the conception the individual has of himself. Thus, the individual will strive to direct his behavior to obtain a positive reaction from his significant references. . . .

GOODS AS SYMBOLS

. . . A more meaningful way of understanding the role of goods as social tools is to regard them as symbols serving as a means of communication between the individual and his significant references. Defined as "things which stand for or express something else," symbols should be thought of as unitary characters composed of signs and their meanings.[6] If a symbol is to convey meaning it must be identified by a group with which the individual is associated whether the group consists of people or an entire society, and the symbol must communicate similar meaning to all within the group. The nature of goods as symbols has been attested quite adequately by Veblen,[7] Deusenberry,[8] and Benedict.[9]

SYMBOLS AND BEHAVIOR

If a product is to serve as a symbolic communicative device it must achieve social recognition, and the meaning associated with the product must be clearly established and understood by related segments of society. This process is in reality a classification process where one object is placed in relation to other objects basic to society.

The necessity for any group to develop a common or shared terminology leads to an important consideration; the direction of activity depends upon the particular way that objects are classified.[10]

---

[5] Hall and Lindsay, *Theories of Personality*, p. 483.

[6] Lloyd Warner, *The Living and the Dead* (New Haven, Conn.: Yale University Press, 1959), p. 3.

[7] Thorstein Veblen, *The Theory of the Leisure Class* (New York: Mentor Books, 1953).

[8] James S. Duesenberry, *Income, Savings, and the Theory of Consumer Behavior* (Cambridge: Harvard University Press, 1949).

[9] Ruth Benedict, *Patterns of Culture* (New York: Mentor Books, 1934).

[10] Anselm Strauss, *Mirrors and Masks: The Search for Identity* (Glencoe, Ill.: The Free Press of Glencoe, 1959), p. 9.

Classification systems are society's means of organizing and directing their activities in an orderly and sensible manner. . . .

GOODS AND SELF-ENHANCEMENT

The purchase and consumption of goods can be self-enhancing in two ways. First, the self-concept of an individual will be sustained and buoyed if he believes the good he has purchased is recognized publicly and classified in a manner that supports and matches his self-concept. While self-enhancement results from a personal, internal, intra-action process, the effect on the individual is ultimately dependent upon the product's being a publicly-recognized symbol. Because of their recognized meaning, public symbols elicit a reaction from the individual that supports his original self-feelings. Self-enhancement can occur as well in the interaction process. Goods as symbols serve the individual, becoming means to cause desired reactions from other individuals.

These two means of self-enhancement are represented in diagrammatic form in Figure 1.

FIGURE 1

Relationship of the consumption of goods as symbols to the self-concept

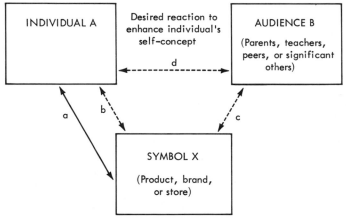

A MODEL OF CONSUMING BEHAVIOR

The following qualitative model is proposed to clarify the systematic relationship between self-theory and goods as symbols in terms of consumer behavior.

Consumption of symbols: A means of self-enhancement

1. An individual does have a self-concept of himself.
2. The self-concept is of value to him.

3. Because this self-concept is of value to him, an individual's behavior will be directed toward the furtherance and enhancement of his self-concept.
4. An individual's self-concept is formed through the interaction process with parents, peers, teachers, and significant others.
5. Goods serve as social symbols and, therefore, are communication devices for the individual.
6. The use of these good-symbols communicates meaning to the individual himself and to others, causing an impact on the interaction and/or the interaction processes and, therefore, an effect on the individual's self-concept.

Prediction of the model

7. Therefore, the consuming behavior of an individual will be directed toward the furthering and enhancing of his self-concept through the consumption of goods as symbols.

This model becomes the theoretical base for a conceptual means to understand consumer behavior. The self-conception approach to understanding consumer behavior is not all-inclusive but does provide a meaningful conceptual framework for the systematic ordering and comprehension of consumer behavior. Of further importance is that this model, although general, can be an aid to the marketing decision-maker and a guide for future research. . . .

SELF-CONCEPT THEORY OF BEHAVIOR AND MARKETING MANAGEMENT

Firms can and should identify and/or segment their markets in terms of differentiated self-concepts. Recent research has indicated significant differences in self-concepts of different consuming groups both for product classes and for different brands.[11] Identification of self-concept segments may be a key element in the determination of marketing strategy and how, where, and to whom the exact tactics should be directed to achieve the desired goals.

Of real importance to the success of a brand of product is the development of a commonly understood symbolic meaning for the product. This means that management of a firm should carefully control the marketing of a product so that the relevant segments of the market properly classify the product and, therefore, behave toward the product in the

---

[11] Edward L. Grubb, "Consumer Perception of 'Self-Concept' and Its Relationship to Brand Choice of Selected Product Types" (unpublished D.B.A. dissertation, University of Washington, 1965), pp. 120–24.

manner desired by the marketer. Through product design, pricing, promotion, and distribution the firm must communicate to the market the desired clues for consumer interpretation and, therefore, develop the desired symbolic meaning for the brand. . . .

Why do people buy? Marketing strategies are based upon assumptions concerning both motivational and overt aspects of buyer behavior. A consumer's purchasing behavior is a function of several influences, all processed by the buyer's psyche. Five "partial" behavioral models are presented, and their application to marketing is discussed.

---

8. BEHAVIORAL MODELS FOR ANALYZING BUYERS*

Philip Kotler †

In times past, management could arrive at a fair understanding of its buyers through the daily experience of selling to them. But the growth in the size of firms and markets has removed many decision-makers from direct contact with buyers. Increasingly, decision-makers have had to turn to summary statistics and to behavioral theory, and are spending more money today than ever before to try to understand their buyers.

Who buys? How do they buy? And why? The first two questions relate to relatively overt aspects of buyer behavior, and can be learned about through direct observation and interviewing.

But uncovering *why* people buy is an extremely difficult task. The answer will tend to vary with the investigator's behavioral frame of reference.

The buyer is subject to many influences which trace a complex course through his psyche and lead eventually to overt purchasing responses. This conception of the buying process is illustrated in Figure 1. Various influences and their modes of transmission are shown at the left. At the right are the buyer's responses in choice of product, brand, dealer,

* Reprinted from "Behavioral Models for Analyzing Buyers," *Journal of Marketing*, Vol. 29, No. 4 (October 1965), pp. 37–45.
† Northwestern University.

FIGURE 1

The buying process conceived as a system of inputs and outputs

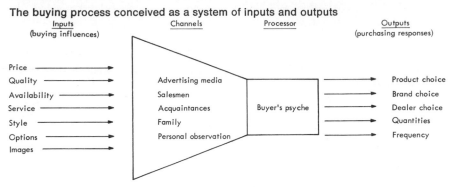

quantities, and frequency. In the center stands the buyer and his mysterious psychological processes. The buyer's psyche is a "black box" whose workings can be only partially deduced. The marketing strategist's challenge to the behavioral scientist is to construct a more specific model of the mechanism in the black box.

. . . The human mind, the only entity in nature with deep powers of understanding, still remains the least understood. Scientists can explain planetary motion, genetic determination, and molecular behavior. Yet they have only partial, and often partisan, models of *human* behavior.

Nevertheless, the marketing strategist should recognize the potential interpretative contributions of different partial models for explaining buyer behavior. Depending upon the product, different variables and behavioral mechanisms may assume particular importance. A psychoanalytic behavioral model might throw much light on the factors operating in cigarette demand, while an economic behavioral model might be useful in explaining machine-tool purchasing. Sometimes alternative models may shed light on different demand aspects of the same product.

What are the most useful behavioral models for interpreting the transformation of buying influences into purchasing responses? Five different models of the buyer's "black box" are presented in the present article, along with their respective marketing applications: (1) the Marshallian model, stressing economic motivations; (2) the Pavlovian model, learning; (3) the Freudian model, psychoanalytic motivations; (4) the Veblenian model, social-psychological factors; and (5) the Hobbesian model, organizational factors. These models represent radically different conceptions of the mainsprings of human behavior.

THE MARSHALLIAN ECONOMIC MODEL

Economists were the first professional group to construct a specific theory of buyer behavior. The theory holds that purchasing decisions are the result of largely "rational" and conscious economic calculations. The individual buyer seeks to spend his income on those goods that will deliver the most utility (satisfaction) according to his tastes and relative prices.

The antecedents for this view trace back to the writings of Adam Smith and Jeremy Bentham. Smith set the tone by developing a doctrine of economic growth based on the principle that man is motivated by self-interest in all his actions.[1] Bentham refined this view and saw man as finely calculating and weighing the expected pleasures and pains of every contemplated action.[2]

Bentham's "felicific calculus" was not applied to consumer behavior (as opposed to entrepreneurial behavior) until the late 19th century. Then, the "marginal-utility" theory of value was formulated independently and almost simultaneously by Jevons[3] and Marshall[4] in England, Menger[5] in Austria, and Walras[6] in Switzerland.

Alfred Marshall was the great consolidator of the classical and neoclassical tradition in economics; and his synthesis in the form of demand-supply analysis constitutes the main source of modern micro-economic thought in the English-speaking world. His theoretical work aimed at realism, but his method was to start with simplifying assumptions and to examine the effect of a change in a single variable (say, price) when all other variables were held constant.

He would "reason out" the consequences of the provisional assumptions and in subsequent steps modify his assumptions in the direction of more realism. He employed the "measuring rod of money" as an indicator of the intensity of human psychological desires. Over the years his methods and assumptions have been refined into what is now known as *modern utility theory*: economic man is bent on maximizing his utility, and does this by carefully calculating the "felicific" consequences of any purchase.

As as example, suppose on a particular evening that John is considering whether to prepare his own dinner or dine out. He estimates that a restaurant meal would cost $2.00 and a home-cooked meal 50 cents. According to the Marshallian model, if John expects less than four times as much satisfaction from the restaurant meal as the home-cooked meal, he will eat at home. The economist typically is not concerned with how these relative preferences are formed by John, or how they may be psychologically modified by new stimuli.

---

[1] Adam Smith, *An Inquiry into the Nature and Causes of the Wealth of Nations*, 1776 (New York: Modern Library, 1937).

[2] Jeremy Bentham, *An Introduction to the Principles of Morals and Legislation*, 1780 (Oxford, Eng.: Clarendon Press, 1907).

[3] William S. Jevons, *The Theory of Political Economy* (New York: Macmillan Co., 1871).

[4] Alfred Marshall, *Principles of Economics*, 1890 (London: Macmillan Co., 1927).

[5] Karl Menger, *Principles of Economics*, 1871 (Glencoe, Ill.: Free Press, 1950).

[6] Léon Walras, *Elements of Pure Economics*, 1874 (Homewood, Ill.: Richard D. Irwin, Inc., 1954).

Yet John will not always cook at home. The principle of diminishing marginal utility operates. Within a given time interval—say, a week—the utility of each additional home-cooked meal diminishes. John gets tired of home meals and other products become relatively more attractive.

John's *efficiency* in maximizing his utility depends on the adequacy of his information and his freedom of choice. If he is not perfectly aware of costs, if he misestimates the relative delectability of the two meals, or if he is barred from entering the restaurant, he will not maximize his potential utility. His choice processes are rational, but the results are inefficient.

Marketing applications of Marshallian model

Marketers usually have dismissed the Marshallian model as an absurd figment of ivory-tower imagination. Certainly the behavioral essence of the situation is omitted, in viewing man as calculating the marginal utility of a restaurant meal over a home-cooked meal.

Eva Mueller has reported a study where only one-fourth of the consumers in her sample bought with any substantial degree of deliberation.[7] Yet there are a number of ways to view the model.

From one point of view the Marshallian model is tautological and therefore neither true nor false. The model holds that the buyer acts in the light of his best "interest." But this is not very informative.

A second view is that this is a *normative* rather than a *descriptive* model of behavior. The model provides logical norms for buyers who want to be "rational." Although the consumer is not likely to employ economic analysis to decide between a box of Kleenex and Scotties, he may apply economic analysis in deciding whether to buy a new car. Industrial buyers even more clearly would want an economic calculus for making good decisions.

A third view is that economic factors operate to a greater or lesser extent in all markets, and, therefore, must be included in any comprehensive description of buyer behavior.

Furthermore, the model suggests useful behavioral hypotheses such as: (*a*) The lower the price of the product, the higher the sales. (*b*) The lower the price of substitute products, the lower the sales of this product; and the lowest the price of complementary products, the higher the sales of this product. (*c*) The higher the real income, the higher the sales of this product, provided that it is not an "inferior" good. (*d*) The higher the promotional expenditures, the higher the sales.

The validity of these hypotheses does not rest on whether *all* individuals act as economic calculating machines in making their purchasing decisions. For example, some individuals may buy *less* of a product

---

[7] Eva Mueller, "A Study of Purchase Decisions," Part 2, *Consumer Behavior, The Dynamics of Consumer Reaction*, edited by Lincoln H. Clark (New York: New York University Press, 1954), pp. 36–87.

when its price is reduced. They may think that the quality has gone down, or that ownership has less status value. If a majority of buyers view price reductions negatively, then sales may fall, contrary to the first hypothesis.

But for most goods a price reduction increases the relative value of the goods in many buyers' minds and leads to increased sales. This and the other hypotheses are intended to describe average effects.

The impact of economic factors in actual buying situations is studied through experimental design or statistical analyses of past data. Demand equations have been fitted to a wide variety of products—including beer, refrigerators, and chemical fertilizers.[8] More recently, the impact of economic variables on the fortunes of different brands has been pursued with significant results, particularly in the case of coffee, frozen orange juice, and margarine.[9]

But economic factors alone cannot explain all the variations in sales. The Marshallian model ignores the fundamental question of how product and brand preferences are formed. It represents a useful frame of reference for analyzing only one small corner of the "black box."

THE PAVLOVIAN LEARNING MODEL

The designation of a Pavlovian learning model has its origin in the experiments of the Russian psychologist Pavlov, who rang a bell each time before feeding a dog. Soon he was able to induce the dog to salivate by ringing the bell whether or not food was supplied. Pavlov concluded that learning was largely an associative process and that a large component of behavior was conditioned in this way.

Experimental psychologists have continued this mode of research with rats and other animals, including people. Laboratory experiments have been designed to explore such phenomena as learning, forgetting, and the ability to discriminate. The results have been integrated into a stimulus-response model of human behavior, or as someone has "wisecracked," the substitution of a rat psychology for a rational psychology.

The model has been refined over the years, and today is based on four central concepts—those of *drive, cue, response,* and *reinforcement.*[10]

---

[8] See Erwin E. Nemmers, *Managerial Economics* (New York: John Wiley & Sons, Inc., 1962), Part II.

[9] See Lester G. Telser, "The Demand for Branded Goods as Estimated from Consumer Panel Data," *Review of Economics and Statistics,* Vol. 44 (August 1962), pp. 300–324; and William F. Massy and Ronald E. Frank, "Short Term Price and Dealing Effects in Selected Market Segments," *Journal of Marketing Research,* Vol. 2 (May 1965), pp. 171–85.

[10] See John Dollard and Neal E. Miller, *Personality and Psychotherapy* (New York: McGraw-Hill Book Co., 1950), chap. 3.

Drive.   Also called needs or motives, drive refers to strong stimuli internal to the individual which impel action. Psychologists draw a distinction between primary physiological drives—such as hunger, thirst, cold, pain, and sex—and learned drives which are derived socially—such as cooperation, fear, and acquisitiveness.

Cue.   A drive is very general and impels a particular response only in relation to a particular configuration of cues. Cues are weaker stimuli in the environment and/or in the individual which determine when, where, and how the subject responds. Thus, a coffee advertisement can serve as a cue which stimulates the thirst drive in a housewife. Her response will depend upon this cue and other cues, such as the time of day, the availability of other thirst-quenchers, and the cue's intensity. Often a relative change in a cue's intensity can be more impelling than its absolute level. The housewife may be more motivated by a 2-cents-off sale on a brand of coffee than the fact that this brand's price was low in the first place.

Response.   The response is the organism's reaction to the configuration of cues. Yet the same configuration of cues will not necessarily produce the same response in the individual. This depends on the degree to which the experience was rewardiing, that is, drive-reducing.

Reinforcement.   If the experience is rewarding, a particular response is reinforced; that is, it is strengthened and there is a tendency for it to be repeated when the same configuration of cues appears again. The housewife, for example, will tend to purchase the same brand of coffee each time she goes to her supermarket so long as it is rewarding and the cue configuration does not change. But if a learned response or habit is not reinforced, the strength of the habit diminishes and may be extinguished eventually. Thus, a housewife's preference for a certain coffee may become extinct if she finds the brand out of stock for a number of weeks.

Forgetting, in contrast to extinction, is the tendency for learned associations to weaken, not because of the lack of reinforcement but because of nonuse.

Cue configurations are constantly changing. The housewife sees a new brand of coffee next to her habitual brand, or notes a special price deal on a rival brand. Experimental psychologists have found that the same learned response will be elicited by similar patterns of cues; that is, learned responses are *generalized*. The housewife shifts to a similar brand when her favorite brand is out of stock. This tendency toward generalization over less similar cue configurations is increased in proportion to the strength of the drive. A housewife may buy an inferior coffee if it is the only brand left and if her drive is sufficiently strong.

A counter-tendency to generalization is *discrimination*. When a housewife tries two similar brands and finds one more rewarding, her ability to discriminate between similar cue configurations improves. Discrimination increases the specificity of the cue-response connection, while generalization decreases the specificity.

Marketing applications of Pavlovian model

The modern version of the Pavlovian model makes no claim to provide a complete theory of behavior—indeed, such important phenomena as perception, the subconscious, and interpersonal influences are inadequately treated. Yet the model does offer a substantial number of insights about some aspects of behavior of considerable interest to marketers.[11]

An example would be in the problem of introducing a new brand into a highly competitive market. The company's goal is to extinguish existing brand habits and form new habits among consumers for its brand. But the company must first get customers to try its brand; and it has to decide between using weak and strong cues.

Light introductory advertising is a weak cue compared with distributing free samples. Strong cues, although costing more, may be necessary in markets characterized by strong brand loyalties. For example, Folger went into the coffee market by distributing over a million pounds of free coffee.

To build a brand habit, it helps to provide for an extended period of introductory dealing. Furthermore, sufficient quality must be built into the brand so that the experience is reinforcing. Since buyers are more likely to transfer allegiance to similar brands than dissimilar brands (generalization), the company should also investigate what cues in the leading brands have been most effective. Although outright imitation would not necessarily effect the most transference, the question of providing enough similarity should be considered.

The Pavlovian model also provides guidelines in the area of advertising strategy. The American behaviorist, John B. Watson, was a great exponent of repetitive stimuli; in his writings man is viewed as a creature who can be conditioned through repetition and reinforcement to respond in particular ways.[12] The Pavlovian model emphasizes the desirability of repetition in advertising. A single exposure is likely to be a very weak cue, hardly able to penetrate the individual's consciousness sufficiently to excite his drives above the threshold level.

Repetition in advertising has two desirable effects. It "fights" forgetting, the tendency for learned responses to weaken in the absence of practice. It provides reinforcement, because after the purchase the consumer becomes selectively exposed to advertisements of the product.

---

[11] The most consistent application of learning-theory concepts to marketing situations is found in John A. Howard, *Marketing Management: Analysis and Planning* (Homewood, Ill.: Richard D. Irwin, Inc., rev. ed., 1963).

[12] John B. Watson, *Behaviorism* (New York: The People's Institute Publishing Co., 1925).

The model also provides guidelines for copy strategy. To be effective as a cue, an advertisement must arouse strong drives in the person. The strongest product-related drives must be identified. For candy bars, it may be hunger; for safety belts, fear; for hair tonics, sex; for automobiles, status. The advertising practitioner must dip into his cue box —words, colors, pictures—and select that configuration of cues that provides the strongest stimulus to these drives.

THE FREUDIAN PSYCHOANALYTIC MODEL

The Freudian model of man is well known, so profound has been its impact on 20th century thought. It is the latest of a series of philosophical "blows" to which man has been exposed in the last 500 years. Copernicus destroyed the idea that man stood at the center of the universe; Darwin tried to refute the idea that man was a special creation; and Freud attacked the idea that man even reigned over his own psyche.

According to Freud, the child enters the world driven by instinctual needs which he cannot gratify by himself. Very quickly and painfully he realizes his separateness from the rest of the world and yet his dependence on it.

He tries to get others to gratify his needs through a variety of blatant means, including intimidation and supplication. Continual frustration leads him to perfect more subtle mechanisms for gratifying his instincts.

As he grows, his psyche becomes increasingly complex. A part of his psyche—the id—remains the reservoir of his strong drives and urges. Another part—the ego—becomes his conscious planning center for finding outlets for his drives. And a third part—his super-ego—channels his instinctive drives into socially approved outlets to avoid the pain of guilt or shame.

The guilt or shame which man feels toward some of his urges— especially his sexual urges—causes him to repress them from his consciousness. Through such defense mechanisms as rationalization and sublimation, these urges are denied or become transmuted into socially approved expressions. Yet these urges are never eliminated or under perfect control; and they emerge, sometimes with a vengeance, in dreams, in slips-of-the-tongue, in neurotic and obsessional behavior, or ultimately in mental breakdown where the ego can no longer maintain the delicate balance between the impulsive power of the id and the oppressive power of the super-ego.

The individual's behavior, therefore, is never simple. His motivational wellsprings are not obvious to a casual observer nor deeply understood by the individual himself. If he is asked why he purchased an expensive foreign sports-car, he may reply that he likes its maneuverability and its looks. At a deeper level he may have purchased the car to impress others, or to feel young again. At a still deeper level, he may be purchasing the sports-car to achieve substitute gratification for unsatisfied sexual strivings.

Many refinements and changes in emphasis have occurred in this model since the time of Freud. The instinct concept has been replaced by a more careful delineation of basic drives; the three parts of the psyche are regarded now as theoretical concepts rather than actual entities; and the behavioral perspective has been extended to include cultural as well as biological mechanisms.

Instead of the role of the sexual urge in psychic development— Freud's discussion of oral, anal, and genital stages and possible fixations and traumas—Adler [13] emphasized the urge for power and how its thwarting manifests itself in superiority and inferiority complexes; Horney [14] emphasized cultural mechanisms; and Fromm [15] and Erikson [16] emphasized the role of existential crises in personality development. These philosophical divergencies, rather than debilitating the model, have enriched and extended its interpretative value to a wider range of behavioral phenomena.

Marketing applications of Freudian model

Perhaps the most important marketing implication of this model is that buyers are motivated by *symbolic* as well as *economic-functional* product concerns. The change of a bar of soap from a square to a round shape may be more important in its sexual than its functional connotations. A cake mix that is advertised as involving practically no labor may alienate housewives because the easy life may evoke a sense of guilt.

Motivational research has produced some interesting and occasionally some bizarre hypotheses about what may be in the buyer's mind regarding certain purchases. Thus, it has been suggested at one time or another that

— Many a businessman doesn't fly because of a fear of posthumous guilt—if he crashed, his wife would think of him as stupid for not taking a train.
— Men want their cigars to be odoriferous, in order to prove that they (the men) are masculine.
— A woman is very serious when she bakes a cake because unconsciously she is going through the symbolic act of giving birth.

---

[13] Alfred Adler, *The Science of Living* (New York: Greenberg Publisher, 1929).

[14] Karen Horney, *The Neurotic Personality of Our Time* (New York: W. W. Norton & Co., Inc., 1937).

[15] Erich Fromm, *Man For Himself* (New York: Holt, Rinehart & Winston, Inc., 1947).

[16] Erik Erikson, *Childhood and Society* (New York: W. W. Norton & Co., Inc., 1949).

— A man buys a convertible as a substitute "mistress."
— Consumers prefer vegetable shortening because animal fats stimulate a sense of sin.
— Men who wear suspenders are reacting to an unresolved castration complex.

There are admitted difficulties of proving these assertions. Two prominent motivational researchers, Ernest Dichter and James Vicary, were employed independently by two separate groups in the prune industry to determine why so many people dislike prunes. Dichter found, among other things, that the prune aroused feelings of old age and insecurity in people, whereas Vicary's main finding was that Americans had an emotional block about prunes' laxative qualities.[17] Which is the more valid interpretation? Or if they are both operative, which motive is found with greater statistical frequency in the population?

Unfortunately the usual survey techniques—direct observation and interviewing—can be used to establish the representativeness of more superficial characteristics—age and family size, for example—but are not feasible for establishing the frequency of mental states which are presumed to be deeply "buried" within each individual.

Motivational researchers have to employ time-consuming projective techniques in the hope of throwing individual "egos" off guard. When carefully administered and interpreted, techniques such as word association, sentence completion, picture interpretation, and role-playing can provide some insights into the minds of the small group of examined individuals; but a "leap of faith" is sometimes necessary to generalize these findings to the population.

Nevertheless, motivation research can lead to useful insights and provide inspiration to creative men in the advertising and packaging world. Appeals aimed at the buyer's private world of hopes, dreams, and fears can often be as effective in stimulating purchase as more rationally-directed appeals.

THE VEBLENIAN SOCIAL-PSYCHOLOGICAL MODEL

While most economists have been content to interpret buyer behavior in Marshallian terms, Thorstein Veblen struck out in different directions.

Veblen was trained as an orthodox economist, but evolved into a social thinker greatly influenced by the new science of social anthro-

---

[17] L. Edward Scriven, "Rationality and Irrationality in Motivation Research," in Robert Ferber and Hugh G. Wales (eds.), *Motivation and Marketing Behavior* (Homewood, Ill.: Richard D. Irwin, Inc., 1958), pp. 69–70.

pology. He saw man as primarily a *social animal*—conforming to the general forms and norms of his larger culture and to the more specific standards of the subcultures and face-to-face groupings to which his life is bound. His wants and behavior are largely molded by his present group-memberships and his aspired group-memberships.

Veblen's best-known example of this is in his description of the leisure class.[18] His hypothesis is that much of economic consumption is motivated not by intrinsic needs or satisfaction so much as by prestige-seeking. He emphasized the strong emulative factors operating in the choice of conspicuous goods like clothes, cars, and houses.

Some of his points, however, seem overstated by today's perspective. The leisure class does not serve as everyone's reference group; many persons aspire to the social patterns of the class immediately above it. And important segments of the affluent class practice conspicuous underconsumption rather than overconsumption. There are many people in all classes who are more anxious to "fit in" than to "stand out." As an example, William H. Whyte found that many families avoided buying air conditioners and other appliances before their neighbors did.[19]

Veblen was not the first nor the only investigator to comment on social influences in behavior; but the incisive quality of his observations did much to stimulate further investigations. Another stimulus came from Karl Marx, who held that each man's world-view was determined largely by his relationship to the "means of production." [20] The early field-work in primitive societies by social anthropologists like Boas [21] and Malinowski [22] and the later field-work in urban societies by men like Park [23] and Thomas [24] contributed much to understanding the influence of society and culture. The research of early Gestalt psychologists—men like Wertheimer,[25] Kohler,[26] and Koffka [27] —into the mechanisms of perception led eventually to investigations of small-group influence on perception.

---

[18] Thorstein Veblen, *The Theory of the Leisure Class* (New York: Macmillan Co., 1899).

[19] William H. Whyte, Jr., "The Web of Word of Mouth," *Fortune*, Vol. 50 (November 1954), pp. 140 ff.

[20] Karl Marx, *The Communist Manifesto*, 1848 (London: Martin Lawrence, Ltd., 1934).

[21] Franz Boas, *The Mind of Primitive Man* (New York: Macmillan Co., 1922).

[22] Bronislaw Malinowski, *Sex and Repression in Savage Society* (New York: Meridian Books, 1955).

[23] Robert E. Park, *Human Communities* (Glencoe, Ill.: Free Press, 1952).

[24] William I. Thomas, *The Unadjusted Girl* (Boston: Little, Brown & Co., 1928).

[25] Max Wertheimer, *Productive Thinking* (New York: Harper & Bros., 1945).

[26] Wolfgang Köhler, *Gestalt Psychology* (New York: Liveright Publishing Co., 1947).

[27] Kurt Koffka, *Principles of Gestalt Psychology* (New York: Harcourt, Brace & Co., 1935).

Marketing applications of Veblenian model

The various streams of thought crystallized into the modern social sciences of sociology, cultural anthropology, and social psychology. Basic to them is the view that man's attitudes and behavior are influenced by several levels of society—culture, subcultures, social classes, reference groups, and face-to-face groups. The challenge to the marketer is to determine which of these social levels are the most important in influencing the demand for his product.

Culture

The most enduring influences are from culture. Man tends to assimilate his culture's mores and folkways, and to believe in their absolute rightness until deviants appear within his culture or until he confronts members of another culture.

Subcultures

A culture tends to lose its homogeneity as its population increases. When people no longer are able to maintain face-to-face relationships with more than a small proportion of other members of a culture, smaller units or subcultures develop, which help to satisfy the individual's needs for more specific identity.

The subcultures are often regional entities, because the people of a region, as a result of more frequent interactions, tend to think and act alike. But subcultures also take the form of religions, nationalities, fraternal orders, and other institutional complexes which provide a broad identification for people who may otherwise be strangers. The subcultures of a person play a large role in his attitude formation and become another important predictor of certain values he is likely to hold.

Social class

People become differentiated not only horizontally but also vertically through a division of labor. The society becomes stratified socially on the basis of wealth, skill, and power. Sometimes castes develop in which the members are reared for certain roles, or social classes develop in which the members feel empathy with others sharing similar values and economic circumstances.

Because social class involves different attitudinal configurations, it becomes a useful independent variable for segmenting markets and predicting reactions. Significant differences have been found among different social classes with respect to magazine readership, leisure activities, food imagery, fashion interests, and acceptance of innovations. A sampling of attitudinal differences in class is the following:

Members of the *upper-middle* class place an emphasis on professional competence; indulge in expensive status symbols; and more often than not show a taste, real or otherwise, for theater and the arts. They want their children to show high achievement and precocity and develop into physicists, vice-presidents, and judges. This class likes to deal in ideas and symbols.

Members of the *lower-middle* class cherish respectability, savings, a college education, and good housekeeping. They want their children to show self-control and prepare for careers as accountants, lawyers, and engineers.

Members of the *upper-lower* class try to keep up with the times, if not with the Joneses. They stay in older neighborhoods but buy new kitchen appliances. They spend proportionately less than the middle class on major clothing articles, buying a new suit mainly for an important ceremonial occasion. They also spend proportionately less on services, preferring to do their own plumbing and other work around the house. They tend to raise large families and their children generally enter manual occupations. This class also supplies many local businessmen, politicians, sports stars, and labor-union leaders.

Reference groups

There are groups in which the individual has no membership but with which he identifies and may aspire to—reference groups. Many young boys identify with big-league baseball players or astronauts, and many young girls identify with Hollywood stars. The activities of these popular heroes are carefully watched and frequently imitated. These reference figures become important transmitters of influence, although more along lines of taste and hobby than basic attitudes.

Face-to-face groups

Groups that have the most immediate influence on a person's tastes and opinions are face-to-face groups. This includes all the small "societies" with which he comes into frequent contact: his family, close friends, neighbors, fellow workers, fraternal associates, and so forth. His informal group memberships are influenced largely by his occupation, residence, and stage in the life cycle.

The powerful influence of small groups on individual attitudes has been demonstrated in a number of social psychological experiments.[28] There is also evidence that this influence may be growing. David Ries-

---

[28] See, for example, Solomon E. Asch, "Effects of Group Pressure upon the Modification and Distortion of Judgments," in Dorwin Cartwright and Alvin Zander, *Group Dynamics* (Evanston, Ill.: Row, Peterson & Co., 1953), pp. 151–62; and Kurt Lewin, "Group Decision and Social Change," in Theodore M. Newcomb and Eugene L. Hartley (eds.), *Readings in Social Psychology* (New York: Henry Holt Co., 1952).

man and his coauthors have pointed to signs which indicate a growing amount of *other-direction,* that is, a tendency for individuals to be increasingly influenced by their peers in the definition of their values rather than by their parents and elders.[29]

For the marketer, this means that brand choice may increasingly be influenced by one's peers. For such products as cigarettes and automobiles, the influence of peers is unmistakable.

The role of face-to-face groups has been recognized in recent industry campaigns attempting to change basic product attitudes. For years the milk industry has been trying to overcome the image of milk as a "sissified" drink by portraying its use in social and active situations. The men's-wear industry is trying to increase male interest in clothes by advertisements indicating that business associates judge a man by how well he dresses.

Of all face-to-face groups, the person's family undoubtedly plays the largest and most enduring role in basic attitude formation. From them he acquires a mental set not only toward religion and politics, but also toward thrift, chastity, food, human relations, and so forth. Although he often rebels against parental values in his teens, he often accepts these values eventually. Their formative influence on his eventual attitudes is undeniably great.

Family members differ in the types of product messages they carry to other family members. Most of what parents know about cereals, candy, and toys comes from their children. The wife stimulates family consideration of household appliances, furniture, and vacations. The husband tends to stimulate the fewest purchase ideas, with the exception of the automobile and perhaps the home.

The marketer must be alert to what attitudinal configurations dominate in different types of families, and also to how these change over time. For example, the parent's conception of the child's rights and privileges has undergone a radical shift in the last 30 years. The child has become the center of attention and orientation in a great number of households, leading some writers to label the modern family a "filiarchy." This has important implications not only for how to market to today's family, but also on how to market to tomorrow's family when the indulged child of today becomes the parent.

The person

Social influences determine much but not all of the behavioral variations in people. Two individuals subject to the same influences are not likely to have identical attitudes, although these attitudes will probably converge at more points than those of two strangers selected

---

[29] David Riesman, Reuel Denney, and Nathan Glazer, *The Lonely Crowd* (New Haven, Conn.: Yale University Press, 1950).

at random. Attitudes are really the product of social forces interacting with the individual's unique temperament and abilities.

Furthermore, attitudes do not automatically guarantee certain types of behavior. Attitudes are predispositions felt by buyers before they enter the buying process. The buying process itself is a learning experience and can lead to a change in attitudes.

Alfred Politz noted at one time that women stated a clear preference for G.E. refrigerators over Frigidaire, but that Frigidaire continued to outsell G.E.[30] The answer to this paradox was that preference was only one factor entering into behavior. When the consumer preferring G.E. actually undertook to purchase a new refrigerator, her curiosity led her to examine the other brands. Her perception was sensitized to refrigerator advertisements, sales arguments, and different product features. This led to learning and a change of attitudes.

THE HOBBESIAN ORGANIZATIONAL-FACTORS MODEL

The foregoing models throw light mainly on the behavior of family buyers.

But what of the large number of people who are organizational buyers? They are engaged in the purchase of goods not for the sake of consumption, but for further production or distribution. Their common denominator is the fact that they (1) are paid to make purchases for others and (2) operate within an organizational environment.

How do organizational buyers make their decisions? There seem to be two competing views. Many marketing writers have emphasized the predominance of rational motives in organizational buying.[31] Organizational buyers are represented as being most impressed by cost, quality, dependability, and service factors. They are portrayed as dedicated servants of the organization, seeking to secure the best terms. This view has led to an emphasis on performance and use characteristics in much industrial advertising.

Other writers have emphasized personal motives in organizational buyer behavior. The purchasing agent's interest to do the best for his company is tempered by his interest to do the best for himself. He may be tempted to choose among salesmen according to the extent they entertain or offer gifts. He may choose a particular vendor because this will ingratiate him with certain company officers. He may shortcut his study of alternative suppliers to make his work day easier.

In truth, the buyer is guided by both personal and group goals; and this is the essential point. The political model of Thomas Hobbes

---

[30] Alfred Politz, "Motivation Research—Opportunity or Dilemma?", in Ferber and Wales, *Motivation and Marketing Behavior* at pp. 57–58.

[31] See Melvin T. Copeland, *Principles of Merchandising* (New York: McGraw-Hill Book Co., 1924).

comes closest of any model to suggesting the relationship between the two goals.[32] Hobbes held that man is "instinctively" oriented toward preserving and enhancing his own well-being. But this would produce a "war of every man against every man." This fear leads men to unite with others in a corporate body. The corporate man tries to steer a careful course between satisfying his own needs and those of the organization.

Marketing applications of Hobbesian model

The import of the Hobbesian model is that organizational buyers can be appealed to on both personal and organizational grounds. The buyer has his private aims, and yet he tries to do a satisfactory job for his corporation. He will respond to persuasive salesmen and he will respond to rational product arguments. However, the best "mix" of the two is not a fixed quantity; it varies with the nature of the product, the type of organization, and the relative strength of the two drives in the particular buyer.

Where there is substantial similarity in what suppliers offer in the way of products, price, and service, the purchasing agent has less basis for rational choice. Since he can satisfy his organizational obligations with any one of a number of suppliers, he can be swayed by personal motives. On the other hand, where there are pronounced differences among the competing vendors' products, the purchasing agent is held more accountable for his choice and probably pays more attention to rational factors. Short-run personal gain becomes less motivating than the long-run gain which comes from serving the organization with distinction.

The marketing strategist must appreciate these goal conflicts of the organizational buyer. Behind all the ferment of purchasing agents to develop standards and employ value analysis lies their desire to avoid being thought of as order-clerks, and to develop better skills in reconciling personal and organizational objectives.[33]

SUMMARY

Think back over the five different behavioral models of how the buyer translates buying influences into purchasing responses.

Marshallian man is concerned chiefly with economic cues—prices and income—and makes a fresh utility calculation before each purchase.

Pavlovian man behaves in a largely habitual rather than thoughtful

---

[32] Thomas Hobbes, *Leviathan*, 1651 (London: G. Routledge & Sons, 1887).

[33] For an insightful account, see George Strauss, "Tactics of Lateral Relationship: The Purchasing Agent," *Administrative Science Quarterly*, Vol. 7 (September 1962), pp. 161–86.

way; certain configurations of cues will set off the same behavior because of rewarded learning in the past.

Freudian man's choices are influenced strongly by motives and fantasies which take place deep within his private world.

Veblenian man acts in a way which is shaped largely by past and present social groups.

And finally, Hobbesian man seeks to reconcile individual gain with organizational gain.

Thus, it turns out that the "black box" of the buyer is not so black after all. Light is thrown in various corners by these models. Yet no one has succeeded in putting all these pieces of truth together into one coherent instrument for behavioral analysis. This, of course, is the goal of behavioral science.

The marketing concept emphasizes the importance of the consumer in marketing strategy development. A model that unifies all of the factors and forces affecting consumer behavior would provide a clearer understanding of the consumer. It would also aid significantly in the formulation of marketing plans, strategies, and tactics. A brief overview of one model which includes several of the most important variables is presented in the following article.

9. A SYNTHESIS: THE THEORY OF BUYER BEHAVIOR*

William Lazer †

The complexity of buyer behavior is evident from the number of demographic, psychological, and sociological factors involved. It is difficult indeed to provide an integrated mosaic representing the situation. Howard and Sheth, however, offer an excellent general overview and model for coordinating the factors that have been discussed in detail on consumer behavior.[1] Their model (Chart 1) describing the theory

---

* From William Lazer, *Marketing Management: A Systems Perspective* (New York: John Wiley & Sons, Inc., 1971), pp. 518–20.

† Michigan State University.

[1] John A. Howard and Jagdish N. Sheth, *The Theory of Buyer Behavior* (New York: John Wiley & Sons, Inc., 1969), p. 30.

CHART 1

A simplified description of the theory of buyer behavior.

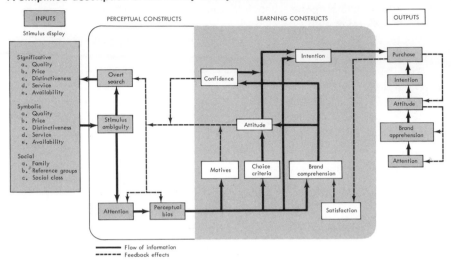

deals with four sets of variables: input variables, output variables, hypothetical constructs, and exogenous variables. The least abstract of the variables are the input and output variables that refer to such inputs as price, service, and quality, and such outputs as purchases, attitudes, and brand awareness. The hypothetical constructs focus on mental states related to buying decisions and encourage theorizing about them. The exogenous variables are powerful influences referring to the contexts in which buying behavior occurs. The flow of information and feedback that have a great impact on buyer behavior are shown by the solid and broken lines.

C.

Life styles and values

THE DIMENSIONS of consumer life styles provide the marketer with insights into consumer behavior. They reflect an all-encompassing conception of consumers' values and priorities as they pertain to their style of living. How people want to live, what they feel is important, and what they want out of life are good indicators of their needs and desires. In total, consumer life styles have direct implications on the ability of a firm's product, service, and communication mix to adequately satisfy consumers' needs.

However, consumer life styles are dynamic, not static, dimensions of consumer behavior. The forecasting of future life styles can provide valuable marketing intelligence to the alert firm. Furthermore, the measurement and projection of evolving trends can be decisive inputs into the marketing planning activity of the firm. This information will enable marketers not only to react to potential changes but also play an active role in influencing those changes most beneficial to the firm.

In the following articles Lazer begins by discussing the relationship of life styles and marketing. In the second article, Kelley examines life styles and technology and their implications to the firm. The third article, by Yankelovich, looks at developing life styles and its meaning to market planners. The final selection, by Smallwood and others, explores some projected life styles of this decade.

Life style is an important concept for marketers, since marketing activities deal not only with products but also act as

113

> *a determinant of life style. Life style analysis facilitates the understanding, explanation and prediction of consumer behavior. In our economy of abundance, marketing functions have contributed to establishing a specific life style and value system.*

---

10. LIFE–STYLE CONCEPTS AND MARKETING *

William Lazer †

A general concept, referred to vaguely as "life style," is being used by behavioral scientists, especially sociologists. The precise nature and scope of the concept is not clear. However, in interviews about life style, several behavioral scientists revealed that they understood its general meaning and its significance for research purposes. They were also willing to discuss relevant life-style research projects and to recommend a body of literature that reflected a life-style orientation. They did not, however, define the concept specifically, and none of the recommended literature contained a definition.

THE LIFE–STYLE CONCEPT

What is life style? Life style is a systems concept. It refers to the distinctive or characteristic mode of living, in its aggregative and broadest sense, of a whole society or segment thereof. It is concerned with those unique ingredients or qualities which describe the style of life of some culture or group, and distinguish it from others. It embodies the patterns that develop and emerge from the dynamics of living in a society.

Life style, therefore, is the result of such forces as culture, values, resources, symbols, license, and sanction. From one perspective, the aggregate of consumer purchases, and the manner in which they are consumed, reflect a society's life style.

Following this definition it is logical to speak of the American life style, our family life styles, consumer life styles, the life style of various social strata, and the life style of specific groups in different stages of the life cycle.

In marketing we have been particularly interested in consumer life styles in terms of the way people individualize, and identify themselves

---

* Reprinted from "Life Style Concepts and Marketing," *Proceedings of the Winter Conference of the American Marketing Association,* 1963, pp. 130–39.

† Michigan State University.

as members of various groups, and the resulting patterns of living. For example, we have gathered and analyzed data on consumer incomes, age groups, and expenditure patterns for decades. The goal is not one of assembling statistics for the sake of statistical information. Rather it is one of translating statistical findings about consumers into models of consumer life styles that will permit us to understand and predict various dimensions of consumer behavior, particularly purchase behavior.

A life-style hierarchy may be charted consisting of:

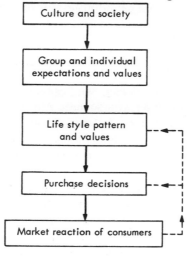

Life style, therefore, is a major behavioral concept for understanding, explaining, and predicting consumer and business behavior. It is a more generalized concept than existing concepts of consumer behavior that have been advanced in marketing. Such topics as mobility, leisure, social class, life cycle, status, conformity, mass, and the family as a consuming unit are all part of the life-style fabric. As a result, life-style studies could foster the unification of findings and theories related to consumer behavior. In fact, life style is a point of interdisciplinary convergence among marketing and such subject-matter areas as sociology, social and cultural anthropology, psychology, demography, and social psychology.

Economists and marketing people seem to have a different perspective on the value of life-style concepts and findings. In most economic studies the life style of a society is usually assumed or ignored. It is part of the "state of the art" and "other things being equal," statements. (One striking exception is Veblen who developed such concepts as vicarious consumption and vicarious leisure.)

By contrast, in marketing, *life-style factors are viewed as among the most important forces influencing and shaping economic activity.* They are the very focus of a major part of marketing. Foote, for instance, has suggested that in essence marketers are becoming taste counselors.[1] If this is the case, marketing and life style are surely intertwined.

Since ours is a materialistic, acquisitive, thing-minded, abundant economy, marketing becomes one of the cores for understanding life styles. Therefore, marketing is in a position to make a significant contribution to a number of life-style-oriented disciplines. Moreover, since our life style is being emulated in other parts of the world, such as Europe, Japan and Latin America, a better understanding of our life style may also enhance economic development theory.

MARKETING AND THE LIFE STYLE OF ABUNDANCE

When we think of abundance, we usually perceive of the physical capabilities and potentialities of a society. Abundance, however, is also a result of the culture itself since it stems partly from physical factors and partly from cultural forces. In large measure, our economic abundance results from certain institutions in our society which affect our pattern of living.

Potter maintains that advertising is the institution identified with abundance, particularly American abundance.[2] However, the institution that is brought into being by abundance without previous emphasis or existence in the same form is the institution of marketing. It is marketing expressed not only in advertising forms, but in such forms as the emphasis upon consumption in our society, marketing research, marketing planning, the marketing concept, new approaches to product development, credit, the management of innovation, the utilization of effective merchandising techniques, and the cultivation of mass markets: that is the institution of abundance.

Ours is a business-dominated society. Hence, business influences our life styles as profoundly as any other force. One of the unique characteristics of American business, however, is the distinctive approach it adopts to marketing. Marketing has reached its most mature form and has had its greatest impact on life styles in the American economy.

Other cultures have made significant contributions to business thought and practice in such areas as business law, ethics, accounting, finance, production systems, and organization theory. By contrast, marketing progress to date is uniquely attributable to the American life style, and it is being studied and emulated in other parts of the world. Such institutions and techniques as self-service, supermarkets, discount houses, mar-

---

[1] Nelson Foote, "The Anatomy of the Consumer," in Lincoln H. Clark (ed.), *Consumer Behavior, The Dynamics of Consumer Reaction* (New York: New York University Press), pp. 21–24.

[2] David M. Potter, *People of Plenty* (Chicago: University of Chicago Press, 1954), p. 167.

keting research, credit plans, and packaging are spreading part of the American life style in many parts of the world.

In a life-style sense, marketing is an institution of social control. It is an institution of social control in the same sense the school and the home are. It exerts an extensive influence on our life style which I maintain is for the betterment of our social and economic life. Moreover, since marketing is responsibale to a very large extent for our standard of living it is impossible to understand our culture fully, and hence our life style, without some comprehension of marketing.

The impact of marketing on our patterns of living, particularly advertising, has not been ignored. Advertising has been criticized pointedly. Toynbee, for example, writes that if it were demonstrated to be true:

> that personal consumption stimulated by advertising is essential for growth and full employment in an economy of abundance . . . it would also demonstrate to my mind that an economy of abundance is a spiritually unhealthy way of life, and that the sooner we reform it the better . . . The moral that I draw is that a way of life based on personal consumption, stimulated by advertising, needs changing." [3]

These are strong indictments of unfavorable marketing influences on our life style and are reinforced by the writings of such people as Warne, Galbraith, and Schlesinger.

When abundance prevails, however, the limitations and constraints upon business and other parts of our life style shift. Potter writes: "The most critical point in the functioning of society shifts from production to consumption . . . the culture must be reoriented to convert the producer's into a consumer's culture . . . and the society must be adjusted to a new set of drives and values of which consumption is paramount." [4] This becomes the challenge of marketing in altering life styles in an abundant economy. *Marketing becomes an instrument for changing production-oriented value into consumption-oriented norms.*

Marketing and values

Our basic value system determines the nature and significance of various social institutions. These fundamental values, moreover, are not merely the result of the whims of marketers. It is true that we live in a sensate culture, one which stresses sensory enjoyment, materialism and utilitarianism.[5] Consumers desire and can own those items and symbols that are associated with status, achievement, and accomplishment. Material values have become important. Marketing responds to, and rein-

---

[3] *"Toynbee vs. Bernbach:* Is Advertising Morally Defensible?" *Yale Daily News,* Special Issue, 1963, p. 2.

[4] Potter, *People of Plenty,* p. 173.

[5] See Pitirim A. Sorokin, *The Crisis of Our Age* (New York: E. P. Dutton & Co., Inc., 1946), especially chap. 3.

forces, such values in our abundant culture, and in so doing appeals to the senses and emphasizes materialism.

The life-style question still to be answered, however, is one concerning the relative desirability of our life style with such emphases as contrasted with other life styles. Great materialistic stress and accomplishment is not inherently sinful and bad. Moral values are not vitiated as many critics seem to think by substantial material acquisitions. In reality the improvement of material situations can lead to a greater recognition of intrinsic values, the lifting of general tastes, the enhancement of a moral climate and the direction of more attention to the appreciation of art and esthetics.

This I would suggest is occurring today. It has also been the pattern of the past. In history great artistic and cultural advancements are at least accompanied, if not shaped, by periods of flourishing trade and commerce.

The next marketing frontier may well be an inner one—the market of the mind and the personal development of consumers.[6] Marketing in the future may be geared to filling the needs of this inner frontier. One of its roles may be that of encouraging increasing expenditures by consumers, of both dollars and time, to develop themselves intellectually, socially, and morally. This has already been accomplished to a limited degree: witness the increasing demand for classical records, good books, the attendance at symphony concerts, the purchase of good oil paintings through mail order catalogues, and the support for the arts in general. Social critics, while prone to point out the undesirable impact of marketing on our life styles, have neglected to indicate the progress and contributions that have been made.

LIFE STYLE AND CONSUMER EXPECTATIONS

Part of the American life style may be referred to as the American Dream. A big difference exists between the American Dream with its expectations and the dreams and expectations of other countries. The gap, however, is narrowing.

The American Dream as a life-style concept includes a belief in equality of opportunity to obtain a good standard of living, to acquire status and success in a community through individual initiative, determination, sacrifice and skill. It involves the contradictory concepts of equality for all and the rank and status orderings that result in the social ladders so characteristic of the functioning of our complex society. It requires the maintenance of an open society with opportunity for upward economic and social movement and the availability of education which is a root for

---

[6] For a discussion of this point, see William Lazer and Eugene J. Kelley, "Editorial Postscript," *Managerial Marketing: Perspectives & Viewpoints* (rev. ed.; Homewood, Ill.: Richard D. Irwin, Inc., 1963), p. 683.

social achievement, occupational advancement, and higher incomes on a widespread basis. These aspects of the Dream are reflected in our life style.

In general, American consumers, especially younger consumers, in living out the Dream exude optimism for the future. They feel sure that tomorrow will be better than today. American consumers believe that they can continue to expand their consumption and increase their relative amount of pleasure rather than merely limit desires. They feel sure they can continue increasing the area of purchasing power under their control.

One result of this optimistic outlook is that American consumers see virtue not so much in curbing desires, but rather in realizing oneself by acquiring the necessary goods and symbols. This optimistic life style has a historical root, for as Kraus has pointed out, unlike the European who only hoped that tomorrow would be no worse than today, Americans felt cheated if tomorrow were not better than today.[7] This orientation is supported and reflected in such marketing concepts and techniques as programmed innovation and product development, installment credit, advertising, sales promotion and merchandising activities.

Life style and change

In our life style we do not accept institutions, techniques, and products as permanent. Our society contains a rich tradition of expecting and anticipating change. This anticipation results from a conscious belief that changes are normal, useful, helpful, and good. We seem to accept what appears to be good today and anticipate that it will be superseded by items that are superior tomorrow. The rather trite expression "innovate or perish" has rich meaning for businesses trying to meet the demands of our pattern of life.

Such an attitude is one of the foundations of aggressive marketing. Girod has written that in our culture, "Innovation, change, mobility, and movement are permanent traits," and that, "In stressing the need for innovation, Americans are fighting for the maintenance of this aspect of their way of life for permanency of the one thing to which they are attached." [8]

By contrast, some other cultures which are more restrictive in their anticipations do not expect, hope for, or plan for any great change in their environment. They strive to maintain the status quo. In these cultures which are resolute against the suggestion of new ideas, new products, and new processes, marketing tends to play but a minor role.

---

[7] See Michael Kraus, "The United States to 1865" (Ann Arbor, Mich.: University of Michigan Press, 1959).

[8] Roger Girod, "Comment on Consumer Reaction to Innovation," in Lincoln H. Clark (ed.), *Consumer Behavior, Research on Consumer Reactions* (New York: Harper & Bros., 1958), p. 10.

To date, technological changes have had the greatest effect on our life styles. Changing methods of marketing are, however, very significant. Consider the effect on our life style, and the life style of other cultures, of supermarkets, self-service, discount houses, shopping centers, automatic vending machines, credit plans, new products, packages, and new communications techniques. Such process and service innovations will have an even greater effect in the future.

CONSUMERS, CONSUMPTION, AND LIFE STYLE

In the scheme of our life style, because of a previous production orientation, the relative significance of consumers and consumption as economic determinants has been underemphasized. The importance of maintaining physical production is, of course, widely recognized. Only limited reference, however, is made to the corresponding necessity of maintaining consumption. *The critical nature of consumption in an abundant economy demands that consumption should not be considered as a happenstance activity.* We must establish the necessary conditions for consumption to proceed on an adequate and orderly basis.

Until recently, even the relative significance of consumer investment in our economy was greatly underemphasized. Business investment, which is certainly a most significant factor in influencing business conditions, received almost all the attention. Katona points out, however, that "growth and expansion of the American economy are dependent on consumer investment as well as business investment . . . business investment and consumer investment are equally important forces which either stimulate or retard the economy." [9]

What must also be recognized is the important fact that consumer investments are not merely the function of increased income. They stem from and reflect life styles.

A distorted picture has been presented of consumers and the purchase and consumption process. Consumers have been portrayed in much of the non-marketing literature as emotional, irrational, uninformed beings, manipulated at will through marketing devices. It is held that conformity, followership, waste, ostentation, and meaningless style changes have been foisted upon consumers by marketers. Rokeach points out, however, that marketers have been using the wrong psychological theory. He emphasizes that the theory that consumers are irrational creatures who must be appealed to only on an emotional level is outmoded. Modern psychological theories view man as "not only a rationalizing creature but also a rational creature curious, exploratory and receptive to new ideas." [10]

---

[9] George Katona, *Michigan Business Review* (July 1961), pp. 17–20.

[10] "Advertising: A Wrong Psychological Limb?" *New York Times* (November 7, 1963), p. 60.

Competition as part of our life style

Essentially, competition is directly related to and can be defined only in terms of the culture and nature of the environment that surrounds it. Competition has its fullest meaning in the marketing environment of a consumeristic economy rather than in a controlled, planned, or cooperative environment such as exists in many other countries.

In thinking about competition, however, we tend to be retrospective and do not relate it to current life styles. In interpreting laws and in our economic analysis we often cling to past or previous models of competition and competitive situations. For example, we often conceptualize competition in terms of an emerging industrial society rather than a maturing industrial society, in terms of price competition neglecting convenience and service competition, in terms of an economy of scarcity with relatively low consumer purchasing power rather than an economy of abundance with widespread discretionary purchasing power; in terms of manufacturers and distributors controlling and dominating the market place rather than an economy governed (or at least influenced to a large extent) by customer sovereignty; and in terms of intra-industry competition rather than inter-industry competition.

In particular, there is a misplaced emphasis, stemming from past economic models, on *price* as the key competitive weapon. This does not mean that price competition is no longer important in our mode of living. Certainly it is. It does mean, however, that ours is a competitive situation in which *price obscurity* and not price clarity seems to be the rule and in which other variables including convenience and service are very important.[11]

We seem to take competition for granted as one of the inherent aspects of our life style. J. M. Clark points out, however, that "There can be no certainty that competition will remain vigorous in American business," and that "The necessary conditions are a fascinating subject for speculation." The necessary and sufficient condition for the existence of keen, vigorous competition, however, is clear. *It is aggressive marketing.* Changes in price, advertising, products, and channels of distribution tend to keep things stirred up and prevent competition from lapsing into routine passivity.[12]

CONCLUSION

To a large extent our marketing technology sets us apart from other cultures. It is a motivating force behind our competitive system and

---

[11] See Eugene J. Kelley, "The Importance of Convenience in Consumer Purchasing," *Journal of Marketing* (July 1958).

[12] J. M. Clark, "Competition: Static Models and Dynamic Aspects," *American Economic Review*, Vol. 45, No. 2 (May 1955), p. 462.

characterizes our life style. Marketing in the future must be recognized as a major institution in our way of life as well as a force that can contribute greatly to the influence of international life styles.

Yet analysts of our culture and life styles have virtually ignored marketing. It is often regarded as but a minor type of activity which is not important enough to be investigated. It has been neglected by psychologists, sociologists, social and cultural anthropologists, economists, and historians. It is treated as though it were a side issue in our economic activity, when in essence, it is one of the core or focal points.

Marketing is one of the longstanding institutions in our society. Its impact reverberates throughout our culture. It has shaped our life styles and has affected everyone of us significantly. The inextricable intertwinement of marketing and our life style was emphasized by a theologian who wrote, "The saintly cannot be separated from the market place for it is in the market place that man's future is being decided, they must be schooled in the arts of the market place as in the discipline of saintliness itself." [13]

Several pertinent issues concerning consumer behavior and satisfaction arise during life-style analysis of the values and objectives of individuals in their normal social settings. Information resulting from the study of such issues is vital to efficient marketing decision making. Life-style forces and technology interact with each other and the firm to create marketing problems and opportunities. Several researchable questions are posed within the framework of the life-style concept.

11. COMMENTARY ON LIFE STYLE*

Eugene J. Kelley †

Marketing in its broadest sense is the medium through which the material goods and culture of a society are transmitted to its members. As

---

[13] Louis Finkelstein in Conference On The American Character, *Bulletin, Center For The Study of Democratic Institutions* (October 1961), p. 6.

* Reprinted from "Discussion," *Proceedings of the Winter Conference of the American Marketing Association, 1963,* pp. 164–71.

† The Pennsylvania State University.

the style of living of members of a society—consumers—changes, the media of distribution and the products and services marketed must also change, or be replaced. All social institutions face the threat of obsolescence in a period of rapid change. Life-style analysis can help marketing institutions both to minimize the risk of lagging behind cultural needs and to render more effective consumer services profitably.

Marketing's concern with the satisfaction of consumer needs explains why concepts, insights, or tools useful in understanding consumer satisfactions and behavior should receive the thoughtful consideration of all marketing people. . . .

The idea of product symbolism has been accepted for some time. But to think of a consumer life as a symbol, or as a family living a patterned way of life, living a family theme and image, opens several research possibilities for academic marketers and marketing research practitioners. A manufacturer, for instance, could ask such questions as:

What are the firm's concepts about consumers and their ways of living?

What assumptions about consumer life styles underlie the advertising and marketing decisions made recently in the firm?

How do these assumptions check out with the realities of consumer life-style patterns?

How can our concepts of consumer behavior be sharpened through life-style analysis?

Life-style analysis reminds us that the consumer is indeed a complex person operating in a complex world. The approach forces an examination of the values and objectives of individuals under social settings in which consumers live. Perhaps one of the great values of life-style analysis is that it raises certain questions about consumers and that it can bring information about such questions into marketing decision making.

Two of the greatest forces for change in the world today have life-style dimensions. The movement to full citizenship of the American Negro is basically an ethical and social matter. But a movement which directly involves one tenth of our population is also bound to affect the style of living of the remainder. The revolution of rising expectations among people of the developing nations also represents life-style movements just as basic to marketing men and to society as technological change. Less dramatic than these revolutionary social changes in the domestic and international markets are the changes in life styles of nearly all Americans. These changes will have a major impact on established institutions and firms, particularly those who do not develop and distribute consumer-satisfying products and services appropriate to changing technologies and modes of living. . . .

The gap between technology and modes of living seems to be widening. The problem is becoming both more complex and important because of the tremendous advances in technology which have taken place in recent years and the growing complexity of internal business operations within the firm. Management has a difficult task keeping up with technological changes and coping with complex internal problems resulting from the increasing scale of operation. When to this is added the rapid obsolescence of existing engineering, management, and marketing knowledge, we can see why management's attention had been diverted from studying changes in the style of living of consumers toward the problems of changes in the style of management of business.

The marketing concept suggests that this may well be the wrong emphasis. Marketing-minded firms might do well to begin with the life-style needs of consumers and then attempt to integrate their technological research and development with these life-style needs rather than the other way around. . . .

The essence of marketing today is innovation, and life-style analysis suggests many areas of profitable innovistic opportunity. In some cases, a study of consumption patterns in life-style terms may suggest a substantial departure from traditional methods of marketing and doing business.

The implications are clear for a seller whose marketing thinking is geared to meeting the needs of old life styles. Until quite recently many department stores resisted the new needs of a suburban population and continued to gear operations to their image of apartment dwelling consumers completely oriented to the central business district. American automobile manufacturers were quite slow to move to the compact car because they did not understand the new life-style needs of an important market segment. . . .

Life style translates into symbols, so the symbolic meaning of products and services is something to be examined constantly by marketing people. Symbols are not merely status symbols, but symbols of a style of life. In an affluent society, the use to which people put products takes on more and more symbolic value. Professor Levy has earlier suggested the importance of symbols in the marketing world, particularly in regard to age, sex, and social class. As indicated earlier, *marketers are not selling isolated products which can be viewed as symbols; they are selling, or consumers are buying, a style of life or pieces of a larger symbol.*

The consumer can be perceived as following a system of living, a family style. The job of marketing then becomes one of providing consumers with models of styles of living and the ingredients in which they, if they are so minded, can compose their own style of living, to reach their own inner frontiers as they satisfy material needs.

The question of applications of life-style research is of interest. The prime value may be in the insights and perspectives the authors have stimulated. One of the greatest needs in marketing is for new concepts, and this concept seems most promising.

Life-style analysis is valuable not only in terms of product development and adjustment, but once understood can be very effective in terms of the communications mix. Many marketing communication efforts are wasted because they emerge from an assessment of the style of living of consumers which misses reality.

How well do advertising and marketing men understand the nature of changing patterns of life style? Undoubtedly a great deal is known about consumers. Whether the right questions are asked is another subject in itself. Many advertisements seem to fly in the face of an elementary understanding of life-style needs. The people in the ads are unreal, and the way in which they live is unreal. Browse through any consumer magazine and you can see the advertisers have a standard American life style in mind. They visualize, or seem to, their market as made up of beautiful and handsome people with several idealized children in an award-winning suburban setting. Happily such families are numerous in America today. But, *consider how many people are not living this style of life or do not aspire to it.* Where are the minority groups? Where are the poor people? Where are the senior citizens? Where are the non-Hollywood types? Where are the working wives? Where are the housewives who don't look as though they have two-car garages, all-electric kitchens, and white-collar husbands? [1]

Life-style approaches make it a little easier to take a new and longer special look at consumer behavior. Focusing on the future to anticipate the nature of life-style changes over a five- or ten-year period can bring a new dimension to marketing planning. The study of life-style patterns can help sophisticated sellers see consumers as they exist today and are likely to look tomorrow. The danger of the kind of advertising mentioned is that it is self-deceptive to advertisers and marketers. We begin to believe it ourselves after a while and, therefore, to sell to consumers as we believe them to be.

Nelson Foote has suggested a question about how marketing fits into the changing life style of consumers. He asked whether we are correct in thinking that the consumer is an individual with constantly expanding needs, and that the job of marketing is just to move more goods and services, to build more shopping centers, stuff more homes, to keep turning out the goods which clog the closets, attics, and basements of America as well as its living rooms.[2] As one speculation, is it possible that before the year 2000 the life style of consumers may not be as product oriented as it is today? It is possible, as Foote suggested, that we are seeing a pattern develop in which the consumer is devoting more of his attention to the satisfaction of wants that do not require consumption or production or distribution in the ordinary sense, but to inner satisfactions of a

---

[1] For some examples indicating areas of advertising ignorance of the consumer, see Marya Mannes, "How Well Do Advertisers Know the Consuming Public?" *Proceedings, Thirty-Fifth Annual Boston Conference on Distribution, 1963,* pp. 75–81.

[2] Nelson N. Foote, "The Image of the Consumer in the Year 2000," *Proceedings, Thirty-Fifth Annual Boston Conference on Distribution, 1963,* pp. 13–18.

variety of kinds. He also pointed out that the customer of 2000 will experience as his first constraint not income, but time; as a second constraint, learning. Our very term "consumer" is a seller-defined term. People are not as likely to see themselves as consumers in the future, but as something else—perhaps as individuals creating their own style of living by using the services of business.

Several researchable questions suggested by David G. Moore are paraphrased below.[3] Such questions may be heard in consumer marketing research more often in the future.

1. What are the life problems and challenges perceived by various market segments in different life cycle stages as they relate to the product mission and opportunities of the firm?
2. How are these life problems and challenges likely to change over the next five to ten years for various market segments as defined in both economic and social terms?
3. How do our present and programmed products and services help consumers deal with these challenges and problems? How can our products be improved in life-style terms during the next five- to ten-year product-planning period?
4. How do customers use the products now available to them in their daily routines, as tools of activity, in their personal, social, and recreational lives, and as symbolic expressions of their desires and interests?

Such questions may challenge some marketers to do more work in defining consumer groups in life-style and systems terms, establishing the goals of various market segments, and doing a more effective job of generating products and services which will help consumers deal with their most important problems. By moving in such directions, marketing can continue to fulfill its promise as an important social discipline concerned with the advancement of economic and social life.

Changing values affect the lives and purchasing patterns of individual consumers. Such changes must be anticipated, evaluated, and acted upon by the marketing strategist to insure that his firm will continue to efficiently function optimally in the marketplace. Illustrations of some of these major changes are grouped into five major categories of social trends that have influenced and will possibly further influence future consumption patterns.

---

[3] See David G. Moore, "Life Styles in Mobile Suburbia," *Proceedings of the Spring Conference of the American Marketing Association, 1963*, pp. 151–63.

12. WHAT NEW LIFE STYLES MEAN TO MARKET PLANNERS*

Daniel Yankelovich †

Mr. and Mrs. Alfonsin, both in their early fifties, decided that they no longer wished to maintain a big house. They moved into a smaller apartment with fewer home repairs and "labor-saving" devices. They bought a smaller car. They now entertain less formally. Mr. A has dropped his subscription to *Business Week*, and purchases his suits at a local department store instead of having them custom made. Mrs. A serves frozen vegetables and desserts for dinner, and with the leisure gained from having less cleaning and cooking to do, she has enrolled in an exercise class. She also finds that she has more time to devote to her physical appearance and to making travel plans for her husband and herself.

The Alfonsins are part of a social trend we call Life Simplification. *They—and people like them—are a matter of concern for a wide swath of companies in home building and furnishing, appliances, transportation, clothing, food, cleaning products, health products, and travel industries.*

Mary Beaton, age 23, secretary, stopped wearing a bra when she isn't at work and has changed her lipstick, perfume, and hairstyle. She pesters her parents about the artificial preservatives and chemicals in the food they eat, and brings home "natural" foods from a small specialty food store. She wants to chip in for the down payment on a farm in the country where their family can go to get out of the city. She has bought a small handloom and is learning to weave fabric from which she has made some of her weekend outfits.

Mary is part of a Return to Nature *social trend, and a major source of concern to the makers of foundation garments, textiles, cosmetics, toiletries, food, leisure-time equipment, and others.*

Michael Carter, age 29, lets his sideburns grow, borrows on his life insurance policy, and smokes "grass" at weekend parties, which gives him a craving for cheese, crackers, Fresca, and other snacks he's never wanted before. He has traded in his Pontiac for a Volvo, purchased a new stereo, an old Borsalino hat, and a subscription to *Psychology Today*. He has begun to complain at home about the meaninglessness of his well-paying job and has started to talk his wife out of having a third child.

---

* Reprinted from "What New Life Styles Mean to Market Planners," *Marketing/Communications* (June 1971), pp. 38–45.

† Daniel Yankelovich, Inc.

Michael is up to his neck in many of the new social trends, including Personalization, The Quest for Meaningful Work, Living for Today, Pleasure for Its Own Sake, The Acceptance of Stimulants and Drugs, *and* The New Romanticism. *He is of no small interest to the life insurance people, magazine publishers, makers of fine whiskies, cars, phonograph equipment, and clothing. He is a source of anxiety to the baby food and toy industries—and to his employer.*

The Alfonsins, Mary Beaton, and Michael Carter are living through a period of wrenching changes in American life styles.

How many people are like them?

How many are strongly involved in each trend, how many moderately or not at all?

Which trends that now affect sharply defined groups in the population —college students, middle class blacks, the affluent with grown children —are spreading to the general population?

Which trends are mushrooming and which are creeping forward at an almost imperceptible pace?

Which trends are here to stay and which are passing fads?

What *are* the major social trends as contrasted to the eccentric life styles that affect only a small group of people?

For convenience in reporting, the 31 trends included in Monitor 1970 have been organized into five broad categories. . . .

. . . The organization of the trends into categories is essentially for convenience in reporting and analysis. The categories represent our judgment as to the common source or root of a given set of trends. While conjecture about the underlying forces that have generated the trends is of scholarly interest, these forces probably are too general in nature to be meaningful for practical, marketing purposes. . . .

Summary of trends

Psychology-of-affluence trends, reflecting the increasing assumption that the essentials of economic survival are assured, leading to a focus on having more or doing more to improve the quality of living.

Personalization	Personal creativity
Physical self-enhancement	Anti-materialism
Physical fitness and well-being	Meaningful work
Social/cultural self-expression	

Anti-functionalism trends, reflecting reaction to the emphasis on the functional and "scientific," seen as leading to drabness and boredom in everyday life.

Mysticism   Introspection
Sensuousness   Novelty and change
New romanticism   Beauty in the home

Reaction-against-complexity trends, reflecting the belief that life has become excessively complicated, that the individual has lost control of his destiny, and that there is much to be gained by returning to a more natural and more simple style of life.

Return to nature   Scientism and technocracy
Simplification   Ethnic orientation
Anti-bigness   Local community involvement

Trends related to the weakening of the "Protestant Ethic," reflecting questioning of a value system, termed the "Protestant Ethic" by sociologists, which, put very simply, is based on the belief that ambition, striving, hard work, self-sufficiency, self-denial, and other familiar virtues will lead to a successful life.

Living for today   Liberal sex attitudes
Hedonism   Blurring of the sexes
Away from self-improvement   Acceptance of drugs
Noninstitutional religion

Trends reflecting permissiveness in child rearing, deriving from the psychological guidelines which have been widely used in the upbringing of our current youth population. These guidelines were based largely on concern about the negative after effects of a rigid, demanding, punishment-oriented childhood.

Anti-hypocrisy   Female careerism
Rejection of authority   Familism
Tolerance for chaos and disorder

Survival and growth are basic objectives of any firm. In a dynamic market of vigorous competitors neither survival nor growth are assured. Where are the highly efficient manufacturers of horse-drawn buggies of the past? Making automobiles, perhaps? Or perhaps they were caught unaware of the influence of the changing times and fell into oblivion. The anticipation of changing consumer needs, life styles, and values is a necessity for any firm. The following article examines some emerging changes and suggests their relevance to the firm.

---

13. LIFE STYLES AND VALUES OF THE 1970s *

John Smallwood, William Lazer, William Henry, Dennis Knight, Lee Rainwater, and George Stolnitz

WHERE'S THE REVOLUTION?

Considerable attention has been focused on the revolutionary changes occurring within the common body of our society in the 1970s. Our society is viewed as being in a state of flux with major pressures influencing and shaping new and different life styles, wants, needs, motives. The main thrust of the change appears to surface in the young and the about-to-be family classes. However, some hard questions about such change must be raised including: Who is changing? In what ways? How basic and significant are the changes? What impact will they have, if any, on the relationship of products, motives and on consumer purchases?

Despite all the attention being given to changes and technological developments, the most striking fact is that life styles and values of various social classes, will demonstrate great stability. Life styles of the 1970s will continue to highlight the dominant characteristic of the existence of core values, of permanence stability, and in general a lack of change in *basic* belief and value systems.

This does not mean that changes will not occur—for they will—as is emphasized throughout this report. However, social changes and their impact on life styles are more likely to be subtle, implicit, low in profile, or even superficial. Rather than changes in values, they will represent adaptations of basic values and patterns of relationships to new social technological, ecological, economic, and political situations. Constant re-interpretation of the meanings and uses of products and services, new and old, will occur to make them consistent with the basic core themes of life styles. In this way the stability of the basic fabric of our life styles will be maintained. The result will be stability within change—a factor often disguised by the emphasis given to rebellion and innovation.

* Reprinted from John Smallwood, William Lazer, William Henry, Dennis Knight, Lee Rainwater, and George Stolnitz, *CELS–80: A Report on Consumer Environments and Life Styles of the Seventies* (Benton Harbor, Michigan: Whirlpool Corporation, 1971), pp. 18–31. The authors are from these respective institutions: Whirlpool Corporation, Michigan State University, University of Chicago, University of Wyoming, Harvard University, and Indiana University.

Major markets will continue to a large extent to be comprised of the mid-age, mid-income, mid-majority consumer. They encompass the traditional stable American family that with its children and extended kin represent the basic purchasing units. These are the homebound people who exhibit standard morality and standard values. This suggests that in the 1970s there will be more apparent variations on the surface of values and life styles than really significant basic shifts.

CONSUMER CHOICES

Consumers of the 1970s will be more knowledgeable and cosmopolitan. They will be more cognizant of national and world-wide trends in tastes, styles and products and will be more sophisticated and discerning. Their life styles will be built out of a rapidly expanding multiplicity of product and service choices. They will be even less fettered by socio-economic constraints than they are currently. The variety of available products and services will be enriched greatly with a resulting broader range of life-style alternatives.

A set of pluralistic standards legitimizing a wider range of living in the U.S. of the 70s will emerge. A more widespread acceptance, recognizing the legitimacy of differences of ways of life of various social segments (black, brown, red, etc.) will exist. This will foster the tailoring of life styles more suited to individual choices and desires rather than the development of life styles conforming with those of "traditional or respectable people."

Not only will nonconforming behavior be more widely accepted but increased prosperity will result in greater economic security. More secure people are willing to express individual differences and life-style preferences. This does not negate, however, the maintenance of a stable body of core values and themes for the mid-majority.

A broad range of choices—both product and life style, does not automatically generate consumer satisfaction. It can also generate anxiety, frustration, and uncertainty. Consumers may well feel the oppression as well as the joy of choices. Being confronted with more complex products, less service, an increasing range of product alternatives, and not knowing how to assess properly or maximize the value expected of purchase decisions, can heighten the consumer frustrations already evidenced in the trend to consumerism.

THE YOUTH CULTURE

The most visible and striking social changes are those attributed to changes in the life styles of younger groups. Although the present disenchanted youth are probably not just one group representing one life style, some general tendencies seem to pervade. The young often talk as though they have given up all achievement-oriented goals, all money-produced objects for the realization of an inner life and a real concern with sensual immediences. In essence they have not. The basic product relations have not been altered. They have not given up products, convenience, or things per se, for their life style is packed full of products and conveniences of life.

The apparent and obvious changes in clothing styles, methods of expressions and new living arrangements of some of the young are evident to all. Such developments and tendencies should be monitored. But the young do not represent the coming of age. Moreover, when the young reach 35 they will act, think, and have values more like present 35-year-olds than like 20-year-olds.

The young have not abandoned the values of achievement and ability. They have abandoned a few symbols, and resent particular products as representative of the current establishment. As the young mature, they will stabilize themselves in the job market, marriage, the family and the home. They will become materialistic, object bound, money bound, and part of the establishment.

However, because things change slowly, and a little change in styles of self-expression does not presage product-disenchantment, does not mean that no change should be assumed, or that changes occurring should be ignored. It is sound to monitor the product/meaning systems of not only the mid-majority but of the young. Dimensions along which the new young become different from "us" are worth reviewing. Product cues from the young, their households and furnishings, their purchase preferences, actual and ideal, could result in valuable product—market—purchase information.

The youth culture has been diagnosed for its ills and praised for its human discoveries. Their foci are often useful, hopeful, and reflective of a burden of societal cares. Their impact in the 1970s will be evolutionary and not revolutionary. Among their major issues are:

1. *Resistance to the rationality of restraint now for later gratification, and emphasis on expressivity.* The "now" logic has heavy elements of need for feeling, empathy, concern for the poor and underprivileged. This movement to help others, however, is often more self-serving and self-determining than other-determining. It is usually directed at self rather than being aimed at social action and complaints against external societal objects—it reflects getting in touch with one's own feelings.

2. *Resentment of achievement drives and symbols.* The young often reject normal routes to achievement and social/job mobility. It is, however, a reaction against establishment logic rather than against achievement/mobility per se. It is a question of old symbols and their connection with the establishment rather than specific value rejections.

3. *Reduction in object accumulation.* As has been noted, although some products and property have lost value among the younger groups, other

objects have taken on value. There is no apparent reduction in either the accumulation of, or involvement with, products—particularly appliances. The younger groups do accept the credit culture rather than thrift. A small part of the youth movement has the view that people should not be bound or burdened by possessions.

4. *New styles of protest.* What will be the impact of hippie styles, freedom movements, youth protests, and riots? Will college radicals, for example, go to business and engineering schools and accept standard life styles? Relevant research findings and scholarly opinion indicates that the basic attitudes of most of the protestors will eventually become similar to those of the mid-majority establishment. But, as a solid accomplishment of this generation, many long held prejudices and constructive "hang-ups" will be greatly diminished.

A rather curious perspective on the desire and tolerance for social changes is associated with increasing incomes. For it is not only the young, the lower income groups, nor even the more affluent skilled labor groups, white or black, that consistently tolerate or lead the way for broad changes. Rather, it is both the young and the majority of the most affluent Americans—the over-$15,000 income group—which is most concerned with such changes as consumerism, the achievement of social objectives by business, the realization of integration and equality among the races. The over-$15,000 group includes a substantial majority of professionally-oriented people who no longer unequivocally adhere to conservative corporate norms, organization loyalty and slogans, or a standpat perspective of life and their environments. It is noteworthy that by 1980 those families that are in the over-$15,000 income bracket *and* under 45 years of age will almost triple in numbers. They will comprise almost 21% of all families by 1980 compared to less than 9% in 1970.

WOMEN'S LIB AND THE WOMAN'S PLACE

What effect will Woman's Lib have? Is the woman's place in the home? What will her role in the family be in the 1970s? Are significant social changes occurring?

Considerable ambivalence exists among middle-class women about whether they are servants of their families, hidden bosses, or a family member of equal status with major responsibilities of keeping the home running smoothly. Given the mechanization of the home, the increasing complexities of home-centered family activities, the wide and rich assortment of sophisticated products from which family purchases are to be made, the wife's role of general manager of a productive center and a life maintenance section will, in the future, become more apparent.

Yet wives have the problem that the values of society do not define this work as productive and useful in the same sense that work external to the home is defined to be so. A trend exists for women to enter the work force as was discussed. By so doing they accept more clearly defined jobs as contrasted with the unending and unambiguous housework, and they gain self-respect and money. Yet with increasing demands for personal services in the 1970s, there will be even more pressures on the limited supply of household help, so that the labor necessary to maintain homes will become even more expensive. "Women's work" will be considered even more valuable. Opportunities to automate further household duties will increase.

The new feminism contains three strains of thought and aspiration for women. First a great self-consciousness exists among women about their subordinate status in the home and world. A drive for more autonomy, self-expression and self-respect is underway. Second, the established notion that a woman's place is really in the home is being challenged. In this regard even the objectives of members of the Women's Liberation Movement may be misconstrued. Most women are much concerned with their ability to fill the homemaker role in a personally gratifying way—in a way that allows for the development of autonomy, self-respect, and a sense of a valid identity than they are in denying or abrogating this role. Third, women are seeking equal opportunity and equal pay in job opportunities. Considerable progress will be made in this latter thrust in the 1970s.

The result of such aspirations and thought will be a continuation of the trend to achieving greater equality between husband and wives in their functioning and roles in the family. There will be more sharing of power and duties in the 1970s. The division of household labors will not be so clearly defined in the sense of kitchen or cleaning duties being the exclusive province of the wife.

The response to the combination of affluence and a continuing emphasis on feminine equality will likely vary among social classes. In the working and lower middle class groups women will realize a greater sense of worth and will be encouraged to assume more autonomous functioning within the homemaker role. In the upper middle class there may be an increasing emphasis on careers or community activities to realize self-expressive goals. This will be added to those "outside the home activities," paid and unpaid, in which upper middle class women now engage. Thus a strong premium will be placed on home appliances that save time and labor. For while homes in the 1970s will be more complex and elaborate, women will want to spend less time living in and maintaining them.

WILL FAMILIES SURVIVE?

Evidences exist of some marked changes in the family structure and way of life in the 1970s. Included are changes in age of marriage, birth rates, sexual relationships, contraception and size of family. However, the basic husband-wife primary household unit will exhibit great stability.

In the 1970s adults will likely spend less time in the "full-nest stage" of the family life cycle and more time as "empty nesters." This will stem from later age at marriage and birth of the first child, unchanging age of birth of the last child, and an unchanging or even declining birth rate and earlier age at which children leave home.

Young people will marry at a later age than they did in the 1950s and 60s. Although research findings do not show evidence of a major revolution in the extent of pre-marital sexual relationships, some significant changes in the pattern of these relationships are occurring. Pre-marital sex is likely to be more open, accepted, frequent and institutionalized within peer group rather than furtive hidden activities. This legitimization will provide alternative means to marriage for establishing maturity and adulthood, and so reduce pressures for early marriage. At the level of the "class mass" relationships, young single couples living together, will become more widespread. The development of a wide range of "singles institutions" will allow the achievement of adulthood without marriages.

Contraception, coupled with widespread legalized abortion, will also result in fewer unwanted children. Both may lead to smaller families and the planned spacing of children. Although the fertility desires of the future are difficult to predict, a continued trend to lower fertility rates seems likely.

The changes in mating behavior indicate that, on the average, in the 1970s women will start their families later than they do now. They will complete their fertility in their late twenties. Children will be grown and old enough to leave home while their parents are somewhat younger than is the case now. Life-style patterns and consumption behavior both prior to marriage, "singles styles" and those of the "empty nesters" will be affected.

THE FAMILY SCENE

The family dominated scene in the 1970s will give way to a peerage by age cohorts. Children will shift relationships more to outside peer groups rather than merely bringing friends into the family circle. Individuality of family members will be stressed more. Increasing solidarity of the husband-wife relationship will be stressed at the expense of mother-children relationship. The trend will be to a continuation of democratic parent-child relationships, stressing the value of friendship rather than authoritarianism.

In line with these developments is the trend away from the "family meal." Adults will more commonly eat with adults, and children with their own age cohorts. Technology, a more casual and quickie approach to food, and the wide range of prepared foods available reinforce this tendency. The mother-directed stove is being replaced by instrumentally specific appliances.

In the 1970s reduced preferences for mother-centered food preparation and family-dominated meals will change family reactions. New products and arrangements will make the kitchen an eat, cook, wash, clean, entertainment, and social life center. The home will be seen as a system involving shelter, production processes, furnishings, maintenance, waste generation, and family care. The interconnections between various parts of the home system will be restructured and the home will become a more capital-intensive place.

Two seemingly opposing food trends are emerging and will be reinforced in the 1970s. The first is an upgrading of food tastes with the purchase of more expensive foods. It includes the development of more epicurean and cosmopolitan tastes, and more expensive processing and preparation of foods. The second is the simplification of food preparation and the fast meals which trade off quality and taste for convenience. Frozen foods, take-home items, and other non-home-prepared foods cater to this trend.

In reality the average standard of American cuisine in the home is improving and will likely continue to do so. Greater emphasis will be given to gourmet cooking and foods. At the same time growing market segments for convenience foods and fast foods, but not necessarily traditional American food, will also exist.

MOBILITY

Since families will be smaller, and less monolithic, the mobility or portability of families in the 1970s will be enhanced. Markets for a whole range of activities, products, and services will stem from the emphasis of exploring the wider world. Needs for both more stimulation and privacy will occur.

The fascination with the wider world leads to two tendencies. First, an interest in bringing into the home more products and services that reflect, symbolize, and express the wider world. Second, a stronger interest in travel—going out and exploring the wider world rather than bringing it home. The impact of both of these sets of needs will be a freeing of the family in its life style from a particular territorial base and local set of products and tastes.

The 1970s will see a growing emphasis on the mastery of space and distance and the availability of amenities so that the family can pursue more gratifying activities. Environments will be more tailor-made to fit family interests, moods, and desires. Technology will foster the decentralized development of entertainment and educational centers in the home. The mastery and control of environments for stimulation and relaxation will occur. New and preferred experiences will be brought right to the home. At the same time there will be a direct impact on travel and the products and services associated with travel including multiple home or condominium ownership, trailers, and camping equipment.

Given greater sophistication, communications, travel and exposure, the mid-majority consumer will also feel a need to pull back, to disengage, to get "away from it all," to get "back to nature." This will strengthen commitments to the "home as the castle." It will encourage vacations in tranquil, isolated, and private settings. The steady growth of camping and its technology and the increasing trend to ownership or use of vacation homes is likely. The pressures on both vacation land and home building, both permanent and mobile, are evident.

SERVICES

The rise of family affluence in the 1970s will have a direct impact on the range of services that can be afforded. Consumers will be better able to purchase services, such as medical and dental services, that they had to forgo previously. Also their own time will take on greater economic value. They will be more willing to hire others to perform tasks, if such help is available at reasonable prices. This is evidenced in the increasing demand for food preparation outside the home; lawn, snow, pool, and window services. This is part of a tendency to eliminate some services from the home, and homeowners pass them on to specialists who can perform them more efficiently. Part of the appeal of the popular condominium is just that.

A large expansion of services will occur in the public sector—municipal, state and federal. Cleaning up the environment, protecting consumers by the provision of information on products by government are examples. Day care institutions, nursery schools, and other children's services, nursing homes, antipoverty programs, etc. will be confronted with increasing demands. Thus homemaking kinds of activities are likely to be carried out by a wide range of "nonhome" institutions.

Similar considerations apply to the demand for services necessary to maintain and repair the capital-intensive home system. Not only will there be an even greater scarcity of competent service personnel, but the costs of services will increase. Products will be redesigned to simplify servicing, to permit the consumer to do it himself, to eliminate the care required to maintain products, to permit early and simple diagnosis of product problems. Monitoring devices that predict wear and trouble, and locate problems, coupled with modular components that can be replaced by consumers, will be developed.

AFFLUENCE AND VALUES

What will the basic impact of affluence be? Do consumers who attain increased purchasing capabilities buy different kinds of objects? Do they think of them differently? Will different meanings be associated with products such as appliances by those who cannot afford them today but will be able to do so in the 1970s? Will social and demographic changes result in new life-style inventories of goods?

Increases in affluence will not result in the purchase of different kinds of products, entirely new life styles, or different product associations and meanings in the 1970s. Rather, consumers will purchase what they have always wanted but could not afford. The result will not be a major change in life style but an accumulation of objects already valued.

The dominant trends of each social class, so discernible since World War II, can be expected to continue to be important in the 1970s. For the working class the dominant theme has been the solidification of the nuclear family base much enmeshed in kinship, ethnic, and peer group ties. In the modern working class family, husband and wife interaction in closer and less rigid ways will occur, with these families directing themselves to attaining a secure, comfortable, and pleasant home as a focus of their lives. Their consumption goals in the 70s will be oriented toward investment in the home. The modern working class will adopt the styles of the lower middle class.

The focus of the lower middle class life style pivots on the necessity to achieve and maintain respectability. As a result of affluence, communications, higher education, etc. the modern lower middle class will strive for wider horizons. However, they will be pursued from a very solid family-oriented base and the traditional base of family togetherness of the lower class family in the 70s will not be challenged. The result will be a wider range of experiences and possessions than that which previously characterized lower middle class tastes and styles.

The upper middle class will intensify the push outward to the external world. They have always been more egocentric and more oriented towards self-sufficiency and self-gratification than the classes below them. They will be in an even better position in the 70s to explore, evaluate elaborate life-style innovations and achieve fuller self-realization.

A NEW POVERTY OF TIME

The major constraint on consumption in the 1970s may be shifting from money to time. Time will become a more significant factor in product selection and use. Paradoxically, increasing affluence will result in less rather than more free or uncommitted time. There will be more alternatives competing for the consumers' time. This does not mean increasing leisure for consumers in the sense that they will do nothing. Rather it means greater amounts of discretionary time—time they need not spend supporting themselves. Hours of work will not decrease greatly if at all. Indeed where shorter work hours have occurred in the past, so has moonlighting.

As more and more products and services are purchased, increasing pressures exist on the time available to consume them. Competition for consumer's limited time will become keener in the 1970s. Products, therefore, that increase the efficient use of time will find more favorable markets. People will become less patient with routine instrumental activities that require great time relative to the gratification generated.

Purchasing itself will become an even more time-consuming activity. The complexity and sophistication of products, bolstered by the expanding variety and assortment will add to time demands. It will also increase consumer frustration.

The care and maintenance of products (mentioned under servicing) will be an important purchase consideration. It is expected that the demand for durable products will be decreasingly influenced by price and increasingly by the time required to care for and use them. Ordinary care and operation should be reduced to an absolute minimum since consumers will increasingly seek to maximize satisfaction received per given time period—to enjoy the use of their affluence. A use-utility orientation rather than an ownership orientation will be more widely held.

AN OLD POVERTY OF SPACE

Coupled with the scarcity of time will be the increasing scarcity of usable land. Such land will be in shorter and shorter supply. Land costs will be one of the principal impediments to developing economical housing. More families in the 1970s will live in multifamily dwellings and condominium developments. While single-family residences are expected to increase from 47 to 51 million in the decade, multiple-family residences will increase from 19 to 22 million. Mobile homes will show the greatest percentage growth in the 70s increasing 100% from 2 to 4 million. Dwelling size relative to possessions will continue to contract, which will affect home design and product usage. Miniaturization, multipurpose appliances and communal use, may be fostered. The scarcity of land and pressure on house space may make older homes and their renovation more attractive.

Problems of poverty, deprivation, and racial discrimination will remain in the 1970s. There are signs that they will be reduced in severity. Income distribution will be directly affected. By 1980, if not before, government income maintenance programs will be introduced to help low-income families participate more fully in the life style enjoyed by American middle classes.

Urban problems of the 1960s will persist. Without a major change in the distribution of income and the concentration of the very poor and those in the central core of cities, the problems will continue to rise. The more affluent will retreat from such areas and try to "wall themselves off."

There will be a rapid rise in the rate of property crime. An association exists between the amount of property crime and the amount of property available to be taken. Also it is not likely that a higher proportion of criminals apprehended will be sentenced. We can expect, therefore, that private efforts to secure property will increase. Although individuals may be better able to afford property losses—the threat, insult, and trauma of property theft, the social-psychological costs, will not decrease.

Although people will seek increased security few people are likely to be sufficiently exercised about crime threats to substantially rearrange their lives, or to spend a great deal of money on protection. Also it should be remembered that products associated with anxiety provoking events, such as crime, can themselves become anxiety provoking. Because of this, the task of producing products that will both offer security *and* gain consumer acceptance will be surprisingly difficult.

ECOLOGY AND ENVIRONMENTS

Ecologists, their causes and viewpoints are currently in vogue. The environment/ecological movement (E/E) which has grown to a major life-style consideration in the past three years is as fashionable as any. Prompted by increasing publicity being given to polluted air, water, beaches, and wildlife, and by such factors as crowded cities, contaminated food, environmental ugliness, and overpopulation, E/E factors and the quality of life have become the concern of citizens and governments. They will continue to be in the forefront throughout the decade of the 1970s.

Ecologists often depict consumers as people who are more conscious of what they are "losing or sacrificing" because of their increasing consumption. Individuals and families are often portrayed as being willing to curb their wants, to "do without," to incur inconveniences, for the improvements of environments and the future quality of life of succeeding generations. This has not been the case, nor will it be so in the 1970s. In general, consumers will not trade the convenience of private autos and clogged roads for public transportation and less highway congestion and unpolluted air. They will not give up the convenience of packages and throwaway bottles for the bother, expense, and fuss of reducing waste. They will not *voluntarily* pay higher prices for products that improve the ecology. Such ecological hopes do not seem to be compatible with the cherished habits and life-style values of consumers in the 1970s.

In the next decade the public will be more informed about ecological-environmental systems than they are currently. Companies, therefore, might do well to conduct ecological audits of products and process. They should calculate social costs of products produced and not merely direct corporate costs.

Direct governmental action will be required in the 1970s to maintain environmental quality. Competitive business enterprise cannot be expected to accept the responsibilities and associated costs voluntarily. Consumers will not voluntarily change their behavior significantly to do so. Even if they do not, the "doom and gloom" predictions of impending environmental catastrophe during the next decade seem unrealistic. Technological applications will alleviate a number of E/E problems including automobile emissions and sewage. Consumers in the 1970s will accept the need for substantial governmental spending for environmental improvement. They will also be more attuned, to the purchase of substitute household products with fewer undesirable environmental side effects.

In the 1970s it will be advantageous for industry to utilize more waste products and recycled resources. New systems will evolve for handling sewage and garbage. Homeowners will be encouraged to perform activities in the home that will aid in recycling at community and industry levels. The major impact, however, may be new awareness, attitudes, and opinions on the part of consumers, particularly housewives, rather than drastically changed life styles, homes, and kitchens to meet ecological parameters.

Bibliography

ANDREASEN, ALAN R. "Attitudes and Customer Behavior: A Decision Model," in *New Research in Marketing*, ed., LEE E. PRESTIN, Institute of Business and Economic Research, University of California, Berkeley (1965), pp. 1–16.

BENNETT, PETER D. and KASSARJIAN, HAROLD H. *Consumer Behavior*. Englewood Cliffs, N.J.: Prentice-Hall, Inc., 1972.

CLAWSON, JOSEPH. "Lewis's Psychology and Motives in Marketing." in *Theory in Marketing*, ed. R. Cox and W. ALDERSON (1950). Published by Richard D. Irwin, Inc., under sponsorship of the American Marketing Association.

ENGEL, JAMES F.; KOLLAT, DAVID T.; and BLACKWELL, ROGER D. *Consumer Behavior*. New York: Holt, Rinehart & Winston, Inc., 1968.

FESTINGER, LEON. *A Theory of Cognitive Dissonance*. New York: Harper & Row, Publishers, 1957.

HAINES, GEORGE H., JR. *Consumer Behavior: Learning Models of Behavior*. New York: Free Press, 1969.

HAMILTON, DAVID. *The Consumer in Our Economy*. Boston: Houghton Mifflin Co., 1962.

HOWARD, JOHN A., and SHETH, JAGDISH N. *The Theory of Buyer Behavior*. New York: John Wiley & Sons, Inc., 1969.

KASSARJIAN, HAROLD H., and ROBERTSON, THOMAS S. *Perspectives in Consumer Behavior*. Glenview, Ill.: Scott, Foresman & Co., 1968.

MASLOW, ABRAHAM H. *Motivation and Personality*. New York: Harper & Row, Publishers, 1954.

MASSY, WILLIAM F.; MONTGOMERY, DAVID B.; and MORRISON, DONALD G. *Stochastic Models of Buying Behavior*. Cambridge, Mass.: M.I.T. Press, 1970.

NICOSIA, FRANCESCO. *Consumer Decision Processes*. Englewood Cliffs, N.J.: Prentice-Hall, Inc., 1966.

SHERIF, CAROLYN W.; SHERIF, MUZAFER; and NEBERGALL, R. E. *Attitude and Attitude Change: The Social Judgment-Involvement Approach*. Philadelphia: W. B. Saunders Co., 1965.

SHERIF, MUZAFER, and HOVLAND, CARL I. *Social Judgment: Assimilation and Contrast Effects in Communication and Attitude Change*. New Haven, Conn.: Yale University Press, 1961.

SHETH, JAGDISH N. "A Review of Buyer Behavior," *Management Science*, Vol. 13, No. 12, August 1967, pp. B–718, B–786.

3 MARKETING MANAGEMENT ACTIVITIES: THE SYSTEMS APPROACH

IN PERFORMING his tasks as a manager of change, the marketing manager must fulfill two roles: he must be both an agent of change and a change agent. As an agent of change, the manager must be an environmentalist; he must consider inputs which provide measures of social, technical, legal, and political change. The marketing manager recognizes the firm is a subsystem of the total environmental system. This recognition is neither altruistic nor a token acknowledgment of consumer veto power, but rests on the concept that the firm's survival, growth, and profits depend on the proper management of change. (See Figure 1.)

Once the marketing manager has assessed environmental forces, he must turn to the task of being a change agent in his organization. As a change agent, the marketing manager must establish effective organizational, communication, and feedback policies in order to manage the marketing concept in the firm. The task is, in summary, to effectively read and translate environmental inputs into the firm's marketing opportunity assessment, planning, organizing, and controlling functions and apply these concepts to local markets or multinational markets.

The four functions of marketing management are described in this chapter. These functions are marketing opportunity assessment, planning, organizing, and controlling. Two other areas of concern for marketing management are also treated here; information systems and multinational marketing. The "information explosion" phenomenon has forced managers to reevaluate their traditional concept towards the use of total management information systems. The growing importance of international activities and markets has caused more corporate attention to be given to the area of multinational marketing.

143

Marketing opportunity assessment is the crucial task of matching the resources of the firm with the market opportunities selected on a continual basis. Changes in the environment create new and destroy old opportunities for the firm. Social, technical, legal, and political indicators are critical information inputs which aid in the assessment of opportunity created by change. No marketing task is perhaps so difficult, and yet so necessary for the firm's growth, profit, and survival.

Market planning and programming is the development of goals, objectives, and strategy to translate marketing opportunity assessment into action. Increasingly, the firm is under pressure to plan and forecast for longer periods. A planning horizon of five or ten years or longer is not uncommon for many leading corporations. Many firms are engaged in "future casting" activities in recognition of the importance change plays in market opportunity.

Future orientation places pressure on the organizational structure. To meet this pressure, the organization must be prepared. Free flows of communication and feedback require an environment and leadership style based on trust and democratic individualism.

As computer software becomes more sophisticated and as the manager becomes more skilled at using the latest innovations, the important task of monitoring the firm's efforts will become easier and more accurate. The second decade of marketing information systems is a reality, and the promise of having a complete system is clearly on the horizon. Such systems will aid the marketing manager in his vital role of planning, controlling, and auditing the performance of marketing programs.

The multinational marketing scene presents a more difficult task for companies engaged in international marketing activities. The firm faces different environments and the inputs variables are more complex than the domestic case. Organizational functions should be adjusted to this broader setting.

FIGURE 3–1

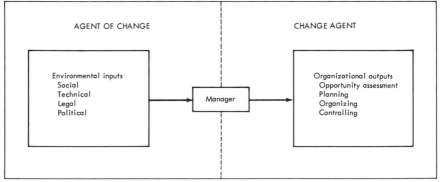

a.

Marketing decisions and information systems

THERE ARE a growing number of variables that must be accounted for in determining marketing policy. The expansion and diversification of many firms have vastly increased the number of multiproduct multinational companies. Marketing managers are currently seeking answers to questions not even considered a short time ago. Computer technology and quantitative techniques are being used to bring order to this situation and to more effectively utilize information in the decision-making process.

As the quantity of information expands to the point where marketing has been described as being in the center of an "information explosion," the ability of managers to adequately handle this information tends to decrease. Marketing information systems are increasingly being employed to accumulate, organize, store, and efficiently disperse masses of relevant information. Selective feedback of more and useful information from the entire marketing system can be incorporated into the information system supplying decision makers with essential and current information. Through the use of mathematical and statistical techniques, marketing models are being employed to yield more scientific solutions to complex marketing problems. The nature of the decisions required has made the decision-making system much more complex; however, the procedures that have been developed to collect and analyze the data have resulted in more precise and sophisticated decisions.

In the first article, Lazer examines the decision-making process as it relates to the marketing mix. The next article, also written by Lazer, explores the role of models and model building in marketing. Berenson

145

discusses the benefits, needs, requirements, and limitations of marketing information systems in the last selection.

Marketing managers must make decisions in the context of product, technological, market, and societal uncertainties. A systems approach to decision making encourages the marketer to evaluate a change in each marketing variable after the impact on the total firm is considered. A logical and systematic approach to the complex marketing decision-making process is described in this selection.

---

14. MARKETING DECISIONS: PROCESSES AND ACTIVITIES *

William Lazer †

MARKETING DECISIONS

The marketing manager must constantly analyze and evaluate alternative situations and choose among them. To do so requires the simplification of marketing reality and the resolution of conflicts. Given conflicting marketing situations, choice is often difficult and involves balancing risks and payoffs, knowledge, attitudes, opinions, feelings, judgments and facts, and current situations and future opportunities. The decision-making process includes more than the decision—the actual choice or cut-off point per se. It is concerned with solving problems and applying decision criteria. The decision-making process shapes a company's destiny, since today's decisions are a prelude to tomorrow's marketing situations.

In recent years, more effective decision making in marketing has been advanced through the application of the behavioral sciences, computers, and quantitative techniques. Many aspects of marketing are emerging from a "hit-or-miss" stage and are becoming quantifiable, measurable, and more scientific. Linear programming, dynamic programming, Markov processes, and expected value theory are used to increase the effectiveness of the problem-solving and decision-making processes.

---

* William Lazer, *Marketing Management: A Systems Perspective* (New York: John Wiley & Sons, 1971), pp. 186–90, 192–96.
† Michigan State University.

The general decision situation can be simply stated: The marketing manager tries to reach decisions that minimize the inputs required to achieve specified outputs or to maximize outputs from specified inputs. As a decision maker, he is concerned with marketing decisions that alter the scope and direction of the whole firm as well as those that pertain directly to marketing. For example, the relationship between the inputs of the marketing mix affect profitability, corporate image, and reputation, as well as market share, sales volume, and customer satisfaction.

Decisions have been classified in many ways. A common classification distinguishes between decisions related to objectives and those that pertain to more specific goals. The latter can be judged on the basis of efficiency; the former depend on normative values. Strategic decisions regarding major directions of an organization are contrasted with tactical decisions that carry out the strategies. Reciprocal decisions, in which one individual interacts with another and causes a reaction (such as competition), are distinguished from controlling decisions, in which one person's actions control the actions of another without interaction. Sequential decisions involving multiple actions and reactions, like those in the marketplace, are differentiated from single decisions.

Marketing decisions form a spectrum from the programmed or highly rigid, routine, repetitious, specific type at one extreme to the nonprogrammed, less definite, unknown, uncertain, loosely constructed type at the other. The former can be handled by habit, clerical routines, standard operating procedures, and mathematical calculations, whereas the latter require creativity, intuition, judgment, and persuasive problem-solving techniques.[1] While there may not be perfect solutions to complex marketing problems, there may be optimal solutions to a number of subproblems or at least acceptable solutions to the total problem.

Marketing decisions may also be classified according to management's degree of certainty or information about choices, as shown in Chart 1. Where "complete" information is assumed, the decision is made under conditions of certainty. Here the outcomes of each management action can be announced explicitly, and the particular state that will exist in the future can be completely identified. Wrong decisions can be eliminated.

At the other extreme, decisions may be made under conditions of complete uncertainty. The decision maker brings nothing to the actual choice by way of experience or marketing information that helps in selecting among choices. This situation is an unrealistic one and is closely approximated in marketing by an absolutely new product with no marketing-research information available. Choices here might be made on a random basis, such as by a flip of a coin.

As a rule, the actual situation lies between these extremes. Often, through evidence gained from experimentation or statistical inference,

---

[1] See Herbert A. Simon, *The New Science of Management Decision* (New York: Harper & Row, Publishers, 1960), p. 8.

CHART 1

Decision spectrum: Certainty and risk

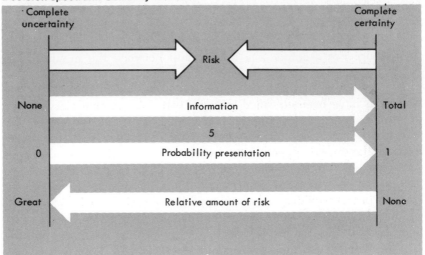

management can assess both the probabilities and the consequences of outcomes and reduce ignorance.

Marketing decisions are usually made under conditions of considerable risk, and it is impossible for an executive to be sure that any specific decision will turn out to be the best one. All the decision maker can hope to do is obtain information to restrict the elements of indecision in a situation. Managers are forced to accept risks; they must gamble.

Marketing executives are placed in the uncomfortable situation of having to choose the best course of action by evaluating relevant factors on the basis of imperfect information at a specific point in time. They know that the decision may eventually prove to be a poor one. The "right" decision consists of choosing the best possible course at a particular time regardless of how the results may be evaluated in the future.

Examples of problems involving marketing in which decisions must be made under conditions of risk are the following:

1. The host of inventory problems in which the demand for a perishable commodity (style or physical) is not known and orders must be placed well before the actual occurrence of demand.
2. The investment problem in which sales are unknown and a choice must be made among investment opportunities.
3. The product-line problem in which decisions about the addition of new products must be made long before consumer acceptance can be gauged accurately.
4. The problem of allocating promotional effort when the impact of the promotional media is not known.

5. The location problem in which a company must decide where to establish retail or wholesale outlets before its distribution pattern is known.

What are the essential characteristics of these marketing problems? The decision maker is faced with the need to choose among a number of possible acts. From his choice, profits or losses will accrue, the amount determined by conditions that the decision maker cannot predict with certainty.

Given perfect information, there would be no need for evaluations or judgment. Wrong decisions would result only from mistakes. But perfect information is not available, and the difficulties and rewards of decision making stem partly from the inadequacy of information. For instance, it is difficult to predict what competitors will do in the face of various strategies, and their actions greatly influence decision outcomes.

When uncertainty exists and no alternative tends to be clearly superior to others in all aspects, decision behavior involves subjective evaluation and judgment. By using formal or informal devices, or both, marketing executives must somehow reach a cut-off point—they must decide and select an alternative. When they do, further decisions will be pending, since marketing conditions are constantly shifting and presenting new opportunities.

Marketing plans and action are rooted in a logical consideration of an uncertain future. The complexity of the factors facing marketing managers makes decision making a risky, frustrating, subjective process. For most decisions, an extensive set of choices confronts them. Yet, for any specific company, the number of feasible alternatives is limited. Decision constraints exist. Marketing actions are confined to a fixed range of possibilities and the responsibility of the decision maker is to choose within this realistic range.

Decision constraints may be organizational, environmental, or personal. Organizational constraints depend on the scale and type of company operations. External or environmental constraints stem from such factors as the socioeconomic, technological, political, psychological, and physical aspects of the company's environment. Personal constraints depend on the personality and characteristics of the decision maker.

Marketing decisions are often made from a different basic perspective than decisions in other organizational areas. The perspective of the marketplace is adopted, and the marketing executive tries to perceive his alternatives and decisions through the eyes of consumers. Environmental constraints prove critical, requiring marketing decisions to be adjusted creatively to the environmental changes in order to match company resources with opportunities in the marketplace. In consequence, there is a continuous redesigning of the business.

We have indicated that marketing decisions fall into three major categories: (1) Decisions affecting the product and services mix, including product line, branding, pricing, credit, customer service, guarantees, and warranties. (2) Decisions affecting the communications mix, including personal selling, advertising, sales promotion, displays, telephone sales, and catalogs. (3) Decisions affecting the distribution mix, including number and types of channels of distribution and physical distribution—handling, packing, warehousing, transporting, and storing.

THE DECISION-MAKING PROCESS

The decision-making process consists of that complex of activities by which an executive seeks to overcome obstacles to the attainment of his goals by adjusting activities through his decisions. Chart 2 depicts the decision-making process in marketing management. It indicates the main decision activities and their flow in choosing a course of action. Like all graphic models, it is a simplification that leaves much to be desired in terms of the dynamics of a real decision situation. It does, however, present a useful summary of the major activities in the making of marketing decisions and what is involved in them. The major decision activities are (1) appraisal of the marketing-decision situation; (2) determination of alternatives; (3) evaluation of alternatives; and (4) making the decision.

The first phase, appraisal of the decision situation, is concerned with determining problematic situations and specifying the problems to be solved. This stage relies heavily on assessment of the information concerning both company goals and actual situations, as well as the discrepancies between them. Company goal may be conceived in such terms as profitability, market share, sales volume, reputation, rate of return on investments, and industry position. By gathering information about performance and assessing it against management standards, executives may spot symptoms of problems and discern the problems themselves. To help management recognize marketing problems, such standards as product-line goals, sales quotas, territorial quotas, productivity ratios, and advertising objectives are established. But the executive must be sure to use them properly to distinguish symptoms from problems. For example, decreasing profits or sales volume, increasing sales costs, and costs of distribution are not problems—they may be symptomatic of problems. Effective decision making is based on the operational definition of problems. The feedback of information on a regular basis provides the marketing manager with information for assessing and reevaluating market position.

Phase two of the decision process is concerned with the determination of alternatives. In attempting to make a decision and solve problems, marketing managers, either explicitly or implicitly, must specify available alternative solutions. The solutions perceived will be limited by management's insight, creativity, and experience. Although no manager will

CHART 2

Decision-making process

I Appraisal of marketing decision situations

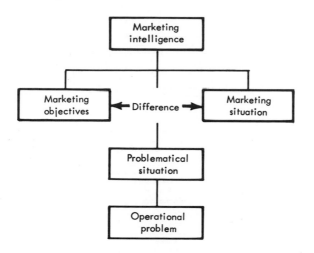

II Determination of alternatives

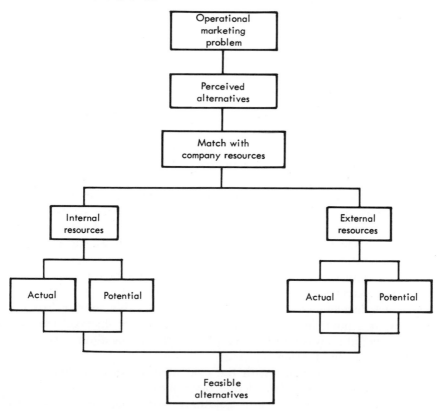

CHART 2 (Continued)

III Evaluation of alternatives

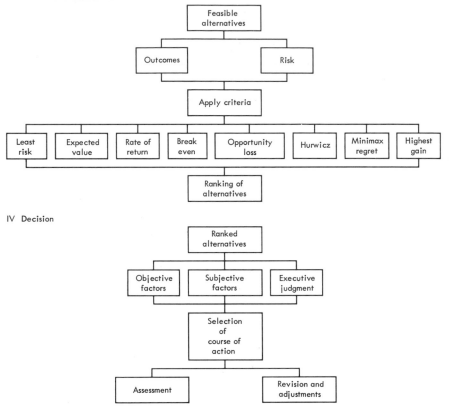

IV Decision

perceive all the choices available, this is not a severe handicap. Companies can consider the most practicable solutions as they are detected by experienced management.

Perceived alternatives must be matched with company resources, actual and potential, to determine their feasibility. The resources include the internal human, physical, and financial ones, as well as the external resources available to the firm such as wholesalers, advertising agencies, and transportation agencies. Through matching, a set of feasible courses will be determined and the most practicable ones will be established. For instance, a perceived alternative may involve an extensive expenditure on product development. It may not be a practicable solution for the company at a point in time, owing to current heavy financial commitments. It would be wasteful to attempt to evaluate this alternative, since it is not within the decision set of the executive.

Phase three is concerned with the evaluation of various alternatives. Here value theory and a knowledge of applicable decision criteria are useful. Given the feasible set of solutions, marketing executives must determine the "relative value" of each choice. Obviously this cannot be determined precisely; yet the task must somehow be accomplished.

If a decision maker chooses a course without explicitly evaluating the relative effects of each, he has in essence imputed a value, and indicated that his choice is the "best" one. It seems desirable, therefore, to evaluate .the alternative choices of action on some more formal basis, according to criteria that the decision maker specifies. This leads to a more objective selection of courses of action and permits more scientific decision making.

The fourth and final phase of the decision process concerns the actual choice or decision. Here the executive assesses the evaluated options, applies his executive judgment, and chooses a course of action. Once a choice is made on the basis of particular criteria, it might not prove to be the best decision after the fact, owing to unforeseen or unexpected circumstances. However, whether a decision is a good one or a poor one really depends on future situations and evaluations. All a decision maker can do is reach the best possible decision, given his incomplete information at a point in time.

CHART 3

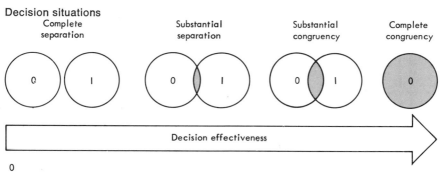

Decision situations

| Complete separation | Substantial separation | Substantial congruency | Complete congruency |

Decision effectiveness

0

I   Individual goals

Making marketing decisions is a subjective process. The decision maker must exercise judgment in specifying problems and their dimensions, in associating probabilities and payoffs with various courses, and in assessing outcomes. The process is one of narrowing the field of possible actions until the choice of the best one is achieved. Various tools and techniques that formalize these processes are useful, but insight and creative abilities are still among the greatest decision-making assets of executives.

DECISION SITUATIONS

Whether a marketing decision proves to be effective depends not merely on whether the process used in arriving at a choice is a logical one. It also depends on the implementation of the actual decision. Management action after a decision is made can have a great effect on the outcome.

When a marketing manager's individual goals are completely congruent with those of the organization, then great effort may be extended in implementation, and even "poor choices" may prove to yield good results. Similarly, where a complete separation exists between a marketing manager's goals and those of the organization, formidable barriers may be erected, and "good choices" may yield poor results. Various decision situations ranging from complete congruency to complete separation of individual and organization goals are shown in Chart 3.

What are marketing models? How relevant are models and systems to marketing problems? This selection defines marketing models, and two approaches to model building are described. Generalizations concerning the role of models in marketing science are discussed.

---

15. THE ROLE OF MODELS IN MARKETING *

William Lazer †

Behavioral sciences and quantitative methods are both in the forefront in the current development and extension of marketing knowledge. It is no mere coincidence that both make frequent reference to two concepts: models and systems. Certainly models and systems have become powerful interpretive tools.[1]

Models and systems have relevance to such significant marketing problems as: (1) developing marketing concepts and enriching the marketing language by introducing terms that reflect an operational viewpoint and orientation; (2) providing new methods and perspectives for problem solving; (3) conducting marketing research and designing experiments;

---

* Reprinted from "The Role of Models in Marketing," *Journal of Marketing*, Vol. 26, No. 2 (April 1962), pp. 9–14. See also W. J. Baumol, *Marketing and the Computer* (Englewood Cliffs, N.J.; Prentice-Hall, Inc., 1963), pp. 202 ff.

† Michigan State University.

[1] Paul Meadows, "Models, Systems and Science," *American Sociological Review*, Vol. 22 (February 1957), pp. 3–9, at p. 3.

(4) developing marketing theories; (5) measuring the effectiveness of marketing programs.

Although they may not be recognized as such, marketing models are fairly widely applied by both practitioners and academicians. The use of analogies, constructs, verbal descriptions of systems, "idealizations," and graphic representations are quite widespread in marketing. For example, pricing models, physical distribution models, models of marketing institutions, and advertising models are useful marketing tools.

DEFINITION OF MARKETING MODELS

A model is simply the perception or diagramming of a complex or a system. In marketing, it involves translating perceived marketing relationships into constructs, symbols, and perhaps mathematical terms. For example, an internally consistent set of statements concerning wholesaling, advertising, merchandising, or pricing comprises a model. It relates in a logical manner certain constructs or axioms that are envisaged.

Models are really the bases for marketing theories, since they are the axioms or assumptions on which marketing theories are founded. They furnish the underlying realities for theory construction. Where the perceived relationships are expressed in mathematical terms, we have a mathematical model. In this sense, any consistent set of mathematical statements about some aspect of marketing can be regarded as a model.

All marketing models are based on suppositions or assumptions. These assumptions do not correspond exactly with the real marketing world. Usually they are employed to simplify an existing marketing situation. Therefore, models cannot depict marketing activities exactly. Moreover, no matter how precise mathematical models may be, they do not correct themselves for false assumptions.

MODEL BUILDING

There are two approaches to the construction of marketing models: *abstraction* and *realization*.[2]

In abstraction, a real world situation is perceived and it is mapped into a model. If it is mapped into a mathematical system, a mathematical model results. This is illustrated by Figure 1.

In abstraction, the model builder must perceive of a marketing situation in a way that permits him to recognize the relationships between a number of variables. For example, he may perceive of relationships between transportation costs, customer satisfaction, and the location of distribution centers; the number of sales calls and resulting sales and profits; the

---

[2] See C. H. Coombs, H. Raiffa, and R. M. Thrall, "Some Views On Mathematical Models and Measurement Theory," in R. M. Thrall, C. H. Coombs, and R. L. Davis (eds.), *Decision Processes* (New York: John Wiley & Sons, Inc., 1954), pp. 20–21.

FIGURE 1

Model building by abstraction

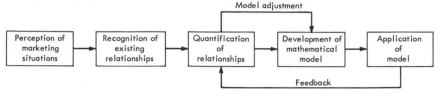

allocation of advertising expenditures and the achievement of favorable consumer response.

Based on this, the model builder will become aware of logical conceptual relationships which he is able to state fairly succinctly and clearly. These relationships may then be quantified through the use of available records and data, experiments, or simulations. The basis for the establishment of a mathematical model is obtained.

Once the mathematical model is determined, it may be applied in "the real world." Feedback will result which will provide the basis for a further alteration of the quantification of the conceptual relationships perceived. It will lead to a refinement and improvement in the mathematical model.

As an example of model building by abstraction, consider the construction of a model representing consumer response to company advertising expenditures.[3] Through observation, analysis of relevant data, and experience, the model builder may recognize that with little or no advertising expenditures consumer purchases of a product are very small. Then it may appear that, as expenditures increase over a certain range, purchase responses increase quite sharply. While response increases even further with additional advertising expenditures, it is noted that eventually it tapers off and tends toward some limit.

The resulting model may be depicted graphically as in Figure 2. Through research these relationships may be quantified and expressed in terms of mathematical formulas. A model is thus developed which represents the relationships existing between advertising expenditures and consumer response. Such a model has been constructed and with further mathematical refinements was used to determine the optimum allocation of advertising expenditures.[4] The model also proved to be useful in developing advertising-response curves, analyzing the impact of time lags in advertising effect, evaluating the interaction of competing promotional effort and estimating the impact of varying promotional resources.

---

[3] A. P. Zentler and Dorothy Ryde, "An Optimal Geographical Distribution of Publicity Expenditure In A Private Organization," *Management Science,* Vol. 2 (July 1956), pp. 337–52.
    [4] Ibid.

FIGURE 2

Relationship of consumer response to advertising expenditures

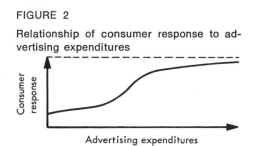

Model building by realization

In realization, the process of model building is reversed. The model builder starts with a consideration of a logically consistent conceptual system. Then some aspect of the real world can be viewed as the model of the system. It is a process of going from the logical system to the real world.[5] This is portrayed in Figure 3.

FIGURE 3

Model building by realization

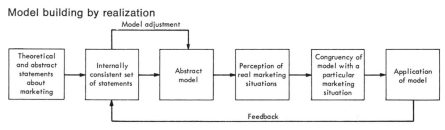

Model building by realization may be illustrated by considering the mathematical model known as a Markov process. This process is a model that is useful in the study of complex business systems. It studies the present state of a marketing system and what has happened through some transition time. For example, it can be of help in studying the users and nonusers of a product (the present state of the system), and what has happened as advertising is applied over a time period (the state transitions). It is a theoretical, logically consistent, and abstract model.

Starting with this model, the model builder may perceive that such marketing situations as the use of advertising to switch brand loyalties of consumers, or to change consumers from the state of nonusers to users, deal with the current state of a system and the transition of the system through time. Therefore, he may use the Markov process to study the

---

[5] Coombs, Raiffa, and Thrall, "Views on Mathematical Models," p. 21.

effects of advertising impact. As experience from application of the model is developed, feedback will result and the model can be adjusted. In using this procedure, the model builder has gone from a logical mathematical system to the world of marketing.

Herniter and Magee and also Maffei have discussed the application of Markov process models.[6] Their research indicates that such models are extremely useful in determining the choice of promotional policy for maximizing profits in the long run; in specifying the kinds of experimentation required to measure the impact of promotional effort, and in calculating cost and revenue changes resulting from the use of alternative marketing strategies over time.

KINDS OF MARKETING MODELS

It is difficult to classify marketing models since there are many dimensions and distinguishing characteristics that may be used as criteria for classification.

Mathematicians, for instance, might classify marketing models according to the type of equations used. They could distinguish among algebraic, difference-equation, differential-equation, and mixed-difference and differential equation models.[7] Physical models can be distinguished from abstract models. Loose verbal models may be contrasted with precise mathematical models. Models that take into consideration changes in factors through time are referred to as dynamic models and are distinguished from static models. Deterministic models are differentiated from stochastic models (models in which some of the variables are random factors and cannot be completely determined). Micro marketing and macro marketing models exist, as do linear and non-linear models. Perhaps one of the most meaningful distinctions from a marketing point of view is that of goal models and systems models.

Systems models and goal models

A distinction has been made in the behavioral science literature between *systems models* and *goal models*.[8]

---

[6] Jerome Herniter and John F. Magee, "Customer Behavior as a Markov Process," *Operations Research,* Vol. 9 (January–February 1961), pp. 105–22. Richard B. Maffei, "Brand Preferences and Simple Markov Processes," *Operations Research,* Vol. 8 (March–April 1960), pp. 210–18.

[7] This breakdown is taken from an unpublished paper prepared by Dr. Paul Craig, at the Institute of Basic Mathematics for application to business, sponsored by the Ford Foundation at Harvard University during 1959–60. The actual classification of models was suggested by Dr. Samuel Goldberg.

[8] Amitai Etzioni, "Two Approaches to Organizational Analysis: A Critique and A Suggestion," *Administrative Science Quarterly,* Vol. 5 (September 1960), pp. 257–78, at p. 258.

In marketing, a goal model or end-means model starts with a marketing task to be achieved. For instance, it focuses on the marketing objectives and the uses of company resources to achieve them as efficiently as possible. It is the achievement of marketing goals, and not necessarily corporate goals, that become important.

The goal model does not lend itself readily to a representation of a multifunctional unit. The marketing department is not viewed as being comprised of a number of different departments with possible conflicting goals, but rather as one over-all unit with a major goal. The implication here is that if we increase the marketing means, we thereby increase our effectiveness in achieving marketing goals. In this model, moreover, the effectiveness of the marketing department is measured by the devotion to the achievement of marketing goals. Although the goal model is useful, it is Utopian and unrealistic.

In the systems model, the starting point is not a goal. The starting point is the model of a total functioning system, for example, the marketing department. It is the model of a marketing unit capable of achieving goals. The systems model recognizes that there can be many conflicting objectives within an organization and that concessions must be made. In this model, the multifunctional units involved in achieving marketing goals are recognized. This model also considers that some means must be allocated to non-goal directed effort, such as the resources necessary to maintain the marketing organization. Given certain marketing conditions and resources, the main consideration is—how can they be programmed to achieve the optimum position for the total business system?

The systems model is the superior model for marketing management. It is the model that the operations researcher uses when he perceives of a business as an over-all system of action as when he plans the optimal use of resources. The systems approach to the study of marketing is appearing in the literature and should result in a better understanding of the existing interrelationships among marketing elements, a clearer grasp of marketing behavior, and a more effective allocation of marketing resources.[9]

Models and marketing theory

The terms "models" and "theories" are often used interchangeably. An interesting and useful distinction for marketing can be drawn from an idea expressed by Coombs, Raiffa, and Thrall; "A model is not itself a theory; it is only an available or possible or potential theory until a

---

[9] See Wroe Alderson, *Marketing Decisions and Executive Action* (Homewood, Ill.: Richard D. Irwin, Inc., 1957); William Lazer and Eugene J. Kelley, "Interdisciplinary Contributions to Marketing Management" (Bureau of Business and Economic Research, Michigan State University, 1959); William Lazer, "Transportation Management: A Systems Approach," *Distribution Age,* Vol. 59 (September 1960), pp. 33–35; and John F. Magee, "Operations Research in Making Marketing Decisions," *Journal of Marketing,* Vol. 25 (October 1960), pp. 18–24.

segment of the real world has been mapped into it. Then the model becomes a theory about the real world." [10] As a theory, a marketing model can be accepted or rejected on the basis of how well it actually works. The actual model itself, however, is "right or wrong" (internally consistent) on logical grounds only.

One can distinguish between models and theories by considering marketing-research techniques. A stipulated technique for marketing measurement may be called a model. For example, the forecasting technique known as exponential smoothing, or forecasting by exponentially weighted moving averages, has proved to be a useful forecasting model.[11] As a model it need only be internally consistent. It is a potential marketing theory.

When data are actually measured by the exponential smoothing technique and are mapped into the model, then the model becomes a theory about the marketing data. The resulting theory may be a good one or a poor one.

The relationship between marketing models, theories, and hypotheses now follows directly. Within a theoretical framework, we are able to test certain hypotheses. The assumptions of a marketing model itself, however, need not be subjected to tests, whereas hypotheses should be tested. It should be noted that assumptions in one model may be hypotheses in another.

USES OF MODELS IN MARKETING

Five major uses for models in marketing can be suggested.

1. *Marketing models provide a frame of reference for solving marketing problems.* They suggest fruitful lines of inquiry and existing information gaps. Marketing models do this by playing a descriptive role. The descriptive model does not go beyond presenting a representation or picture of some aspect of marketing activity. However, it serves an extremely important function in the extention of marketing thought. The use of flow diagrams in depicting existing relationships or in developing a logical computer program is an example of the use of descriptive models.

2. *Marketing models may play an explicative role, and as such they are suggestive and flexible.* Such models are more than simple metaphors; they attempt to explain relationships and reactions. The marketing scientist not only is interested in describing marketing phenomena and examining them, but he desires to explain existing relationships and frames of references. For example, "switching models" often attempt to explain the relationships between advertising and brand loyalty.[12]

---

[10] Coombs, Raiffa, and Thrall, "Views on Mathematical Models," pp. 25–26.

[11] Peter R. Winters, "Forecasting Sales by Exponentially Weighted Moving Averages," *Management Science*, Vol. 6 (April 1960), pp. 324–42.

[12] See footnote 9.

3. *Marketing models are useful aids in making predictions.* For instance, in answer to the question why models should be used, Bross explains that the real answer to this question is that the procedure has been followed in the development of the most successful predicting systems so far produced, the predicting systems used in science.[13] Marketing practitioners and scientists wish to predict and consequently employ various types of forecasting models and inventory models. These models become more than just an explanation and a representation of an existing situation. They become means of presenting future reality.

4. *Marketing models can be useful in theory construction.* Formulators of marketing models may hypothesize about various aspects of marketing as they might exist. Thereby, we have "reality" as it is hypothesized. Simulation, for example, which really involves experimentation on models, can lead to valuable insights into marketing theory. In the same vein an ideal may be developed as a model. Although the ideal may not be achieved, it provides a useful vehicle for extending knowledge.

5. *Marketing models may stimulate the generation of hypotheses which can then be verified and tested.* Thereby, it furthers the application of the scientific method in marketing research and the extension of marketing knowledge.

Benefits of mathematical models

Why should marketing scientists and practitioners utilize mathematical models rather than other kinds of models?[14] Perhaps the most important reasons are four:

1. *The translation of a model from a verbal to a mathematical form makes for greater clarification of existing relationships and interactions.* It is a rigorous and demanding task; and conceptual clarity and operational definitions are often achieved. The models developed may also become more generally applicable.

2. *Mathematical models promote greater ease of communication.* Within business administration and related subject-matter areas, there is the difficulty of cross-communication because of the terminology used by specialized disciplines. Through the use of mathematical models, all of the disciplines may be reduced to a common mathematical language which may reveal interrelationships and pertinence of research findings not previously known.

3. *Mathematical models tend to be more objective, while verbal constructs lean heavily on intuition and rationalizations.* Scientific marketing can be advanced through the application of objective mathematical analysis.

---

[13] Irwin D. J. Bross, *Design for Decisions* (New York: Macmillan Co., 1953), p. 169.
[14] See footnote 7.

4. *Analyses that are not feasible through verbal models may be advanced through mathematical models.* Mathematics provides powerful tools for marketing academicians and practitioners. Mathematical models lend themselves to analysis and manipulation. In the manipulation of verbal models, the interrelationships and logic are easily lost.

CONCLUDING OBSERVATIONS

The usefulness of a marketing model is a function of the level of generalization the model achieves and the degree of reality it portrays. Symbolization is used in model building to achieve greater internal consistency and more correspondence with reality. The greater the level of symbolization, and the fewer the restrictions, the more adequate and more generally applicable is the model.

For example, it is true that linear-programming models are more abstract, more general, and more valuable than are mere descriptive models representing a factory and warehousing complex. However, it may well be that the linear-programming model is by no means more widely used.

All marketing models are based on simplifications and abstractions. Only by making assumptions is a model molded to fit reality. Sometimes the reality beyond the boundaries of the model, however, is much greater than the reality within the boundaries. The model then becomes severely limited by the assumptions on which it is based.

To be effective, marketing models should be plausible, solvable, and based on realistic assumptions. The current level of model building in marketing is not yet a sophisticated one. It cannot compare favorably with the level of model building in the physical or biological sciences. As the discipline of marketing matures, however, it will use an increasing number of models and will develop more complex models that have broader application.

Marketing information systems are part of the marketing wave of the future. The author provides insights into the need for marketing information systems and discusses their benefits, organizational and structural requirements, and general limitations. Current marketing information systems are discussed.

---

16. MARKETING INFORMATION SYSTEMS *

Conrad Berenson †

During the past several years the words "marketing information systems" have appeared with increasing frequency in the marketing literature. Unlike some other words which are in vogue and then disappear from sight, this phrase has prevailed and, indeed, provided a great deal of substance and meaning for the entire marketing community.

This paper focuses on marketing information systems, examines them vis-à-vis the traditional market research function, studies the background of the needs which initiated the development of such systems, and reviews the benefits, pitfalls, myths, and structure of marketing information systems. Obviously, with so many critical facets to cover in such a brief period of time, one can do little more than indicate the major considerations that fall within the purview of any of these categories. A comprehensive analysis of marketing information systems requires far more attention than just a brief paper.

Let us turn first to a definition of "marketing information systems." This is defined as an interacting structure of people, equipment, methods, and controls, which is designed to create an information flow that is capable of providing an acceptable base for management decisions in marketing.

The question that logically arises when definitions of marketing information systems are presented is "How does it differ from the traditional function of marketing research?" Market research ordinarily follows an eclectic path—one time examining the prices of one product line, and at another time reviewing competitors' packaging innovations, and the like. Usually, the marketing research department provides only a fraction of the data needed to make marketing decisions which have great and far-reaching impact upon the company. This is not to be construed as a criticism of marketing research; all too often marketing research in both consumer and industrial areas fails to receive either adequate budgets, or adequate organizational support.[1]

Furthermore, its mission is different from that of a marketing information system. The latter differs from marketing research in that it provides,

---

* Reprinted from "Marketing Information Systems," *Journal of Marketing*, Vol. 33, No. 4 (October 1969), pp. 16–23.
† City University of New York.
[1] Philip Kotler, "A Design for the Firm's Marketing Nerve Center," *Business Horizons*, Vol. 9 (Fall 1966), pp. 63–74.

for example, *continuous* study of the marketing factors which are important to an enterprise—not just intermittent examination. It utilizes far
more data sources—both internal and external—than does marketing
research; and it accepts the responsibility for receiving, analyzing and
distilling a far greater volume of information inputs than market research
is structured to do.[2]

The market research department should be considered to be one part
of the marketing information system. The latter would also include or
work very closely with such organizational units as: economic research,
operations research, long-range planning, the controller, the computer
center, marketing planning, and sales management.

Marketing research's traditional role as the primary supplier of information to management for marketing decisions is, consequently, somewhat different in firms with a marketing information system. In the latter,
market research concentrates more upon spot projects, fire-fighting, new
areas in which the inputs to the system have not yet been established, on
data other than that likely to be found in the controller's office or the
billing department, and on utilizing a variety of techniques in order to
study a particular area which is of momentary interest to the firm. In
firms without a marketing information system, market research concentrates more upon such routine information as sales analysis by product
line and customer, determination of end-use patterns, and the projection
of price and demand trends. It does this on a somewhat eclectic basis.

THE NEED FOR MARKETING INFORMATION SYSTEMS

It is not at all surprising that at this time there is a good deal of
discussion and development of marketing information systems. Long-term
trends, both in marketing and in business in general, are intersecting in
the present time to crystallize the systems activity which is presently
taking place. Some of these trends are outlined below:

1. The increased complexity of business calls for more data and for
better performance. Markets are no longer local but are national in scope.
The organization that previously may have had firm control of its business
in a limited area such as New England, now finds itself on uncertain
grounds when competing with similar enterprises in the Midwest, on the
West Coast, and in the South.

2. Product life cycles have become far shorter—thus requiring more
skillful management in order to extract a profit during the reduced time
available.

3. The marketing concept, in which the various marketing functions of
the enterprise are organized under one individual—the marketing manager—has taken root in American industry. Since one manager now more

---

[2] Lee Adler, "Systems Approach to Marketing," *Harvard Business Review,* Vol. 45
(May–June 1967), pp. 105–18.

than ever before has the responsibility for integrating a far-ranging variety of marketing activities, he needs a good deal more information so that this can be done effectively.[3]

4. More companies have grown so large that unless they make an intensive effort, such as the development of marketing information systems, their existing marketing information will be dispersed in so many places that its effective use will be virtually impossible.

5. The speed with which today's business decisions have to be made has increased, and therefore marketing systems must be developed to provide information for such rapid decision making.[4]

6. The advent of techniques which can provide information for effective decision making has gone hand-in-hand with the development of marketing decision tools. Thus, Bayesian analysis, PERT, decision trees, and factor analysis, all require more information than could previously be made available by normal market research approaches.

7. Although the marketing information system is not entirely dependent upon the use of computers, nonetheless the evolution of these machines to the role of a relatively commonplace article in many enterprises, and the concomitant development of qualified personnel to work with these computers, means a good deal of information which previously could not be handled by more archaic methods, now can be effectively organized and retrieved.

BENEFITS OF A MARKETING INFORMATION SYSTEM

An effective marketing information system may provide the following benefits:

1. It may provide more information within the time constraints required by the firm. Concomitantly, better performance could be achieved by the entire enterprise.

2. It may permit large and decentralized firms to use the information which is scattered in many places, and integrate it into a meaningful perspective.

3. It may permit fuller exploitation of the marketing concept.

4. It may provide selective retrieval of information—users can be given only what they want and need.

5. It may provide quicker recognition of developing trends.

6. It may permit far better use of material which is ordinarily collected by many firms in the course of their business activities; for example, sales by product, by customer, and by region.

7. It may permit better control over the firm's marketing plan; for example, it may raise warning signals when something is amiss in the plan.

---

[3] D. Maynard Phelps and J. Howard Westing, *Marketing Management* (Homewood, Ill.: Richard D. Irwin, Inc., 1968), pp 9–11.

[4] Kotler, "Design for Firm's Marketing Nerve Center." p. 63.

8. It may prevent important information from being readily suppressed; for example, indications that a product should be withdrawn.

THE ENVIRONMENT NEEDED FOR A SUCCESSFUL SYSTEM

In a speech presented to the American Marketing Association, Arnold Amstutz of M.I.T. has suggested that successful marketing information systems need four environmental characteristics.[5] First, the system must be designed to provide information in a form which can be used in the present management decision processes. The information given to management, furthermore, must be refined to the point where management is capable of acting upon it. In other words, management must not be deluged with mountains of paper.

Second, management must participate in creating the parameters of the system's capability. After all, it is management that will be using the information derived from this system. Therefore, it is this same management that must undertake the specification of what is needed and how it will be used.

Third, the information which is gathered by the system must be filed in what is known as a disaggregated data file. In such a file new information input is maintained together with previously received input. The net effect of such procedure is that all previous transactions can be recreated by the system at any time. This is particularly important with new systems, since such information systems are bound to change, and an aggregated file, that is, one in which all information is combined, may have to be completely discarded as being unsuitable for the changes made in the system. A disaggregated file, however, contains the inputs in such a way that they are adaptable to any form of system change.

Finally, the system must be designed so that it can evolve to fit the continually changing needs of the enterprise. Obviously, when the system is first introduced it will only use a few of the many techniques that are available. As the system users become more familiar with its capabilities, their needs will evolve. Thus, the system must be designed so that it too can cope with these new needs.

ELEMENTS OF THE MARKETING INFORMATION SYSTEM

Figure 1 shows a graphical representation of the marketing information system.[6] The input and output shown in that figure are illustrative only. Obviously, they will change, depending upon the need of the enterprise.

---

[5] Arnold E. Amstutz, "The Marketing Executive and Management Information Systems," in Raymond M. Haas (ed.), *Science, Technology and Marketing* (Chicago: American Marketing Association, Fall 1966), pp. 69–86.

[6] Walter Buckley (ed.), *Modern Systems Research for the Behavioral Scientist* (Chicago: Aldine Publishing Co., 1968), passim.

Not only will they change within any one firm over a period of time, but they will differ from one enterprise to the next.

The inputs to the system are those items of information which can be used to generate the required output. The output consists of that information which is needed by marketing management for decision-making purposes. The illustrative outputs shown in Figure 1 can be considerably augmented by an effective system. For example, the sales category shows

FIGURE 1.

The marketing information system

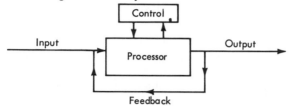

Invoice	Sales	Profitability
price	by product	by product
quantity purchased	by product line	by product line
customer name	by customer class	by customer class
customer location	by cost center	by salesman
credit terms	by region	
method of delivery	by salesman	Life cycle
date of order	by competitors	Analysis

Annual reports	Market share
of customers	Inventory
of competitors	Forecasts
of suppliers	Technical service

Trade association data	Marketing personnel
Payroll	turnover ratio
Departmental budgets	hiring ratio
Manufacturing cost	transfers
reports	promotions
Accounts receivable	absenteeism
Accounts payable	
Inventory reports	Financial
Trade journals	credit
Sales call reports	discount analysis
Manning tables	(by customer,
Personnel department	region, etc.)
reports	promotional
Census data	allowances
Marketing cost reports	budgets

Market research inputs, e.g.,	Customer lists
audit and panel data	New accounts
special projects	Etc.
customer demand schedules	
questionnaire replies	

that the sales volume will be indicated by product, by product line, by customer class, and by region. For each of these categories we can also design the system so that it will print out the budgeted or forecasted sales figure, the cumulative sales to date, and a graphical representation of curves of cumulative sales, both actual and forecast. Similar expansion of output can be obtained for the profitability data.

The section of the chart marked "Processor" is the system itself. This system consists not only of hardware and software, but of the human machinery which is necessary to carry out the mission of the system, and to accomplish the required marketing objectives. The "Processor" sector contains a number of sub-systems, each devoted to a different facet of the input and output sectors. Thus, there could be a sub-system dealing with price, one with marketing personnel, another with life cycle analyses, and others with sales, profitability, market share, and advertising effectiveness.

There are several types of *controls* which can be imposed upon a system.

1. The MIS can be managed by some group within the firm.
2. The MIS can be at a higher stage on the information-decision hierarchy than merely the "information system" stage—the stage at which the system provides timely, reliable, and sufficient information for managerial decisions. It may have advanced to the stage at which *control* capabilities are coupled to the system in the form of remote consoles, cathode ray tube terminals, and other devices by which the manager and the information system are joined into an *interactive man-machine problem-solving network.*[7]
3. *Control* or "limits" exist which are set by the market and the environment in which the firm operates; examples are social, legal, political, economic, financial, technological, and temporal.
4. The "feedback" loop also serves as a control. It monitors the output so that the nature of the input can be varied in order to provide subsequent output in accordance with the current decision-making needs of the marketing executive.

It should be noted that the third type of control mentioned above is utilized in the *processor* of the system shown in Figure 1. For example, if we are concerned with an information system for an enterprise manufacturing women's bathing suits, we know we need a system which has an extremely fast capability for gathering and processing information. Markets such as those for bathing suits change with extreme rapidity, and last week's information is of relatively little value. On the other hand, if we were dealing with the manufacture of office furniture, the system would be quite different; although there are style changes and technolog-

---

[7] G. W. Dickson, "Management Information–Decision Systems," *Business Horizons,* Vol. 11 (December 1968), pp. 17–26.

ical advances in such a business, these changes are, relatively speaking, far slower. The information system's controls, accordingly, must be changed to correspond with this different sort of market.

WHO IS RESPONSIBLE FOR THE SYSTEM?

One of the basic decisions which has to be made early in the program of any company that wants to develop a marketing information system is that of fixing the responsibility for the daily operation of the system. There are several aspects to this that must be considered.

The primary support for the system must come from top management. Unless the principal executives of the organization, both in marketing and in other areas, are firmly convinced and will support fully the operation and the implementation of a marketing information system, it is bound to fail.[8] Beyond this concept of top management support is the problem of whether or not the system should be run on a daily basis by either a specialist in data processing, or an operating manager who is more of a generalist and is consequently more knowledgeable within the area of marketing itself.

Both the specialist and the generalist have their supporters and critics. The advantages of specialist managers are obvious. They have the technical skills for running a system. On the other hand, their deficiencies are equally obvious. Too often the specialist simply has not had a sufficient background in marketing so that he can properly handle the principal flows of information that are relevant to the important marketing decisions. As a result, costly mistakes are inevitable. Also some specialists overemphasize the system at the expense of the job which the system is designed to accomplish.

The generalist, or operating manager, has the advantage of a detailed knowledge of the areas about which decisions are being made. This can be extremely valuable in designing the system output. The manager, however, is handicapped by his lack of knowledge relative to information-handling techniques. Such generalists tend to concentrate upon information which will provide immediate profit to the marketing sector at the expense of the long-run profitability.

Responsibility for the system should rest with the top marketing executive who, after all, is accountable for the performance of the entire marketing sector of the enterprise. This is not intended to infer that the specialist-technician should not have a good deal of responsibility; nonetheless, the task which is being performed is a *marketing* task and it is the marketing manager's responsibility to supervise all marketing activities. In consequence of the duality of roles, the last several years have

---

[8] Donald F. Cox and Robert E. Good, "How to Build a Marketing Information System," *Harvard Business Review*, Vol. 45 (May–June 1967), pp. 145–54.

seen the development of a new position title in many business firms, that of director of marketing information services. This title is ordinarily held by an individual who is primarily a technical specialist who, hopefully, has some marketing knowledge as well, and who is capable of utilizing expert staff assistance in marketing. This individual usually reports to the marketing manager who, as stated above, really bears the ultimate responsibility for all facets of the marketing task.

ORGANIZATIONAL PROBLEMS OF MARKETING INFORMATION SYSTEMS

In the few years in which marketing information systems have been used, it has become obvious that there are some typical organizational problems which occur unless extensive foresight, as well as care in execution of the system, is exercised. These are briefly discussed below.

1. Faulty integration between sub-systems

It must be recognized that the marketing information system is just *one part* of a total management information system; the other part embraces such areas as finance, production, and personnel. Too great an emphasis upon the objectives of any one of these parts without constant realization that it is the entire enterprise's efficiency which must be optimized can result in a failure of the system to achieve its objectives economically. The problem sometimes becomes particularly acute when the output from one organization is needed as part of the input for the other.

2. Changes in jobs and skill requirements

The implementation of a marketing information system will require the marketing department to bring new skills into its organization and to create new job functions to utilize these skills. In addition to these totally new jobs and skills, there will certainly be changes in existing work patterns. After all, many new documents and new information will be generated, and the traditional ways of handling information will probably no longer be adequate. Consequently, we are going to have problems of personal conflict, of adjustment to new types of work, of dissatisfaction with new work environments, of human inertia, of obstruction, and the like.

3. Relationships between the system's designers and the system's users

Those who are using the system's outputs must get involved with the system's design—otherwise there will be excessive friction at the interface between designers and users. Some marketing decision makers with authoritative positions in the enterprise must be assigned to work with the system's designers. It must be borne in mind that the users must develop plans for utilizing system output. They should not simply expect a mass of data to be deposited with them several times each day, and then sit around and wonder what to do with it.[9]

THE SYSTEM'S RELATION TO OTHER CORPORATE FUNCTIONS

One question that must be raised is "What is the relationship of the marketing information system to the other functions of the organization?" The easiest way to present this relationship is in the form of a chart, and this is shown in Figure 2. Here, it can be seen that the marketing infor-

FIGURE 2.

Organizing for marketing Information systems

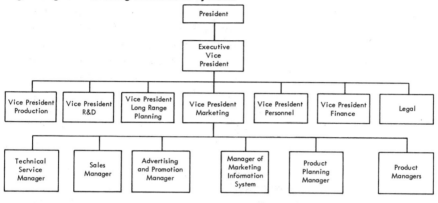

mation system is a part of the marketing area. The latter area is led by a single marketing executive who, ordinarily, would have a title such as vice president of marketing, or marketing manager. The organization shown is one for a company which is organized along what has come to be known as the marketing management concept. This concept requires all of the marketing operations of the enterprise to be so organized that one individual only has responsibility for all such operations and that he be equal in rank with other top corporate executives. The latter relationship is also shown on the chart and indicates that the vice presidents of production, research and development, finance, and so forth are in the same echelon as the top marketing executive.

RELATION TO THE MARKETING PLAN

The marketing plan is the basic working document by which the marketing department conducts its activities. Obviously, every facet of this

---

[9] Emanuel Kay, "Some Organizational Problems Which Arise as the Result of Large-Scale Information Systems," in Samuel V. Smith, et al. (eds.), *Readings in Marketing Information Systems* (Boston: Houghton Mifflin Co., 1968), pp. 323–29.

plan requires information so that appropriate decisions can be made. The output of the marketing information system hence provides the input to the marketing plan for these marketing decisions. Therefore, the relationship of the information system to the marketing plan is two-fold: (1) the marketing plan uses the output of the information system, and (2) provides control criteria for the marketing information system.

A BRIEF LOOK AT SOME OPERATING SYSTEMS

Chemstrand

The Chemstrand Company has an advanced marketing information system. For example, the Chemstrand system will provide detailed sales analyses by product, by category of product, by sales district, type of process, type of end-use, the type of mill, and so on. Reports are sent to the company's salesmen concerning their transactions with their customers; different marketing groups get specific reports which are relevant to their particular sphere of interest. For example, product managers receive analyses of the marketing operations of their particular area of responsibility. Records are kept of consumer behavior in 7500 households which represent a sample of the national market, so that these socioeconomic backgrounds and attitudes can be analyzed to determine buying trends and other related information.[10]

The system also keeps close tabs on Chemstrand's competitors and, in addition, also turns out a number of short-, medium-, and long-range forecasts. These forecasts are made by industry, by company, and by end users. Projections are made for approximately 400 different products on a short-term basis.

Lever Brothers

Lever Brothers has a system that produces 2500 different pages of daily reports, 3000 pages of weekly reports, and 40,000 pages of monthly reports. Thus, managers have daily tabulations for the sales of their brands by geographic districts. Data are also provided as to whether the sales quota is being achieved, and how close to this the salesman is coming. It is possible to compare brands by zones, by districts, and by regions.[11]

Every month there are reports on more than 3000 important customers and, best of all, they are available during the first week of the new month. These reports show a variety of information such as how well a particular account is doing vis-à-vis its performance in a prior year.

---

[10] Phyllis Daignault, "Marketing Management and the Computer," *Sales Management,* Vol. 95 (August 29, 1965), pp. 49–60.

[11] Ibid., pp. 58–59.

RCA

Another example can be found with RCA, whose system can provide sales analyses by product, by territory, comparisons with quota, and so forth. They have a program to determine the amount of each model of the product line which is to be sold to each distributor. It is based on the distributor's sales history, and the knowledge of his territory's market potential, as well as RCA's market share within that area.

Another program combines 100 variables to determine the gross margin for individual models or families of products. In addition, there are monthly reports which show sales by product, by dealer county area, and by distributor. These outputs represent, of course, only a fraction of the output of the RCA system.[12]

MYTHS AND PITFALLS OF MARKETING INFORMATION SYSTEMS

Because there has been so much talk about marketing information systems and very little hard fact concerning how well they have operated under a variety of industry types and conditions, a number of myths have evolved concerning the nature and capabilities of marketing information systems. Of course, there are some pitfalls that are well recognized, since they are generally the same as those associated with other information systems, such as management information systems.

Several of these myths and pitfalls are briefly discussed below:

1. Not every firm should have a computer-oriented marketing information system. While it is true that it is fashionable to talk about one, there are some companies that are equipped neither to run one nor to utilize the output. For these firms the expenditure on the development of this system would be a waste.

2. The marketing information system should not be based solely on the computer. While this is a vital tool, there are still many "old-fashioned" forms and procedures which are quite good.

3. Be careful of a revolutionary effect upon the enterprise. The firm simply may not be able to handle both the personnel problems and the output of the system.

4. The marketing information system is not a substitute for basic market research of the traditional type. Such market research is still required for specific studies of particular marketing problems and for handling information needs which are outside the sphere of interest of the system.

It is too easy to accept a computer printout with 100% confidence, simply because it is neat and voluminous. However, this does not make it right and the marketing manager must remember that outputs are only as good as the inputs used to generate them.

---

[12] Ibid., pp. 59–60.

6. Marketing information systems are not new. Obviously, they have existed for some time, since managers have for a long period had reliable and comprehensive and timely sources of information. What we do have at the present time is a capability for making the system far more comprehensive and for equipping it to handle vastly increased quantities of input with effectiveness and promptness.

7. The same marketing information system cannot serve all levels of management, nor can all levels benefit equally from such systems. The top managers, for example, require information which is of such a nature that it permits them to make strategic choices. Middle managers and lower level supervisors require different types of information.[13] Within any one level, the sophistication of the system must be selected carefully so that it is compatible with the managers who will use it.

8. Because computers have such an enormous capacity, there is a tendency to make the information too detailed and wide-ranging. This is a mistake. The marketing manager should be provided with an amount of information sufficient for decision making and no more. If there is too much information, that which is relevant and useful will be hidden in the mass of excess input and output.

Insofar as the marketing manager is concerned, the proper design of the marketing information system is one which emphasizes not the outpouring of great masses of data, but rather the filtration, condensation, and evaluation of masses of information into more manageable form.[14]

9. You cannot expect to develop at one time a total system that will handle all of the marketing information needs of your enterprise. Instead, the system must be developed and implemented in small, manageable stages. How much time is required for the development of the system to its fullest capacity is very difficult to state. One company may be able to implement a fairly comprehensive system in one year, while other companies may require five or ten years before their systems are fully operational.

10. There is a danger in the fact that many marketing managers do not know what information they really need, yet one of the precepts of designing a good marketing information system is that the marketing manager must be consulted. Unfortunately, the great tendency is for people to demand more information about areas of which they are uncertain. The result, of course, is that in those decision-making areas about which the marketing managers are not too confident, they require the system designers to provide far more information than they really need.

11. Do not take it for granted that simply because your marketing personnel will be given more information than they had previously they will know what to do with it. Therefore, during design of the marketing

---

[13] Ridley Rhind, "Management Information Systems," *Business Horizons*, Vol. 11 (June 1968), pp. 37–46.

[14] Cox and Good, "How to Build a Marketing Information System," p. 152.

information system, firm steps must be taken to insure that the managers are prepared to use the output of that system effectively.

12. The final pitfall is that too often managers feel that they do not have to understand how the system works, but merely to take advantage of its capability. While this is true to a certain degree, nonetheless it requires them to place too much faith in a system which simply may not be functioning properly insofar as their decision needs and marketing objectives are concerned. While the managers who use the system need not be specialists in its design and implementation, they must be sufficiently aware of the mechanics of the system so that they can evaluate its output and provide suggestions for improvement of the system.

SUMMARY

Marketing information systems are part of the marketing wave of the future. They are important, and they are beginning to function very well. However, like any radical change imposed upon an organization, they can be very expensive and have great potential for damage. Hence, they must be used carefully and with a recognition of their potential for damage. The rewards of struggling with the many problems of developing a successful system are, however, well worthwhile.

b.

Marketing opportunity assessment

Assessing, marketing opportunity involves the identification of corporate goals, the appraisal of available present and potential resources and capabilities, and the systematic analysis of established and new profit opportunities. A creative and innovative approach is essential for successful marketing opportunity assessment.

Environmental changes and technological developments emerging at an increasing rate place firms in competitive situations of high risk. Diverse forces such as higher costs of market development, high break-even points, and environmental changes of new types have made it necessary for firms to adopt innovative approaches to marketing and particularly to new product development and market opportunity assessment. As a result, firms have accepted the concept of programmed innovation as a prerequisite for survival and growth. Thus, marketing opportunity assessment reflects directive efforts of management to plan, organize, and control product and process innovation.

In the first article, Lazer and Bell explore the process of innovation, and summarize theories of new product and process acceptance from a marketing point of view. Kelley and Lazer emphasize the concept of anticipating and adapting to change. Muse and Kegerreis propose managerial techniques to integrate research and development into the marketing process. Lazer then examines sales forecasting as a basic component in marketing planning and in assessing marketing opportunities.

The programmed introduction of new or improved products and processes has become an essential part of the planning and strategy of many firms. It is a difficult task which requires a realistic evaluation of existing product lines, markets, trends, and competitive positions. This article defines and describes the different categories of innovation and various theories of the innovation adoption process.

17. THE CONCEPT AND PROCESS OF INNOVATION *

William Lazer† and William E. Bell‡

DIMENSIONS AND INNOVATION

Marketing and innovation are closely intertwined. Successful innovation is a necessary condition for effective marketing.[1] "Innovate or perish" is a trite statement, but one which has rich meaning for business operating in a consumeristic economy.

Marketing as an adaptive process seeks greater correspondence between the opportunities reflected in environments and a company's marketing mix. Since environments change continuously, and since technological developments are emerging at an increasing rate, greater attention is being directed at innovation. The result has been an acceptance of the concept of programmed innovation—the regular introduction of innovations to markets on a planned basis.

The significance of technological discovery to innovation has long been recognized. Now, in addition, the complementary and critical role of marketing in achieving successful innovation is underscored. The result is more market-directed research and development, the organization of marketing planning departments, and the extension of the activities and scope of marketing research departments.

This article explores innovation from a marketing point of view. It defines different categories of innovation, discusses the stages of the inno-

---

* Commissioned contribution.
† Michigan State University.
‡ Merrimack College.

[1] William Lazer, "Competition, Innovation, and Marketing Management," in Taylor W. Meloan and Charles M. Whitlo (eds.), *Competition In Marketing* (Department of Marketing and Business Logistics, University of Southern California, Los Angeles, 1964), p. 10.

vation process, and summarizes a few theories of new product and process acceptance.

THE INNOVATION PROCESS

Innovations are often distinguished from inventions. They are referred to as successful inventions. An innovation, essentially, is the act of developing a novel idea into a process or product. For an innovation to be successful, the process or product must be feasible and have commercial acceptability.[2]

Successful innovations go through three major phases: the idea, the implementation, and market acceptance. The idea is defined as the invention, and it is the result of creative work often done by researchers. Implementation refers to the development of the idea from its conceptual stage to an output—a developed product or service. This phase has received the greatest attention by business firms. Market acceptance, the third stage, is, by definition, crucial to any successful innovation.

The first two phases of the innovation process can be partially controlled by the firm. The acceptance decision, however, is largely exogenous to the firm. It depends upon consumers and their reactions. Although promotional and other marketing influences may be exerted, the decision per se is in the hands of potential consumers.

REASONS FOR INNOVATIONS

Innovations can be troublesome, risky, and may meet with great resistance. They require change on the part of manufacturers, distributors, and consumers. Yet innovation has become an integral part of modern marketing operations. Why do companies innovate?

Management innovates to solve problems—problems in the sense of untapped opportunities and not just immediate company difficulties. Innovations afford opportunities for: [3] (1) the use of excess plant capacity, (2) the use of available manpower, (3) better use of sales organization, (4) the utilization of by-products, (5) the employment of surplus capital, (6) the provision of a hedge against slack seasons, and (7) the counteraction of declining market for a company's basic products.

Although risks may be great, the financial rewards for innovations can also be very large. Increasingly, a greater proportion of the earnings of many companies come from new products and processes. Effective innovation assures corporations a niche in tomorrow's business setting. Simi-

---

[2] William E. Bell, "Consumer Innovation: An Investigation of Selected Characteristics of Innovations" (unpublished D.B.A. dissertation, Michigan State University, 1962), p. 7.

[3] Grey Matter, Grey Advertising Agency, Inc., National Advertiser's Edition, Vol. 31 (January 1960), p. 2.

larly, inadequate innovation can render a company vulnerable to competitors' actions.

Company growth can be maintained through innovations. In fact, companies in industries classified as "growth industries" typically are oriented toward new product and process innovation. Examples of such industries are: chemicals, drugs, and electronics. For them, "It is about 'par' to have around 50 per cent of sales in products that are new since the war." [4]

Programmed innovation is also a defensive strategy. As old products decay and suffer loss of markets, new ones must be ready to accept the slack. The costs of not innovating can prove to be excessive. Given a competitive situation, a firm cannot hold its current market and profit position for long without innovating.

ADAPTIVE, FUNCTIONAL, AND FUNDAMENTAL INNOVATIONS

Innovations vary in both degree of complexity and application. The complexity of innovations may vary from minor adjustments to major technological breakthroughs. Minor product alternations, such as changes in packages or colors, constitute small changes in a product. They may, however, account for significant changes in the marketing task. At the other end of the continuum are completely novel products, such as missiles, laser beams, and computers. They may generate totally new industries and hitherto unrecognized markets.

Three main categories of innovation based on consumer reactions can be delineated: adaptive, functional, and fundamental. The least complex type of innovation is an adaptive innovation. It refers to the minor alteration of an existing product. Alterations in packages, color, design, trim, size, and style are examples. The adaptive innovation does not perform new functions for the user or the purchaser. It does not require any change in consumer behavior patterns or new consumer skills to use it. Adaptive innovations usually require the least investment in research expenditures, less ingenuity on the part of the firm, and little change on the part of consumer behavior. They constitute the most common type of innovation and also the easiest to emulate. ·

The second type of innovation is functional innovation. These are more complex for both consumers and producers than adaptive innovations. Functional innovations are those in which the product or service remains the same but the method of performing the function is new. For example, electric and gas clothes dryers, or electric knives, perform the same functions for consumers as wringers and clotheslines, and ordinary knives,

---

[4] Ralph W. Jones, "Management of New Products," *The Journal of Industrial Engineering*, Vol. 9, No. 5 (September–October 1948). Reprinted in William Lazer and E. J. Kelley (eds.), *Managerial Marketing: Perspectives and Viewpoints* (rev. ed.; Homewood, Ill.: Richard D. Irwin, Inc., 1962), p. 444.

but do so in a different manner. Consumers, therefore, satisfy a previously fulfilled want in a new and better way.

Functional innovations can require considerable adjustments on the part of consumers. They may result in the purchase of tangible products to perform functions previously not requiring a physical product. For example, an electric or gas clothes dryer requires a different behavior pattern on the part of the consumer than did previous methods of drying clothes. Also a firm may need new processes or raw materials to effect such a change.

The third group of innovations are fundamental innovations. They are the most complex and rare of the three classes. Fundamental innovations incorporate original ideas or concepts which perform new functions for the consumer. They represent a complete break with the past on both the part of the consumer and the firm. They fulfill a need which was not previously recognized, or if recognized, was not previously fulfilled.

Fundamental innovations do not involve direct substitution, but focus on complete newness. Therefore, a firm may be faced with developing new raw materials and/or processes, as well as developing primary demand. The cultivation of markets and achievement of customer acceptance can be a difficult, expensive, and timely task for fundamental innovations.

An example of a fundamental innovation is the dehumidifier. The previously unsatisfied want or need is comfort in muggy or chilly weather, and freedom from the expense and nuisance of mildew. It had not been fulfilled previously. A new set of habits is required in the use and operation of this new product.

Any classification scheme of products or services suffers from the inability to establish categories that are mutually exclusive in all cases. There is some overlap in the categories established. It may even be more realistic to think in terms of an innovation spectrum ranging from various kinds of adaptive innovations at one extreme to several classes of fundamental innovations at the other. Yet, for purposes of understanding market reaction, the three categories suggested are useful.

Do products necessarily move from one category to another over time? For instance, does a fundamental innovation become an adaptive innovation? Part of the answer depends on how one defines a new product. If television, for example, is considered a completely new product, it is a fundamental innovation. But it may also be considered as an extension of radio with just the addition of sight to sound. Thus, the dilemma of what is new must be resolved before ascertaining whether or not a product started at the fundamental level.

A product or service does not necessarily have to move along the innovation continuum from category to category. All products need not emanate as fundamental innovations. On the other hand, it seems that the majority of them do at least move from functional to adaptive types of innovations. Few products do not have some kind of adaptation with regard to size, variety, number of parts, packaging, branding, and the like.

FIGURE 1

Classification of product innovations by type of innovation

	Fundamental	Functional	Adaptive
CHARACTERISTICS	Requires: 　Absolute newness 　No substitutability 　Habit change 　New process 　New markets May Require: 　New skills 　New resources 　New consumption 　　patterns 　New distribution 　　systems	Substitutability Improved product or 　process New or changed 　production Change in consumption 　patterns New or changed distri- 　bution systems	New in minor aspects: 　e.g., weight, color, 　design, package Much substitutability Limited production 　change No changes in con- 　sumption pattern No change in distribu- 　tion required Greater convenience
EXAMPLES	Missiles Dehumidifiers Airplanes Televisions Lasers Computers	Clothes dryers Electric knives Electric sharpeners Automatic dishwashers Jet planes	Flip-top box Filter and mentholated 　cigarettes New brands
MARKETING TASKS	Create primary 　demand Create new con- 　sumption habits New production 　facilities　and/or 　processes Overcome resistance 　to change Gain acceptance	Create selective demand Change consumption 　habits New or changed 　production New service facilities Extend markets	Meet competition Extend markets Create selective demand Specialize product for 　market segments Differentiate product Create image of 　newness

In Figure 1, some of the salient considerations of fundamental, functional, and adaptive innovations are presented in tabular form. The characteristics of each innovation category, various examples of each, and a number of the marketing tasks are summarized.

ACCEPTANCE OF INNOVATION

Several theories have been advanced to explain the process of new product and process acceptance by consumers. In general, there has been no attempt to differentiate between types of innovations and their effects on consumer acceptance.

The "trickle down" theory is one of the most widely referred to explanations of the acceptance of innovations. The essence of this theory is that product or process acceptance starts at a top echelon of consumers, the upper income groups or social class, and trickles down until it reaches the lower echelons—the masses or lowest income groups. The acceptance of fashion is often explained in this way. While this theory has great appeal and may be useful in developing marketing strategy, it is an oversimplification and does not have applicability to all products.

A second theory might be called the theory of random selection. Proponents of this theory would assert there is a unique core market who will purchase an innovation regardless of socio-economic characteristics. The propensity to buy newness does not depend on the product but only on the fact that it is new and provides status, prestige, and recognition for the owners. A rational assessment of product characteristics is not involved in these purchases.

A third theory holds that there are opinion leaders and influentials within every peer group and these people are the tastemakers or pace setters within their own groups. They determine the acceptance of innovations for their respective groups.

The distinction between this theory and the "trickle down" theory is that each peer group will have its own pace setters, and product or process acceptors can be found within each. Further, the proponents of this theory argue that these opinion leaders are extremely influential in determining whether a product will achieve market acceptance. This approach has the benefit of matching kinds of innovations with different types of consumers.

THE ADOPTION PROCESS

An adoption process has been hypothesized by numerous researchers.[5] This process covers the steps that a consumer goes through in determining the feasibility of buying new products. The steps are described as

> 1. Awareness   4. Trial
> 2. Interest   5. Adoption
> 3. Evaluation

Awareness. At the awareness stage, a person first learns about a new idea, product, or practice. He has only general information about it. He knows little or nothing about any special qualities, its potential usefulness, or how it would likely work for him.

---

[5] H. V. Lionberger, *Adoption of New Ideas and Practices* (Ames: Iowa State University Press, 1960), pp. 22–23.

Interest. Here he develops an interest in the new things that he has learned about. He is not satisfied with mere knowledge of its existence. He wants more detailed information about what it is, how it will work, and is inclined to actively seek the information desired. It makes little difference whether we call this the information or the interest stage. The personal need of the individual making the decision remains much the same.

Evaluation. At the evaluation stage a person weighs the information and evidence accumulated in the previous stages in order to decide whether the new idea, product, or practice is basically good, and whether it is good for him. In a sense, he reasons through the pros and cons mentally, and applies them to his own situation. Perhaps this stage could very well be referred to as the "mental trial stage." To be sure, evaluation is involved at all stages of the adoption process, but it is at this stage that it is most in evidence and perhaps most needed.

Trial. At this stage the individual is confronted with a distinctly different set of problems. He must actually put the change into practice. This means that he must learn how, when, where, how much, etc. Competent personal assistance may be required in putting the innovation to use. The

FIGURE 2

Comparison of profiles: Adaptive and functional innovators

Variable	Adaptive Innovators	Functional Innovators
Age		
Head	Very young	Young
Spouse	Very young	Young
Occupation		
Head	Dispersed between Professional-Managerial and Craftsmen-Foremen	Highly concentrated in Professional-Managerial
Spouse	No difference	No difference
Education		
Head	Above average education	Very highly educated
Spouse	Above average education	Very highly educated
Family Income	High income	Very high income
Ethnic Group	Negro, French, Italian	Jewish, British, German
Home Characteristics		
Ownership	Slightly higher than average	Very high
Structure	Highly concentrated in single units	More highly concentrated in single units
Home Value	High value	Extremely high value
Rent	High rent	Very high rent
Number in Family	Dispersed	Dispersed

Source: William E. Bell, "Consumer Innovations: A Unique Market for Newness," *Proceedings of the Winter Conference of the American Marketing Association, 1963,* p. 92, with adaptation.

usual pattern of acceptance is to try a little at first, and then to make large-scale use of it if the small-scale experiment proves successful.

Adoption. Here a person decides that the new idea, product, or practice is good enough for full-scale and continued use. A complete change is made with that end in view.

CHARACTERISTICS OF INNOVATORS

Do those who accept different kinds of innovations vary in their characteristics, or are the innovators the same regardless of the kind of innovation? Some research has shown that there are differences. Figure 2 presents several socio-economic characteristics of innovators for selected adaptive and functional innovations.

Management must recognize the necessity for planning, organizing, and controlling product and process innovation in the development of market opportunities. Marketing managers must develop a framework for analysis of the problems and opportunities involved in programmed innovation. Activities basic to innovation management are identified and related to two examples of the innovation process.

---

18. MANAGING INNOVATION IN MARKETING *

Eugene J. Kelley † and William Lazer ‡

Despite all the speeches made about "marketing orientation" or "customer orientation," most businesses are still primarily product- or process-oriented rather than market-oriented.[1] Few firms today construct and

---

* Reprinted from "Managing Innovation in Marketing," *Advanced Management-Office Executive* Vol. 1, No. 7 (July 1962), pp. 10–13. For a discussion of managerial marketing functions, see Thomas A. Staudt, "The Managerial Function of Marketing," in William Lazer and Eugene J. Kelley, *Managerial Marketing: Perspectives and Viewpoints* (rev. ed; Homewood, Ill.: Richard D. Irwin, Inc., 1962), pp. 385–92. Also see Thomas A. Staudt and Donald A. Taylor, *A Managerial Introduction to Marketing* (Englewood Cliffs, N.J.: Prentice-Hall, Inc., 1965), pp 17–26.

† The Pennsylvania State University.

‡ Michigan State University.

[1] Peter F. Drucker, quoted in Hector Lazo and Arnold Corbin, *Management in Marketing* (New York: McGraw-Hill Book Co., Inc., 1961), p. vii.

execute corporate plans and strategy on the basis of careful study of market needs, forces, and opportunities. Competition will accelerate the change to a genuine marketing concept in more firms in the next few years, and stimulate more interest in the process of managing change through programmed innovation management. Programmed innovation will increasingly become the foundation of business strategy. The basic managerial response to accelerating change must be innovation.

In this article, nine activities of innovation management are identified and are applied to the function and process of innovation. Experience in a number of firms indicates that while innovation may rest basically on the creative and managerial powers of a relatively limited number of individuals, innovation can be stimulated, produced, and managed by systematic attention to the task. The risks and costs of non-innovation are tending to overcome the fear of loss on unsuccessful innovations in more competitive situations in large and small firms.

Managers in all industries must produce and manage innovation on a scale sufficient to absorb unused and growing production capabilities and to achieve differential advantage in the market. To do this job, each manager must develop a framework for analysis of the problems and opportunities involved in innovation management. Increased understanding of the function and process of innovation is a basic requirement of executive and corporate growth.

To managers the fundamental notion underlying innovation is clear, i.e., the addition of something new and different to an existing situation. The managerial problem is administering the systematic injection of appropriate new insights, concepts, and techniques into existing business situations. Programmed attention to each of the following activities characterizes the innovation-directed firm. Their neglect is more typical in non-innovation-minded enterprises.

ACTIVITIES OF INNOVATION MANAGEMENT

1. Acceptance of the inevitability of change and innovation by management.
2. Programmed perception of new market needs and of dysfunctioning in the system.
3. Relating market opportunity to corporate resources.
4. Specifying innovistic opportunities of the firm.
5. Identifying practical alternative strategies.
6. Determining the expected profitability of each of the major strategies.
7. Making a decision on innovative action.
8. Promoting the innovation.
9. Assuring market acceptance of the innovation.

The relation of these nine activities is discussed below.

1. Acceptance of the inevitability of change and innovation by management

This is primary and pervasive. Acceptance of the inevitability and necessity of change and innovation in a period of accelerating technology is a basic management and organizational responsibility. The point of view that change is accelerating, normal, and constructive must be held by the leadership of an enterprise. This is essentially a directorship responsibility which requires an awareness on the part of top management of the need for discerning unsatisfied market demands. Top management's tasks include provision of a motivated organization and a permissive environment for innovation. Innovation can not only be encouraged, but discouraged by top-management attitudes.

2. Programmed perception of new market opportunities and of dysfunctioning in the system

The perception of new market needs, future market opportunity, and system dysfunctioning is a prerequisite for business dynamism. This perception grows out of an attitude of dissatisfaction with present performance. Market opportunity and dysfunctioning is recognized by comparing market response to products and services with market wants and needs. The discrepancy is one measure of innovistic and market opportunity. The discrepancy is measured through a combination of various techniques of consumer and market research and managerial judgment and vision.

The early stages of the innovation process require people able to perceive areas of human dissatisfaction as market opportunities. One of the major problems confronting corporate management committed to the generation of innovation is to identify, stimulate, and encourage the people in the system who are perceivers of dysfunctioning. Innovation and creativity do not flourish in overstructured situations. Perceivers can exist among customers and salesmen as well as executives and researchers. Management must plan to broaden the base of perceivers of dysfunctioning by stimulating and rewarding such people wherever they are found in the organization.

3. Relating market opportunity to corporate resources

Perception of market needs does not mean an opportunity exists for any particular company. Available opportunities must be related to the particular company's resources including its personnel, financial, and physical resources. Profitable courses of action vary with individual corporate postures and goals. The overwhelming majority of innovative opportunities will be rejected. But it is necessary to screen the many to find the few that do relate to the resources and the mission of the company.

4. Specifying innovistic opportunities of the firm

This function of innovation relates to specifying the company's innovistic opportunity by identifying the various practical alternatives which exist to remedy the discovered dysfunctioning. This is a job where the technician can assume a major responsibility. An analysis of total company operations and methods in light of market opportunities is helpful in sifting the opportunities to arrive at the few that are most relevant and profitable for the company's current situation.

5. Identifying practical alternative strategies

Having specified the available opportunities, the company is in a position of being able to outline alternative strategies for the profitable pursuit of innovistic opportunity. It can thereby indicate various courses of action that could be followed to overcome the market dysfunctioning or meet a new market need.

6. Determining the expected profitability of each of the major strategies

One logical method of selection of the right strategy is to determine the expected dollar values in following each of the practical strategies. For example, market opportunity might indicate that five products could satisfy market wants at a particular point in time. Each product has inherent advantages and disadvantages, but each is capable of serving market demands. The question becomes one of determining the expected dollar values of each of the five strategies. The expected dollar value is determined by two items.

1. The anticipated dollar outcomes of following each of the five strategies.
2. The estimated profitability of success of each of the five strategies.[2]

Management usually does not know with certainty the likelihood of success of following any given strategy nor the exact payoff. However, it should attempt to determine specific values for them. A value of this approach is that management is forced to place an expected dollar value on the outcomes of each of the strategies. If the objective is to maximize profits, then the decision choice for the innovation becomes one of choosing that strategy which has the highest expected dollar value.

---

[2] For example, if it is estimated that the dollar value of following strategy "A" is a million dollars, this dollar value times the estimated probability of success of the strategy determines the expected dollar value. Therefore, if the probability of success is 0.5, the expected value of strategy "A" is $500,000.

7. Making a decision on innovative action

Once the expected dollar values of alternative decision choices have been arrayed, a logical choice is facilitated. The expected returns, however, must meet corporate criteria before an innovation is adopted.

If the expected dollar return of the best alternative does not meet the rate of return or profit expectations of a company, or if the risk of the alternatives is too high, the innovistic opportunity may then be passed up by the company. The opportunity finally selected will determine the specific marketing program adopted.

8. Promoting the innovation

This might be more broadly considered as marketing the innovation to the audience for which it has been designed. It is in this area, for instance, that advertising, salesmanship, and all the elements of the marketing mix must be coordinated to effectively cultivate the particular market. To promote an innovation to the market place, a firm must cultivate awareness on the part of consumers, build up its image, and overcome the natural resistance to innovation.

9. Assuring market acceptance of the innovation

The last stage is the adoption of the innovation. The gradual overcoming of the resistance to change to any innovation becomes the focal point for management effort. Factors leading to possible refinement of the innovation are evaluated through appraisal of information fed back from the market. Such market feedback will enable management to measure market responses to innovation and help to indicate new market opportunities. Market acceptance of an innovation results not in a new equilibrium but in a new situation in which the seeds of further dysfunctioning exist.

THE PROCESS OF INNOVATION

Chart 1 illustrates one model of the innovative process and indicates the activities required at various managerial levels. It may suggest that different talents are needed at each stage of the process. The skills of the entrepreneur, the manager, the technician, the distribution expert, and the salesman are called for at various action stages of the innovative process.

The innovation time scale is collapsing. The period from the perception of dysfunctioning to the acceptance of the innovation has been consistently decreasing. This means more pressure will be placed on management to understand more fully the process of managing change through

CHART 1

The Process of Innovation

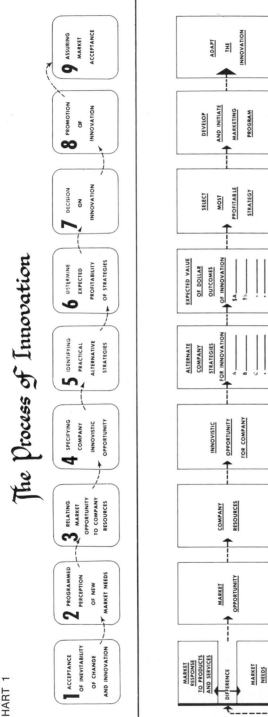

1 ACCEPTANCE OF INEVITABILITY OF CHANGE AND INNOVATION

2 PROGRAMMED PERCEPTION OF NEW MARKET NEEDS

3 RELATING MARKET OPPORTUNITY TO COMPANY RESOURCES

4 SPECIFYING COMPANY INNOVISTIC OPPORTUNITY

5 IDENTIFYING PRACTICAL ALTERNATIVE STRATEGIES

6 DETERMINE EXPECTED PROFITABILITY OF STRATEGIES

7 DECISION ON INNOVATION

8 PROMOTION OF INNOVATION

9 ASSURING MARKET ACCEPTANCE

MARKET RESPONSE TO PRODUCTS AND SERVICES — DIFFERENCE — MARKET NEEDS

MARKET OPPORTUNITY

COMPANY RESOURCES

INNOVISTIC OPPORTUNITY FOR COMPANY

ALTERNATE COMPANY STRATEGIES FOR INNOVATION
A
B
C
:
R

EXPECTED VALUE OF DOLLAR OUTCOMES OF INNOVATION
$A
$B
:
$R

SELECT MOST PROFITABLE STRATEGY

DEVELOP AND INITIATE MARKETING PROGRAM

ADAPT THE INNOVATION

FEEDBACK

managing knowledge and the process of programmed innovation. Innovation approaches manageability when participation in the process becomes part of the continuing responsibility of all levels of management. Only then can a firm hope to deploy its resources profitably and be envisioned to meet the challenge of change.

INNOVATION ILLUSTRATIONS

Marketing innovation is influenced by technology and the physical sciences and by diverse social changes. Basic technological and social change combine to generate new areas of innovistic opportunity in marketing.

Marketing innovations occur in two main areas:

1. Product and service developments.
2. The facilitation of the processes of marketing.

An application of the innovative process in the introduction of a new product follows.

PRODUCT INNOVATION IN THE DRUG INDUSTRY

The drug industry offers many examples of product innovation. The competitive and social environment of the drug industry stimulates an acceptance of the inevitability of change and innovation. Individual drug companies typically recognize the nature of innovative opportunity and establish systematic programs for the perception of new market needs and the development of products to satisfy those needs. Research and development in drugs is based on the recognition that medical researchers, physicists and chemists must point towards the frontiers of knowledge in certain defined areas.

Basic research is usually encouraged. But, it is usually guided towards areas of strength of the company to relate new knowledge to corporate resources and marketing opportunities. For example, one drug company may have advanced research in steroids further than any competitor or any research group. Market opportunities in the development of steroids will present a particular innovistic opportunity for such a company. Top management in such a company tends to become more concerned with evaluating alternative strategies designed to achieve innovative opportunities in steroid drugs. For instance, four or five particular products with a steroid compound may be developed which seem likely to lead to successful treatment of particular diseases. With limited resources, the company must decide which is the most profitable and desirable opportunity to follow. Expected profit is usually the criterion in innovation-minded industries; it is only through profitable returns on innovation that further research and innovation are insured.

It becomes relatively simple to decide on the particular innovations to pursue within a specified time period after determining which steroid opportunity is likely to deliver the greatest expected value. The particular drugs developed as a result of this process are then tested and marketed with a complete program. In drugs this will require specific innovative promotion through advertising in medical journals, the publication of learned papers, and field promotion. Distribution through drug stores, hospitals and physicians produces information fed back from consumers and medical men. Adjustments may take place in either the product itself or the form of the product. The product may become an injection or a pill, or of varying dosages, depending to some extent on the reaction of the market to the innovation.

PROCESS ILLUSTRATION—THE PLANNED SHOPPING CENTER

Innovation is also essential in the activities that must be performed to distribute goods and services efficiently and economically. Several process innovations in marketing of a basic nature have appeared in recent years. These include the shopping center, the discount house, automatic vending machines, physical distribution changes, new credit concepts, and new organizational developments growing out of the marketing concept. The process of innovation operates in all. One specific illustration which has followed the pattern of innovation outlined in this article is the planned shopping center.

The early developers of shopping centers were among the first to recognize the marketing changes required to adapt to the evolving needs of Americans caught up in the suburban population movement. Early shopping center developers recognized almost intuitively that changes in the population distribution and living style of suburban Americans meant that consumers could not be as well served by the existing retail structure located in the central business district of the metropolitan area. They visualized the area of difference in marketing opportunity terms between the shopping needs of new suburbanites and the existing retail facilities available to serve those needs. This area of marketing opportunity was further defined through various kinds of studies. When evidence supported the belief that existing concentrations of retail stores were not adequate to serve new market needs, early developers attempted to relate those unmet needs to individual company or developer resources. In some cases, the developers were large department stores, such as J. L. Hudson in the Detroit metropolitan area. In other cases, real estate developers were the basic innovators.

Shopping center management requires identifying specific innovative opportunities at several levels. Decisions must be made on the size of the shopping center, nature of the center, number of stores and types of stores. The question of location and site selection is also one of analyzing specific innovative opportunities.

In site selection and locational innovation the problem becomes one of identifying various sites and attempting to determine the expected profitability of a location at each site. This involves trading area analysis, time-distance studies, and other efforts to get at the expected value of the dollar outcomes of locating shopping centers on a given site.

As with other process innovations, the decision once made must be promoted, not only to consumers, but to bankers, merchants, and others in the system. Finally, the innovation is modified through changes in the tenant mix or merchandise mix to fit more precisely the needs of the consumers served by the innovation.

Process innovation will be recognized as more important in marketing in the future. Fundamental concepts of marketing are changing and the entire field is being reoriented. The attitude of retailers, particularly, toward innovation is changing. The retailer must adapt to changes in the basic dynamic areas of consumer behavior, technology, changing competitive practices, and constantly altering business-governmental relationships.

CHANGE AND INNOVATION

All managers today must recognize product and process change as the constant in planning, organizing, and controlling marketing activity. Management's responsibility becomes that of anticipating, adapting, and innovating under accelerating change conditions. The emphasis, in many enterprises in the future, is not likely to be on operations. It will have to be on anticipating and adapting to change. Innovation is the essential element in such a strategy.

Little direction to R&D efforts and the lack of a marketing orientation have contributed to the high failure rate in new product introductions. The authors discuss some of the problems in new product development and suggest three approaches as partial solutions for the dilemmas in management organization, executive behavior, product analysis and the planning process.

---

19. TECHNOLOGICAL INNOVATION AND MARKETING MANAGEMENT: IMPLICATIONS FOR CORPORATE POLICY *

William V. Muse† and Robert J. Kegerreis‡

With steadily increasing expenditures on research and development in American industry, why is the rate of new product failures still quite high? Can the productivity of this vital area be improved? This paper discusses factors that may have contributed to the low productivity of R&D efforts and offers operational suggestions that might improve the payoff from technical research.

R&D and new product development

It is estimated that expenditures on research and development in the United States will reach $25.9 billion during 1969. Of these funds, approximately 35% or $9 billion is expected to be supplied by industry.[1] When these projections are overlapped with the estimate that business firms spend over $10 billion annually on the planning, research, and marketing of new products, the magnitude of the effort to provide technological development and convert these developments into marketable and successful products is evident.[2]

Yet there have been some indications that the productivity of the research and new product development process is low. A recent study by the management consulting firm of Booz, Allen, & Hamilton found an overall ratio, in a variety of industries, of 40 to 1 from the screening stage of new product ideas to successful introduction.[3]

---

* Reprinted from "Technological Innovation and Marketing Management: Implications for Corporate Policy," *Journal of Marketing*, Vol. 33, No. 4 (October 1969), pp. 3–9.

† Ohio University.

‡ Wright State University.

[1] W. Halder Fisher and Leonard L. Leaderman, *Probable Levels of R&D Expenditures in 1969: Forecast and Analysis* (Columbus, Ohio: Battelle Memorial Institute, December, 1968).

[2] Taylor W. Meloan, "New Products—Keys to Corporate Growth," in Martin L. Bell (ed.), *Marketing: A Maturing Discipline* (Chicago, Ill.: American Marketing Association, 1961), p. 29.

[3] *Management of New Products* (Chicago, Ill.: Booz, Allen, and Hamilton, 1960), Chart 7, p. 11.

At the same time, there is some evidence that the new products introduced also have a high failure rate. The National Industrial Conference Board in a study of 87 firms reported that one out of every three products put on the market failed. Other reports indicate that failure rates may even exceed this estimate.[4]

Trends in R&D expenditures

A number of studies revealed that the turnover rate in a firm's product line is high and that significant sales volume tends to be derived from the newest products marketed.[5] These results seem to indicate that the rate of R&D efforts or technological innovation has a direct effect on the marketability of new products and the profitability of the firms involved. The implication is plain: either develop new products or succumb to obsolescence and an inability to remain competitive.

The response to this challenge has been steadily increasing expenditures on R&D efforts both by the federal government and industry, particularly in the last ten years. However, the dedication to R&D expenditures as the panacea for new product competition seems to be lessening. A number of influential voices in industry have begun to question the productivity of the substantial expenditures on research and development.[6] This has been a contributing factor to a decline in the growth rate in R&D expenditures over the past four years.[7]

It is recognized that various R&D efforts are directed not only toward the development of new products, but also toward improvements in such areas as productive efficiency. Likewise, some government-sponsored investigations may be directed more toward basic or pure research rather than applied. While the need for basic research is not minimized, the primary concern here is with that portion of the R&D effort applied to new product development.

THE LACK OF MARKETING MINDEDNESS: SOME BACKGROUND

In this area of new product research and development, there all too often appears to be a lack of sensitivity to marketing implications on the part of the technical personnel involved. This condition is usually accompanied by an isolation of marketing personnel from these technicians, which leads to a significant gap in organizational communications and to a reduced level of net "realized" productivity in R&D operations.

---

[4] Ralph S. Alexander, James S. Cross, and Richard M. Hill, *Industrial Marketing* (Homewood, Ill.: Richard D. Irwin, Inc., 1967), p. 198.

[5] See *Management of New Products*, p. 1. Also Steven J. Shaw, "Behavioral Science Offers Fresh Insights on New Product Acceptance," *Journal of Marketing*, Vol. 24 (January 1965), p. 9.

[6] Conrad Berenson, "The R&D Marketing Interface—A General Analogue Model for Technology Diffusion," *Journal of Marketing*, Vol. 32 (April 1968), p. 11.

[7] Fisher and Leaderman, *Probable Levels of R&D Expenditures in 1969.*

One of the authors has developed a handy measurement technique for detecting the relative isolation of marketers from the technological research section of their firm. This measurement is based on the following series of questions directed to the marketing management sector concerning their utilization of a ubiquitous technical resource, that of computer services:

1. Do you use the computer service department in developing marketing plans? Or in carrying out marketing research projects? In model building or simulations of markets, new product adoption patterns, competitive strategies, and the like?
2. Was a series of programs provided for you when the computer was installed? If not, has this been done since the installation occurred?
3. Under whose auspices (department, title of executive, etc.) was the entire computer-based information system designed?

Typical responses to these questions demonstrate a persistent separation of marketing from technology in most firms. Because it is new, "technical," and conspicuous, the computer offers a convenient focal point for spotlighting this blind spot in modern management. If the marketing management segment of a firm is found to have little contact with the company computer sections, it is invariably found also to have relatively little influence over R&D activities. The correlation appears to be significant, although more research is needed on this point.

Another example is worth citing because of its representativeness. In the role of a consultant, one of the authors made a comprehensive study of a research establishment in order to evaluate its communications activities, both internal and external. The external phase of his analysis covered for this organization the same function known in conventional firms as marketing. The principal finding was that both the quality and quantity of communications by these technical researchers were critically low. The marketing orientation of this group was close to the vanishing point. They saw no utility (for them) either in a closer association with marketers, or in learning to use some of the principles of contemporary marketing science. They had developed to an extreme degree a behavior pattern quite familiar to academicians—the tendency to talk and write in a special language which the authors call "status patois" and which is designed to limit communications to a controlled professional peer group. The result is that an expensive mystique is created which purports to say to outsiders "Don't bother us, you wouldn't understand."

In this relatively mature and long-standing situation the consultant prescribed a simple remedy—a cybernetic translator who could provide transformations in both directions—to researchers from management and also the reverse. This sort of patchwork solution can be avoided by providing at the outset the kind of managerial framework which forces all subsystems to be "open," to have a common language, and to be amenable to common goal orientations.

A HYPOTHESIS

There are obviously a number of factors, like those cited in the situations above, that account for or influence the high mortality rate of new products and new product ideas. It is hypothesized, however, that the low "conversion rate" may be largely explained by two interrelated factors:

1. A lack of specific direction to R&D efforts; that is, the philosophy that all research is good and, hence, greater expenditures of research funds will result in an increased flow of profitable new products.
2. A lack of marketing orientation on the part of R&D personnel (engineers, scientists, etc.), the principal instigators or formulators of technological innovation.

As a response to the problems implicit in these two generalizations, this paper attempts to develop three managerial techniques which are described in the following sections. The three approaches become partial solutions for dilemmas in management organization, executive behavior, product analysis and the planning process. These are: (1) new direction for R&D management supplied through the infusion and involvement of marketing executives; (2) application of the "Test of Marketing Feasibility" in the allocation of R&D effort; and (3) adherence to a very deliberate, profit-motivated marketing orientation throughout the stages of new product development.

OPERATIONAL PROPOSALS

New direction for R&D through the "co-involvement" process

No two persons can provide sufficient experience from which to generalize over a whole society. However, both the consulting and business experience of the two authors lead to the conclusion that the managerial technique most needed at the interface of marketing and technological innovation is "co-involvement." At the earliest stage of overall planning, and at every subsequent stage, both marketing managers and researchers should be involved in the process as participants, not observers. The sharing of the planning process at each level is educational and convincing for both "sides." Such an experience displays for the researcher all the variables at work in the forward thrust of a dynamic firm. It convinces him that he cannot operate in isolation. It illustrates the need for communication, not just among managers, but a flow of communication from the world of the consumer to the milieu of the technological innovator.

FIGURE 1

Typical table of corporate organization

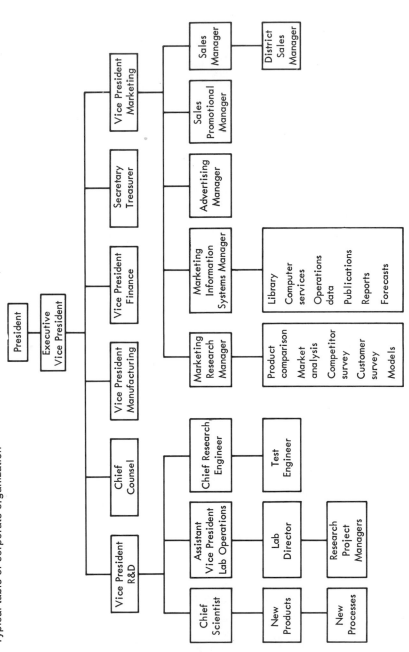

Note: Selected second-level positions and functions are shown only for Marketing, Research, and Development.

FIGURE 2

Levels of interaction among organizational positions

LEVEL 1.	**RESEARCH COMMITTEE**	Chairman: Executive Vice President	
	Fields: Allocation of resources Budgets Long range planning Short run directions and control	Members: Vice President, R&D Chief Scientist Senior Lab Director Chief Engineer Design and Testing	Vice President Marketing Marketing Research Director Marketing Information Director Vice President Finance
LEVEL 2.	**NEW PRODUCT COMMITTEE**	Chairman: Vice President, R&D	
	Fields: Feasibility test Cost effectiveness studies Evaluate potentials Develop priorities Product budgets Establish controls	Members: Assistant Vice President for Lab Operations Chief Scientist Chief Engineer New Product Lab Director	Sales Manager Marketing Research Director Marketing Information Director Sales Promotion Manager
LEVEL 3. Example of single new product committee	**PROJECT "X" COMMITTEE**	Chairman: Assistant Vice President for Lab Operations Members: Lab Director Project "X" Lab Director Assistant Chief Engineer Assistant to Chief Scientist	Assistant Director Marketing Research Assistant Director, Marketing Information Assistant Advertising Manager
	Fields: Progress review Forecast results Adjust schedules Cost analysis Evaluation		

A graphic example of one possible scheme for co-involvement is presented in Figures 1 and 2. In Figure 1 a typical organizational chart is shown, but with extra detail provided for the two critical areas of marketing and R&D.

Figure 2 consists of a three-stage development of horizontal, organizational interaction between the two groups. In level 1, committee members from marketing contribute analyses of (1) the external environment, (2) situational factors, (3) actions of competitors, and (4) marketing by salesmen, customers, and researchers. The financial representative provides a summary of available resources, and the R&D group contributes its special expertise and information about the technical state of the art. The activities involved in the three levels of committees are described by the sector labeled "Fields." The scope of the committee in level 3 is confined to a single new product development.

Each level in Figure 2 illustrates a type of horizontal involvement via committees composed of appropriate representatives of both the marketing and R&D sectors of the firm. Via a sharing of ideas, philosophies, and information at these three stages of new product development, substantial improvement in the penetration of a marketing orientation into the planning process should be effected.

This practical implementation of the marketing concept should obviously begin at the top, be accompanied by deliberate horizontal involvement, and be followed by suitable guidelines for product development, such as a feasibility test (see "Fields," level 2, Figure 2).

A marketing feasibility test

A "Test of Marketing Feasibility," in whatever form it assumes, may not be easy to apply, given the difficulty in specifying the nature of the new product or innovation that might result from a research effort. However, it is hypothesized that deliberate attempts must be made in this regard—at least in giving priority to areas of investigation— for the following reasons:

1. Those most likely to advance the threshold of scientific or technological knowledge are least apt to be concerned with its commercial use. The experimental scientist may be more excited by the chase (the exploration of the frontier of knowledge) than with the catch (the resulting innovation). Once the breakthrough has been accomplished, the job of the scientist is completed. He may be uninterested in questions as to the commercial use of the innovation, or in the implication that the value of the results may be diminished by the lack of opportunities for commercial exploitation of the innovation.
2. The producers of scientific and technological innovations seem persistently to possess a "mousetrap myopia"—that is, the concept that a better product will automatically create its own demand. There would seem to be sufficient evidence to invalidate this conclusion and to indicate that such a "product-orientation" is also dangerous, but such an attitude appears amazingly resilient.
3. Without strong direction, research efforts are apt to be tied to a technological base—that is, investigation is conducted in those areas in which researchers are most interested or in which they have the greatest familiarity. However, the most beneficial results would seem to emanate from research that reflects expressed or perceived consumer needs and desires rather than technology alone.

It follows that a major responsibility of those who manage or influence the direction of efforts to develop technological innovations would be to employ a marketing orientation or the "Test of Marketing Feasibility" to the allocation of research efforts. Such a test might require answers to these questions prior to the funding of the investigation:

1. What is the objective of the research? What is most likely to be the nature of our results—new product, improved process, etc.?
2. Who is most likely to be the benefactor or user (the potential customer) of this innovation?
3. What is known about the potential customers? How many are there? Where are they located? Are they large enough in number and purchasing power to create a market of sufficient size to make the investment worthwhile? What needs or wants of the customer will be satisfied by the innovation?
4. What change (if any) will be required in the behavior pattern of the potential users or customers in order to try, adopt, and use the proposed innovation?
5. What form should the innovation take (size, design, price) in order to increase the probability of adoption?

As an example of an appropriate situation in which the feasibility test could be administered, consider the following case:

Two prominent competing companies recently introduced into the market slightly different versions of an electronic letter writer, a consumer item that represented the application of an in-house technological advance. The incentive for the product creation arose partly from research which indicated that most consumers regarded writing letters as a chore, and felt guilty about always being "behind" in their correspondence.

The new battery-powered gadget was designed to convert consumers from letter writers to letter recorders by enabling the sender to dictate his message into a handheld transcriber which produced a mailable disc. The recipient used an identical device to listen to the message and later to dictate a reply. Each participant needed a separate machine, although the addressing of the envelopes and the use of postage stamps were still part of the overall process.

Confusion was encountered at every stage of the marketing plan—channel selection, promotional campaign, pricing, even the departmental location within the retail stores. However, the consumer was the most confused of all. Was he expected to buy one of these fairly expensive electronic gadgets for every person to whom he now wrote letters? Would the disc be standardized? How long would the batteries last? Was it very complicated, did it need a lot of service, who would do the servicing, what about long letters, short letters, could you erase the disc and start over? The questions were numerous, the level of consumer skepticism was high, and the product became another input to the mounting list of new product failures.

Profit-motivated marketing orientation

Allied conceptually with a test of marketing feasibility is a marketing orientation that is pervasive throughout the organization. This basic commitment on the part of management is necessary to provide the most profitable direction to research activities.

Bruce has ventured the thought that "one of the major false assumptions of our age is that change, by definition, is good." [8] One might also say the same about technological innovation. The implication is, unless an innovation can be applied in such a way that it will result in useful products or services which will contribute either to a higher standard of living or to an improvement of the social welfare, the *social value* of the time, energy, and money spent can be questioned, not to mention its bearing on the rate of return on the corporate investment. From a practical viewpoint, this system currently supplies a very impartial measurement of social service; that is, the social value gained from the innovational results of R&D.

As is typical of numerous companies, one can only conclude that many corporate leaders think of marketers as product sellers not product creators, or as order takers rather than demand analyzers. This class of manager continues to separate technological research from those individuals who are best suited to provide critical information relating to the optimal direction of that staff activity.

One way to insure the application of a marketing orientation to technical research might be to use only contract research where control over the research organization and the product of its efforts is more absolute. In any case, questions need to be raised about the need for in-house research establishments. Why is an R&D department necessary after all? Some of the typical responses are: all our competitors have R&D staffs; R&D means progress, you have to believe in it; we always need new ideas and new product suggestions.

It is interesting that very few respondents ever say that the wholly-owned research department is the least expensive source of new technological advances. More exploration needs to be made of the alternatives to in-house research. Many corporations have found significant advantages in leasing equipment and services. In many cases it might be equally advantageous for firms to contract for research as needed rather than to maintain a full-fledged R&D capability of their own. There are numerous independent R&D firms who are willing to bid on every phase of research, including the taking of a new product concept from the talk stage through to pilot production and test marketing. In this manner costs are known in advance, control is maintained, and marketing evaluation is sometimes easier.

---

[8] Robert D. Bruce, "Marketing and the Management of Technological Change," in Raymond M. Haas (ed.), *Science, Technology and Marketing* (Chicago, Ill.: American Marketing Association, 1966), p. 36.

Finally, contract research removes this vital operation from the corporate political system and permits the marketing concept to provide the focus of orientation for new product planning. A standard caution should be entered here. Contract research is not a panacea for problems at the interface between marketing and R&D activities. Furthermore, there are many companies who have a volume of research requirements that make in-house facilities a necessity.

OTHER APPROACHES

In this article, three managerial perspectives or techniques are presented that can help direct R&D activities more productively. Other observers in a variety of disciplines have also displayed their concern with this same problem area in management.

One example is the attention devoted to the development of means to increase the *transfer* of technological knowledge into marketing action. Kenneth Boulding has been quoted as saying "the gravest danger facing mankind is the lag between scientific technology and social institutions." [9] The passage of the State Technical Services Act to assist small businesses in using technological information is also evidence of the concern of the federal government over "technology transfer." [10]

Berenson has made a significant conceptual contribution by comparing "technology diffusion" with mass transfer in a physical system and by the development of an analogue model.[11] Cook has advocated the use of a program appraisal staff as a means to make R&D efforts more productive.[12] Clewett suggests the adoption of the "Entrepreneurial Concept of Integrating Science, Technology, and Marketing" which is related to the idea advanced in this paper, that is, penetration of a marketing orientation into the R&D operation.[13] Levitt and Talley both discussed a separate marketing R&D department staffed with highly competent personnel, to increase the flow of information and processes from the technical to the marketing area.[14]

SUMMARY AND CONCLUSIONS

During the late 1950s and early 1960s, considerable lip service was given to the "Marketing Concept" by top management in U.S. corporations; yet, the evidence indicates that there is much room for an expansion

[9] "Heretic Among Economists," *Business Week*, January 4, 1969, p. 82.
[10] S. 949, U.S. Senate, 80th Cong., 1st sess., July 1, 1965.
[11] Berenson, "The R&D Marketing Interface," pp. 8–15.
[12] Leslie G. Cook, "How to Make R&D More Productive," *Harvard Business Review*, Vol. 44 (July–August 1966), pp. 145–53.
[13] Robert L. Clewett, "Integrating Science, Technology, and Marketing: An Overview," in Haas, *Science, Technology and Marketing*, pp. 3–20.
[14] *Ibid.*, p. 18.

of its acceptance.[15] The largest percentage of top managers is still those with an engineering, production, or technical background developed independently from marketing.[16] Hence, the problem of developing greater "marketing sensitivity" or "marketing orientation" among top management would still seem to be of consequence. Moreover, for this concept to pervade the core of the scientists' bailiwick—the R&D operation—it would appear essential that top management assume the leadership in infusing a marketing philosophy into the arena of technical research.

In the opinion of the authors, this infusion may be obtained by means of a new direction for R&D efforts through the "Co-Involvement Process," the application of a "Test of Marketing Feasibility," and the adoption of a "Profit-Motivated Marketing Orientation."

In addition to these broad proposals, the following suggestions might also be considered, either as a means to make the broad proposals operational or as an added dimension of application.

1. Those who are responsible for stimulating, managing, or directing efforts designed to produce technological change or innovation could become more cognizant of and familiar with the process via which innovations are adopted and diffused. The growing body of literature in adoption and diffusion theory should be of considerable interest to top managers and research directors in identifying possible problems that are likely to be encountered in getting an innovation accepted and used by potential customers.

2. Berenson has suggested increased mobility of personnel as a device to enhance technological diffusion.[17] However, the primary movement that he advocates is one-way—technically trained engineers and scientists moving into marketing jobs. It might also be advocated that it would be profitable to generate a reverse movement—that is, marketing-trained people moving into the technical R&D area, as members of planning committees, or in managerial positions, or even in staff roles. The experience of both authors tends to indicate that this latter movement or involvement has a better chance of achieving our suggested objectives than does the Berenson plan (see Figure 2, above).

3. Efforts to increase the contact of the marketing department and the R&D staff via deliberate procedures have been advocated.[18] It would seem highly desirable to have an integration of the marketing research function (and staff) with the R&D function before a new product idea reaches the production stage, with possibly the marketing staff performing the "Test of Marketing Feasibility" at this point.

---

[15] Richard T. Hise, "Have Manufacturing Firms Adopted the Marketing Concept: An Overview," in Haas, *Science, Technology and Marketing*, pp. 3–20.

[16] William P. Dommermuth, "On the Odds of Becoming Company President," *Harvard Business Review*, Vol. 44 (May–June 1966), p. 67.

[17] Berenson, "The R&D Marketing Interface," p. 14.

[18] Ibid.

In conclusion, it can be seen that there is an important and critical interrelationship between marketing and the effort to produce technological innovations. A marketing orientation, properly employed in management decision, could make a major contribution toward improving the efficiency of research efforts and accelerating the adoption and use of technological innovations.

Marketing planning, based on an assessment of market opportunity, is one of the key concepts of the marketing management approach. Sales forecasting furnishes "future information" for planning purposes. A comprehensive sales forecasting program is one of the essential ingredients in an integrated approach to marketing.

---

20. SALES FORECASTING: KEY TO INTEGRATED MANAGEMENT *

William Lazer†

Business organizations are increasingly adopting the marketing management concept. This philosophy of business operation places greater emphasis on marketing planning and forces business executives to design marketing strategies and program marketing effort to achieve realistic and predetermined objectives.

Sales forecasting can aid management greatly in implementing the marketing management approach. It is a basis for developing coordinated and goal-directed systems of marketing action. The sales forecast is one of the vital tools of marketing planning since adequate planning and the effective deployment of marketing resources are based on sales forecasting data.

Sales forecasting promotes and facilitates the proper functioning of the many segments of a firm's total spectrum of business and marketing activities. It influences almost every other prediction of business operations. It is used in establishing budgets and marketing controls. Sales forecasts help determine various limiting conditions for management decisions and programs and are useful tools for coordinating the integral aspects of business

* Reprinted from "Sales Forecasting: Key to Integrated Management," *Business Horizons*, Vol. II, No. 3 (Fall 1959), pp. 61–67.
† Michigan State University.

operations. They provide bases for evaluating the functioning and productivity of various segments of business activity. They can guide marketing and other business action toward the achievement of implicit and explicit objectives.

This article investigates three aspects of sales forecasting as a key to integrated management action: (1) sales forecasting as a component of the marketing planning process, (2) sales forecasting as a focus for integrative planning, and (3) the basic components and procedures of a comprehensive sales forecasting program.

FIGURE 1

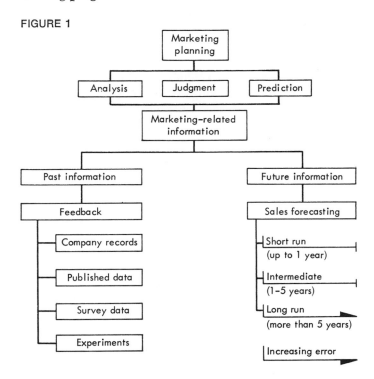

IN MARKETING PLANNING

Figure 1 illustrates the strategic role of sales forecasting in gathering information for marketing planning. Effective planning of marketing activities can be achieved only if adequate marketing-related information is available. Marketing planning is concerned with the application of analysis and judgment to available information and the prediction of likely occurrences and trends during some future period.

Marketing-related information can refer to either the past or the future. Information about past activities is often referred to as factual information. Information about the future is anything but factual, and might be characterized as assumptive. Past information is available to every business if it has an adequate record-keeping process. It is also available from other secondary data sources, such as information reported by governmental bureaus, university research bureaus, and trade associations. Past information may also be assembled through the use of various primary data-gathering research tools, such as surveys and experiments.

Future information requires the utilization of forecasting techniques and processes. Nevertheless, it is based on past data and is usually the result of the application of predictive tools to available past information.

Whenever a business gathers future data, varying degrees of error are bound to exist. Regardless of the forecasting techniques used and the degrees of sophistication achieved, future conditions will always deviate to some degree from the predictions of the forecasters. Thus, management must expect future information to contain some error.

For effective marketing planning, both types of information must be available for executive use. From a planning and decision-making point of view, future, or nonfactual, information may be more significant than information about the past. This becomes clear if one considers that plans and decisions made today are actually based on executive expectations of what will happen during some future period.

If we consider sales forecasting from the point of view of furnishing marketing-related information, we can state that management gathers information as a result of two complementary processes: feedback and sales forecasting. Feedback consists of relating information about past events and relationships back to management. Through the use of such factual data, management can adjust existing operations and plans and thereby improve the effectiveness of all business action.

Sales forecasting furnishes management with information about what market conditions will probably be like during a future period. Management can then use this information as a basis for planning broad company goals and the strategies to achieve them. Sales forecasting data are used in establishing various types of potential volume and profit targets that become the bases for guiding and controlling operations.

Past and future information, however, are constantly blending. A sales forecast, although it furnishes future information, eventually takes the form of feedback information. Once this happens, a comparison may be made between actual and forecast sales for a specific period. Through such an audit, deviations may be noted and explanations sought for them. This information can, in turn, help refine the assumptions about future sales forecasts and increase the total effectiveness of the forecasting procedure.

The various predictions made may take the form of short-run sales forecasts of less than a year, intermediate forecasts of from one to five years, and long-run forecasts for periods of more than five years. Generally, the longer range the predictions, the greater the forecasting error.

IN INTEGRATIVE PLANNING

Another facet of sales forecasting and its role in marketing planning is its position in the integrative planning process. A sales forecast is a useful tool for integrating the external business environment with the internal forces of the company. It reduces to workable management dimensions the external business environment over which management has relatively little control. It delimits those constraints that establish the boundaries within which a company must make decisions and operate and translates them into company programs.

FIGURE 2

Noncontrollable and partially controllable external factors

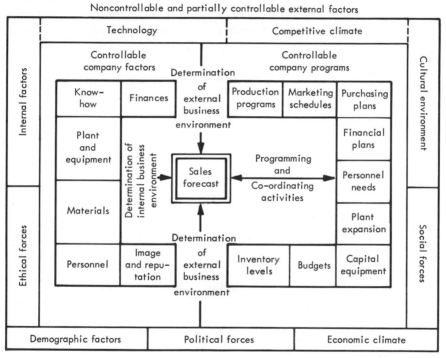

Figure 2 portrays sales forecasting as an aid to integrative planning. It indicates the controllable, partially controllable, and noncontrollable factors that management should integrate and take into account in making effective sales forecasts.

The noncontrollable forces determine the broad environmental limits within which the company will operate. These factors include cultural forces, the economic environment, demographic forces, political factors, ethical and social forces, and various international conditions. They cannot be influenced to any degree by company action; at best, they may be recognized and appraised in an intelligent manner.

In Figure 2, broken lines separate the competitive environment and technological factors from other noncontrollable factors. This is to indicate that management action may have some influence over at least these two external forces, which are considered partially controllable factors. However, even though company action can affect competition and technology, the forces *beyond* company control generally have a more significant impact.

As forecasts become longer run in nature, the necessity of recording the existing external climate becomes more imperative since, in the future, it will be these noncontrollable factors that set the over-all constraints and boundaries within which companies survive and grow or fail. Through an evaluation and projection of external forces, management attempts to make realistic assumptions about the future environment. These assumptions about noncontrollable and partially controllable factors are the foundations of sales forecasts, and intelligent sales predictions can be made only by implicitly or explicitly assuming relationships about these factors.

Management should not consider this initial step of determining the external company environment as merely a theoretical exercise that is of little use in practical sales forecasting. The external variables are factors that must be dealt with practically and realistically. Their influence cannot be ignored.

As an example of the importance of external forces, consider the development of a controlled shopping center. Several years may elapse from the initiation of the original idea and the first inquiry concerning site location until the actual opening of the center. Choices must be made from among alternative sites, and considerable negotiations may follow to obtain the property and construct and finance the center. Then there are a host of operating details to attend to, including the actual leasing of stores.

The profitability of the total investment and the sales realized by retail stores in the shopping center will be affected by external forces. Existing and potential competition, for example, can have great influence on future sales. Demographic and economic forces in the form of population shifts and income trends will shape the retail sales potential of the center. Existing and potential industrial development of the surrounding territory will influence employment and income and will be reflected in marketing opportunity.

Municipal, state, and federal regulations will have an impact on future pricing tactics, on the use of various promotional devices including trading stamps, on store hours, and even on the types of merchandise that may be sold in particular kinds of stores.

Other examples could be presented concerning such industries as wood products, chemicals, mining, petroleum, transportation, the power industry, and communications.

After determining the external business climate for a future period, the sales forecaster must estimate the impact that internal business factors will make on potential markets. This involves an evaluation of those factors over which the company has direct control. They can be adjusted over the longer run by the company itself.

For an effective forecast, the company's know-how, its financial position, the plant capacity, the material resources and personnel available, and the company's reputation, image, and position in the market place must all be evaluated. The market position that a company eventually earns and the sales that it achieves will depend on the impact made by the internal business factors as they are combined into planned management programs carried out within the external business system. A consideration of both climates, external and internal, will give management some guides by which to judge the potential sales opportunity for a company. Through the use of various analyses and by the application of sound judgment, management may map out a company's future sales position.

Thus, sales forecasting helps integrate the management-controllable and management-noncontrollable factors, or the given elements of a total business system within which the company operates and the internal factors of the business itself.

The sales forecast is also a device by means of which management may integrate its objectives, its operating programs, and its targets with potential market opportunity. This can be done by translating the sales forecast into specific profit and sales-volume goals to be realized in a given future period of time. The sales forecast thus becomes a basis for marketing programs, purchasing plans, financial budgets, personnel needs, production schedules, plant and equipment requirements, expansion programs, and perhaps most other aspects of management programming.

The right half of Figure 2 presents sales forecasting as a vehicle for translating the noncontrollable, partially controllable, and internal business environments into specific controllable management programs. The figure also emphasizes the interrelationships between sales forecasts and company programs.

FORECASTING PROGRAM

Figure 3 outlines the elements of a total sales forecasting program. Four major stages of forecasting, the specific procedures to be followed, and their sequence are presented. These stages are: assembling the forecasting information; evaluating and projecting the data; applying the sales forecast operationally; and auditing the forecast. These four steps are broken down further, and some of the techniques that may be utilized at each stage and the results achieved are described. Figure 3 starts with the noncontrollable business environment and internal business climate and works down through the various predictions about controllable business plans, programs, and objectives.

The first step in a comprehensive sales forecasting program is assembling forecasting information. This involves the recognition of noncontrollable and partially controllable environments through observation and listing of significant external factors. The result is the identification of pertinent social, cultural, ethical, economic, political, demographic, international, technological, and competitive forces that will influence the projections.

Next, information can be assembled about these noncontrollable factors and an investigation made of such outside sources of information as governments, industries, and universities.

The third step in assembling forecasting information is that of gathering information about the controllable company environment, which involves research into company records. This should result in the selection of relevant company forecasting information.

After forecasting information has been assembled, the data must be evaluated and projected. This activity has two components: analyzing the data and making the actual forecast. To analyze the data, such analytical tools as time series analysis, least squares methods of fitting a straight line, fitting curves, simple and multiple correlation, the use of input-output tables, and breakeven charts may be used. This leads to the determination of patterns and relationships through lead and lag indicators, cycles, seasonal indexes, trend lines, and measures of covariation.

The actual sales projections may be made through extrapolation, a straight percentage increase in sales, executive opinion polls, end-use analysis, historical analogy, a panel of experts, the grass-roots approach, samples and surveys, models, experiments, hunches, judgments, and the oft-used crystal ball. After these projections have been made, the prediction and definition of future dollar and unit sales, and maximum and minimum sales ranges are possible.

Then the forecast must be applied operationally, which involves refining the sales forecast. This is done by breaking it down on the basis of volume and profit control units by product lines, salesmen, customers, territories, and other managerial units. Specific sales targets can thus be established, and sales forecasting data become the basis for programming marketing, production, purchasing, finance, plant expansion, capital equipment acquisition, personnel, and inventory needs. Controllable business programs have now been really determined.

The last step in a comprehensive sales forecasting program is that of auditing the forecast. This involves reviewing the forecast by comparing actual and forecast sales and analyzing any deviations or discrepancies. The purpose here is to determine the reasons for the deviations. Then future

FIGURE 3

A total sales forecasting program

Stages of process	Techniques	Results
Assembling Information		
Recognize noncontrollable and partially controllable business environment.	Observe and list significant external factors	Identification of pertinent cultural, social, economic, political, demographic, competitive, ethical, international technological forces
Gather information about noncontrollable and partially controllable forces	Investigate outside sources of information	Selection and gathering of data from government, industry, university research, Federal Reserve Board, company records
Gather information about controllable forces.	Investigate company records	Selection of relevant company forecasting information
Evaluating and Projecting Data		
Analyze data	Apply analytical tools: time series analysis, least squares, simple correlation, multiple correlation, input-output tables, breakeven charts	Determination of patterns and relationships: lead and lag indicators, cycles, seasonal indexes, trend lines, covariation
Forecast future sales	Employ extrapolation, constant percentage of increase, end-use analysis, executive opinion, historical analogy, panel of experts, grassroots techniques, surveys, models, experiments, samples, hunches, judgment, and crystal ball	Prediction and definition of future dollar sales, unit sales, maximum and minimum ranges
Operationally Applying Forecast		
Refine sales forecast	Break sales down by volume and profit control units: product lines, territories, customers, salesmen	Establishment of specific sales targets
Translate specific targets into operational programs	Establish and coordinate plans: marketing program, production schedules, purchasing plans, financial requirements, personnel needs, plant expansion, capital equipment budgets, inventory levels	Identification of controllable business environment
Auditing the Forecast		
Review forecast	Compare actual and forecast sales regularly and analyze discrepancies	Determination of reasons for deviations
Modify forecast and forecasting procedures	Re-evaluate projections and adjust forecasting techniques	More accurate sales forecasting

forecasts and even the forecasting techniques can be modified. The end result is more accurate sales forecasts.

The total sales forecasting process is one of refinement. It starts with the more general factors—the external noncontrollable environment and the internal business environment—quantifies them, and finally establishes specific operational goals and targets.

Marketing planning often suffers because management does not develop an effective sales forecasting program. One of the great inducements to ignore or neglect sales forecasting is the difficulty of making predictions. It is a trying task for anyone to try to determine future relationships and their implications for potential sales. It is much more comfortable to turn to the consideration of current operating problems, which are more concrete, are somewhat easier to grasp, and for which some corrective action may be initiated almost immediately.

However, professional marketing management cannot afford to neglect the sales forecasting process. It must become concerned with the development of well coordinated, planned, and forceful systems of business action. It must plan the use of company resources so that a firm can establish itself in the market place and grow.

The future marketing climate is likely to be one of keener competition, an exhilarating pace of market change, heavier fixed costs, and an increasing emphasis on innovation. Adequate marketing planning will become the foundation for integrated marketing action. Since one of the basic components of effective marketing planning is sales forecasting, it seems obvious that in the future an increasing amount of time and resources will be spent by companies in developing more adequate sales forecasts.

C.

Planning and programming market activities

THE PRIMARY purpose of marketing planning is to develop appropriate marketing objectives, strategies, and plans that will enable the firm to take advantage of its market opportunities and to successfully meet its overall goals. Effective marketing plans can be achieved when the technical approaches to information management are integrated with innovative leadership.

Although the past experiences of the firm can serve as a convenient guideline, the planner should not limit himself to the use of historical standards and events. During the last decade, the significant role of statistical and control models in the planning process has been recognized. An understanding and appreciation of these models is imperative for the contemporary planner. However, these tools cannot replace the foresight and creative abilities of the planner.

In the first article, Kelley discusses the broadening scope of marketing planning and its relationship to the entire firm's planning effort. In the second article, Winer describes the key elements in a marketing planning procedure. In the third article, Oxenfeldt describes the necessary steps required to attain a more scientific formulation of marketing strategy.

Effective marketing management is dependent upon sound marketing planning. The marketing plan is the vehicle for the achievement of corporate objectives. This selection describes the broadening scope of marketing planning and discusses the planning concepts of mission, goals, objectives, tactics and strategy.

21. MARKETING PLANNING FOR THE FIRM *

Eugene J. Kelley†

PLANNING: THE BASIS OF MARKETING MANAGEMENT

Planning based on research and design to achieve both customer satisfactions and corporate objectives is basic to the marketing concept. An integrated marketing strategy rests on a management philosophy that is based on planning. Because of its importance and complexity, planning, one of the enterprise functions of marketing management, is discussed in more detail in this section. Planning precedes market action and covers the business tasks that must be carried out before a program is made operational.

The need for financial and production planning has long been recognized in business; formal marketing planning, in the sense of giving systematic attention to careful calculation and coordination of corporate means and marketing ends is a relatively new development. Perhaps the key management concept here is the idea that concrete marketing objectives can be defined and a program of action designed to achieve them. Planning is not a luxury appendage of marketing, but a managerial element that is indispensable for the survival, growth, and profitable operation of the firm.

Any plan involving a change from existing patterns usually encounters substantial resistance. The task of the marketing executive managing change is to recognize the inevitable obstacles, provide ways of overcoming them in his planning, and see that the organization needed to implement the plan is structured to capitalize on the opportunities the plan is designed to meet. This requires drive and persistence from market planners comparable to the drive and persistence required of line executives.

Formal marketing planning is an integrative process which blends cor-

* Reprinted from Eugene J. Kelley, *Marketing Planning and Competitive Strategy* (Englewood Cliffs, N.J.: Prentice-Hall, Inc., 1972), pp. 52–61.
† The Pennsylvania State University.

porate goals and resources with information on opportunities external to the firm. The object of planning is to develop creative and innovative policies to guide corporate efforts in the marketplace. Successful planning involves combining information management and creative leadership to achieve marketing excellence and corporate goals.

Planning as an enterprise function

Marketing planning includes the continuing managerial and technical activities and processes involved in assessing areas of marketing opportunity, determining the marketing mission and goals, developing and coordinating marketing action programs, and evaluating and adjusting all market-related programs. The first two elements of planning are essentially conceptual and analytical; the others are operational.

The enterprise functions of marketing planning are a natural extension and application to the current marketing situation of principles developed in the early history of the field. Henri Fayol, one of the earliest influential management thinkers, divided the field of administration into the elements of forecasting and planning, organization, commanding, coordinating, and controlling. He defined planning as both forecasting and providing a means of examining the future and drawing up a plan of action. A plan of action, according to Fayol, encompasses the goal, the line of action to be followed, the progressive stages, and the methods. He further stated that the plan of action "is a kind of future picture wherein proximate events are outlined with some distinctness, whilst remote events appear progressively less distinct, and it entails the running of a business as foreseen, and provided over a definite period." [1]

Long-range planning

The planning horizon in marketing is constantly being extended. Corporations in the United States are commonly and systematically planning five or more years into the future. In some of the major corporations, there is a trend to look ten and even twenty-five years ahead.

The long-range plan in a company operating under a planning philosophy can be very detailed. A two-inch thick volume that attempts to forecast consumer buying patterns in 1980 serves as one map of the future for General Electric. In 1961 the United States Seel Corporation was estimating how much iron ore it will need in the year 2000. [2]

Effective long-range planning (LRP) requires coordinated planning in all functions and divisions of a firm. Prime consideration must be given to market and customer preference in the planning and decision-making of

---

[1] Henri Fayol, *General and Industrial Management* (New York: Pitman Publishing Corp., 1949), p. 43. (Original published in French, 1909.)
[2] "More Companies Peer into Distant Future, Try to Prepare for It," *Wall Street Journal*, October 25, 1961, p. 1.

all departments that have a potential marketing impact. Because of the competitive necessity for LRP and improvement in the tools of LRP there is every reason to expect that this trend to long-range planning will continue.

In most industries, rapid technological advances have been made in three areas of special interest to marketing planners—data processing euipment, physical distribution concepts and facilities, and communications systems. Increasingly, rigorous competition will force firms to make greater use of integrated automatic processes combining manufacturing, physical distribution, and data processing. This integration may become a minimum basic requirement if a firm is to remain competitive. The magnitude of these changes and the investment required will vary with corporate objectives and skill in scientific long-range planning.

The trend is toward increased acceptance of marketing planning as a fundamental premise of business adjustment to present and future market patterns. As planning becomes a basic management technique and the cornerstone of management philosophy in designing marketing systems, practical methods of linking many market-related decisions and programs will be developed. The firm will be better able to capitalize on areas of market opportunity and profit, thereby achieving corporate goals in the market.

The planning concepts of mission, goals, objectives, and strategy are presented in this chapter. Also considered is the role of innovation in developing a dynamic, action-oriented, environmentally sensitive corporate entity.

SOCIAL SYSTEM ORIENTATION TO BUSINESS PLANNING

During the 1960s many business executives used the marketing concept to help themselves become more responsive to consumers. The current thrust of corporate development is to move beyond the "marketing concept" to a social-system-oriented view of the firm as an integrated technological and marketing system.[3] In the spirit of this total systems approach to business, it is important to recognize business planning as a conscious decision-making network composed of complex and often uncertain information flows. Corporate mission, goals, objectives, and strategy are concepts implicit or explicit in all business decision-making.

These concepts can be differentiated by seeing them in the context of specific planning processes, a number of which have been developed in recent years.[4] Such an approach, however, is situation-specific and premature until a conceptual base applicable to most variations in business planning systems is developed.

---

[3] Eugene J. Kelley, "Marketing Is a New Ball Game," *Sales/Marketing Today*, Vol. 16, No. 4 (1970), pp. 7–10.

[4] For example: Stanford Research Institute, "A Framework for Business Planning," *Business Week*, June 1, 1963, p. 54; Mark E. Stern, *Marketing Planning, A Systems Approach* (New York: McGraw-Hill Book Co., 1966), p. 13; David Luck and Arthur Preil, *Market Strategy* (New York: Appleton-Century-Crofts, 1968), pp. 4–5.

Decisions generated from the assessment of marketing opportunities are blended to form a definition of the corporate mission and to determine current and projected goals of the business. Business objectives, the specific quantifiable ends toward which business activities are directed, are the foundations on which executives establish operational plans. Quantitatively stated objectives outlined in the plans guide specific business activities and programs within each functional business area. Figure 1 illustrates the

FIGURE 1

Planning framework

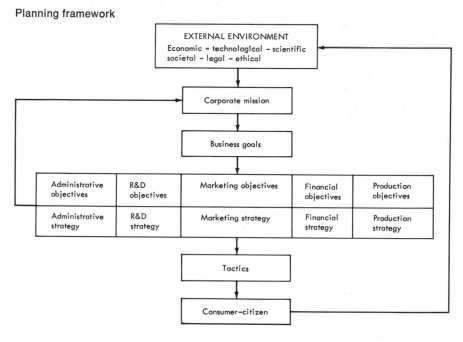

broad planning framework. It indicates that the starting point of a discussion of the planning concept is the external environment in which the firm operates. The environment and changes in it provide the basis for defining and redefining the mission of the firm. Specific business goals are established and various functional objectives and strategies are designed to serve customers profitably.

Mission of the firm

"Who is the company? What is the company?" [5] These questions must be answered not in terms of what the company is going to do, but in terms of

---

[5] Seymour Tilles, "The Manager's Job: A Systems Approach," *Harvard Business Review*, Vol. 41, No. 1 (January–February 1963), p. 75.

what the company is going to be—to stockholders, to management, to customers, to distributors, to competitors, and to the rest of society.[6] These philosophical sounding questions are not nearly as esoteric as one might expect, for the answers to them provide the basis for business planning. They provide the firm with a "corporate mission and self-concept." Social psychologists have used the term "self-concept" to denote a "theory that attempts to explain the conception that the individual has of himself in terms of his interaction with those about him."[7] The basic propositions of the theory of self-concept, which can be adapted to the corporation by environmentally responsive business planners,[8] suggest:

1. The corporate "self-concept" is based on management perception of the way others (society) will respond to the corporation.
2. The corporate "self-concept" will function to direct the behavior of people employed by the company.
3. The actual response of others to the company will in part determine the corporate "self-concept."[9]
4. The "self-concept" is incorporated in statements of "corporate mission" in order for it to be explicitly communicated to individuals inside and outside the company—that is, for it to be actualized.

Historically, the firm has been viewed from an economic perspective. This orientation explains the debates in the 1950s and early 1960s regarding whether profit maximization, optimization, enterprise survival, or some other factor was the "goal/objective" of the company. Whether the term "goal" or "objective" was used proved of little importance at a time when economic guideposts, and profit consideration, were believed to be the major basis of corporate policy. Today a social-environmental perspective is necessary to carry the company to a position of full contribution and growth. The term "corporate mission," with its broader connotations, is used to symbolize this highest level of company self-determination. For the firm, statements of "corporate mission" are essentially a qualitative, broad, basic, lasting, and innovative definition of the company.[10]

Organizational goals

Corporate goals are broad, essentially qualitative, target components of planning. Many beginning business students believe that the basic goal of

---

[6] H. Igor Ansoff, *Corporate Strategy* (New York: McGraw-Hill Book Co., 1965), p. 33.

[7] John W. Kinch, "A Formalized Theory of the Self-Concept," *The American Journal of Sociology*, Vol. 68 (January 1963), pp. 481–86.

[8] From Gilbert Harrell, "Company Mission, Goals, and Objectives" (unpublished manuscript, The Pennsylvania State University, March 1970).

[9] Kinch, *op. cit.*

[10] Theodore Levitt explains "Marketing Myopia" as essentially a failure to properly identify and state "company mission." "Marketing Myopia," *Harvard Business Review*, Vol. 38, No. 4 (August 1960), pp. 45–56.

a business is profit making, and the marketing objective is to maximize sales volume. These are appealing but often dangerous notions; they lead to oversimplified and incorrect analyses of complex business problems. Profits are not so much a business goal as a condition necessary for survival and satisfactory economic performance. Profits reflect the social valuation of the firm's contributions to consumers. Profitability is the rationale of business enterprise, not its goal. Marketing effort is focused on customer service offered in the expectation of earning a profit. Goals, such as service, survival, and growth depend on profitable selling. If this is done effectively, the owners of the firm will receive profits, managers will receive salaries, and employees, wages.

A challenging management task is that of obtaining a balance between short-term profits and long-term profitability. To do this managers must reconcile business goals, the present position and resources of the firm, profit requirements, and potential areas of long-run profit opportunity. Historically, corporate growth goals were achieved by introducing new models or new products to replace or supplement existing products. This has been a pattern of corporate growth throughout American business history. Today, however, the orderly introduction of new models of existing products is usually not enough to secure the growth goals of large firms. The current trend is toward a clear definition of corporate purposes, including plans for supplying a broader spectrum of customer wants and requiring strategies of diversification, acquisitions, and planned growth through serving new markets. The result is a corporate customer- rather than product-orientation.[11] Within this perspective goals are constrained by the corporate mission, but not the reverse.

Some general business goals that interact with corporate mission to form the basis of marketing strategy are:

Survival of the firm or a subfirm organizational unit.
Growth of the firm, division, product line, or product.
Short-term profit of the firm or product.
Long-run profit.
Enlargement of market size.
Maintenance or increase of market share.
Diversification of corporate activity.
Achievement of industry leadership.
Securing a balance between domestic and international business.
Maintaining employment at certain levels in particular plants.
Enhancement of image with various publics.

As this list suggests, the determination of profit and other goals is one of the most difficult conceptual tasks of management, and profit maximization

---

[11] The Marketing Pattern: A Better Way for Business to Grow," *Business Week*, July 14, 1962, p. 60.

is one of several, sometimes conflicting, business goals. This is particularly the case in the multidivisional, multiproduct, multinational business organization. Thus the modern corporation operates with a hierarchy of organizational and personal goals and objectives.

Objectives

Marketing objectives, and indeed any functional level objectives, relate to the firm's business goals, but are also designed to help fulfill its "corporate mission." [12] These objectives should be formulated in quantitative statements specifying what is to be accomplished. They should take into account the internal company situation through an interaction and evaluation of other functional objectives, a true systems perspective. Moreover, they should be analyzed and stated in terms of their relationship to the external environment.

Marketing objectives are statements of the corporate mission as operationalized for a specific time period. They are made specific with regard to market segments and customer needs. Marketing objectives focus corporate wide market related activities. Development of the marketing concept has moved business toward more integrated functional areas.[13]

Determination of strategy and objectives is an important task for individuals as well as corporations. Robert Townsend states that, ". . . money, like prestige, if sought directly, is almost never gained. It must come as a by-product of some worthwhile objective . . . which is sought and achieved for its own sake." [14]

Strategy and tactics

"Strategy," in the broadest sense, is a dynamic, action-oriented blueprint to accomplish "company mission," "business goals," and "functional objectives." Strategy "is the catalyst, the main thread and thrust of the business." [15] Most important, it is the bonding agent that provides the systematic directing force to actualize desired relationships between the firm and the environment. In the more specific contexts used throughout the business community, "strategy" has various shades of meaning, each of which leans toward the description given above but none of which touches it.

The different uses of the term "strategy" by prominent business authors center on how many of the policy-making and activity-directing processes

---

[12] Norton Paley, "Corporate Objective and Marketing Aim: What is the Relationship?" *California Management Review*, Vol. 11, No. 2 (Winter 1968), pp. 59–65.

[13] Robert Ferber, "Marketing Merging into a New Total Business Discipline," *American Marketing Association News*, May 1969, p. 1.

[14] Robert Townsend, *Up the Organization* (New York: Alfred A. Knopf, Inc., 1970), p. 62.

[15] J. Thomas Cannon, *Business Strategy and Policy* (New York: Harcourt Brace Jovanovich, 1968), p. 3.

are included in the definition. One common use of the term is in reference to corporate strategy, which has been defined as "the pattern of objectives, purposes, or goals and major policies and plans for achieving these goals, stated in such a way as to define what business the company is in or is to be in and the kind of company it is or is to be." [16] Such a broad definition could be considered the grand strategy of the business.

Confusion with the concept of strategy usually comes from two planes: (1) the failure to recognize it as a two-level function, and (2) the problem of differentiating it from "tactics." To complete the terminological profile, such a differentiation must be made explicit. "Strategy" is divided into concepts of "grand strategy" and "functional" (i.e., marketing) strategy. "Tactics" are an outcome of "functional strategy."

"Grand strategy" forms an interface with "company mission," "business goals," and "functional objectives." These elements form the result component of grand strategy, which is designed in response to them. Grand strategy is the integrating map that charts the development and use of resources to meet the challenges of fulfilling "corporate mission," "business goals," and "functional objectives."

Functional strategy, a middle management responsibility, grows out of grand strategy and is guided by the functional objectives. At the same time, alternative functional strategies and their probability of success are important inputs in deciding on "functional objectives." The two work as a bivariate subsystem within the larger system. Functional strategy (under the title of strategy) has been the topic of much research. Implicit in it are target components such as sales quotas by market segment and product line, quality control and so forth.[17]

The choice of mission, goals, objectives, and strategy is a simultaneous process involving patterns of information flows. The executive should focus his attention on the company's interaction with its environment, rather than on factors primarily within the corporate framework. To achieve this end strategy designers should have considerable interaction with whatever management personnel set mission, goals, and objectives. In many instances both parties will be part of the same departmental team. Seymour Tilles commented on the difficulties of setting objectives when he wrote:

The general state of the art of setting corporate objectives is an appalling one. By and large, the terms in which managers state their official aspirations are over-simplified deceptions: profit, market share, or return on investment. Each of

---

[16] Liddell Hart, a military strategy expert, provides a foundation for understanding the aberrations. "The role of 'grand strategy'—higher strategy—is to coordinate and direct all the resources of a nation, or band of nations towards the attainment of the political object of war . . . Strategy (conventional) is the art of distributing and applying military means to fulfill the end of policy. . . . Tactics lies in and fills the province of fighting. Strategy not only slaps on the frontier, but has for its purpose the reduction of fighting to the slenderest possible proportions." (Liddell Hart, *Strategy* [New York: Frederick P. Praeger, 1954]), pp. 336–47.

[17] Cannon, *op. cit.*, p. 55.

these indicators still has great appeal to management, despite the extent to which scholars have rejected them as valid bases for performance evaluation. Their appeal lies primarily in the fact that each one sounds simple, since its inherent ambiguities are not obvious; each can be expressed in numbers, and thereby endowed with an aura of objectivity and utility; and each one can be a logical measure of past performance.

The trouble with these criteria is that they entice the general manager to focus his attention where it does not belong: on the company itself, rather than on the relationship between the firm and the broader systems of which it is a part. This is vividly reflected in the design of the information systems. . . . Looking at these systems, one sees a great deal of money and effort devoted to analyzing what went on within the organization itself and very little, if anything, devoted to an analysis of environmental trends. Managers, too, frequently lose sight of the fact that corporate performance is the result of a company interacting with its environment, rather than the result of factors wholly within the company itself.[18]

"Tactics" are the day-to-day use of resources that have already been committed within a strategy. It is no longer a matter of deciding what or how much shall be committed; rather, it is a matter of assigning specific action to be taken, by whom, and when. Tactical planning in marketing directs the efforts of small groups or individuals and indicates the tactics and procedures to be used in a given marketing situation. A salesman may spend hours preparing his tactics for a half-hour sales interview. An advertising copywriter may spend several days on a particular piece of advertising copy. Anyone with management aspirations must first master the principles of tactical planning in his subfunction.

Having discussed corporate mission, goals, objectives, strategy, and tactics, we must ask: What differentiates the outstanding company from the also-rans? The answer is systematic corporate and marketing planning based on an innovative perspective geared to competitive action. The corporate strategic plan is the master plan that provides guidance to all managers about the direction in which the firm wants to go and the position it wants to achieve. This plan sets the boundaries for all other planning. Functional strategy is developed from grand strategy. Marketing strategy is based on corporate marketing objectives (discussed above) and is implemented by a coordinated marketing action program. The ideal marketing strategy would achieve what military strategists refer to as a perfect economy of force. In economic terms, this would be the optimal strategy; that is, all resources of the firm, including personnel, would be utilized so that it would be impossible to improve the efficiency of one part of the operation without decreasing the effectiveness of others. With perfect economy of force the firm would correctly allocate resources, including money, to all marketing elements. But because of the nature of consumption and competition, particularly the uncertain human element, perfect economy of force represents an ideal rather than a practical planning goal.

---

[18] Tilles, *op. cit.*, p. 77.

A sharp division does not necessarily exist in practice between the levels and kinds of planning identified in the foregoing analysis. There is actually an interacting and reciprocal relationship between them, a hierarchy of plans in which corporate strategic planning influences tactical planning, and the results of planned tactical operations influence further corporate planning.

According to the author, few current marketing planning processes follow sound planning principles. Although there are no short-cuts to the development of effective and profitable marketing plans, a sound beginning can be made by following the procedures discussed in this article.

22. ARE YOU REALLY PLANNING YOUR MARKETING? *

Leon Winer †

The biggest problem in marketing planning is the *planning*. Many companies have a marketing "plan," yet few of these plans represent any real planning. To demonstrate this point, five steps will describe practices frequently encountered. These practices were observed through intensive interviews with manufacturing firms and their advertising agencies, and have been reported by executives at meetings and seminars attended by the author.

Step 1: Set the market share objective of your brand by adding to its present market share, depending on how ambitious you are.

Step 2: Project total sales volume, for *all* brands of the products, in dollars, for the following year.

Step 3: Multiply the result of Step 1 by the result of Step 2. (Market share objective × projected total dollar market.) This gives the dollar sales objective for the brand.

Step 4: Subtract from the dollar sales objective: (*a*) total factory cost, (*b*) an allocated portion of the company's fixed marketing costs, and (*c*) desired profit. What is left, if anything, is "planned" marketing expenditure.

* Reprinted from "Are You Really Planning Your Marketing?" *Journal of Marketing*, Vol. 29, No. 1 (January 1965), pp. 1–8.

† IBM Corporation.

Step 5: Compose a "marketing mix" of advertising, marketing research, personal selling, price concessions, public relations, package design, point of sales materials, dealer aids, and so on, that will (*a*) just use up all the marketing funds and (*b*) yield exactly the forecasted sales volume.

These five steps represent the procedures of many companies, yet they are thoroughly unsound, for three reasons:

First, the procedure assumes that an increase in market share is profitable or, for that matter, possible. By definition, not *all* brands of a product can increase their market shares.

Second, this method of marketing planning reverses the cause-and-effect relationship between marketing effort and sales volume. Clearly, the sales volume forecast should depend on the amount of effort expended on marketing, not the other way around.

Third, this method requires the manager to select the "right" marketing mix from among the hundreds, or thousands, of possible marketing mixes. In other words, the manager is given a sales volume objective and a fixed amount of money for marketing, and he is expected to devise the combination of advertising, price reductions, personal selling, marketing research, public relations, point of sale materials, and so on, that will just use up the available money and will attain the sales objective. No human being has the knowledge or the calculating ability to do this, even if it were *theoretically* possible.

If the argument presented above is correct, and widely followed practice is inadequate, what alternatives are available?

To answer this question, a study was made of the marketing planning practices of companies recognized as leaders in this area, and of planning books and articles. The conclusion was that while a certain amount of adaptation is required in each case, a general procedure exists that is applicable to marketing planning. This procedure is presented as a flow model in Figure 1. The discussion of the steps in the model will follow the sequence shown, except that "assigning responsibility for planning" will be discussed last instead of first.

SETTING MARKETING OBJECTIVES

In setting marketing objectives, planners should keep in mind three properties of objectives: (1) multiplicity, the fact that organizations have many objectives; (2) time, objectives need to be set for varying lengths of time; and (3) level, the firm should have many levels of objectives, or a hierarchy of objectives.

Multiplicity

Generally speaking, marketers tend to focus on maximizing next year's profits as being the only proper objective for their efforts. Actually a com-

FIGURE 1

Flow model of a marketing
planning procedure

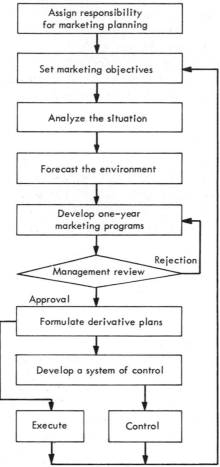

pany may be equally interested in stabilizing profits, or in seeking opportunities for investments for the longer term. Therefore, before doing any marketing planning, it is necessary to explore thoroughly with the company's management what *it* views the company's objectives to be and to derive marketing objectives from those of the company.

Objectives and time

Given the company's objectives, it does not necessarily follow that these can be realized directly. A firm may not be able to capture a larger share of the market, economically, unless it has an improved product. Therefore, in order to attain a more distant objective of increasing its market share, it will set an intermediate objective of developing an improved product.

Since the firm possesses only limited management and financial resources, in setting the objectives described above, it will very probably have to forsake such alternative objectives as entering a foreign market or acquiring a potentially profitable competitor.

Therefore, in setting long-range objectives, and the intermediate objectives that will lead to their attainment, the firm must consider the alternatives it is forsaking, and select those most suitable to its circumstances.

Hierarchy of objectives

Even though a firm sets long-term objectives and determines the appropriate intermediate objectives, that may not be enough. It does not do much good to tell the advertising department that the objective of the company is to increase its rate of return on investment unless this objective is translated into specific strategies. Therefore, it is necessary to develop a hierarchy of objectives.

Development of such a hierarchy of objectives is not a simple task. Careful study is required to make sure that sufficient alternatives are considered at each level and that suitable criteria are discovered for deciding which alternatives are to be selected, or emphasized.

An example, showing how a hierarchy of objectives may be derived through flow-modeling, is shown in Figure 2. This is the case of the business market (offices, factories, stores, hospitals, and so on) of the Interstate Telephone Company (a fictitious name for a real company). At the top of the chart is one of the Company's permanent objectives, that of increasing return on invested capital. A rate of return of 7½% is believed to be attainable. Two possible objectives were derived from this one: (1) increase return, or net profit, and (2) reduce the investment base on which return is computed. The second possibility was not believed to be attainable because of (1) population growth, (2) rapidly growing communication needs, and (3) trend toward mechanization and automation. Therefore, attention was focused on the first.

To increase profits, two objectives may be set, following the reasoning of the Interstate Company: (1) increase billings, or (2) reduce costs. Again, the second objective is unlikely to be attained because one of the important sources of the return on investment problem is the rising cost of labor and materials. (One exception should be noted, however. Costs may be reduced by reducing the rate of disconnections due to customer dissatisfaction, since the cost of installing complex equipment often exceeds installation charges.) This leaves the alternative of increasing billings.

To increase billings, the Interstate Company may (1) try to raise rates and risk reduction in usage, (2) persuade customers to increase usage of existing equipment, or (3) sell additional equipment and services in order

FIGURE 2

Hierarchy of objectives for the Interstate Telephone Company

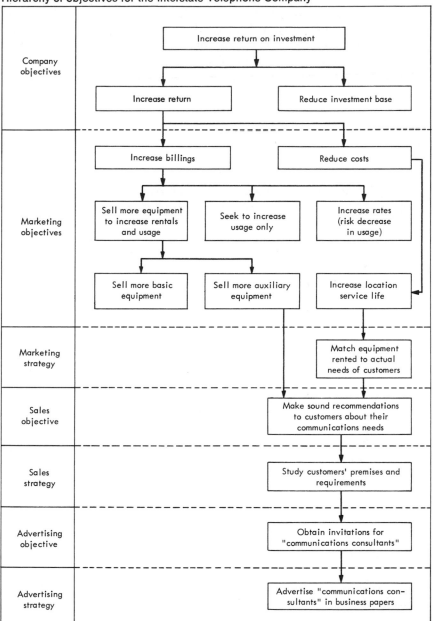

to increase equipment rentals and, to some extent, usage. However, a public service commission will not grant a rate increase unless return on investment is *below* a certain minimum, say 5½%. Then a commission is not likely to grant a raise that will increase return by as much as two percentage points. The next alternative objective, persuading customers to increase usage, has been used as an objective for promotional efforts of the Company. The third objective, that of selling additional equipment and services, has been selected for particular emphasis. In particular, because of the saturation of the business market with respect to basic equipment, the marketing effort has focused on the sale of auxiliary services and equipment, such as "Call Directors," teletype units, modern switchboards, and interior dialing.

To achieve the objective of selling more auxiliary services and equipment, and reducing disconnections due to customer dissatisfaction, the Company needs to match equipment and services to the *needs* of the customers, by making recommendations based on careful study of these needs. To do this, it seeks to persuade customers, through advertising, to invite "Communications Consultants" to survey their communications problems. In this way, by deriving a hierarchy of objectives, Interstate identifies the specific marketing strategies that will lead to attainment of the Company's highest objectives.

ANALYZING THE SITUATION

Once the planner has a well-developed set of objectives, the next step is to begin discovering ways of attaining them. To do this, he has to form some ideas about what *actions* of the firm, under what *environmental conditions,* have brought about the *present* situation. He will then be able to identify courses of action that may be used in the future.

Logan [1] has suggested a four-step procedure for conducting the situation analysis:

Investigation—A wide range of data that may be relevant should be sought, with care being taken to distinguish between facts and opinions.

Classification—The planner sorts the data collected during the investigation.

Generalization—Classes of data are studied to discover relationships. Statistical techniques, such as correlation analysis, are used to determine whether dependable associations exist between types of events. For example, a distributor may find that leased outlets are more profitable than owned outlets to a degree that prevents attributing the differences to chance.

Estimate of the Situation—Causes are sought for the associations discovered in the previous step. The planner now has some ideas about what

---

[1] James P. Logan, "Economic Forecasts, Decision Processes, and Types of Plans" (unpublished doctoral dissertation, Columbia University, 1960), pp. 14–19, 76.

actions under past conditions have resulted in the present situation. In this way he has learned several courses of action that he may follow to achieve his objectives. In the example cited previously, the distributor may find, on searching further, that the higher profitability of leased outlets is caused by the superior location of the leased outlets. In other words, the fact that the outlet was leased was *not* the cause of the higher profitability. Rather *both* the leasing and the higher profitability were caused by a third factor—superior location. (Owners of well-located outlets were not willing to sell them and therefore the distributor had been forced to lease.) Consequently, the appropriate strategy for the future would not be to prefer leasing to owning, but to seek good locations and leasing, if necessary. Inadequate search for causes might have led to very poor results.

Ideally, the situation analysis should cover other firms in the industry, so that the company may benefit from their experiences, both successes and failures.

FORECASTING THE FUTURE ENVIRONMENT

The forecasting problem, from the viewpoint of the planner, is to determine *what* conditions he should forecast and *how* to do it. In this article we will limit ourselves to the first part of the problem because the literature of forecasting techniques is too vast to be reviewed adequately here.

Frey[2] has listed five factors that may affect purchases of a product:

1. Population changes.
2. Improvements in, and new-use discoveries for competing types of products.
3. Improvements in, and new-use discoveries for the company's own type of product.
4. Changed consumer attitudes and habits.
5. Changes in general business conditions.

Howard[3] suggests four criteria for identifying *key* factors:

1. Variability. If a factor is stable over time, there is no need to make a forecast of it.
2. Co-variation. There must be a relationship between changes in the factor and changes in demand.
3. Measurability.
4. Independence. The factor must not be closely related to another factor already considered.

Essentially, this means that the planner has to find out *which* uncontrollable factors, such as personal income, occupation of consumers, educa-

---

[2] Albert W. Frey, *The Effective Marketing Mix: Programming for Optimum Results* (Hanover, N. H.: The Amos Tuck School of Business Administration, 1956), p. 11.

[3] John Howard, *Marketing Management* (Homewood, Ill.: Richard D. Irwin, Inc., 1957), Chap. vi.

tional level, attitudes, affect sales of his brand, and then he has to forecast the future of these factors. Here, as in situation analysis, statistical methods must be used with care, to avoid erroneous conclusions.

DEVELOPING ONE-YEAR MARKETING PROGRAMS

Development of marketing programs requires three steps: (a) formulating alternative courses of action, (b) examining these alternatives, (c) comparing alternatives and selecting the ones to be recommended.

Formulating alternatives

The first step in conceiving alternative courses of action was described in an earlier section on situation analysis. We reviewed a four-step process for discovering factors that had brought about the present situation, and presumably could be manipulated to achieve future objectives.

However, in addition to the cause-and-effect relationships discovered in situation analysis, there is usually room for innovation, or the development of new courses of action.

The importance of the creative process cannot be underestimated, because a plan can only be as good as the best of the alternatives considered. Therefore, it is highly rewarding to spend time evolving alternatives. Unfortunately, there is a strong human tendency to stop the search for alternatives as soon as an apparently acceptable course of action is discovered. This is a tendency that planners must guard against.

Examining alternatives

This step consists of projecting all the outcomes of each alternative course of action evolved above. The outcomes considered should include (1) desirable and undesirable; (2) immediate and long range; (3) tangible and intangible; and (4) certain and only possible.[4]

Clearly, one of the outcomes that must be projected in every case is sales volume and/or profit. In making this projection, errors in both directions are possible. Eldridge discusses the probable consequences of these errors and suggests a solution to the problem.

If (the marketing manager) overestimates his sales volume and gross profit, and bases his marketing expenditures on that overestimate . . . he is likely to find . . . that profits are running well below the forecast. . . .

If he underestimates his volume and gross profit, he runs the risks of spending less than the product needs—and thereby . . . makes certain that the results are less than hoped for.

---

[4] William H. Newman and Charles E. Summer, Jr., *The Process of Management* (Englewood Cliffs, N. J.: Prentice-Hall, Inc., 1961), p. 302.

Nevertheless, it is probably preferable for the marketing manager, when weaving his way perilously between the devil and the deep sea, to err on the side of conservatism in budgeting sales, his marketing expenditures, and his profits. . . .

For himself, his associates, the advertising agency, and the field sales department, it is wholly desirable that objectives should be set on the high side, in order that the attainment of those objectives shall require "reaching. . . ." [5]

In other words, Eldridge suggests "keeping two sets of books." The implications of this suggestion will be discussed subsequently.

Comparing and selecting alternatives

In this step the planner compares the projected outcomes of the various alternative courses of action. The purpose is to rank the alternatives on the basis of the extent to which they achieve objectives and avoid undesirable results. Then the most desirable alternatives are recommended to management.

This point, after programs are prepared, and before they are reviewed by top management, is suitable for writing down the plans.

On the basis of the argument presented here, the written plan should discuss the following topics, if it is to enable management to evaluate it:

1. Specific objective(s) of the plan.
2. Relationship between the specific objective(s) and the objectives of the firm, or an explanation of the extent to which this plan will advance the higher-level and longer term objectives of the firm. Quantitative measures should be included, if possible.
3. Other specific objectives considered, and the planner's opinion of the relative values of these specific objectives. This evaluation should also include quantitative measures, if possible.
4. Costs of executing the plan.
5. Forecasts of the firm's environment.
6. Course of action recommended: first, briefly, then in detail.
7. Alternative courses of action and reasons why they were considered inferior to the action recommended.
8. Projected results of the plan, if it is executed.
9. Listing of control standards and procedures to be used for controlling execution of the plan.

Before leaving this discussion of preparation of programs, an important point should be emphasized:

Marketing planning should not be done function by function, as has been the tradition for a long time and still is the practice in many firms. (By "functions" we mean the activities normally performed by a marketing

---

[5] Clarence E. Eldridge, "Marketing Plans," in E. R. French (ed.), *The Copywriter's Guide* (New York: Harper & Bros., 1958), pp. 3–28, on pp. 24–25.

department, such as advertising, personal selling, pricing, marketing research, and product and package development. *Within* these functions are many sub-functions. For example, within personal selling is recruitment, selection, and training of salesmen; assignment of territories; design of compensation systems; sales analysis, and so on. At least 50 functions and sub-functions could easily be listed.)

Marketing planning should be oriented to achieving objectives. Of course, if objectives may be fulfilled entirely within one function, the objective-directed plan will also be "functional." But the approach, even then, will still be from objectives to means rather from means to objectives.

MANAGEMENT REVIEW

Criteria of reviewing executives may be grouped conveniently as follows: (1) economic, or financial; and (2) subjective.

Economic or financial criteria, such as return on investment, present discounted value of future income, alternative uses of funds, and cut-off rates, are sufficiently well known that they do not require comment here.

Subjective criteria, on the other hand, may require some discussion. Smith[6] has commented on the role of management as follows: "Management may simply accept the goals indicated. . . . More frequently . . . management's reaction will be one expressed by such comment as: 'Surely we can do better than that. . . .'"

In the case of the National Paper Company (a fictitious name for a real firm), during one year, management reduced the recommended marketing expenditures by 23%, *without* reducing the sales volume objective. Other, similar, reviewing actions could be cited. Therefore, it appears that management, in reviewing marketing plans, asks itself: "How much 'fat' does this plan contain?" and answers the question somehow, probably subjectively.

Are **such** reviewing actions justified? In other words, is it fair to the planner to suspect him of "padding" his plan? We have noted earlier the view that: ". . . when it comes to budgeting (setting sales, profit and marketing expenditure goals), the situation is different (from setting objectives for the advertising agency, the sales force, and the like). The forecasts for financial budgeting should be sufficiently conservative that . . . they are certain to be made. . . . "[7] This commentator appears to be suggesting that the planner should overstate consistently the expenditure needed to achieve the goals of the plan. This appears to recognize that a conflict may exist between the objectives of the planner and those of the firm.

The management literature has emphasized repeatedly that differences exist between the objectives of the employee and those of the employing

---

[6] Wendell R. Smith, "A Rational Approach to Marketing Management," in Eugene J. Kelley and William Lazer (eds.), *Managerial Marketing: Perspectives and Viewpoints* (rev. ed.; Homewood, Illinois: Richard D. Irwin, Inc., 1958), p. 154.

[7] Eldridge, "Marketing Plans" in *The Copywriter's Guide*, pp. 3–28, on pp. 24–25.

organization. Therefore, it seems fair to conclude that the planner, in trying to achieve his personal goals of continued employment and approval of his superiors, may undermine organizational objectives such as maximum return on marketing expenditures. Following this, the problem of the reviewing manager would then appear to be not to decide *whether* there is "fat" in the plan, but rather to estimate the percentage.

FORMULATING DERIVATIVE PLANS

Ultimately, at the lowest level in the hierarchy, the result of planning has to be a list of actions, or a program, to be carried out.

For drawing up this program, Newman and Summer[8] suggest six steps:

1. Divide into steps the activities necessary to achieve the objective.
2. Note relations between each of the steps, especially necessary sequences.
3. Decide who is to be responsible for each step.
4. Determine the resources needed for each step.
5. Estimate the time required for each step.
6. Assign definite dates for each part.

In formulating its derivative plans, the Finchley (a fictitious name for a real company) Drug Company, uses the individual plans prepared for each of 50 products. The pertinent information is pulled out of each product plan and reassembled in three derivative plans: (*a*) detailing (personal selling) schedule, (*b*) advertising program, and (*c*) financial summary. These derivative plans are described below:

Detailing Schedule—The Detailing Schedule is structured very much like a calendar. For each month, three products are listed in the order in which they are to be presented to physicians. The schedule serves as a working document for the sales force. As the year passes, 500 copies of each page are made and distributed to Finchley's detail men to be carried out.

Advertising Program—The Advertising Program describes several thousand items of direct mail and journal advertising to be prepared during the course of the year. The items are arranged by month and by day of the month when they are to appear, or to be mailed. As the year progresses, this information is used by technicians and artists in the Advertising Department and the Company's agency to prepare advertisements, buy space and materials, and so on.

Financial Summary—The Financial Summary, unlike the other two documents, is not used by any functional department as a basis for action. Instead, it is essentially a communication and control device. Probably the best way to describe the contents of this document is to list the information presented for *each* actively promoted product:

---

[8] Newman and Summer, *The Process of Management*, p. 302.

1. Total market ($).
2. Company's share (%).
3. Company's sales ($).
4. Advertising expenditure ($).
5. Allocated detailing cost ($).
6. Total marketing cost ($).
7. Marketing cost as a % of sales.
8. Gross profit ($).
9. Gross profit as a % of sales.

This information is presented both for the current year and the following year.

As plans are executed, the Financial Summary is used for comparing actual results with plans, or controlling the execution of the plan. The point is that advertising, sales, and financial plans are derived from objective-directed product marketing plans and *not* prepared independently by the separate functions: Advertising, Sales, and Finance.

DEVELOPING A SYSTEM OF CONTROL

A system of control should (1) establish standards, (2) measure activities and results, (3) compare these measurements to standards, and (4) report variances between measurements and standards.

Control is relevant to planning because control standards have a greater effect in determining actual results than the objectives of the plan. Therefore, it is necessary that the standards which *are* set, reflect very closely the objectives of the plan.

In addition, a system of control informs the planner of the results obtained from execution of his plans. This is helpful because it becomes possible to change plans if they are found to be ineffective either because (1) the cause and effect premise on which they were based turns out to be faulty, or (2) the actual environment is sufficiently different from the forecast environment.

In the first instance, the objectives are still valid, but the method of attaining them needs to be changed. In the second instance, the objective may no longer be appropriate. Therefore, new objectives and strategies may be required, and with them, new courses of action.

ASSIGNING RESPONSIBILITY FOR MARKETING PLANNING

In practice, the management decision of assigning responsibility for marketing planning is the first step performed. In this paper, we have postponed discussion of this topic until the end, because organization of the planning function may depend on the kind of planning to be done. Therefore, it was necessary to describe first the steps in marketing planning.

Writers on the subject of marketing planning organization have described several alternatives:

1. Delegation of planning to functional executives, such as managers of the advertising, sales, pricing, sales promotion, marketing research divisions of the marketing department.
2. Planning done by a planning staff group.
3. Planning done by everyone who has a part to play in marketing the brand, including outside organizations.
4. Planning done by brand, or product managers.

However, criteria are lacking in the literature for selecting the appropriate planning organization.

Leading firms often rely on product managers, or brand managers for planning, although the practice is not universal, and where such managers are used, their responsibilities are not always the same.

To illustrate this point:

1. At the drug company discussed earlier, product managers plan advertising of two kinds, and personal selling.
2. At the household paper products company, brand managers plan consumer advertising and temporary reductions in price charged to retailers and consumers.
3. The telephone company, on the other hand, does not employ product managers. Instead, planning is assigned to sales and advertising executives for their individual functions.

Possibly these differences in planning organization can be attributed to differences in the means used for communicating with the market. The telephone company needs to communicate with business market customers (that is, business firms, government agencies, and so on) on an individual basis. The reason is that no two customers (other than the very smallest) are likely to need exactly the same combination of products and services. Therefore, a centrally conceived, uniform approach, used alone, would not be suitable. The household paper products company and the drug company deal with mass markets where the potential profit made from individual customers is small. This rules out the possibility of tailoring a specialized approach to each customer. In addition, the needs and desires of large numbers of potential and actual customers are relatively similar. Therefore, grouping large numbers of customers into a market for a brand is an economical way of approaching the planning problem.

It follows that the "brand" manager is really a *market* manager, the market being the totality of actual and potential consumers of the brand. We may conclude, therefore, that a brand or product manager has a role to play whenever there is an opportunity to use standardized appeals in communicating with numerous customers.

Nevertheless, not all firms require brand managers, even though they may use mass communication media. For example, the Interstate Telephone Company permits all the advertising planning to be done in its advertising department, and delegates the major part of its sales planning to sales executives. The question arises then: what are the key differences that cause such marked differences in planning organization?

The answer that suggests itself is that there are important differences in the marketing objectives of these firms. Two illustrations can be given.

1. At the paper company, two of the important objectives are increase in market share, and product distribution in certain areas. Programming for these objectives requires crossing of functional lines. Therefore there appears to be a need for a special planning executive.

2. At the telephone company the important marketing objectives are: (1) to increase auxiliary equipment and service billings; and (2) to increase location service life of auxiliary equipment. These objectives are interpreted to require that "communications consultants" survey the operations and premises of business market customers. To achieve this, the company tries to persuade customers to avail themselves of the free services of these consultants. Thus, we have three levels of objectives: (a) persuade the customer to invite the communications consultant, in order to (b) have the communications consultant advise the customer, in order to (c) increase billings and service life.

Achieving objectives (a) and (b), the objectives that can be achieved by direct action—(c) obviously cannot—does not require any coordination among functions. Objective (b) is achieved by the Sales Department, and objective (a), by the Advertising Department.

The conclusion is that the planning organization should mirror the hierarchy of objectives: a planning manager is needed wherever there is an objective whose achievement requires coordination of, or selection from among, several functions. In practice, the existing organization may satisfy this requirement, in which case, no new responsibilities need be assigned. However, if existing planning responsibilities do not allow for this type of selection, or coordination, new ones need to be created.

IMPLICATIONS FOR MARKETING MANAGERS

When a new idea or concept is presented to the business world, its *form* often receives more attention than its *substance*. While attempts are made to adopt the new concept, old habits of thought, and procedures, are continued even though they may not be consistent with the new idea.

The central idea of marketing planning is to develop marketing objectives that will lead to attainment of the objectives of the firm, and then to devise programs and controls that will help to achieve these marketing objectives. In deciding to plan its marketing activities, a business firm has to stand ready to scrap its traditional budgeting and functional planning procedures and to re-think and reorganize its marketing. Only those methods and procedures should be retained that fit logically with the pattern of starting with the highest objectives of the firm and refining successive steps of instrumental objectives until courses of action are specified. Any other approach, or procedure, will give inferior results.

Admittedly, it is much easier to go through the five steps outlined in the first few paragraphs, and say that marketing is being planned, than to follow the procedure described in the body of this paper. However, in this instance, as in most, there are no easy short-cuts to the development of good, effective, and profitable plans. Also, there really is no escape from the need to plan conscientiously. Leading companies *are* planning in this way, with obvious financial success. Those who wish to attain similar success will have to apply themselves equally. Successful procedures will not be developed overnight, or even in one year. Most likely, it will take from three to five cycles of planning to establish an effective, smoothly working procedure. However, nothing will be accomplished if a sincere beginning is not made.

Clearly defined corporate objectives are the starting point of scientific management. Marketing strategy formulation requires translations of the firm's missions and goals into marketing objectives. Once objectives have been set, the scientific method for making marketing decisions can be applied to the development of a market strategy. This article explains what a market strategy consists of and how it can serve as a potent organizing tool for decision-making.

---

23. THE FORMULATION OF A MARKET STRATEGY *

Alfred R. Oxenfeldt †

I. INTRODUCTION

Business management has been called many things: it commonly is described as an art; some describe it as a guessing game. Perhaps the height of wisdom on this subject is contained in the phrase, "business is business," for business is not like anything else. Clearly, success as a busi-

---

* Commissioned contribution.
† Columbia University.

ness executive requires what some people describe as "artistry" and intuition—though these probably are far less vital than just plain luck. In addition, as this paper endeavors to prove, successful business management demands careful and maximum application of the scientific method.

The scientific method obviously needs no defense; only an eccentric will maintain that guesses are more valid bases for decision than careful observation and experimentation. However, the phases of business management that *are* amenable to scientific methods are far from obvious.

II. IS THERE A SCIENCE OF BUSINESS MANAGEMENT?

Little is to be gained by pointing a finger at businessmen for having left managerial decision-making in a relatively primitive state until recently while production men applied the fruits of science to achieve miracles in the factory. The very large number of business failures and high turnover among business executives have been punishment enough. However, the contrast between the methods by which managerial and production decisions are made deserves emphasis, for there exists an influential body of executives—and some academicians—who find the main ingredient of business success to be "good judgment and practice of the managerial art." These phrases are question-begging unless one is able to define what is meant by good judgment and the managerial art. Moreover, such a view deprecates the importance of fact-gathering, rigorous reasoning, hypothesis-testing—and all elements of the scientific method that can be applied to many of the problems faced by businessmen.

It may appear pretentious to link business management with the scientific method. When one speaks of "scientific management" or "scientific marketing" he simply means that business decisions should have the maximum benefit of factual support, close rigorous reasoning, and empirical test; also, that every conclusion reached should be open to challenge and be capable of rational defense. There is no room in this concept for bowing to authority, deference to the intuitions or "experience" of older men or persons associated with the business for a longer time; it requires that decisions be made on the basis of facts and logical argument rather than by appeal to authority.

No one familiar with business dreams that it will become an "exact science" which rests upon a body of proved principles analogous to what has been produced by the chemist and physicist. Everyone knows that duplicatable experiments cannot be the main technique employed for arriving at generalizations applicable to business. The methods available to business executives for solving concrete problems are, at best, relatively crude, unreliable and unproved by the standards of most physical sciences. However, they are vastly more reliable than reliance on hunch, intuitions, feel and guess, or appeal to authority.

The scientific method, or the most scientific techniques applicable to business—however one prefers to express it—is not to be confused with the use of the conference or committee method of decision-making. All too often, these methods are applied in a manner that brings several uninformed people together to pool their thoughts and hammer out a common agreement. A "bull session," no matter by what elegant title it may be dignified, will not produce valuable results unless at least some participants are very well informed. Once maximum use is made of observation and experimentation, discussion will generally prove very valuable; however, it certainly cannot substitute for the collection and analysis of facts.

Practitioners in most fields—especially those who practice for a fee—understandably are anxious to persuade others that their fields of specialization are sciences. Only recently, however, have some persons specializing in business fields claimed to be "applied" scientists. To understand what they claim, one must also know what they disavow. Almost all admit their inability to remotely approach the accuracy, predictability and even objectivity of most physical sciences. But they maintain that there do exist data, methods of data collection, experimental and testing procedures, and methods of analyzing and testing findings whose application to business would greatly increase the proportion of correct managerial decisions. Rather than *great* accuracy in absolute terms, these people claim to be relatively accurate in a field where attempts at systematic and rigorous answers to problems remain exceptional.

III. HOW CAN BUSINESS MANAGEMENT BE MADE MORE SCIENTIFIC?

To make business management into an applied science, executives must first clarify their firm's objectives. Although the selection of *ultimate* business objectives is necessarily unscientific, for they express the fundamental values of individuals who establish broad policy, operating objectives stated fully, clearly, and concretely are indispensable if one is to make managerial decision-making amenable to the scientific method. Once objectives are known, the *selection of means* becomes the task of appraising, by the best means available, the relative effectiveness of alternatives.

A. *Statement of a Firm's Broad Objectives.* Business objectives can be stated on a variety of levels; one must begin with the ultimate—the broadest and most general—and work back to the more narrow and specific ends that they imply. The two most widely expressed ultimate objectives of corporate managements these days are: first, to make maximum profits for the firm over the life of the enterprise and strictly within the limits of the law; and, second, to conduct operations in a manner that gives equal weight to the claims of: stockholders, labor, consumers and government. Both of these broad objectives must be translated into more specific market goals if they are to be very helpful to executives responsible for making concrete business decisions.

B. *Statement of Market Objectives.* In pursuit of maximum profits, for example, management might set its operating objectives at: a maximum of dollar or unit sales; a maximum share of total or of particular geographic markets; maximum profit figured as a percentage of net worth or of sales; it might set itself the objective of a steadily increasing return on sales or profits; or the goal of an increasing market share. But even if narrowed this far, the objectives are not as helpful as they can be made. It is possible to state market objectives in a form that facilitates an application of the scientific method.

Market objectives are best expressed as customer types—narrowly defined—whose patronage the business will try especially to win. (Of course, it will not turn away others desiring to buy.) Once objectives have been refined to this point, management is in a position to formulate more specific problems in a manner that makes it readily amenable to solution by the scientific method.

A determination of the types of customers the firm should try to serve in particular does not flow simply and logically from a firm's ultimate objectives. A careful consideration of alternative markets must underlie the selection of those markets to be cultivated intensively.

IV. CONCEPT OF A "MARKET STRATEGY"

Put differently, use of "scientific" methods for making marketing decisions calls for what is here termed a "market strategy." The main purpose of this paper is to explain what a market strategy consists of and how it can serve as a potent organizing tool for the decisions of business executives. It may well assist students of marketing by giving a central structure to various facets of the study of business.

A market strategy consists of two parts: (1) the definition of market targets—selecting the types of customers whose patronage will be sought; and (2) the "composition of a marketing mix"—picking a combination of sales promotion devices that will be employed. Market targets represent the operating objectives (which are subject to change of course) of top management; the marketing mix represents a combination of instruments by which these objectives are pursued.

The scientific method finds its greatest potential application to marketing by calling for a rigorous appraisal of the relative effectiveness of alternative means of winning the patronage of particular types of potential customers. The scientific marketer must assemble the best evidence available, determine what additional evidence should be gathered, subject all information collected to rigorous analysis, formulate and test hypotheses regarding the effect on unit sales of such things as: price changes, changes in the quality of the product, advertising outlays, number of salesmen, margins offered retailers, number of retail outlets, etc.

It will be acknowledged at the outset that no generalizations about these matters can be applied to all or even to many products. Answers to specific marketing problems probably differ for each individual business—and will not even be stable for it over long periods of time. Thus, top management must reconcile itself to an unending study of the relative effectiveness of sales promotion devices. Management's success in achieving the market targets it sets itself will, it is maintained here, depend upon the scientific rigor with which it conducts this endless study—rather than upon the artistry and intuition of its top executives.

The steps involved in the formulation of a market strategy will be discussed in broad general terms in this paper. First, the determination of market targets will be taken up; thereupon, the composition of a marketing mix will be discussed.

A. *Definition of Market Targets.* No one can hope to please everybody! Persons who attempt to win the friendship of everyone are likely to have few friends, for they will lack individuality and basic personality. Many will doubt their sincerity and almost everyone will get an uneasy feeling in their presence and think that there is something "fishy" about them. Businesses who try to sell to everybody risk a similar fate. If they attempt to convince their prestige conscious customers that their product represents the highest possible quality and the brand that customers buy if they do not have to worry about cost, they may repel potential customers who are extremely concerned about economy. But, if they claim that the product represents both the highest possible quality and the lowest price, they will be believed by almost no one.

No business needs to sell to *all* potential customers. A fraction of the total market is all any firm need hope for—and the Department of Justice frowns on those with more ambitious hopes. It is almost always wise for a management to select consciously the types of customers it will try to win as their firm's main patrons; in so doing, management can mobilize the full resources of the firm to a clearly defined task. To make such a selection, management should first divide the total potential market into its "significant" segments.

Potential customers must be divided into groups that have some significance *from the standpoint of what management can and should do about them.* The most important criteria for segmenting the market for any product are: (1) strength of their need or desire for the product; (2) channels (media, distribution outlets, etc.) through which they can be reached; (3) "appeals" (lines of argument) to which they are responsive; (4) degrees of responsiveness to particular types of sales appeal (that is, their ability to be influenced by price considerations, availability of credit, sales talk of salesmen, etc.); and (5) physical location.

The most significant market segments vary widely from product to product. Customers must be classified according to the many special features of the product in question and of the circumstances under which it is sold. In almost every case, however, there are two types of criteria that should be employed: the first are the features traditionally used by market analysts. These generally can be measured and include such things as: incomes, marital status, size of family, religion, age, size of community, whether or not the product is already owned, the age and condition of the product owned, etc. The second are social and psychological characteristics that almost always are unmeasurable and apply particularly to the product in question. For example, one might divide potential customers of most products into: the self-confident and those who are unsure of themselves; the adventurous and those craving the familiar; the ostentatious and the modest, etc. In addition, particular attitudes are confronted in the marketing of some products but have no bearing upon others. For example, it seems to have been established that the use of instant coffee is associated in the minds of many housewives with neglect of a wife's proper duties. This attitude is not likely to have any bearing upon the sale of women's hats, however.

As already indicated, the criteria by which potential customers are divided should meet two tests: (1) they should reflect differences which indicate or affect the actions that businessmen should take in trying to win their patronage; and (2) they should apply to the particular product in the specific markets in which they are being sold. In classifying potential customers, one should err, if at all, in the direction of dividing them into too many rather than too few groups. Both measurable and unmeasurable characteristics should be combined into one scheme of classification. It is likely that one will end up with many scores of market segments; as stated, the more the better.

Those segments should then be scrutinized carefully to determine: (1) which ones are least adequately served at present; (2) those which the particular firm is best qualified to attract—because of its product, personnel, tradition, reputation, standing in the customer's mind, etc.; and (3) those that management would like to make the core of the business over the future, simply on grounds of personal taste.

By scrutinizing the total potential market broken down into segments possessing significance for action, a management may well find that several parts of the market had gone relatively uncovered. If so, it may profit by cultivating those particular markets, using measures especially effective in winning their patronage.

Management should also select the market segments to cultivate intensively by matching its own resources against what is needed to "sell" particular types of prospective customers. Special qualities about a firm's management, location, past performance, design of product, company tradition, etc., may make it particularly effective in serving certain market segments. To match the firm against market segments involves a realistic appraisal of the firm's strengths and weaknesses and of the factors that influence the purchase of each potential customer group. Often a firm will find itself especially suited to win patronage from particular types of customers—which may also be actively cultivated by some of its competitors. Not infrequently, there is a conflict between market targets that are uncovered and those for which the firm has special talent. A choice must be made, and often it will not be an easy one.

Businessmen are people! They have likes and dislikes that do and should influence their decisions. The most profitable markets may be found in regions which require location in uncomfortable climates or uncongenial social environments. In part, a selection of market segments for intensive cultivation must be influenced by such considerations. However, management cannot long follow its inclinations if they would result in persistent losses.

To summarize what has been said up to this point, a scientific market strategy first requires that a business formulate general and broad objectives. These must then be translated into operating objectives, by specifying the particular market segments the firm will cultivate most intensively.

To make such a decision, which is among the most crucial that management must make, requires an exhaustive division of all potential customers into segments which possess marketing significance—that is, they are best cultivated in different ways. The selection of the particular segments that the firm should cultivate intensively should be made on grounds of the extent to which they are being neglected at present, the special qualifications that the firm possesses to serve them, and the taste of the business owners.

B. *Composition of the Marketing Mix.* Once the firm's market targets have been specified, management faces the task of selecting measures most likely to achieve them. In modern marketing parlance, we must discuss the "marketing mix."

The "marketing mix" is composed of a large battery of devices which might be employed to induce customers to buy a particular product. The same devices are involved whether one is thinking of inducing altogether new buyers to purchase the product or of shifting customers from rival brands to one's own. These devices are here termed "sales promotion devices" and include a wide variety of instruments. It is wise to list separately those which are at the disposal of the manufacturers and those which may be employed by distributors and dealers.

Sales promotion devices that might be used by manufacturers to induce customers to buy their products include such things as: quality of product, special product features, amount of advertising outlays, lines of advertising appeals employed, types of advertising media used, number of personal salesmen employed, quality of salesmen, distributive channels employed, quality of distributors used, number of distributors, location of sales effort (geographically), product guarantees, servicing arrangements, credit and accommodations supplied.

Distributors and dealers might use the following instruments to induce customers to patronize them: price inducements, advertising, number and quality of salesmen, location, air conditioning, location of merchandise departments in the store, breadth of selection offered customers, width of aisles, hours of operation, return privileges, credit accommodation, delivery service, etc.

Even though the foregoing lists of sales promotion devices are far from complete, they are long. And, what is especially significant, managements must make decisions regarding almost every one of them. Either consciously or by default, a management decides whether or not to employ each device and in what form and to what degree.

Although a firm may concentrate on one particular sales promotion device, it almost invariably employs many of them to some degree. Even firms which rely primarily upon the appeal of low price must do some advertising; if they were not to do so, their low price offerings might not be noticed by many customers. Moreover, they are generally compelled to give some assurance of acceptable quality (by guarantees or return privileges). The point urged here is that each firm must employ a combination of sales promotion devices, rather than only one, and that the overriding task of marketing management consists in selecting the optimum combination. The formulation of a combination of sales promotion devices is sometimes described as the "composition of a marketing mix" for an actual firm.

1. The selection of a marketing mix must be made very explicitly in terms of the particular market segments whose patronage is to be sought most intensively.
2. To a considerable degree, the individual sales promotion devices are substitutes for one another. One could spend more on advertising or to hire personal salesmen of higher quality, or to build more quality into the product, etc.
3. Almost every one of the possible sales promotion devices must be employed in some form and to some degree. No single line of appeal for patronage will suffice.
4. In deciding how much to rely upon each sales promotion device, the following general rules should be applied:
   a) Never expend sums for sales promotion unless you anticipate that they will produce enough additional revenue to cover all of the costs incurred to obtain that revenue—including the sales promotion outlay. (One must take account of the effect of a sales promotion outlay on future sales as well as their immediate impact.)
   b) Compare alternative sales promotion devices that might be employed to obtain any specified increase in sales volume and employ that one which involves least cost.

V. CONNECTION BETWEEN "SCIENTIFIC MARKETING" AND MARKET STRATEGY

Executives with responsibility in the marketing area will find maximum opportunity to apply the scientific method if they consciously endeavor to formulate a concrete market strategy. Preferably, this formulation will take a written form, and be quite explicit and detailed. A market strategy combines explicit ends and the means selected to achieve them; the scientific method can be employed to a considerable degree to assess the effectiveness of alternative measures for attaining any given objective.

Specifically, top marketing executives will be entitled to regard themselves as "scientific" if they carry out the following steps:

1. Formulate each problem clearly and sharply, and in a form that lends itself to maximum verification by the use of evidence.
2. Gather available evidence bearing on the problem.
3. Arrange for the collection of additional information that would contribute to a solution to the problem—within the financial means of the firm.
4. Organize and analyze the information gathered in a manner that will shed maximum light on the solution to the original problem.
5. Formulate conclusions suggested by the evidence into hypotheses, each of which implies a potential solution to the original problem.
6. Test the hypotheses to the fullest extent possible.
7. Make a list of alternative solutions to the problem that has been discarded in favor of the one selected.

VI. HISTORICAL ANTECEDENTS OF THE MARKETNG STRATEGY CONCEPT

When a new concept stands by itself, its meaning and significance often are unclear. If contrasted with other views and seen as part of a general progression of ideas, it generally can be understood and appraised rather easily. Accordingly, the notions which preceded the marketing strategy concept will be described very briefly. Historians recording the process of intellectual discovery invariably conclude that thought develops in an orderly, step-by-step method. Whether this view is valid or is the creation of the historians themselves sometimes is unclear. Consequently, the following sketch of the marketing strategy concept's development may not describe how individuals came by their ideas; it does, however, describe the state of thinking at successive points in time.

The marketing strategy concept attempts to organize the factors that determine the sales of individual products. We must therefore seek its antecedents among the writings of men who were interested in explaining or actually influencing the volumes of sales. The earliest probably would be the merchants of ancient times and the early Greek philosophers who occasionally wrote about commercial affairs. Given the modest purposes at hand, this review will pass over the early writings and will start with the "Classical" economists.

Although they doubtless knew that they were oversimplifying the matter, classical economists based their explanations of sales solely on the effect of price. (All other possible influences were held constant and left unexplored.) They offered a simple and monolithic view of the determination of sales that was later incorporated into the demand schedule. In their view, sales varied inversely with price—at any given time and with all other things remaining equal; later economists summarized the relationship between sales and price in the "Law of Demand."

The second stage in the attempts of professional economists to explain the determinants of sales might be dated from the publication of Edward Chamberlin's *Theory of Monopolistic Competition*.[1] It was during this stage that academic economists first took explicit account of nonprice influences on sales. Professor Chamberlin explored the effects of advertising on sales and explained this factor in the traditional manner common to formal economics. Despite the fact that the *Theory of Monopolistic Competition* was written over a quarter of a century ago, many academic discussions of sales still proceed as if price were the overwhelmingly important determinant of sales. Little attention is devoted even now to nonprice influences on sales by economists, although several books have been written by academic economists on the subject of individual nonprice influences on sales.

At this stage, the development of concepts to explain product sales reached a fork in the road. One prong continued the application of traditional techniques to take account of a larger number of influences on sales. An important step in this direction was taken in 1941 when Professor Kenneth Boulding[2] treated sales efforts and costs in the same way that theorists had handled production costs; this theoretical framework contained the implicit analogy between the top marketing executive and the engineer. Economists have not built on this major breakthrough, however. An article by P. J. Verdoorn in 1956[3] represents perhaps the high point of this line of development, which is characterized by the use of geometric tools of analysis.

Further developments along this traditional route are in the hands of persons with a mathematical orientation. The field of operations research known as "programming" handles many sales promotion activities without serious difficulty, because mathematics is vastly more powerful than geometry. Programming of sales activity is not being explored by formal economics but represents the contribution of marketing specialists in the main.

The second fork in the road reached after the writing of the *Theory of Monopolistic Competition* might be termed the checklist approach to the sales problem. It was along this road that the term "marketing mix" was introduced for the first time by Professor Neil Borden in approximately

---

[1] Cambridge, Mass.: Harvard University Press, 1933.

[2] See his *Economic Analysis*, (New York: Harper & Bros., 1941).

[3] See his "Marketing from the Producer's Point of View," *Journal of Marketing*, January 1956.

1953.[4] Writers who have followed this route were concerned with two major factors: first, they sought to itemize the large number of influences upon sales that marketing executives must take into account; second, they were interested in facilitating practical application of the concept to concrete operating problems. Foremost among the writers who adopted this approach were Professors Neil Borden and Albert Frey.[5] The latter attempted to relate the marketing mix concept directly to the development of marketing programs in his publication, which carries the subtitle, "Programming for Optimum Results."

With the development of the checklist approach, the enormity of the problem confronting the top marketing executive became apparent. The task of balancing a very large number of variables (even if one ignores their interdependence) clearly is huge. Paucity of evidence about the productivity of individual sales promotion devices, and the difference between present and future markets, inevitably makes the task of the chief marketing executive overwhelming, if not impossible. The inability to set down a workable method of composing a marketing mix is not a failing of the concept itself; the concept *does* describe what the top marketing executive should attempt to do. It certainly represents a substantial improvement over earlier views that took explicit account of only a few factors influencing sales. The complexity of the sales function is real and not a figment of the imagination of the concept builders.

Doctrine discussing determinants of sales had reached this state when the concept of marketing strategy was first set down in 1957. This concept differs from earlier thought on the subject by relating customer targets directly to the marketing mix. (It may be regarded as another step down the road from the checklist approach to the sales problem.) It emphasizes that an effective marketing mix requires top management to be explicit about the kinds of customers to whom the business is trying to sell because specific sales promotion devices that appeal to some customers will bore others and even repel some.

The addition of customer targets to the concept of the marketing mix partly overcomes the difficulties in implementing the concept caused by a lack of information. When a marketing specialist is explicit about his target customers and informs himself thoroughly about their needs, desires, perceptions, habits, attitudes, assumptions, economic situation, etc., he can guess more confidently about the productivity of different sales promotion devices than if he thinks in terms of so unrealistic an abstraction as "the average customer."

The marketing strategy concept also directed attention to a major omission in the thinking of many business executives. When the marketing

---

[4] Professor Borden first introduced the concept in his presidential address to the American Marketing Association in 1953.

[5] Professor Frey dealt with the subject in a pamphlet entitled, *The Effective Marketing Mix*, and published by the Amos Tuck School of Business Administration in 1956.

strategy concept was reduced to writing, even as today, the greatest marketing errors resulted from the failure of sellers to be explicit and selective about customer targets.

The concept of marketing strategy certainly does not represent the pinnacle of thought about the determinants of sales. It is intended primarily for businessmen who must make operating decisions — rather than for mathematicians or econometricians. Superior methods of formulating the sales problem are certain to be developed. Nevertheless, this view of sales determination may explain the sales and marketing function more clearly and suggest how to deal with it more effectively than did earlier views.

d.

Marketing organization and leadership

EACH FIRM is a complex social system comprised of personal and corporate goals, values, structure, communication patterns, and management styles. Within this complex system, the marketing planner must implement and translate proposed marketing action programs. Success in reaching targeted goals depends on full cooperation from other members of the organization. This is the essence of an effective organization.

The major requirement for effective organization and leadership within a firm is the recognition and handling of specific traditions and established relationships. The marketing planner has to "market" his ideas to the organization. He must often ignore traditional patterns in order to accomplish what he thinks is best. To do this, he must know and understand the executive behavior system within the organization. To achieve planned targets, organizational attitudes which may block effective marketing planning must be overcome. Furthermore, a total system commitment to the plan is required. Without supportive attitudes and system commitment, organizational goals and plans cannot be achieved.

Buzzell, in the first article, explores the trends of the 1970s and their effects on the marketing organization. Douglas discusses the relationship between McGregor's Theory Y and the marketing concept and related implications for marketing. Thorelli, in the last article, presents a model of a transacting ecosystem to aid in the development of a total marketing system.

Contemporary changes will demand different approaches to marketing. The trends toward bigness, greater diversifica-

tion, international expansion, and increasing environmental pressures will have an impact on the marketing organization and its methods. The following article explores the meaning of these trends for marketing managers.

---

24. WHAT'S AHEAD FOR MARKETING MANAGERS? *

Robert D. Buzzell †

How will the problems and practices of marketing managers change during the 1970s? The only certain prediction is that there *will* be change, reflecting shifts in industry and company structures and in the social and economic environments within which marketing executives must function. I shall first look at these two areas and then discuss several trends and their likely effects on the practice of marketing management in the next decade.

INDUSTRY AND COMPANY STRUCTURES

The economies of the United States, Canada, and Western Europe will increasingly be dominated by large, highly diversified, multinational corporations operating at all levels of manufacturing and distribution. The marketing problems of these corporations will differ from those of traditional companies that operate on a more limited scale within a narrower range of products, markets, and production stages.

Marketing executives will thus be faced with new challenges and pressures within their industry and company structures, resulting from increasing corporate size, greater diversification, and expanded internationalism.

Increasing size

The continuing trend toward bigness in American industry has been measured, discussed, lauded, and lamented since the depression-ridden 1930s. The only constant factor in the controversy over increasing dominance of large corporations has been the trend toward bigness itself, which has continued unabated.

Statistics can be cited to show the increased importance of large firms in the American economy. For example, by 1966 the companies included in the *"Fortune* 500"—the 500 largest U.S. industrial firms—accounted for

---

* Reprinted from "What's Ahead for Marketing Managers," *Journal of Marketing*, Vol. 34, No. 1 (January 1970), pp. 3–6.

† Harvard University.

almost two-thirds of our total national employment.[1] These firms employed 9.3 million persons in 1961, for an average of 18,500 each. By 1966, employment had increased 40% to 13.1 million, and the average per company had grown to 26,150 employees.

The relationship between the nature of marketing management and company size is not well enough understood. It is clear, however, that increasing size does bring new problems and calls for new approaches. It seems virtually certain that many companies will enter new stages of their growth cycles during the 1970s, and will have to reconsider established marketing methods.

Greater diversification

Both a cause and an effect of greater size is the continuing diversification of products and services within large corporations. The so-called "pure conglomerates" represent, perhaps, a special case. But even in more traditional firms such as Armour, General Mills, and R. J. Reynolds, the extent of product and service diversification has increased markedly during the 1960s and will probably continue to do so in the next decade.

A good example of the diversification trend is Beatrice Foods. Traditionally a dairy products producer, this firm acquired 100 other companies between the mid-1950s and the mid-1960s. It presently distributes a wide range of industrial and consumer products including camping trailers, lubricants, and barbecue grills, as well as its many kinds of food products.[2]

Diversification is also changing the retailing landscape, and major companies which once specialized in food or general merchandise distribution seem likely to evolve into "retail conglomerates." These distributors are also increasingly involved in control or ownership of manufacturing facilities. Thus the once sharply drawn distinction between "manufacturer marketing" and "distributor marketing," is becoming less and less meaningful.

International expansion

Increasing emphasis on international marketing activities is, in effect, another kind of "diversification." Throughout the 1950s and 1960s, companies based in North America have dramatically increased their foreign operations by establishing subsidiaries, building plants, and by undertaking more aggressive marketing efforts, especially in Western Europe. For some companies, sales and profits in foreign markets now exceed those earned domestically.

---

[1] *The Fortune Directory* (New York: Time, Inc., August 1962, October 1966, and June 1968).

[2] "Beatrice Foods Savors a Zestier Cupboard," *Business Week*, December 16, 1967, pp. 122, 126, and 128.

During the 1970s, expansion of international operations will probably continue at a somewhat lower rate of increase than in the preceding decade. More important, management approaches to foreign markets will mature. U. S. companies, particularly, have often regarded overseas markets as a strange kind of novelty, and some have committed egregious blunders through their marketing policies. Like tourists who have already visited Paris several times, they will now start to feel and display a greater savoir faire.

ENVIRONMENTAL PRESSURES

As industry and company structures change during the 1970s, managers will also be faced with new pressures from the social and economic environments. . . . I shall briefly mention three kinds of environmental changes that are of great importance to marketing organization and management.

First, technological change will almost certainly continue at a rate equal to or greater than that of the period 1950 to 1969. In many areas, new combinations of previously unrelated materials and processes will be developed. Traditional boundaries between areas of technology will become less meaningful.

Second, there will be an acute shortage of qualified managers. Simple projection of population figures in different age groups indicates that in 1975 there will be a decrease in the absolute number of men between 30 and 45 years of age of about 7% from the 1965 figure. The decline will obviously be much greater in relation to the increasing scale of business activity.

Third, there will be continued improvement in computer efficiency and in the quality of computer-based models and systems. To date, progress in the latter area has been discouragingly slow, but some basic problems have been solved, and a good foundation has been laid for future development.

EFFECTS ON MARKETING

The following predictions of the effects of structural and environmental challenges and pressures on marketing management and organization in the 1970s cover only several of what seem the most likely trends. These trends are based on conditions and changes evident in the late 1960s. Although the list is surely incomplete and probably somewhat conservative, perhaps at least it will stimulate discussion and encourage the flexibility of thinking which is the only real means of dealing with change.

1. *The trend toward decentralization of authority within large firms will continue, and probably accelerate.*

With occasional interruptions, this trend has been going on since the late 1940s. It is a direct consequence of increasing company size and diversity.

A substantial number of companies will discover what Du Pont, General Electric, and others already know: that top managers of large, diversified firms simply cannot acquire sufficient knowledge or maintain enough contact to participate effectively in all major decisions, for all products and markets. A good example is the Pillsbury Company, which has been decentralizing its management structure since the mid-1960s. In 1969, Pillsbury designated each of its product divisions as a separate "company," reflecting the substantial autonomy granted division managers.

During the 1950s and 1960s, the primary basis for decentralization has been products; product divisions, product groups, and product managers have all gained in importance. In the next decade, more emphasis is expected to be placed on markets as a basis for company organization. Ames has noted that differences in the needs, buying practices, locations, and other attributes of industries and other customer groupings are often more significant than those among a company's products.[3] This is likely to become true in more and more cases, particularly where changes in technology obscure traditional product boundaries.

The values and limitations of the "market manager" form of organization are not yet well understood. Although they will be discovered primarily by trial and error, more intensive studies of the companies that have already tried this approach will also isolate the issues involved.

2. *A critical shortage of qualified marketing management talent will develop.*

Indeed, many executives feel that such a crisis already exists. The decline in males aged 35 to 49, coupled with the demands created by newer types of company activities—such as urban development—will surely create a "talent squeeze" for most or all of the traditional management fields.

Beyond this, marketing may have special problems attracting the more competent younger men, because marketing careers seem inconsistent with the social goals and ideals advocated by the "Protest Generation." (To be sure, the most vocal critics of business are today's college students, who will not be 35 until after 1980. The substance of their ideas also has a powerful effect on their older brothers and sisters.)

How can business alleviate the shortage of marketing managers? Improved and accelerated management development is one obvious answer. Massive amounts are already being spent on university programs, short courses, and other educational efforts. Yet very little is known about what kinds of results can be achieved by various kinds of programs under different conditions. There is a clear need for research in this area.

Another avenue for expanding the supply of younger executives may be greater utilization of women. Already, of course, many women are engaged in marketing jobs, notably in advertising and retailing. During the 1970s, manufacturers and consulting firms may also give greater consideration to female candidates than in the past.

3. *Top-level management will rely increasingly on formal corporate planning systems.*

---

[3] Charles B. Ames, "Payoff from Product Management," *Harvard Business Review*, Vol. 41 (November–December 1963), pp. 141–52.

Formal planning systems, usually computer-based, are used most extensively by large, diversified, multinational firms, such as General Electric, IBM, and the major oil companies. Utilization of formal planning, including quantitative estimation and measurement of key marketing variables and results, is not a substitute for decentralized management. Rather, it is a logical corollary.

As such, top management delegates wide-ranging authority to division, product, and market managers; however, it must retain control over the goals of each unit, and must have some means of measuring performance. The more diverse and scattered a company's operations, the less headquarter's executives can rely on personal experience and direct contact—and the more it is forced to employ formal systems.

The development and use of formal planning systems may alter traditional approaches to marketing management. For one thing, most of these systems are designed to enable decision makers to estimate the "total effects" of an action. Traditionally, many marketing decisions have been made on the basis of "direct effects"—for example, sales force programs are appraised in terms of predicted or actual sales volume and selling costs, without full and explicit consideration of manufacturing costs, physical distribution costs, employment effects, and so on.

During the next decade, more and more firms will try to implement what is termed the total system viewpoint, and some will become reasonably skilled in doing so. It is not clear how this will affect traditional marketing practices, but it seems likely that changes will occur.

4. *Some companies will have to modify their selling methods to meet the needs of large, diversified, multinational customers, both manufacturers and distributors.*

The increasing size and diversity of both marketers and customer firms will greatly aggravate problems of duplication in sales contacts and intracompany competition. Often the various product divisions of large diversified firms have separate sales forces calling on the same customers. As these divisions themselves diversify their product lines, they become more and more competitive with each other. During the 1970s, corporate executives in many firms will be confronted with the problem of balancing economy and coordination of sales activities with the advantages of specialization and divisional autonomy.

At the same time, there is increasing interest among industrial buyers in "procurement systems" in which individual products and transactions are related to a broader context of supply needs and costs. Some companies have recently modified their organizational structures in order to offer coordinated "packages" of goods and services to system-minded customers. Others can be expected to follow suit in the decade to come.

5. *There will be extensive experimentation in the definition of a proper role for corporate marketing units.*

Among large, diversified companies there appears to be considerable uncertainty about the nature and extent of authority that should be assigned to corporate marketing executives in relation to divisions or other "operating" units. For example, among 76 divisionalized companies covered by a National Industrial Conference Board study, 24 had *no* marketing units whatsoever at the corporate level and 12 had only small, specialized staff units. In the other 40 companies the functions of corporate marketing ranged from more extensive staff activities to direct line authority.[4]

Some of this variation is no doubt natural and proper, but the comments of executives in some companies reflect feelings of uncertainty about the role of corporate marketing. Should it be an internal consulting group? A firefighting squad? A training school? A watchdog, advising top corporate management? Whatever its role, what methods should be employed to achieve it?

During the 1970s, various approaches to corporate marketing coordination will be tried. This trial-and-error process might be facilitated by careful study of the experiences of selected companies which have already tested different organizational arrangements.

The relationship between McGregor's Theory Y, concerned with human resources management, and the marketing concept are explored, and some implications of the relationships are examined. The underlying theme of both the marketing and Theory Y concepts is dependence upon participation and cooperation of subordinate units. Both theories need to be extended to their broader ramifications before widespread acceptance occurs.

---

25. A COMPARISON OF MANAGEMENT THEORY Y WITH THE MARKETING CONCEPT *

John Douglas †

One of the most important problems faced by men in all professions is that of "keeping up." For the executive, this means reading in a multi-

---

[4] Harold Steiglitz and Allen R. Janger, *Top Management Organization in Divisionalized Companies* (National Industrial Conference Board, Studies in Personnel Policy No. 195 [New York, 1965]).

* Reprinted from "A Comparison of Management Theory Y with the Marketing Concept," *Quarterly Review of Economics and Business*, Vol. IV, No. 3 (October 1964), pp. 21–32.

† University of Kentucky.

tude of areas. Wendell Willkie's One World concept has descended upon business. As interrelationships and interdependencies appear, the scope of the businessman's "specialty" broadens. To keep up in his reading, the executive must not only read but also develop the criteria for sifting through the volume of materials.

The acquisition of an up-to-date posture is difficult at best. So time-consuming can this be that the most important questions rarely are formed. How does this report relate to the one read last week? What implications do the new empirical research findings pose for the future? How valid are the assumptions underlying the newer theories?

This article represents an attempt to gain this broader vision. In an effort to approach current business topics in such a manner, this writer focuses upon two recent major developments in business—the newer management and marketing theories. The following paragraphs contain a discussion of these theories organized around four basic questions. What are the management and marketing theories that are receiving attention in current literature? What are the similarities of these theories that suggest a more basic trend or characteristic? How is this basic trend identified? What are the implications of this trend for marketing and management operations and therefore for society? Starting with the first question, then, the following discussion will attempt to relate these theories and to present possible implications.

THE CONTEMPORARY THEORIES

The new management theory

In 1960, Douglas McGregor of the Massachusetts Institute of Technology presented in book form some ideas that represented the more advanced management thought of the time.[1] In particular, Professor McGregor emphasized the management thought that related to the managing of the human resources of the firm—a topic appearing in more and more academic and professional journals[2] and one which gains international attention daily. In McGregor's words,

This volume is an attempt to substantiate the thesis that the human side of enterprise is "all of a piece"—that the theoretical assumptions management holds about controlling its human resources determine the whole character of the enterprise. They determine also the quality of its successive generations of management.[3]

---

[1] Douglas McGregor, *The Human Side of Enterprise* (New York: McGraw-Hill Book Co., 1960).

[2] See, for example, David W. Belcher, "Toward a Behavioral Science Theory of Wages," *Journal of the Academy of Management*, Vol. 5, No. 5 (August 1962), pp. 102–17; Perry Bliss, *Marketing and the Behavioral Sciences* (Boston: Allyn & Bacon, Inc., 1963); Rensis Likert, *New Patterns of Management* (New York: McGraw-Hill Book Co., 1961).

[3] McGregor, *The Human Side of Enterprise*, pp. vi–vii.

In his book McGregor stated that every managerial act rests on theory and that theory and practice are inseparable; thus, he suggested that the assumptions about human nature and human behavior (and so also the statements underlying managerial decisions and thus theory) should be clearly delineated and expressed. In short, McGregor contended that the traditional management practice (Theory X) should give way to a more contemporary Theory Y.[4] He built his case by analyzing the basic assumptions of both the traditional and the "called for." A brief summary of the major points will provide a common reference point.

THEORY X ASSUMPTIONS

The assumptions about human behavior are

1. The average human being has an inherent dislike of work and will avoid it if he can.
2. Because of this human characteristic of dislike of work, most people must be coerced, controlled, directed, threatened with punishment to get them to put forth adequate effort toward the achievement of organizational objectives.
3. The average human being prefers to be directed, wishes to avoid responsibility, has relatively little ambition, wants security above all.[5]

With these assumptions as a base, McGregor held that traditional methods actually stress direction and control of subordinates since the direction and control of operations includes people as well as things. Although this pattern seems to have expressed the management practice of past years, McGregor contended that these practices should change because the basic assumptions of Theory X are in error and also are lacking in validity.

This is a brief summary of some of the characteristics of the traditional theory of management; a review of what McGregor hoped would replace it will follow.

Theory Y assumptions and practice

The more appropriate assumptions about man should be

1. The expenditure of physical and mental effort in work is as natural as play or rest.
2. External control and the threat of punishment are not the only means for bringing about effort toward organizational objectives. Man will exercise self-direction and self-control in the service of objectives to which he is committed.

---

[4] When McGregor uses the term "theory" he means certain managerial assumptions about the behavior of subordinates.

[5] McGregor, *The Human Side of Enterprise*, pp. 33–34.

3. Commitment to objectives is a function of the rewards associated with their achievement.
4. The average human being learns, under proper conditions, not only to accept but to seek responsibility.
5. The capacity to exercise a relatively high degree of imagination, ingenuity, and creativity in the solution of organizational problems is widely, not narrowly, distributed in the population.
6. Under the conditions of modern industrial life, the intellectual potentialities of the average human being are only partially utilized.[6]

The central principle which derives from these assumptions is that conditions should be created to encourage subordinates to achieve their own goals best by working for the success of the enterprise.

In summary, McGregor believed that the traditional management practice is based upon assumptions about human nature which are the *consequences* of a management practice using organizational concepts derived from early military and church organizations—authority through direction and control. If management were to change its practices, the proponents of Theory Y say, the truer nature of man would be revealed. This position, of course, gains support from psychology and sociology research. The manager under Theory Y would create positive conditions or a climate wherein the subordinate would see that fulfilling the needs of the organization would in turn enable him to fulfill his own personal needs. The subordinate, therefore, would become much more involved in the matters that affect his work behavior. He would plan, organize, direct, and maintain self-control over work that was his responsibility.

This review presents only the highlights of the newer management theory presented by Douglas McGregor—a theory finding widespread acclaim, acceptance, and expression in other articles, in executive development courses, and in graduate and undergraduate curricula.

Now, let us turn to the development of another new theory—one representing changing thought in the marketing field. At the moment, there should be no attempt by the reader to compare the new marketing concept with Theory Y; this discussion will occur later in the article.

The new marketing concept

This new theory sounds almost naïve in its simplicity; that is, all marketing activity should start with the consumer. While the consumer has always been important, he has not always been the key figure in the design and manufacture of the product. In past years, the problems of reducing cost and increasing efficiency have required the major efforts of the corporation; however, a new focal point is being discussed. No longer can the engineer demand the most attention. The important man on the emerging scene is now the consumer.

---

[6] Ibid., pp. 47–48.

In some instances, men have expressed the newer concept as part of an evolutionary process.[7]

The function of marketing is still growing within the corporate organization, and it will continue to grow for some time to come. Business has come a long way since the day when most corporations were production-oriented manufacturing companies. The swing to the customer-minded philosophy has brought the marketing-oriented manufacturing company into full bloom today.[8]

But not all the experts hold the newer marketing theory to be a natural evolutionary outgrowth. Much more urgency and change is expressed by such persons as Robert J. Keith. In his article, "The Marketing Revolution,"[9] Mr. Keith likens the relationship between the new marketing concept and the traditional one to the revolution in science created by Nicolaus Copernicus. "The market is the center of the economic universe as the sun is the center of our universe." A similar picture is expressed by Fred J. Borch, new president of the General Electric Company. "Under marketing, the customer becomes the fulcrum, the pivot point about which the business moves in operating for the balanced best interests of all concerned."[10]

The operating idea in the last statement quoted is supported by those persons who look at the marketing concept in terms of the decision process of the corporation. Peter Drucker, long associated with dealing with the managerial problems of firms, suggests that even (perhaps he meant to say *especially*) the corporate officers should view marketing as the starting place for policy, for criteria in decision-making, and for the testing of corporate effectiveness.[11] Professors Lazo and Corbin go so far as to say that the new marketing concept means that all business decisions (whether made by marketing personnel, engineers, research and development workers, or financiers) should be made with the market in mind; the decision should be viewed in terms of the impact upon the market.[12] And finally, A. P. Felton has stated that the marketing concept is

---

[7] The evolutionary character of the concept found expression in a recent article "AMA Beats the Drum for Innovation," *Business Week*, No. 1764 (June 22, 1963), pp. 88–91. The retiring president of the American Marketing Association, Donald R. Longman, said, "It's not a revolution, but a rapid evolution."

[8] "Transition to a Marketing Company," *Sales Management*, Vol. 87, No. 2 (July 21, 1961), pp. 36–38 and 102.

[9] Robert J. Keith, "The Marketing Revolution," reprinted from the *Journal of Marketing*, Vol. 24, No. 3 (January 1960), pp. 35–38, in Parker M. Holmes, Ralph E. Brownlee, and Robert Bartels (eds.), *Readings in Marketing* (Columbus: Charles E. Merrill Publishing Co., 1963), pp. 65–70.

[10] Fred J. Borch, "The Marketing Philosophy as a Way of Business Life," in *The Marketing Concept: Its Meaning to Management* (Marketing Series, No. 99 [New York: American Management Association, 1957]), p. 4.

[11] Peter Drucker, *The Practice of Management* (New York: Harper & Bros., 1954), pp. 37–41.

[12] Hector Lazo and Arnold Corbin, *Management in Marketing* (New York: McGraw-Hill Book Co., 1961). These authors also mention that some persons believed it was not the early efforts of educators like Paul Converse, J. F. Pyle, and R. S. Vaile nor the efforts by Ralph Cordiner at General Electric to act on marketing matters that ushered in the marketing concept. Rather, it may have been "the graduated taxes, high wages, and inflation which followed in the wake of World War II which finally made management focus its attention on the importance of marketing" (p. 9).

A corporate state of mind that insists on the integration and coordination of all the marketing functions which, in turn, are melded with all other corporate functions, for the basic objectives of producing maximum long-range corporate profits.[13]

Thus, the marketing concept has been viewed from a number of different bases: an evolutionary concept, a revolutionary concept, an integrating concept, and others. Common to all views is this important thought: while the movement toward the new theory or concept will be a function of the type of industry, the character and vision of top management, the nature of the product, and other factors, the movement is inevitable. Marketing in its many ramifications must start with the customer.

The preceding paragraphs have served the purpose of answering the first question: What are the contemporary management and marketing theories that represent newer trends of thought? With this material as a framework, we are now ready to ask, What are the similarities of these theories that suggest a more basic trend or movement?

SIMILARITIES OF THE NEW THEORIES

Timing

Perhaps it was not unusual that the new management theory and the new marketing concept came on the scene about the same time. The fields of management and marketing almost by definition tend to overlap each other in both day-to-day operations and longer-range policy matters. Because the marketing activity of a firm must be managed, the management concepts relate to all processes of marketing. Similarly, the higher levels of management (divisional level and up) must be concerned with marketing matters—products, prices, markets, competition, and so on. This relationship probably explains the emergence of the two new ideas at approximately the same time—the early fifties.

Heralds of new truth

Both theories have received so much attention and acclaim that the outsider might feel that major breakthroughs had been accomplished and that the search for truth had ended. Theory X represented the traditional management thought and although no analogy has been made to the coin, there is the feeling that the other side of Theory X is Theory Y. Theory Y is presented as *the* theory for the management of human resources.

Often the new marketing concept, too, is presented as an absolute or ultimate law: ". . . once the importance of marketing has been accepted *as a matter of survival*, the company creed itself will undergo vital

---

[13] Arthur P. Felton, "Making the Marketing Concept Work," *Harvard Business Review*, Vol. 37, No. 4 (July–August 1959), p. 55.

changes. . . ."[14] A business executive of General Electric has said that the reason many older business firms had been successful was that "their businesses were customer-oriented because they knew that this was the only way to run a business!"[15] As a final example of the critical nature of the concept, J. W. Keener believes that "the marketing-oriented organizations will be the winners in the exciting, risk-filled, and opportunity-filled decade ahead."[16]

Both these concepts, therefore, represent advanced stages in the respective fields. Both also are described as major changes in emphasis and direction incorporating the latest information from the allied fields of economics, psychology, and sociology.

Shift in emphasis

Figure 1 shows the pre-concept relationship of both the marketing area in its relationship to the market and the management area in its relationship through supervision.

From Figure 1, we see that communications and decisions have flowed downward through the organization, the subordinate and the consumer responding with feedback. In management circles, the subordinate feedback has been in the form of productivity; in the marketing context, the consumer has responded with his feedback in terms of the purchasing dollar.

Theory Y and the new marketing concept seem to suggest that the orientation needs revision; the new emphasis should be on customer or market orientation. In management, the new emphasis should be on employee orientation to the management process. In both these concepts the call is for greater involvement by the lower-level units (i.e., the subordinate or the consumer).

If the new relationships were to be diagrammed, they would appear as in Figure 2.

Communications are now (or would be) originating in two areas: the boss and the corporation; the subordinate and the market or consumer. Each is to be a more equal partner in the relationship. Feedback also stems from both as information concerning needs and wants as well as reactions to decisions are continually transmitted to both parties. Decisions emanate from the bottom and flow upward with the subordinate and the consumer having a more direct influence in the decision process. These figures should illustrate the influence of the newer concepts upon communication and decision patterns. No longer would the main stream of ideas and communi-

---

[14] Lazo and Corbin, *Management in Marketing*, p. 30.

[15] Borch, "The Marketing Philosophy . . . ," in *The Marketing Concept . . .*

[16] J. W. Keener, "Marketing's Job for the 1960s," reprinted from the *Journal of Marketing*, Vol. 24, No. 3 (January 1960), pp. 1–6, in Holmes et al., *Readings in Marketing* p. 174.

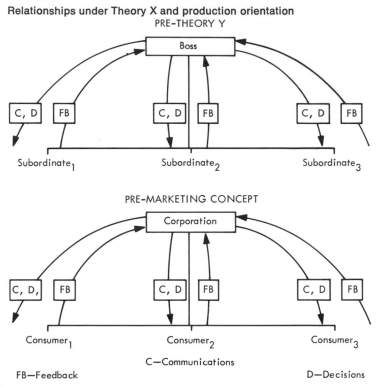

FIGURE 1

Relationships under Theory X and production orientation

PRE-THEORY Y

cation be downward. Under the new plans, the pattern would be modified in favor of a bottom-to-top direction.

The preceding paragraphs have served to suggest that many similarities exist between the new marketing and management theories. These newer theories began to be discussed about the same time. The supporters of both the management and the marketing theories claim the presence of new or ultimate truth in these ideas. And both theories represent a shift of emphasis in decision and communication patterns.

The presence of many common elements, then, points to the possibility of a more basic relationship or factor common to both movements. Thus far, such a relationship has merely been suggested, but the following section will directly support a case for the common element. This time the question is, How is this basic characteristic identified?

THE COMMON CHARACTERISTIC

To me the underlying theme permeating both the marketing concept and the management concept is the dependence upon participation. The

FIGURE 2

Relationships under Theory Y and consumer orientation

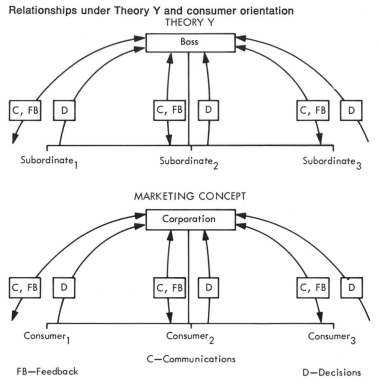

C—Communications

FB—Feedback   D—Decisions

new concepts call for the subordinate and the consumer to participate in activities once reserved for those persons in higher management levels and positions.

Participation in management

The rationale in management thought follows logically in this way: Who should perform the management process? Who should do the planning, organizing, directing, and controlling of activities? In earlier days the answer might have been a resounding "the boss," but today many would say "the subordinate." Many consultants know that solutions to company problems exist within the ranks of the company personnel and that the consultant's job is to clarify the problem, locate the persons with the solutions to these problems, and then convince top management of the value of the solutions. This very characteristic is basic to the participation concept. Theoretically, the subordinate manager, who has to work on the project, is best able to plan the project and set the objectives he believes are attainable. If the subordinate manager is best able to plan the operation that he will perform, it follows that he will be the one who can best organize and direct it. In the process of performing these management functions, the subordinate applies control, which has become self-control. Under this kind of system of subordinate participation in the management process, the primary role of the executive manager or boss is in the *coaching* of the subordinates as they participate and in the *coordination* of the activities of the subordinates.

Participation in marketing

The American economic system has always had an element of consumer participation in it. As put forth in the basic economic texts or even in the contemporary language of Robert Heilbroner's *The Making of Economic Society*,[17] America chose the market system (as opposed to tradition and command) for finding an economic answer to such questions as what is to be produced, how it is to be produced, and to whom it should be distributed. In the market system, the consumer is supposed to have the greatest voice by actually deciding whether to purchase or not. The dollar is the consumer vote. This point is relevant to the marketing concept.

The role of the consumer is theoretically elevated through the implementation of the new marketing concept. This is not a drastic step, as the consumer role is already on a high plane. In 1944, Ludwig von Mises wrote:

Within the market society the working of the price mechanism makes the consumers supreme. They determine through the prices they pay and through the amount of their purchases both the quantity and quality of production. They determine directly the prices of consumers' goods, and thereby indirectly the prices of all material factors of production and the wages of all hands employed.

. . . in that endless rotating mechanism the entrepreneurs and capitalists are the servants of the consumers. The consumers are the masters, to whose whims the entrepreneurs and capitalists must adjust their investments and methods of production.[18]

If the American economic system has already given the consumer such an elevated role, how does the newer theory stress greater participation by the consumer?

It appears that the major difference between the consumer roles under the traditional market system and under the new marketing concept is that the consumer in the past has participated in response to corporate activity (through buying or not buying the products) whereas the new marketing concept describes consumer participation in the *planning phases* of production as well as in the setting of the criteria for decision-making throughout the total enterprise.

---

[17] Robert Heilbroner, *The Making of Economic Society* (Englewood Cliffs, N. J.: Prentice-Hall, Inc., 1962).

[18] Ludwig von Mises, *Omnipotent Government* (New Haven, Conn.: Yale University Press, 1944), pp. 49–50.

This participation in the new marketing concept is manifested in two ways.[19] The consumer now assumes a much greater role and voice in the decision-making processes of the firm *and* those persons involved with the marketing activity assume a much more important place among the executive elite. Most writers, when describing the implementation of the marketing concept in the firm, speak in terms of the change that must take place within the organization. The "proper state of mind" or the "changed attitude" refers to that of the corporate officials, who must be willing to see the significance of operating *from* the market rather than *to* the market. Thus this type of participation (the other was consumer participation) is an internal type where the person in charge of marketing activities becomes more involved.

Considerable effort has been devoted to illustrating where this new, greater stress upon participation occurs in the new marketing and management theories. This is not to say that these newer theories contain no other factors or ideas in common; however, basic to them both and crucial to their implementation is consumer or subordinate participation. It is this dominant characteristic which permeates both trends.

The identification of this common denominator is important for two reasons. First, it enables us to see more easily the relationship of these newer theories to others outside the business area. Certainly, participation or ego involvement is an important term in many fields. The newer art expression rests upon it; education and training insist upon it; and psychology thrives upon it. To this extent, then, Theory Y and the new marketing concept are part of a broader social trend. This insight helps to understand better the "why" of the newer theories.

The second reason for identifying the common characteristic is more directly relevant to the final topic of the implications of the newer theories. If the theories are perceived as being related to other movements also stressing participation, a possible danger presents itself. Because of the inertia created by similar movements, the newer theories may be acclaimed and accepted before their merits have been investigated extensively. Participation is neither good nor bad. It must be weighed with a specific set of conditions in mind. There are many questions of limitations and extent. Therefore, the next question is, What are the implications of this increased participation for marketing and management and indirectly for the whole of society?

The following discussion is intended to locate probable problems if the greater-participation trend is supported. This is not to say that the raising of questions necessarily denies the point. In other words, the succeeding paragraphs are not included to condemn participation but to provide an awareness of the more far-reaching consequences of participation by

---

[19] In the Foreword to Lazo and Corbin, *Management in Marketing*, p. v, Peter Drucker uses the terms "marketing view" and the "management of marketing" to convey a similar idea.

greater numbers of people in decisive areas of management and marketing. It is hoped that such an examination of problem areas may aid the reader in evaluating the newer theories from a broader and wiser base.

IMPLICATIONS OF PARTICIPATION

Benefits

Many claims have been made by the proponents of the participation movement as to its advantages. These proponents, coming primarily from the university ranks as social scientists, believe participation provides significant benefits for both the individual participating and the corporation. Included in these advantages are such items as productivity increases, improvements in morale and motivation, a greater sense of well-being for the participating subordinate, and enhancement of the individual's identification with the corporation goals.[20] The picture that emerges is of an individual growing and developing through participation in the decision process of the enterprise. This individual is a cooperative person and is thus able to find much more meaning in his work and the work of others around him.

These benefits to the individual are not at the expense of the corporation, however, since it too benefits from this participation. The productivity increases of the individual will also improve the cost picture of the corporation; efficiencies from the cooperation of the subordinates should be more attainable; the corporate image becomes more easily accepted by all parties, who, because of their participation, become salesmen for the enterprise.

Problems and criticisms

Not everyone agrees that the benefits just described are the natural extension of participation. The first charge thrown at the participation proponents is that of manipulation.[21] The social scientists, particularly the newer group of behavioral scientists who have worked in industry, have been labeled by Loren Baritz as the "servants of power." [22] The behavioral servants respond to the wishes of their masters, the corporation executives,

---

[20] See, for example, Victor H. Vroom, *Some Personality Determinants of the Effects of Participation* (Englewood Cliffs, N. J.: Prentice-Hall, Inc., 1960).

[21] Douglas McGregor was well aware of the criticisms of participation. In his Chapter 9, "Participation in Perspective," he criticizes those proponents of participation who believe that the magic formula has been found for the elimination of conflict and disagreement; he also attacks the critics who believe participation is merely manipulation. In his words, ". . . participation is not a panacea, a manipulative device, a gimmick, or a threat. Used wisely, and with understanding, it is a natural concomitant of management by integration and self-control." See McGregor, *op. cit.*, p. 131.

[22] Loren Baritz, *The Servants of Power* (Middletown, Conn.: Wesleyan University Press, 1960).

who have hired them at salaries far above their meager university earnings to conduct "research studies" that will "uncover the truth." Baritz maintains that most of these "findings" are really *post facto* findings: a company needs data to support some point and data are found. The Harwood studies, for example, which are purported to exemplify the benefits to be derived from participation, are seen by Baritz as ingenious methods for having the employees "participate" in a management-planned situation so that the goals of the corporation would be better achieved.[23]

Baritz' criticism has been used here to exemplify some thinking and uneasiness about the use of social findings. Actually, one of two possible assumptions must be made before carrying the discussion further. One assumes that subordinate units can help set objectives in the best interests of the firm or one assumes that they cannot. If the latter position is held, then efforts to guide behavior in the direction of predetermined patterns must be vulnerable to the charge of manipulation. The control of individual behavior is beset with many problems of ethics. The reader can surely extend his thinking along these lines to see how involved this charge of manipulation can become.

But the other assumption may also hold. Perhaps the majority of the proponents of the newer management and marketing theories sincerely believe that goals and methods advocated by subordinate units will in fact work for the greatest good of the organization. What then?

If subordinate units in fact were encouraged to make corporate plans and decisions, the mind would immediately turn to difficulties emerging in many directions. How could responsible leadership be encouraged?[24] How could such units handle complex commodities such as defense mechanisms or drugs? Does the consumer know what he wants?[25] These are only some of the pertinent questions. Even though such reflections conjure up a multitude of problems, the discussion here will center about a broader area. Perhaps the most serious and far-reaching implication of the participation movement is the subtle impact it would have upon the standards of society.

The social system

It has been suggested that the pursuit and questioning of implications is important because so many forces in society (management and marketing, in this case) are striving toward the goal of participation. True, not all factions of the business society may completely achieve this end, but because of the striving, the question of direction is critical.

If a corporation actually becomes consumer oriented, it takes on the values of the consumers. This transformation does not come overnight but

---

[23] Others have raised their voices in protest. See the writings of Arthur Kornhauser, C. Wright Mills, and Wilbert E. Moore.

[24] John Douglas, "Our Lopsided Concept of Accomplishment," *Business Quarterly*, Vol. 28, No. 1 (Spring 1963), pp. 10–18 and 77.

[25] "Tiffany's Off On a Spree," *Business Week*, No. 1727 (October 6, 1962), p. 56.

in the day-to-day attempts to have "the customer's wants become the very criteria for corporate decision-making." What will happen to society when participation encourages the acceptance of mass values? Can society's goals be achieved when mass values may delay the process of innovation and individual creativity? And as Irving Kristol suggests,[26] if segments of our nation resist taking on the values of the masses, the government may become the protector or guardian of these segments—resulting in increased bureaucratic organization.

The point is that the very process of placing participation as *the* goal may erode the forces within this nation that have been balanced basically by our Constitution (the doctrine of checks and balances). The individual's values can be lost to those of the mass. Can minority or individual rights continue to be respected with this greater emphasis upon mass values?

In the same way that followership should be viewed as the countervailing[27] force to leadership, participation should be viewed as the countervailing force to autocratic decision-making, and cooperation the countervailing force to conflict. In more specific terms, the two new theories being discussed contain an emphasis upon participation by subordinate units. In effect, this movement would invest new power in these groups. If the pendulum swings radically to one side, then it would be possible for the new power groups to overbalance the power of the executive organization. To provide an effective and constructive change, then, the new theories must include more specific corollaries relating to limitations, extent, and scope.

SUMMARY

Two concepts, one in marketing and one in management, were reviewed with special attention given to the relationship of each to a more fundamental movement of the times. Stress upon participation by subordinate units in management and marketing and the resulting aim of cooperation among the forces appeared as primary goals. The implications of such goals suggested that the newer theories in marketing and management—indeed, in all areas—need to be extended to their broader ramifications before widespread endorsement occurs.

Exchange is a process of interactions. The central concern of marketing is the interaction process between the organ-

---

[26] Irving Kristol, "Is the Welfare State Obsolete?" *Harper's Magazine,* Vol. 226, No. 1357 (June 1963), pp. 39–43.

[27] See John Kenneth Galbraith, *American Capitalism* (Cambridge, Mass.: Riverside Press, 1962) for the development of the countervailing power concept.

ization and its environment. The term "ecosystem" is used to describe an organization functionally linked to its environment through a pattern of dynamic interactions. A model of a transacting ecosystem is presented to aid in the development of a total marketing system.

26. MARKETING ORGANIZATION: AN ECOLOGICAL VIEW *

Hans Thorelli †

Every biological organism, human being, and organization is dependent on its *environment* for survival. No one is self-sufficient. To obtain necessary sustenance from the environment we all must have something to offer it in exchange. Neither nature nor human civilization is in the end an eleemosynary institution. Conceptually, universal dependence on exchange means that every person, plant or organization (be it a boy scout troop, a government agency or a private firm) is really engaged in marketing.

Exchange is often thought of as a simple swap of "tit for tat," just as many people tend to think of decision-making simply as the flick of a switch in the mind of an executive.[1] To the student of marketing, however, it must be clear that exchange in this narrow sense is the result of a *process of interaction* between the organization and its environment. Indeed, this process of interaction and its determinants is the central concern of our discipline.

The interdependence of organism and environment stems from the incessant drive towards specialization, or division of labor, or nichemanship, as the prime means of survival in a world characterized by an all-prevailing relative scarcity of resources. In the plant and animal world, this specialization is brought about by the glacial interplay of forces resulting in the survival of the fittest. In industrialized societies humanity achieves division of labor primarily through organizations. Organizations whose output is economic utilities are called firms. It is important to emphasize that firms represent a species of organization. Progress in understanding the firm and its behavior is linked intimately with progress in the general area of organization theory.

---

* Commissioned contribution.
† University of Indiana.
[1] We may observe in passing that both of these notions are part and parcel of the classical economic theory of the firm.

ECOLOGY CUTS ACROSS THE DISCIPLINES

An emerging vital strain of thought is aimed directly at linking organization theory and theories of markets and marketing. This development— heralded by some of the writings of John R. Commons, Kurt Lewin, Wroe Alderson and others—involves the application of the concepts and viewpoint of ecology. The term *ecology* originates with that branch of biology which deals with the mutual relations among organisms (or populations of plants or animals) and, especially, between organisms (or populations) and their environment. While the prime attention in biology[2] as well as in the more recent field of "human ecology"[3] generally has been on spatial, demographic and physical aspects of the environment, there is an unmistakable tendency to broaden the concept to apply to the interrelations of an organism with its *total* setting. It is in this latter sense the notion will be used here.

Traditionally, the focal points of inquiry in biological ecology have been succession and evolution and the laws of survival and extinction. Adaptation tends to be viewed mainly as a one-way proposition: the organism which can adapt to a changing environment will survive. Adaptation also tends to be viewed as an objective, largely non-conscious process.

While research on human organization may derive considerable inspiration from plant and animal ecology, there are important distinctions to be made. Humans have long-term objectives, and they have a certain amount of foresight (as well as hindsight). They can plan for and administer change. Man and the organizations he creates are to a certain extent the masters of their own destiny. To some degree we may shape our own environment, and are not merely shaped by it. This is most clearly evident in the case of such powerful entities as national governments or large corporations, but it is actually characteristic of all human organizations.

The fact that in the environment of human organization constraints are less immediate, the range of discretion is greater, and the alternative means to reach given ends are more numerous is of tremendous significance. It provides the explanation for two vital phenomena, largely neglected in economic and sociological theory. The first is the emergence of a multiple goal structure in every organization once its immediate survival seems assured. The second is the viable coexistence of different organization structures and strategies of interaction in the same general environment.

---

[2] Sample references: W. B. McDougall, *Plant Ecology* (Philadelphia: Lea & Febiger, 1931); W. C. Allee, A. E. Emerson, O. and T. Park, K. Schmidt, *Principles of Animal Ecology* (Philadelphia: W. B. Saunders Co., 1949).

[3] Sample references: A. H. Hawley, *Human Ecology; A Theory of Community Structure* (New York: Ronald Press Co., 1950); O. D. Duncan, "Human Ecology and Population Studies," in P. M. Hauser and O. D. Duncan (eds.), *The Study of Population: An Inventory and Appraisal* (Chicago: University of Chicago Press, 1959), pp. 678–716.

THE UBIQUITOUS ENVIRONMENT

A constellation of an organization, or several organizations, functionally linked to its (their) environment through a pattern of dynamic interaction may be labeled an *ecosystem*. At least if the organization is a business firm the principal manifestation of this interaction is found in the *transactions* taking place. Figure 1 represents a model of a transacting ecosystem at what is admittedly a very high level of abstraction.

FIGURE 1

Model of transacting ecosystem

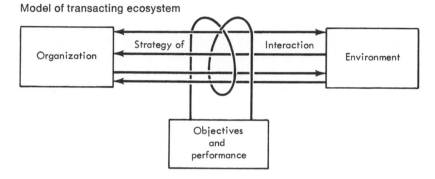

To simplify the representation of interaction between the organization and its environment they are depicted as being entirely distinct. Actually, the organization is totally immersed in the environment, and it is frequently difficult to distinguish the borderlines between them. This is why any "black box" concept of organization is so artificial.

Since little would be gained by studying the entire universe in order to understand the operations of any given organization (for example, a corner drugstore), it is clear that we are also faced with the problem of defining the *relevant* environment. For the time being it may be sufficient to say that the sum of all the factors and phenomena which may affect an organization, or which may be affected by the organization, constitutes the relevant environment.[4]

An action system based on four interdependent sets of variables is envisaged. A sample of variables in each category might include:

---

[4] The question is whether it is the environment as *perceived* by the actors in the situation or as it "actually" manifests itself by objective measurement that counts. Most likely, people's perception of the facts counts most heavily in the short run, while in the long run no one can "fly in the face of the (real) facts." Note, however, that in the meantime our misconceptions of the facts may have caused us to act in ways which will result in a set of "real" facts somewhat different from that which would have resulted if our action had been based on perfect perception of the environment and our own situation in it.

Organization	Interaction strategy	Environment	Objectives and results performance criteria
Size	Product	Size	Survival
Centralization	Promotion	Geographical	Growth
Integration	Place	dispersion	Profitability
Structuring by area, product, function, clients	Price	Competition	Sales volume
		Diversity of	Customer satisfaction
		customers	Productivity
		Stage in growth	
		cycle	

It is frequently useful to speak of three different environmental layers. The first might be labeled *intra-organizational.* It is relevant whenever a semi-autonomous part of a broader organization is studied. A highly relevant sector of the total environment surrounding the Chevrolet Division, for example, is all the other divisions of GM as well as the corporate headquarters of the concern. The second layer is represented by what we might call the *task environment,* i.e., generally the market in which the principal offering (cars of a certain price, performance, quality, prestige, etc.) of the organization is exchanged for the customer dollars on which the survival of the organization directly depends. The third layer includes such factors as the general social, economic, political and technological climate in which the organization finds itself operating.

From the viewpoint of interaction between the organization and its habitat it is pertinent to observe that the factors encountered at each layer of the environment may be divided into parameters and variables. While there is no hard and fast borderline, parameters may be viewed as factors which the organization must regard as given at least in the short run, while variables are factors which may be changed or influenced by the organization, at least in the short run. Generally speaking, the proportion of givens increases as one proceeds from the inner to the outer layers of the environment, while for manipulables the relationship is reversed.

The set of factors labeled Objectives and Performance have been placed in an intermediary, inductive-deductive position between the organization and the environment. This stems from the hypothesis that the objectives of an organization must be meshed with those of relevant groups in its environment. Organization leaders may think their objectives are new and unique. Nevertheless, if they are not in tune with the environment they will either have to be modified or the organization is doomed. Objectives yield performance criteria. If performance is not up to par, objectives are again likely to be revised, as is suggested by psycho-sociological theories about aspiration levels and their revision.

EFFECTS IN SEARCH OF CAUSES

Managerial decision-making as well as scientific inquiry presupposes the existence of at least one independent variable, the action of which affects at least one dependent variable. Even the schematic model of an ecosystem presented earlier is quite powerful as a generator of hypotheses. For example, relating environment to organization we might postulate that increased geographical dispersion is associated with decreased centralization, and that the later stages of the market growth curve tend to be associated with a high degree of integration. Or, relating environment to strategy, we might assume that the greater the diversity of customers, the greater the degree of product differentiation.

To complicate matters, we must assume mutual interaction between all four sets of variables with a cacophony of causal arrows bringing to mind Musorgski's *A Night on Bald Mountain.* The problem of intervening variables is, however, far from new, and improved techniques of handling this difficulty are being developed in the areas of statistics and experimental design. The direction of causal arrows, whenever they happen to be one-way, can frequently be traced by analysis over time.

A further complication stems from interaction *within* each set of variables. Within organizations, for example, it is often held that size and centralization are inversely related. Among objectives, profitability and sales volume often evidence high collinearity. Looking at the strategy variables, marketing men are apt to emphasize the gestalt effect: any marketing strategy worth its salt is something more than a marketing mix; that is, it represents a whole that is greater than an odd conglomerate of so many parts of product, price, and promotion. To some extent the problem may be alleviated by factor analysis, but in the long run it will be handled more effectively once we are able to classify strategies more meaningfully than at present. Until then, there is nothing wrong with studying the effects of individual variables, such as price or advertising, and combinations thereof. Plant ecologists frequently study the effects of climate and soil conditions, taken separately, on plant populations, even though it is clear that there is considerable interaction among climate and soil variables themselves.

MERITS OF ECOLOGICS

The simplified model displayed in Figure 1 may be extended (or contracted) in various ways. It is not difficult, for instance, to nominate twice as many variables signifying dimensions of organization, interaction strategies, and environments, although there is little reason to believe that a great many more are needed for adequate explanation. (On the other hand, no claim is made that the sample of variables given here includes all the most important ones.) The model may also be focused on what Alderson used to call market behavior systems, comprising the entire chain of inter-linked organizations from primary producer to consumer, and the relations between parallel systems. Biologists have made observations concerning food chains and dominant species in plant and animal communities, insights which may prove quite helpful in applying ecological approaches to manufacturer-distributor interaction in channel systems.

A major advantage of eco-models is that they generally lend themselves fairly well to operationalization, that is, to empirical testing. It is true that there are no self-evident or universally accepted measures for almost any of the variables which we have listed by way of example. But for most of them, operational substitutes have been used in many studies which were not ecological in character. Organization theory has several useful measures of "size" and "centralization," economics, "price" (listed, quoted, actual, with and without discount, etc.) and "productivity." Geographers and location theorists have widely used measures of spatial dispersion.

The relative ease with which eco-models lend themselves to operationalization sets them apart from some otherwise intriguing models about the behavior of firms and markets, such as the attempts to explain such behavior as a manifestation of the interplay of interest groups[5] or in terms of Galbraith's countervailing powers. The prime advantage of eco-models in relationship to Operations Research type models is that the former are less ephemeral, less focused on the short term and less casuistic than the later. In relation to classical economic theories of the firm and competition, eco-models would seem to offer quite a set of major advantages:

1. Recognition of the idea of multiple goals, and the related notion of the niche, i.e., the "market within a market."
2. Recognition of the entire arsenal of marketing strategy variables.
3. Recognition of relevant aspects of the environment generally neglected by these economic theories (spatial aspects, differential customer characteristics, market life cycle notions, and so on).
4. Recognition of the fact that competition and cooperation are really two different dimensions rather than simply opposite poles on a continuum of interaction.
5. Recognition of the vital role of structural and functional variables *inside* the organization in conditioning (and being conditioned by) objectives, interactive strategies and the environment itself.

Ecological approaches have already proved to be useful in marketing as well as organization theory. There is every reason to believe that these pioneering efforts will be followed by a tidal wave of intellectual endeavor in the near future, to the benefit of theory and practice alike.

---

[5] H. B. Thorelli, "The Political Economy of the Firm: Basis for a New Theory of Competition?" 101 *Schweizerische Zeitschrift für Volkswirtschaft und Statistik* (1965: 3), pp. 248–62. Also published in Graduate School of Business, Indiana University, *Reprint Series*, No. 15.

e.

Controlling marketing performance

THE CONTROL of marketing systems is influenced by a variety of concepts and techniques. There exists no such thing as a representative marketing control system. The diversity that characterizes marketing operations imposes many different control requirements. However, there are several traits of a general nature that are common to such systems.

First, although control factors encompass a number of operating aspects, they all can essentially be translated into the common denominator of revenue or expense dollars. Second, the last decade has marked the widespread adoption of the systems concept and a resulting awareness of the interdependency of marketing control elements. Finally, the recognition of these complex relationships has been made possible by the advent of the computer and in turn has stimulated the application of computerized operations in the area of marketing control.

The application of computerized operations in the area of marketing control is not enough to achieve efficient control. The complexities of the marketing process require an integrated approach to effective marketing control. The approach must therefore be a systems orientation that views marketing controls as operating in a hierarchy of integrated marketing subsystems.

The first article, by Stasch, deals with the general nature of marketing systems and the related implications for marketing intelligence. In the second article, the coordination of the accounting function with the marketing control activity is discussed by Barry. Finally, DeVos and others discuss the benefits and approaches of marketing profitability analysis.

The control and improvement of marketing performance are two important goals sought by the marketing manager. Their achievement could be greatly enhanced through the successful application of computer and quantitative techniques to marketing. In turn, this objective can be attained through the adoption of a systems approach; which would also facilitate communication between marketers and computer specialists.

27. SYSTEMS ANALYSIS FOR CONTROLLING AND IMPROVING MARKETING PERFORMANCE *

Stanley F. Stasch †

The executive of a very large packaged goods firm was recently quoted: "I don't know of a single case where the computer or operations research has contributed substantially to the solution of any marketing problem."[1] A recent headline read: "Computer's marketing use is in primitive stage, especially in industrial field."[2] In a recent article, Adler comments on the shortcomings of model building in marketing.

There is no better evidence of this than the gulf between the elegant and sophisticated models with which recent marketing literature abounds and the actual number of situations in which those models really work. For the truth of the matter is that we are still in the foothills of this development, despite the advances of a few leaders.[3]

This paper will (1) briefly explore some of the causes of marketing's poor record of computer applications and (2) propose that the systems approach to marketing can greatly facilitate a substantial increase in marketing's use of the computer and appropriate quantitative techniques.

* Reprinted from "Systems Analysis for Controlling and Improving Marketing Performance," *Journal of Marketing,* Vol. 33, No. 2 (April 1969), pp. 12–19.

† Northwestern University.

[1] John J. Cardwell, "Marketing and the Management Sciences," a paper presented to the Chicago Chapter of TIMS (May 24, 1967), p. 1.

[2] "Computer Forces User to Answer Basic Operating Question; More Data Needed," *Marketing Insights,* Vol. 1 (April 10–14, 1967), pp. 10–11.

[3] Lee Adler, "Systems Approach to Marketing," *Harvard Business Review,* Vol. 45 (May–June 1967), p. 115.

WHY THE LAG IN MARKETING?

Why has marketing fallen behind the other business areas in applying quantitative techniques and the computer to problem solving? This lag can be attributed to three factors:

1. Behavioral phenomena are difficult to quantify and hence difficult to computerize. It is to be expected that marketing problems with strong behavioral aspects will not be computerized until they have been quantified, and this development must await further behavioral research.
2. Of the large quantities of marketing data available, only small amounts have been collected, and not all of that in an organized manner.

   Any second or third generation computer can store millions of memory "bits." But what is overlooked by most industrial marketers—and by many of their bosses—is that those "bits" do not come pre-packed in the computer. They have to be gathered painstakingly by the computer user, and this is where most users fall short.[4]
3. Marketing people have not taken the initiative in closing the communications gap between themselves and computer personnel.[5] If the computer—and appropriate quantitative techniques—are to be applied to decision areas in marketing, the nature and structure of those problem areas must be explained *in detail* to the computer specialists. The marketing decision maker must be able to communicate the following to the computer specialists and quantitative analysts:

   a The details of the specific problem.
   b The theoretical structure of the marketing phenomenon, at least as the marketing manager understands it.[6]
   c The alternative decision choices associated with the problem.
   d The specific information, and its form, *required by the decision maker.*
   e The source, form, and frequency of availability of raw data to be used in the decision-making process.

Only when the quantitative analysts and computer specialists have been given all of this information will it be possible for them to apply *their skills* to the problem.

---

[4] Same reference as footnote 2, p. 11.

[5] Donald F. Cox and Robert E. Good, "How to Build a Marketing Information System," *Harvard Business Review*, Vol. 45 (May–June 1967), p. 149; C. W. Plattes, "The Requirements for Problem Solving and Quantitative Aids to Decision-Making in Marketing Consumer Products," remarks made at the panel session on *Using OR Effectively in Advertising and Marketing—Why and How*, at the Thirty-First Annual Meeting of the Operations Research Society of America, New York City (May 31, 1967), pp. 2–3; *op. cit.*, pp. 30–31.

[6] Peter F. Drucker, "The Manager and the Moron," *The McKinsey Quarterly*, Vol. III (Spring 1967), pp. 48–49.

ROLE OF THE SYSTEMS APPROACH

Guided by a list of *management's problems* and the *information needed by management* for solving those problems, data collection can be organized within the framework of an information system.[7] The task of identifying the specific information needed by the decision maker can be facilitated if managers will first organize their thinking according to the five points mentioned above. In so doing, they will have thought through thoroughly all facets of their problems, they will understand their information needs, and they will then be in a position to communicate effectively with non-marketing computer specialists.

Of the three reasons given earlier for marketing's poor record of computer usage, only the first represents a situation which cannot be influenced by management; and a systems approach can be very helpful in dealing with the remaining two. If managers could adequately describe their problems and the information requirements associated with those problems, they would be in a position both to organize their data collection activity and to communicate with non-marketing computer specialists. These simple steps would rectify the second and third causes of marketing's poor record of successful computer applications.

WHAT IS A MARKETING SYSTEM?

A marketing system is comprised of a number of separate sub-systems, each concerned with only one of the marketing activities performed by the firm. The primary purpose of each sub-system is the measurement and evaluation of current performance and, if a marketing activity is not being performed as economically as possible, the evaluation of proposed alternative courses of action to determine which will lead to more economical performance. These goals are attained by bringing together the components shown in Figure 1.

1. An actual operating system based on past decisions

There must be actual or real system currently in use; that is, the firm's marketing functions are currently being performed, and someone or something must be performing them. The firm has warehouses where products are inventoried, transport facilities of some kind are used to ship their products, salesmen are calling on certain customers in certain territories, advertising of a given type is being used in certain media, and still other marketing activities are being performed. These items constitute the actual operating systems of the firm, and each represents a *past decision* made by management.

---

[7] Cox and Good, *op. cit.*

FIGURE 1.

A marketing sub-system

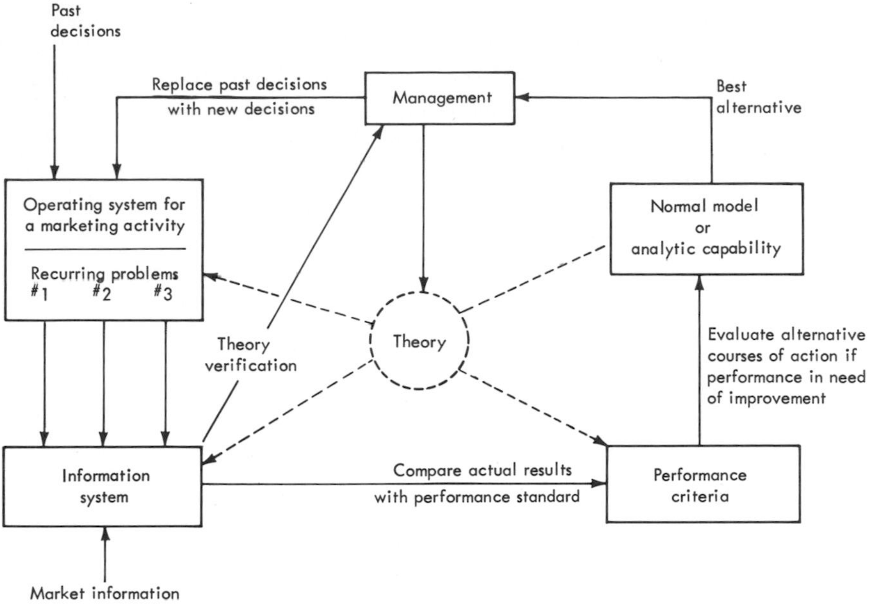

Past
decisions

Replace past decisions
with new decisions

Management

Best
alternative

Operating system for
a marketing activity

Recurring problems
#1   #2   #3

Normal model
or
analytic capability

Theory
verification

Theory

Evaluate alternative
courses of action if
performance in need
of improvement

Information
system

Compare actual results
with performance standard

Performance
criteria

Market information

2. An information system guided by recurring problems

Parallel to an operating system is an information system which records data from a number of sources. Two major sources provide the required information. Data concerning operations and performance of the firm's various marketing activities are obtained directly from those activities. Data describing the firm's markets are obtained from internal sources and external secondary sources. This information-collecting activity is guided by a *specific list of frequently occurring problems or decision areas*. The list of recurring problems is required for the identification of the information managers need when making decisions in each of these problem areas.

3. A theoretical structure required for each recurring problem

The decisions made in the past by management were based upon, or guided by, some marketing theories and concepts which decision-making managers considered applicable to their particular problem areas. This theoretical foundation is necessary if computer specialists are to develop a computerized information system for decision making. These specialists must be informed of the kinds of input data provided for them and how these data should be processed in order to transform them into output information which management can use when making decisions.

In effect, the computer specialist must understand how management conceptualizes the problem phenomenon before he can develop a computer program capable of generating information useful in decision making. Consequently, decision makers should take it upon themselves to provide the computer specialists with (a) the number and kind of variables (data) that constitute the theory on which decision processes are based and (b) a structural relationship of all variables, how they fit together, and how they are interrelated.[8]

This aspect of systems analysis serves two additional purposes. First, it forces the manager to think through his decision-making processes in great detail, probably in greater detail than he has ever done before. Second, it requires that the manager be capable of communicating, or that he develop the ability to communicate, with those who do not have his marketing knowledge or experience.

4. Theory verification through organized data collection

Before decisions based on theoretical concepts can be made operationally effective, the theoretical concepts used must first be measured and verified. For example, a marketing manager may well believe that his firm would experience a diminishing returns effect if sales effort were increased indefinitely. He may even be absolutely certain that this is the case. However, he must know at least one of two things in order to make an intelligent decision concerning the amount of sales effort to be authorized. He must know either the sales volume at which diminishing returns are such that increased effort will no longer be profitable, or he must know the level of sales effort at which this diminishing returns effect will be experienced. If he knows either of these things, he can increase his effort until the critical sales volume is reached, or until the critical level of sales effort is reached. If he knows neither of these things, he can make a decision based only on experience and intuition.

Consequently, management should require that certain data collection procedures designed to verify appropriate theories and concepts be included in each marketing sub-system. Such data should be transformed into information which will permit the quantification of the relationships associated with those theories and concepts.

5. Develop criteria for evaluating performance

Since the purpose of a marketing sub-system is to improve performance, it is necessary to compare the effects of current performance with criteria reflecting a level of performance considered good, or at least acceptable. Such criteria might be the desired number of sales calls or advertising expo-

---

[8] For an illustration, see William F. Massy and Jim D. Savvas, "Logical Flow Models for Marketing Analysis," *Journal of Marketing*, Vol. 28 (January 1964).

sures, actual sales compared with market potential, sales compared with profits, or any one of a large number of other possible criteria. Clearly, these criteria reflect certain marketing theories and concepts embraced by management. In order to make them operational, management must communicate the essence of these criteria to the computer specialist.

The results should be a better measure of both the distance (the separation) between actual and desired performance and the direction in which actual performance should move to attain the desired level of performance.

6. Construct a normative model using analytic techniques

As a result of the foregoing five steps, a manager will know the direction in which to move and how far, but he is told nothing about how this should be done. He may even have a number of alternatives available, each of which might achieve the desired objective. Before he can choose between them, he must evaluate these alternatives and, hopefully, select the best one. However, in this case, he gets no help from the performance criteria suggested above.

This difficulty will be eliminated if the sub-system includes a normative model capable of evaluating the effects of various alternatives without actually operationalizing each alternative. If it is not possible to construct a normative model, some other analytic capability should be devised. Although not as desirable as a normative model, such a capability is likely to be an improvement over the use of a performance criterion based only on theoretical concepts. However, regardless of which is used, the end product should be the joint effort of the manager's knowledge of marketing theory and the computer specialist's knowledge of quantitative techniques.

If such a model were constructed, management could use it to evaluate all alternatives and then select the one alternative which will result in each marketing activity being performed as economically as possible. This information should then be used to improve the performance of the actual operating system. In so doing, management must discard some of the *past decisions* (see number one above), and replace them with the new decisions suggested by the analysis utilizing the normative model. It is only through such analyses that management can be confident that its marketing activities are being performed as inexpensively as possible.

It should be noted that the sub-system illustrated in Figure 1 represents a dynamic process occurring over time. Decisions made in the past influence the system's current performance, and the system's current performance is compared to some standard. Even though performance may have been up to standard last period, the firm is not guaranteed that this period's performance is also up to standard. Changes beyond the firm's control — a change or shift in the number of customers, the emergence of new technology such as railroad piggy-backing, a reduction in air freight rates, or an increase in space rates in a media vehicle, to mention a few—may cause a reduction in current performance. When such developments occur, alternatives should be reevaluated utilizing the normative model in the appropriate sub-system. When such developments result in current performance not being up to standard, past decisions must be replaced with new ones, the current operating system must be modified in some way, and the modified system will then influence future performance. Future performance will, in turn, be compared against a standard, and the procedure described above will be repeated. In effect, this transforms the procedure into a process occurring again and again over time. The result should be a regular and continuous improvement in the performance of the actual operating system.

EVOLUTION OF A MARKETING SYSTEM

How is the systems approach applied to marketing? It appears that the evolution of a marketing system is at least a two-stage process. As an illustration of this process, consider the case of a firm manufacturing products for a large number of geographically dispersed industrial users. The firm sells directly to their customers, and because customers request fast delivery the firm maintains its own distribution facilities. In other words, although personal selling is the primary demand stimulant, fast delivery is an important element in the firm's marketing mix. The marketing system of such a firm might consist primarily of three sub-systems: market potential, personal selling, and distribution.[9]

The first stage in the development of such a marketing system would find the firm concentrating its efforts on the individual sub-systems. When these sub-systems have been developed, management will have an accurate measure of the potential in each of its markets and the capability of (1) measuring the performance of each of its marketing activities—requires an organized data collection effort—and (2) analyzing and improving the performance of those activities not being performed efficiently—requires both the availability of data and the use of appropriate analytic techniques. Once this level of analysis and sophistication has been achieved, management is ready to move on to the second stage in the development of their marketing system.

The second stage calls for integrating the sub-systems into a larger system which utilizes information taken from all sub-systems. Figure 2 illustrates how this might be done. Although not shown specifically, both the personal selling and distribution sub-systems would consist of those components shown in Figure 1. In addition, the market potential sub-system

---

[9] For a more detailed description of these individual sub-systems, see Stanley F. Stasch, "Marketing Systems and Quantitative Analysis," in R. B. Cunningham (ed.), *Dynamic Competition in Utility Marketing* (Chicago: American Marketing Association, 1967), pp. 77–94.

FIGURE 2

Evolution of a total marketing system

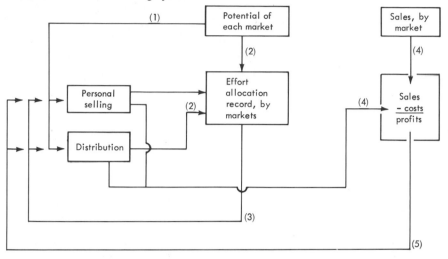

could be quite complex, possibly using such techniques as regression analysis, econometric models, input-output techniques and still others.[10]

Figure 2 is useful in explaining the evolutionary process by which a marketing system takes shape. In the initial phases of the system's development, the information generated by the system will be somewhat incomplete. Nevertheless, because it is still necessary for the firm to make decisions concerning the allocation of its marketing effort, such decisions can only be based on market potential information at this stage of the system's development. In such a case, the effort expended by each marketing activity can be allocated in proportion to the potential believed to exist in each market. (See (1) and (2) in Figure 2.) At the end of the accounting period, information available from each of the sub-systems should verify if, in fact, effort had been allocated in proportion to potential. If it had not, this information should be fed back to each sub-system and an attempt should be made during the following time period to rectify whatever discrepancies existed. (See (3) in Figure 2.)

Because of competition and still other factors, the profitability of various markets displaying the same potential could differ substantially. This suggests, of course, that potential is a useful criterion when nothing better is available, but that it is not necessarily the most desirable criterion. As the

[10] For more detailed descriptions of such sub-systems: R. J. Twery, "The Role of EDP in Sales Forecasting," pp. 21–25; G. B. Hegeman, "The Role of EDP in Market Forecasting," pp. 26–28; S. T. Pender, "LAMBASTE-Determining Market Potentials Statistically," pp. 33–35, all in *Chemical Marketing and the Computer,* Proceedings of the Chemical Marketing Research Association meetings, November 16 and 17, 1965.

first stage of the marketing system nears completion, the firm will begin to have available, for each marketing activity, cost information which accurately reflects the performance of each of those marketing activities. (The firm will, in effect, be performing each of its marketing activities as economically as possible in each of the markets it serves.) When the firm has this capability, it is ready to complete the second phase of this evolutionary process. The profitability of each market, is then a valid criterion for effort

> Marketing Revenue (units sold times manu-
> facturing gross margin)
> *Less:* Marketing Costs Accurately Reflecting
> Effort Expended in That Market
> *Equals:* Market Profitability

allocation *because the costs used in calculating profitability will represent dollars spent in an efficient manner.* Until this is true, that is, until the firm can accurately measure marketing costs and the marketing effort associated with those costs, profits will not accurately reflect each market's response to the firm's efforts. Consequently, market potential should be used initially as the effort allocation criterion. When cost information which accurately reflects performance becomes available, the potential criterion can be replaced with the profit criterion and effort can then be re-allocated to those markets which are more profitable. (See (4) and (5) in Figure 2.)

Because of the second stage—the integration of the individual subsystems into a larger system — the firm will be provided with still more information. One result of the first stage is that the firm will know the proportion of each marketing activity allocated to each of the markets it serves. By selecting a market and summing the amount of effort allocated to *each of the marketing activities used in that market,* the firm can develop a record of how its total marketing effort was allocated to its many markets. In addition, the firm will have a record of how the various marketing activities were combined within each market. This is essentially the marketing mix problem. If the firm knows the profitability of each market, it will then be in a position to make better decisions concerning both the allocation of its marketing effort and the composition of its marketing mix.[11]

ADDITIONAL ADVANTAGES

It has been argued that the use of the systems approach by a firm will encourage the collection of data pertinent to its marketing problems, and that such an approach will facilitate communications between marketers and computer personnel. Both of these developments should lead to an increased use of the computer and appropriate quantitative techniques.

---

[11] An interesting and appropriate discussion of effort allocation can be found in Richard A. Feder, "How to Measure Marketing Performance," *Harvard Business Review,* Vol. 43 (May–June 1965), pp. 132–142.

In addition, management will be in a better position to cope with two significant marketing problems—effort allocation and marketing mix.

There are a number of other advantages which a firm can realize through the use of the systems approach. The literature concerned with quantitative models stresses the fact that a model usually facilitates a "sensitivity analysis"—that is, the ability to ask how much, if at all, the optimum decision would change if certain data were only partially accurate or if certain assumptions were not valid. Another advantage of a quantitative model lies in the fact that it is possible to vary the model's inputs experimentally while observing the changes in the output.

There is wide agreement that model-building and simulation is perhaps the most significant of those things not otherwise possible without a computer. As of now, an electronic digital computer is the only device that can handle variable on top of variable and give management a choice of alternatives while there is still time to make a decision.[12]

Because models and other analytic techniques are an integral part of the individual sub-systems of a marketing system, these same advantages are also realized by the firm utilizing the system's approach. In addition, a firm with a marketing system will enjoy a number of benefits which would be unavailable to them if they did not have such a system. Three of these advantages are discussed below.

1. Frequent or numerous decisions

The marketing manager is concerned with a number of situations wherein decisions must be made periodically, that is, at regular intervals in time such as weekly, monthly, quarterly, and so on. He is also concerned with situations which require that essentially the same decision be made over and over at a given point in time. Such high frequency decisions abound in most marketing-oriented firms. They range from determining the profitability of various products and/or markets to determining the distribution system's ability to service customers within certain time and cost limitations. As more and more of these decision areas are systematized, management will find that they have more time to spend on those problem areas less well defined or less susceptible to quantitative analysis at present.

2. Theory usage and validation

It seems realistic to assume that all managers base their decisions on certain theories and concepts. Although these are likely to be explicit, in many cases they may be implicit. For example, the sales manager is likely to believe that calling on a customer has some effect on the sales eventually

---

[12] "Computers Begin to Solve the Marketing Puzzle," *Business Week*, No. 1859 (April 17, 1965), p. 133.

made to that customer. On the other hand, it is unlikely that he will feel that an infinite number of sales calls will lead to an infinite amount of sales. This indicates that the sales manager, either explicitly or implicitly, believes in the diminishing returns of sales effort.

The real issue facing the manager is whether or not the diminishing returns theory is, in fact, valid and, if so, at what level of operation diminishing returns occur. The manager knows that sales will not approach infinity as effort is increased, but he does not know the scale at which to operate in order to avoid those diseconomies associated with diminishing returns. This cannot be determined without a great deal of empirical data which, generally speaking, is not available today. This then is the situation facing management. If management does not know the shape of the diminishing returns response, they will have no way of knowing if their operations fall within the range of diminishing returns *in spite of the fact that they may be completely certain of the presence of the diminishing returns phenomenon.*[13]

This illustrates the second advantage accompanying the use of a marketing system. Many marketing problems cannot be solved or even analyzed today because of the lack of empirical verification of those theories required for their solution. The use of a marketing system, however, gives management the opportunity to provide for the generation and collection *over time* of the information which will tell them if the theory being used is valid. Thus, the use of a marketing system is a necessary prerequisite in those problem areas where theory verification must precede the use of quantitative analysis.

3. Adaptive considerations

Frequently a given problem can be analyzed in different ways, each of which may utilize a different quantitative technique. Those different techniques usually reflect various levels of quantitative sophistication and input information. The more sophisticated quantitative techniques typically require larger amounts of, and generally less accessible, data. Table 1 lists three different levels of quantitative sophistication, the input data requirements associated with them, and the approximate time span required for the collection of those data. In addition, the column farthest right in the exhibit shows how the problem of determining sales territories might be approached in three different ways.

Many decisions must be made periodically, regardless of how much information has been collected and regardless of what quantitative techniques, if any, are being used to assist in those decision-making processes.

---

[13] An interseting case study illustrating this point can be found in Clark Waid, Donald F. Clark, and Russell L. Ackoff, "Allocation of Sales Effort in the Lamp Division of the General Electric Company," *Operations Research*, Vol. 4 (December 1956), pp. 629–47.

TABLE 1

Quantitative sophistication, data requirements and data collection time

Quantitative sophistication	Data requirements	Data collection time	Illustration of sales territory determination
Little or no quantitative analysis involved.	Readily available from many secondary sources.	Less than one year.	Use managerial judgment in determining the number of salesmen to use. Each sales territory should represent an equal amount (approximately) of sales potential.
Some simple quantitative techniques used.	Uses some data from primary sources. Firm must gather data.	One to three years.	Same as the example above except that historical data are used to determine the amount of sales potential which can be most effectively exploited. This information suggests the appropriate number of salesmen to use. (See reference 1.)
Highly complex quantitative techniques used.	Strong emphasis on primary data collected by the firm.	Three to five years.	The sales effort required to just attain each customer's saturation level is determined and summed over all customers in a territory. This is then compared with the effort available to determine if the territory is too large, too small, or just the right size. (See reference 2.)

References:
1. Walter J. Semlow, "How Many Salesmen Do You Need?" *Harvard Business Review,* Vol. 37 (May-June 1959), pp. 126–32.
2. Arthur A. Brown, Frank T. Hulswit, and John D. Kettelle, "A Study of Sales Operations," *Operations Research,* Vol. 4 (June 1956), pp. 296–308; Clark Waid, Donald F. Clark, and Russell L. Ackoff, "Allocation of Sales Effort in the Lamp Division of the General Electric Company," *Operations Research,* Vol. 4 (December 1956), pp. 629–47.

One consequence of the unavailability of data is that it may be necessary initially to use the least sophisticated quantitative techniques to aid in the decision-making process. At the same time, however, management should be preparing to utilize increasingly more sophisticated quantitative techniques in later years by setting up the systematic procedures which will collect now the data they will require.

This illustrates the third advantage of a marketing system. Some quantitative techniques may never be used by a firm which does not utilize the systems approach for the simple reason that some quantitative techniques require data normally unavailable except after a long period of collection activity. It may therefore be necessary for a firm to be simultaneously collecting data for two or more quantitative techniques in those problem areas wherein a hierarchy of quantitative techniques can be applied. The least sophisticated techniques will be used initially, with the more sophisticated techniques being employed as the required data are collected. A marketing system is ideally suited for facilitating such an adaptive process and for making possible the use of the more sophisticated quantitative techniques.

CONCLUSIONS

This paper has presented the case for utilizing a systems approach in marketing. The main points presented in the foregoing can be briefly summarized.

Marketing has not utilized the computer or quantitative techniques to the same extent as the other functional areas of business. Three factors were seen to account for this lag: the difficulty of quantifying the behavioral aspects of marketing, the lack of a data collection tradition in marketing, and poor communications between marketers and computer specialists. Although the behavioral aspects of marketing may not succumb to the computer for quite some time, other aspects of marketing can be computerized if management structures its marketing problems and decision areas in terms of pertinent marketing theory, and if it then organizes the data collection activity in proper relationship to the structured marketing problems and decision areas. This is the essence of the systems approach, and it will greatly facilitate the application of the computer to marketing.

The collection of pertinent data, and both a more complete description of the marketing problems faced and the underlying theory associated with those problems, will encourage the use of operations research, management science, and other quantitative techniques in marketing. Because these analytic techniques would be an integral part of the individual subsystems within a marketing system, all of the advantages purported to be associated with quantitative techniques and model building would also accrue to a firm using a marketing system. Thus the systems approach might be viewed as a necessary condition for the successful application of quantitative techniques to marketing.

Marketing control is dependent on other parts of the organization for inputs and support. Although there is a logical relationship with accounting, the author suggests this relationship has often been characterized by misunderstandings and lack of communication. He points out the potential bene-

fits of using accounting techniques for marketing control and discusses specific methods of increasing coordination between these two functional areas.

28. ACCOUNTING'S ROLE IN MARKETING *

John W. Barry †

For the management seeking to enhance corporate profitability, marketing is one of the undeveloped frontiers. Marketing as a function should have its own productivity and profitability standards, and an alert accounting staff can play a major part in developing them. However, it takes some special understanding on the part of financial executives to function effectively in this role.

As is well known, the marketing function has been undergoing major changes during the last decade or so. These changes are symbolized by the new name—this function used to be called sales—and by the growing adoption of the so-called marketing concept.

THREE ASPECTS OF MARKETING

In its fullest sense the marketing concept has three aspects: (1) customer orientation, that is, study of customer needs and wants before the selling process (if possible, before the manufacturing process) begins; (2) an organizational structure in which all marketing activities are performed by the marketing department and in which the chief marketing executive is accorded a status equal to that of the top financial or manufacturing executive; and (3) emphasis on improving the profitability and productivity of marketing operations.

As a number of studies have shown, the marketing concept has been adopted to a large extent by both large and medium-size manufacturing companies—but not necessarily to the same extent in all its aspects. Most generally accepted are the first two aspects, customer orientation and high status for the top marketing executive. Attention to the third aspect has lagged.

One recent study[1] showed that while virtually all the companies surveyed measured product profitability, only two-thirds measured territory

---

* Reprinted from "Accounting's Role in Marketing," *Management Services* (January–February 1967), pp. 43–50.
† John W. Barry and Associates.
[1] Michael Schiff and Martin Mellman, *Financial Management of the Marketing Function* (New York: Financial Executives Research Foundation, 1962).

profitability and only a little more than half assessed customer or salesman profitability.

BARRIERS

This points up obvious opportunities for the accounting function. The accountant should proceed with the utmost caution, however, for there are long-standing differences between the two areas. Their relationship is traditionally characterized by lack of mutual understanding and indifferent (if not downright poor) communications.

All too often accountants regard the marketing function as mostly selling, and the marketing men have an image of the accountant as "just a scorekeeper." Sometimes the accountant deserves that label.

Consider the approach taken by a beverage company a few years ago. An analysis of sales costs showed that the cost of maintaining old sales volume (selling to established customers) was 4 per cent of that sales volume while the cost of getting new volume (obtaining new customers) was 50 per cent of that volume. When these findings were noised around, the company decided to abandon seeking new business. In a short time it went broke. Can't you hear the sales-oriented people saying, "I could have told you so?"

The attitude of sales executives was epitomized in a recent speech by the sales vice president of National Cash Register Company. He said, in essence, "I don't know any better way to ruin a good sales organization than to start emphasizing profits. First thing you know, more attention is put on cost-cutting than on business-getting, and when creativity is diverted this way, the business suffers."

BRIDGE-BUILDING

Actually, of course, it is possible to put creativity into both business-getting and cost control. (Please note that we are interested in cost control, not necessarily cost-cutting.) Before a financial executive attempts to establish new cost control concepts in marketing, however, he should build a bridge—perhaps a new bridge—between the finance and marketing functions. The best way to build such a bridge is by undertaking to help the marketing people do a better job in the same terms as those in which they themselves conceive of their job.

TRAINING SALES FORCE

One good approach to this problem is through sales training. The accountant's first reaction to this suggestion may well be, "What do I know about sales training?" But a financial man who participates in any way in final purchase decisions may know a good deal and be in a position to make a significant contribution.

Here is an example cited by Dr. Michael Schiff: [2]

A corporation had a large force of industrial sales engineers who were thoroughly familiar with the technical capabilities and applications of their products. However, the buyers' final decisions were made more in financial terms than in terms of technical capabilities.

Dr. Schiff worked with these sales engineers to help them develop understanding of the fundamental concepts of capital asset acquisition decisions. He taught them how to make a total presentation covering both the technical features and the financial considerations — the investment returns on a payback and discounted flow basis. Thus, the prospective customer got a total business analysis of the advantages of the acquisition, thorough enough to use in raising the funds to finance it.

BRIDGES CREATED

All this was not done easily. The salesmen had to learn to understand depreciation, cash flow, investment, the tax aspects of various depreciation methods, and the like. In some cases Dr. Schiff has made a financial man a permanent part of the sales team to help in this kind of work. Giving help in sales training has paid off in more than increased sales; in these companies real bridges—carrying profitable two-way traffic—exist between accounting and marketing.

Another bridge-building device is to have a member of the controller's staff in the marketing department who has line responsibility to the marketing manager but a close working relationship with the controller. Such arrangements are not uncommon in manufacturing departments; they are less frequently used in marketing.

There are many ways to build closer, more productive relationships between accounting and marketing. The important thing is to make a beginning. Before trying to sell most kinds of profitability ideas, the financial man would be wise to see whether he can first make a contribution to marketing effectiveness in the marketing manager's own terms (and the sales training approach is as good as any). His counsel on profit planning, controls, and reports will be both more knowledgeable and more welcome if he makes this effort—and makes it successfully.

What are some of these profit-enhancing ways accountancy can contribute to marketing profitability? A number of them are suggested by the profit-analyzing deficiencies mentioned earlier: distributor profitability,

---

[2] Dr. Michael Schiff, chairman of the accounting department at New York University, and his brother Jack, professor of marketing at Pace College, have done more to build bridges between the accounting and marketing functions than anyone else. Many useful suggestions can be found in the book cited earlier and in Dr. Michael Schiff's "The Sales Territory as a Fixed Asset," *Journal of Marketing*, October 1960.

marketing channel profitability, salesman profitability, customer profitability, and the like.

TERRITORIAL PROFITABILITY ANALYSIS

One of the most constructive—if it is undertaken in conjunction with the market research department and the traffic department—is to prepare territorial profit and loss statements. This is an old but an under-utilized technique. It involves setting down all the sales costs and profit factors applicable to each sales territory, including advertising, transportation costs, etc., together with data on each territory's market potential.

Every marketing man knows that some sales territories make money and some break even. He knows that still others contribute needed volume or represent investments for the future. He probably has a rough idea of what actions he wants in given areas and which areas he wants to leave alone.

However, a rough idea isn't enough. Too many marketing executives make decisions by reflex, relying solely on rule-of-thumb judgments. Those who don't analyze each of their territories from time to time are overlooking a sound device for improving the profitability of their operations. They are also overlooking a key way to win support for their decisions from above and from below.

HOW TO DO IT

To analyze profit and loss by territory, set down all the sales costs and profit factors applicable to each territory, together with data on each territory's market potential. (The last-named is often left out, although it enters heavily into the marketing manager's thinking. However, his peers and subordinates may suspect him of making decisions in a vacuum if he does not show it.)

For each territory, list the following elements down the lefthand side of a sheet: sales potential, current sales, production cost of product(s), transportation costs, direct selling costs, indirect selling costs, and local factors (such as nearness to competitor's plant, local competition, sales or inventory taxes). Then, to the right of that column, enter the figure that shows how things stand right now. To the right of the second column, list the targeted objectives for each of the elements (with the dates on which you expect to hit the target). In the final righthand column, list the actions you think necessary to achieve your immediate objectives in each area.

In most cases, this analysis will require the combined efforts of the market research department, the traffic manager, and the sales accounting people. This is, in fact, one of its chief benefits. When each of these people sees how the information he provides leads to a marketing decision, he is much more likely to support that decision. The traditional battle lines that tend to separate these functions will melt away.

This kind of analysis clearly points up whether the marketing manager should increase or decrease the sales effort and sales expense dollars entrusted to him—and what the stakes are and the returns should be in each case. Properly done, it differs little from the Schiff principle of treating each sales territory as a fixed asset. The accountant, the marketing manager, and the market research man who collaborate on this kind of an analysis usually complete it with enormously increased respect for one another.

EXAMPLES

One decision made as the result of such an analysis concerned a Midwestern state. Its sales potential for the company making the analysis was high, and so was the expense for national advertising, which was of course, allocated on the basis of circulation. Personal sales efforts were only nominal, however. As a result, sales were quite low, and the territory showed a loss. When these facts were exposed, the decision was to hire enough salesmen for this Midwestern market to achieve at least a breakeven level of sales.

A territorial analysis, of course, needs to be done only once every few years. In general, it should be performed only when there are fresh and informative data available on market potentials.

Here is a case in which territorial profitability analysis helped turn a company around to better profitability:

A company made electrical products for industry. Its annual sales were slightly over $25 million, but it carried a heavy debt load, and profit margins were uncomfortably narrow. The chief marketing executive, a relative newcomer, decided his area needed the most attention. He began probing for soft spots.

Years before, when the company was founded, there was little money for hiring salesmen. Accordingly, management had hired independent agents, offering them a commission rate high enough to ensure their interest in pioneering the company's products. A few years later, in certain sparsely populated areas where no agent could be induced to take the line on a commission basis, direct salesmen were hired.

COMMISSIONS UNREALISTIC

Since this choice of marketing channels had been largely fortuitous, the marketing executive's first step was to analyze territorial potentials and sales costs. His analysis confirmed many previous suspicions, uncovered a few surprises, and, most important of all, justified certain necessary steps.

Some samples from the chart he worked up are shown in Table 1.

The original commission rates may have been low for new products, but they had become unrealistically high now that the products no longer required much pioneering. Territory No. 14 (covered by a direct salesman)

TABLE 1

Territorial analysis

Territory	Total annual industry potential	Annual company sales	Percentage of penetration	Field sales cost $	%
No. 1 Agent	$20,000,000	$1,000,000	5%	$130,000	13%
No. 16 Agent	5,000,000	1,000,000	20	130,000	13
No. 14 Direct salesman	1,000,000	400,000	40	16,000	4
No. 18 Direct salesman (sparsely populated)	200,000	120,000	60	18,000	15

probably represented the ideal situation: The 40 per cent market penetration was considered as high as was realistic to shoot for, and the 4 per cent cost seemed to be the lowest that was consistent with good coverage of the market.

The actions taken were all orthodox as well as humane. The agents in Territories No. 1 and No. 16 (as well as some other agents in territories showing similar figures) were given realistic sales volume and expense quotas. Eventually, both became direct factory branches, retaining the best of the old personnel.

The salesman in Territory No. 14, with 40 per cent market penetration and a 4 per cent sales cost, was given a substantial bonus. The salesman in sparsely populated Territory No. 18 was encouraged to become an independent agent and was given a sub-office in another part of his territory to supervise. The marketing vice president helped him obtain two good product lines from noncompeting companies to sell. The commision rate was dropped slightly. Territory No. 18 probably still remained unprofitable to the company, but management decided not to risk having a marketing vacuum near an adjoining high-potential market area.

As a result of building up the kind of sales force required to meet the company's current market needs, sales rose 30 per cent over the next two years, and profits increased by 50 per cent. During the same period creditors began to give the company better interest rates on the money they had loaned. The turnaround was completed within 30 months.

PHYSICAL DISTRIBUTION

Similar analysis—with similar results—can be made of the profitability of individual salesmen, of products, and of such special factors as various aspects of physical distribution. Here is another case in which accounting collaborated in a marketing turnaround—in this case as a result of a physical distribution system analysis.

This company produced some 7,000 items, about half of which were industrial supplies. The industrial supplies division had yearly sales of about $8 million, nearly all through a chain of company-owned branch warehouses.

With such a wide product line, management had emphasized long production runs to keep manufacturing costs down. This seemingly laudable policy had, unfortunately, put the company in a loss position. Large inventories of slow-selling goods had accumulated. Out-of-stock situations arose frequently. Deliveries of bread-and-butter products were slow, and customers were going elsewhere to get them. Coordination between manufacturing and sales was nonexistent. Salesmen were getting too little of the right goods to sell and too much merchandise they couldn't move.

The marketing vice president decided to act. Since his top management had always stressed cost analysis in evaluating new moves, he decided to do likewise.

1. With the controller, he developed accurate data on the cost of owning finished goods inventories, product group by product group. Not surprisingly, it averaged about 25 per cent of value per year.

2. He developed careful estimates of the amount of business lost by the branches because of lack of the merchandise on order from the plants. He supplemented this by internal studies showing the cost of handling back orders.

3. Finally, with the help of his branch managers, the marketing vice president conservatively estimated the business lost the past year because customers had shifted their business elsewhere and because salesmen had dissuaded some of them from ordering chronically out-of-stock items.

When all his figures were ready, he sent the president a short, well-documented report. It showed, almost incontestably, that:

1. The annual cost of owning the excessive, poorly balanced finished goods inventories—both in factory warehouses and in branches, both those ordered and those shipped unordered—equalled gross profit margins on some product groups and exceeded them on others.

2. The branches were incurring excessive costs because of heavy ill-balanced inventories, lost business, and back orders, and these excess costs approximated the difference between budgeted sales costs and actual sales costs.

The second part of the marketing executive's memo outlined his proposed and already partially tested remedial program. Over the next few months, all its major elements were put into effect, as follows:

1. The company plants agreed to abandon the practice of shipping unordered goods to the branches.

2. Based on sales forecasts, minimum and maximum stock levels and

standard order quantities were established for all the products carried by the branches.

3. Numerous changes were made in the procedures for handling branch stock orders on the plants. Orders were still placed monthly, but they were staggered throughout the month. Orders from the most distant branches were scheduled for placement early in the month, while those for nearby branches were scheduled for later in the month. As a result, plant shipping rooms began to complete the filling of branch stock orders within 48 hours of receipt instead of the three or four weeks that had prevailed before. This improvement was made possible largely by a steady, uniform flow of work in the plant shipping rooms and by the use of new stock replenishment order forms matching factory warehouse layouts, which reduced order picking time.

The marketing executive's system was not intended to be a sophisticated one initially, and many refinements, such as improving sales forecasting techniques and setting up each branch as a profit center, were left to be added later. Even so, the results achieved within about eight months from the time the marketing vice president started his studies were dramatic:

Sales increased 18 per cent, as a result of better merchandise availability.

Finished goods inventories were cut nearly 60 per cent and their annual carrying costs were reduced by some $200,000.

The number of out-of-stock and back-ordered items was reduced substantially, enabling the branches to regain some previously disaffected customers.

The longer-term improvements were also gratifying. Production management, having had its attention called rather forcibly to the importance of total costs rather than just manufacturing costs, initiated a major effort to improve one of the root causes of the problem: its production scheduling.

BROAD-BASED STUDY

Here is an example of an analytical study that covered various aspects of the marketing function:

A company made power generation specialties sold to public utilities, private power generation facilities, and certain process industries. It was a long-established firm, and its products enjoyed an exceptional reputation for quality. However, profits were low. For years annual sales had remained at a relatively static level of about $8 million. There was little awareness of a marketing problem at all until the company hired a brilliant young industrial engineer, who improved production scheduling so substantially that considerable excess productive capacity was disclosed. Management became disturbed about the idle facilities and manpower, and the company's marketing manager decided to find out just what was wrong.

It was generally known that the key individuals specifying the purchase of power generation specialties in customer organizations were the piping draftsman and designers. However, the marketing executive found that neither he nor his salesmen were as familiar as they should have been with the details of the selection and decision-making processes that took place in the drafting rooms.

Investigation showed that these decision makers in the drafting rooms considered the company's catalogs inconvenient to use and often not complete. They had not been modernized in some years. The first step, therefore, was to obtain an appropriation to get the catalogs up to date and complete.

The chief engineer was given this assignment, heading a task force that included one of the younger home-office sales executives who had had recent, intensive drafting room experience. Three chief draftsmen in the employ of friendly nearby customers were persuaded to serve as an informal advisory committee. One of them was a man with unusually inventive ideas on how to make both the selection and the drafting procedures easy and foolproof. They served with the approval of their employers and were compensated for their time. The catalog that finally evolved—in record time—was clear, complete, and attractive; contained numerous innovations; and is now widely regarded in the industry as a model of ease and convenience.

Sales potentials were estimated—the company had not undertaken forecasting in any serious manner before—and the company's sales results were compared with them. This led to the discontinuance of certain manufacturers' representatives who had obviously been lethargic in their activities on the company's behalf, the opening of two new company sales offices in new market areas, and considerable redeployment of sales manpower to accord better with the opportunities for sales. In addition, several house accounts were assigned to the field sales organization to assure more effective coverage.

These moves to improve coverage of the market created opportunities to promote several salesmen. This also helped to stimulate morale.

Two other changes were made that improved the field sales organization. The first involved training; the second, compensation. With the assistance of the most successful company salesman, the marketing department prepared instructional material to guide the sales office managers in showing their men how to explain the use of the new catalog. This new material also showed how the salesmen could be more helpful to the men in the customers' and prospects' companies who were responsible for specifying the choice of power generation specialties. The importance of continuing to cover purchasing executives was also stressed, of course. In revamping the compensation setup, a simple sales incentive plan was installed to replace the previous salary-only policy. It provided a commission on sales over quotas agreed to by the marketing manager and the individual men.

Some of these actions paid off quickly, but most required a few months to show results. The significant achievements were these: a sales increase of 20 per cent; an increase in pretax profits that was more than commensurate with the sales increase, since the increased volume was produced on existing, already depreciated facilities; and full use of the company's previously idle manpower and machinery.

OTHER AREAS

There are many other ways in which accountancy can help marketing, outside the obvious areas of budgeting and forecasting:

Analyses showing profitability at varying sales volumes

Class of trade profitability

Product-group profitability for product managers (making certain to distinguish between those costs they can control and those they can't)

Analyses for special sales managers. (Nearly every business has some of these—national accounts manager, government sales manager, etc.)

The accountant can be very useful in helping the marketing executive determine—and not in too theoretical terms—the most profitable product mix. He also can cost out practical alternatives the marketing manager should consider, different channels of distribution, for example. This sort of analysis is probably done best when the controller has his own man in the marketing department.

Typically, the marketing department is one in which many essentials are nebulously defined. Authority is usually clearly delegated, but responsibility for profit is seldom clear-cut; often the marketing man has little more than profit awareness to go on.

Even more than other departments, marketing tends to be deluged with reports it cannot utilize. Accounting should try to cut down the number of these and devise ways to make those that survive more actionable.

Marketing has, in the main, paid relatively little attention to the profitability and productivity of its own operations. There are enormously fruitful opportunities for the accounting and controllership functions to contribute to improvement in this area. But, to be listened to, to hope for action, be sure you first have a good understanding of your company's marketing activity. An approach modeled after techniques used in manufacturing will almost certainly get you into hot water.

If you can possibly find the opportunity to do so, first see if you cannot make the marketing function more effective in its own terms—this usually means getting more business—by cranking some basic understanding of customer and prospects accounting into your salesmen's thinking and into their sales presentations. This effort can be rewarding not only for its own sake but also for the doors it will open to let you help make the marketing function more profitable.

Marketing profitability analysis offers a significant opportunity for profit improvement. Marketing profitability analysis may be the most important facet of a management information system. The authors cite reasons for the weaknesses in many reporting systems and enumerate the benefits of establishing effective reporting systems.

29. MARKETING PROFITABILITY ANALYSIS *

Henry DeVos,† Martin Isenberg,‡ and Monroe Schaefer ‡

In today's dynamic business environment, there are ever-increasing demands being placed on the organization for more definitive information —for facts about its operations. The pressures being exerted are both internal and external to the organization.

Stockholders and security analysts often raise probing questions about operations and even the adequacy of information required for management decisions. The Securities and Exchange Commission is now attempting to have companies that are registered furnish more sales and earnings data on a segmented basis, e.g.; by product line division or industry grouping.

But more importantly, management itself must have vital information about its operations. At a time when companies are devoting significant effort and costs to complex management information systems and high-speed computers, the availability of basic information, such as the profitability of each segment of the business, is lacking in a surprisingly large number of cases. A marketing profitability analysis provides this information and, in many cases, identifies opportunity for significant profit improvement.

A marketing profitability analysis develops the revenues, costs and profits for each segment of a business. A segment is defined as a component of the business capable of generating a profit—and is therefore susceptible to profit measurement. Examples are products, channels of distribution and customers. The analysis is quantitative in nature. It is based upon a series of comprehensive snapshots of profit results under existing operating conditions.

* Reprinted from "Marketing Profitability Analysis," *Journal of Accountancy* (March 1968), pp. 76–83.
† American Institute of Certified Public Accountants.
‡ Lybrand, Ross Bros. & Montgomery.

Although the analysis usually identifies opportunities for profit improvement, its basic scope does not initially include an evaluation of the effectiveness of all revenue and cost factors. For example, reviews of pricing strategy, purchasing effectiveness or materials control are separate, although perhaps simultaneous, studies. Also, the results of the analysis should not be considered as the sole basis for planning. Many other factors such as market share, consumer demands and competitive strategies must be considered.

Many reporting systems currently in use fail to satisfy management's needs for four apparent reasons:

1. Dynamic aspects or segments of the business are grouped when analyzed. This produces averages for broad sections of the operations, often hiding conditions warranting attention.
2. Certain segments, such as channels of distribution, end markets, customer size and order size, are not analyzed at all.
3. Unsound economic logic is applied through arbitrary allocations of costs to the segments.
4. Only manufacturing costs, and not marketing costs, are identified with the segments.

POTENTIAL BENEFITS

A marketing profitability analysis offers significant opportunity for profit improvement, especially where the following conditions exist:

1. The marketing environment is complex, consisting of many products, channels of distribution, territories, customers, etc.
2. Sales and marketing costs are significant.
3. Any of the above-mentioned shortcomings exist in the present reporting system.

A few examples of profitability problems exposed in various companies through the use of this analysis are presented below. In each case, either a major unprofitable activity was identified, or a misconception of true profitability was clarified.

1. Sixty per cent of the products in the line accounted for only 3% of sales, 1% of profits but 30% of the inventories on hand.
2. Fifteen per cent of the products in the line accounted for 90% of sales and 95% of profits.
3. One of the most profitable products was previously considered to be highly unprofitable.
4. Fifty per cent of the customers sold to in a particular territory accounted for only 7% of sales.
5. Six per cent of the customers sold to accounted for 75% of sales and 80% of profit. Conversely, 94% of the customers accounted for only 25% of sales and 20% of profits.

6. Thirty per cent of the total 800 customers individually accounted for less than 1/100th of 1% of total sales.
7. For 50% of the orders shipped, the company paid excessive freight as the weights were less than that allowed by the minimum dollar charge.

MAJOR STEPS TO PERFORM

There are generally five major steps to perform in developing the analysis:
1. Develop a thorough understanding of the marketing environment.
2. Define the questions.
3. Review the behavior of costs and develop the logic for identifying costs with the marketing segments.
4. Design the report formats.
5. Develop and process the data.
6. Use the information.

The marketing environment

In order to structure the scope of the analysis properly and to evaluate the results intelligently, it is important to have a thorough understanding of the company and its marketing environment. So the first step in the analysis should include a consideration of:

1. Products and/or services.
2. Product mix.
3. Product life cycle.
4. Uniqueness of product, if any.
5. Span of distribution.
6. Channels of distribution.
7. Physical methods of distribution.
8. Seasonality.
9. Sales organization.
10. Pricing and promotion strategies.
11. Market conditions.
12. Competitive position.
13. Customers and ultimate consumers.
14. Cost characteristics.

Conducting an analysis without first having an understanding of the environment often produces misleading or at least incomplete results. For example, many companies perform analyses directed solely to product-line profitability, even though there are various methods used to merchandise and distribute their products. Each of these methods of doing business generally has its own peculiar pricing and cost characteristics causing different measurable effects on the profitability of products. Because of these

EXHIBIT 1

Flow of analysis through marketing profit segments

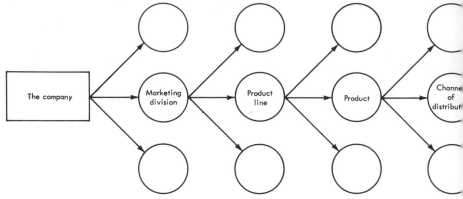

different *businesses,* the analysis should present the profitability of each business, and each product within each business, and each product on a total company basis.

An example of the above is a company which sold basically the same products through six different distribution channels in various parts of the country. These included sales to independent distributors, company owned distributors, retail chains, other manufacturers, consumers through mail orders, and institutions. Major groups of products were produced in different plants. Most selling expenses were incurred by salesmen who sold only to the independent distributors. Both company brands and private label products were sold, the latter mainly to other manufacturers. Advertising was consumer-oriented and therefore was not beneficial to private label or institutional sales. The price of the product varied according to the channel of distribution.

These conditions clearly demonstrate that the method of merchandising and distributing can have a significant effect on the profitability of a product. An understanding of the company's environment is required in order to determine what to analyze, the logic to apply and the results.

Questions to be answered

The questions which should be answered by the analysis should now be defined. They should be directed to points of profit evaluation; i.e., marketing segments. The method of inquiry should resemble a decision-making process by starting with a major segment and flowing to the minor segments comprising it. (See Exhibit 1.)

The sales and marketing personnel should play a key role in defining the questions.

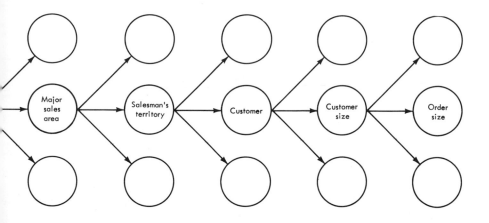

Examples of questions are:

1. What are the sales and profitability of each marketing division?
2. Within each marketing division, what are the sales and profitability of each product line?
3. Within each product line, what are the sales and profitability of each product?
4. For each product, what are the sales and profitability for each channel of distribution?
5. By channel of distribution, what are the product sales and profitability of each major geographic sales area?
6. For each major geographic sales area, what are the product sales and profitability of each salesman's territory?
7. Within each territory, what are the product sales and profitability of each customer?
8. What are the sales and profitability of each order size?

Similar trees of questions can be constructed for key accounts, customers, television areas, salesmen's territories and order sizes by defining a series of questions relevant to the segment selected.

Cost behavior and identification

A major task in the analysis is to identify costs with marketing segments of the business. The analyst should not be concerned with whether he selects direct cost of absorption cost principles, nor should he be confused by attempting to reconcile the true differences between the two. His prime concern should be to use sound economic logic—and identify the "relevant" costs with each marketing segment.

Certain guidelines which may be helpful are as follows:

1. A cost should be identified with a segment only if it has some measurable cause-and-effect relationship to it.
2. Arbitrary allocations of costs to segments should not be performed.
3. Attention should be directed to the most significant costs.
4. Finite accuracy of cost identification need not be stressed.
5. Certain costs will be directly identifiable with one segment and not with others.

The types of costs to be identified with segments will generally fall into the following categories:

Direct variable. A cost which can unquestionably be identified with a segment and which generally varies in direct proportion (linear) to sales volume. A cost which would not be incurred if the segment were eliminated. Examples are variable product manufacturing costs, brokers' commissions, cash discounts.

Direct period or committed. A cost which can unquestionably be identified with a segment but which does not necessarily or generally vary in direct proportion (linear) to sales volume. A cost which would not be incurred if the segment were eliminated. Examples are regional warehousing, product media advertising and product research and development.

Use of resource. A cost which is direct to one segment and not direct to another segment, but the demands on the latter segment are easily measurable. An example is salesman salaries which are direct to the area, district and salesman segments. Although the salaries may not necessarily be direct to a customer segment, the amount of salesman's time (the resource) spent on each customer is measurable.

Benefits available. A cost which is direct to one segment and not direct to another, but the benefit available (not necessarily the benefits obtained) by the latter segment is measurable. An example is television advertising which may be direct to a product segment and to a television area of the country. Although it is not necessarily direct to a particular sales area or city, the benefits available (viewing audience of each area) are ascertainable.

Indirect nonidentifiable. A cost which is not capable of being easily identified with a segment on any sound measurable basis, without performing a complete study of what effect a significant change in a segment or segments would have on the cost. Examples are administrative management and home office rent.

Before performing the actual mechanics of the analysis, it is often helpful to prepare a chart reflecting the approximate amount of costs (by type) identifiable with each marketing segment and the method of cost identification (see Exhibit 2). An understanding of the company's environment and a review of the existing management reports (even if only trial balances) usually provide the basis for such a chart.

EXHIBIT 2

Identification of costs with marketing segments

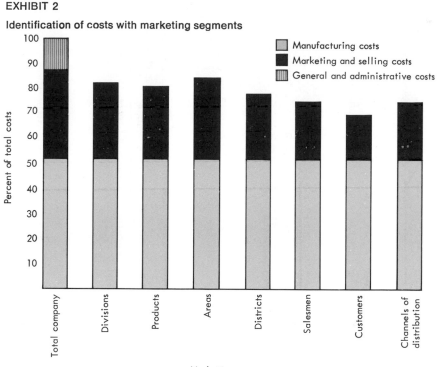

Marketing segments

Report formats

At this point the design of the report formats is quite easy if the prior steps in the analysis have been properly completed. Developing an understanding of the company's marketing environment enables the analyst to define what should be analyzed and which are the significant costs to identify with each of the marketing segments. By defining the questions to be answered by the analysis, the basic structure of the report formats is established. All formats should be reviewed with the key marketing or sales personnel before the data are processed.

There are basically two major types of reports:

1. *Data reports.* This type of report presents, either in summary or detail form, all of the relevant revenue and cost factors for a particular marketing segment, such as a product line. It should be remembered that an analytical report is more probing than a control report, thus warranting more detail. A control report, on the other hand, is generally used to measure performance against a plan.

Although the format of the report should be tailored to the particular company, examples of columnar headings are shown in Exhibits 3 and 4. Significant value can be added to the reports if the actual data are ranked

EXHIBIT 3

Product group profitability analysis (data report)

Product group	Sales	Mfg. gross margin Amount	% to sales	Selling and distribution costs* Amount	% to sales	Profit contribution before advertising Amount	% to sales	Advertising	Net profit contribution Amount	% to sales	Rankings $ Profit	% Profit	% of total Sales	Profit
A	$116	$76	65%	$11	9%	$65	56%	$14	$51	43%	1	36	23%	25%
B	66	36	55	7	10	29	44	—	29	44	2	35	13	14
C	58	40	69	7	12	33	57	5	28	48	3	26	12	14
D	82	32	39	10	12	22	27	3	22	27	4	47	16	11
E	16	10	62	3	19	7	44	1	6	38	5	42	3	3

* Detail reports reflect separate amounts for such items as commissions, allowances, freight and warehouse costs.

EXHIBIT 4

Channel of distribution profitability analysis (data report)

Channel*	Sold in	Sold to	Sales	Mfg. gross margin Amount	% to sales	Allowances	Freight and warehousing	Profit contribution Amount	% to sales	Rank of territory within channel $ Sales	$ Profit
Supermarkets	Territory 17	Customer									
		A	$305	$131	43%	$ 61	$15	$ 55	18%		
		B	187	103	55	37	15	51	27		
		C	170	46	27	34	14	(2)	Loss		
		D	50	15	30	10	3	2	4		
	Total territory		$712	$295	41%	$142	$47	$106	15%	1	12

*This report would be prepared for all channels of distribution, and the territories and customers within each.

by factors such as highest profit amount, highest freight per cent to sales, lowest profit per machine hour or highest profit per cent to sales.

2. Search reports. Electronic data processing equipment enables the analyst to search a mass of data and print reports in reply to specific questions. This does not require mathematical models, nor real time computer systems, nor does it necessarily encompass computer simulation. Examples of data provided by search reports are presented below and in Exhibits 5 and 6.

1. If the profit contribution percentage for territory A is 41%, which customers are above 50% and which are below 30%? How great is the dispersion?
2. If product 101 is unprofitable, which customers buy only that product? Which customers buy other products with higher profits?
3. Which orders are being shipped at a less than minimum freight weight for which a minimum freight rate is being paid?
4. How often are various sized orders shipped from each warehouse?

A method of determining what to search is to develop the simulated profitability of each sales event on a unit basis. For example, compute the profitability of one unit of:

Product A,
Sold to distribution channel B,
In quantities of C, D and E,
By salesman F or broker G,
To customers in location H,
From warehouse I.

By precomputing the profitability of each type of sales event on a unit basis, those events of a low or unprofitable nature can be determined. The computer can then be used to search the actual events and print out both the frequency of occurrence and the marketing segments in which they occurred.

Developing and processing of data

The difficulty of developing the required data will depend upon the adequacy of the company's existing information system and the complexity of its operations. An inventory must first be taken of the data presently available to determine exact form, volumes and relative accuracy.

The following situations are often encountered in developing the cost data required for the analysis.

1. Costs are presently recorded in the books of account by type or nature of expense, and also possibly by department responsible for incurring them. Certain of these costs should be analyzed and individually identified with the marketing segments. An example would be an analysis of advertising

EXHIBIT 5

Customer "low" profitability analysis (search report)

		% profit contribution*		Deviation from average caused by				
Customer	Sales amount	Actual	Deviation from average	Gross margin	Allowances	Freight	No. of products ordered	No. of orders
Customer A	$750	25%	− 5	+ 3	−7	− 1	12	3
Customer B	200	18	−12	− 4	+2	−10	1	2
Customer C	280	10	−20	−10	−3	− 7	2	8

*Average profit contribution of 30% reflects the absence on this report of costs not identifiable with customers, such as product advertising.

EXHIBIT 6

Frequency of minimum orders and possible savings by consolidation (freight search report)

		Profit contribution		Freight		Number of shipments		If shipments consolidated		
									Freight savings	
Customer	Sales	Amount	% to sales	Cost	Weight	Total	With minimum weight charge	Freight cost	Amount	%
ABC	$380	$78	25%	$20	700 lb.	2	1	$17	$ 3	15%
MNO	175	53	30	17	400	3	2	10	7	41
XYZ	195	20	10	40	400	8	8	10	30	75

costs to determine the products and/or territories with which these costs should be identified.

2. Other costs must be identified, first with a function, and then with a marketing segment. An example would be the delivery costs incurred by a company's own trucking operation. The driver's wages and the many truck-related expenses should be analyzed to develop a combined cost per ton-mile or per cubic-foot-mile before delivery expenses are identified with a customer or area.

3. Certain costs are not recorded in the information system in the unit of measure required for the analysis. Examples would be common carrier costs for delivery to a particular customer, or sales allowances for a particular product. This information must be captured from the originating sources such as freight bills.

Automated data processing equipment should be given strong consideration in both developing and processing the data. Exhibit 7 indicates some of the inputs and outputs of a recent marketing profitability analysis which was entirely performed by a computer. Companies not having their own processing equipment could utilize a service bureau.

Use of the Information

Once the quantitative analysis is completed, the decision-making process really begins. This consists of the evaluation of the results of the analysis and the definition and implementation of changes required to the existing practices and policies. It demands the active participation of top management members, as the skills required are significantly different from those used in performing the basic analysis.

This decision-making process would generally include an evaluation of the available alternatives, the effect of any changes on customer demand and relations, probable competitor reaction, and of course the company's basic long-range plans. Estimates of these factors should be defined within ranges, and probabilities of occurrence should be assigned.

THE ANALYSIS IS NOT A COMPLETE INFORMATION OR CONTROL SYSTEM

It is important to point out that a marketing profitability analysis is not, in itself, a complete management information system. A few of the reasons are as follows:

1. The information required for planning differs significantly in scope and timing from that required for control. Analyses should be used to plan more effectively, and not solely for after-the-fact control.

2. A management information system should concentrate on all of the critical factors of a particular company. The definition of a critical factor is: "Lack of attention to it could have a significant effect on profitability and

EXHIBIT 7

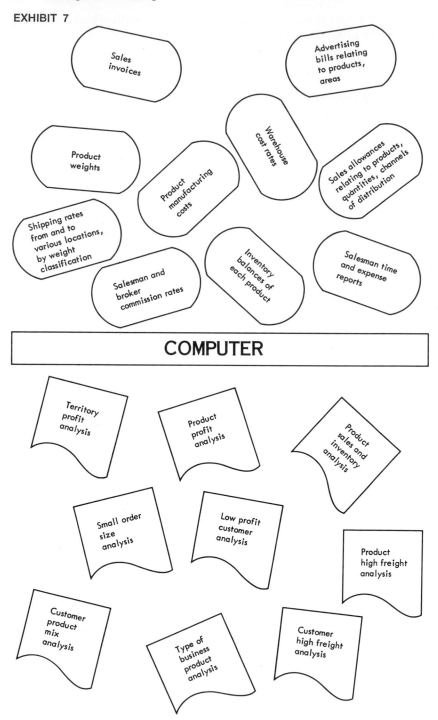

growth." Although critical factors vary significantly by industry and company, examples are customer service, equipment maintenance, material usage control, inventory management and capital investment.

3. The implementation of policy changes resulting from this type of analysis should be fit into a context of managing. This requires defined objectives, policies, organizational structure and responsibilities. Continual use of this analysis to constantly track an uncontrolled environment can be extremely frustrating and often ineffective.

4. A total information system requires operating as well as financial information.

5. A total information system requires data external to the company itself, as well as information concerning its own operations.

6. Information developed by the analysis requires further application of tools and techniques to improve the effectiveness of the factors which were analyzed.

SUMMARY

It is fair to state that the information provided by a marketing profitability analysis is basic criteria for sound decision-making. Most companies will achieve significant profit improvement by performing the analysis and properly acting upon its results. The analysis is a necessity, not a luxury, for any profit-oriented business.

f.

Multinational marketing

THE GROWING importance of American business and government involvement in international business and international marketing is producing changes in marketing policies and practices. The changes include altering the very definition of a business. This change in the way of defining the corporate concept departs from the view of the firm as a national, one-flag business and views the firm as a multinational conglomerate; a firm without a national identity and with multinational management, equity, and manufacturing operations. Marketing management decisions in such a multinational context will continue to grow in complexity as the expansion of multinational corporations continues.

A framework to conceptualize the differences among consumers and institutions in various parts of the world is required. This framework is necessary to provide managers with a base for better marketing decisions in the changing multinational environment. The articles included in this section propose approaches to conceptualizing the dynamic forces and strategies open to management in international operations.

Multinational marketing does not differ in fundamentals from domestic marketing. It could even be said that domestic marketing is a particular case of international marketing. The same basic marketing tools, concepts, techniques, and know-how apply in both cases. Differences arise in terms of consumers, institutions, and economic, social, political, and cultural factors. Dynamic forces and changes may not only contribute to unify various country markets, but they may alternatively differentiate such markets even more. These forces and changes include the emergence of trading blocs, the formation of common markets, population growth, diffusion of technology, urbanization, increased mobility, and the standardization of business practices.

The first selection, by Leighton, points out how the shift toward the internationalization of American business took place and the resulting implications. Lipson and Lamont caution marketers against lumping less developed countries together while ignoring the differences in each individual market. Buzzell then evaluates the potential gains to consider in standardizing various elements of marketing programs used in different areas. Finally, Keegan formulates explicit product and communication strategies according to product use and function.

Changes in management technology and thinking have contributed to the development of large complex international companies. A reevaluation of traditional views of trade, direct investment, and demand considerations are required for marketers who must adapt to the new internationalization of business.

---

30. THE INTERNATIONALIZATION OF AMERICAN BUSINESS—THE THIRD INDUSTRIAL REVOLUTION *

David S. R. Leighton †

Changes in business management have been so vast in the last 15 years that this period might be described as "The Third Industrial Revolution." The principal characteristic of this revolution has been the emergence of corporations of unprecedented size, complexity, breadth and international scope. For example:

1. In 1969, International Business Machines Corporation had total sales of $7.2 *billion* with $2.5 *billion* coming from outside the U.S. This company operated in 108 countries with 99,000 foreign employees, one-third of the company's total payroll.
2. The International Telephone and Telegraph Corporation had worldwide sales of over $5.4 *billion from 200 companies and divisions in 67 coun-*

---

* Reprinted from "The Internationalization of American Business—The Third Industrial Revolution," *Journal of Marketing*, Vol. 34, No. 3 (July 1970), pp. 3–6.
† University of Western Ontario.

tries employing a total of 300,000 persons. It derived 40% of its sales and a substantial share of its $300,000,000 before-tax income from assets outside the U.S.

Manufacturing or service companies of this scale of international operations were virtually unknown 15 years ago, at least in the U.S. Today, these are merely two of several hundred U.S.-based corporations that meet the test of multinationality, owning and operating a significant proportion of their assets abroad. The really substantial movement of U.S. firms abroad that began in the late 1950s marked the true beginning of The Third Industrial Revolution.

This movement continues unabated; growth of U.S. direct investments abroad has maintained a consistent 10% per-annum rate over the last 10 years. A development of this magnitude will inevitably shape the international environment for business in the 70s and beyond. Its implications for academicians, businessmen, and government policy makers have not yet been fully appreciated.

THE THREE INDUSTRIAL REVOLUTIONS

The First Industrial Revolution occurred in England in the last third of the eighteenth century. It was triggered by the invention of the steam engine, the replacement of hand labor, and the shift to more capital-intensive methods of production.[1] This spelled the end of the craft and "putting-out" systems, brought workers together under one roof, led to specialization and the division of labor, and put us on the road toward the industrial world of today.

The Second Industrial Revolution came in the 1880s and 1890s in the United States with the evolution of the national corporation. This was made possible in part by developments in communication, and in part by facilitating legal instruments. These developments enabled multiplant operation, opened markets, provided a vehicle for large-scale financing, and led to the growth of centralized staff and geographically decentralized line operations. They eventually pushed the corporation into large, vertically-integrated structures embracing research and development, marketing and distribution, and manufacturing.[2]

The Third Industrial Revolution began in the last half of the 1950s, with the sudden explosion of U.S. corporations beyond national and continental limits. From a modest level of direct investment of $20 billion in 1955, most of it in Canada, U.S. private direct investment abroad increased to

---

[1] This development has been documented in many books and articles. See, for example, Paul Mantoux, *The Industrial Revolution in the Eighteenth Century* (rev. ed., New York: Harper & Row, Publishers, 1961).

[2] For an excellent summary of these events, see Alfred D. Chandler, Jr., *Strategy and Structure* (New York: Doubleday Anchor, 1966), chap. i.

$65.7 billion by 1968, with Europe the main recipient.[3] This development has helped transform U.S. business inward-looking, parochial point of view to one of considerable international sophistication. At the same time it has wrought an even greater upheaval in the ways of foreign-based firms.

THE CHANGING ECONOMICS OF MANAGEMENT

The point that has been largely missed in writings on the subject is that this recent revolution in business has been primarily a revolution in management. The economics of managing a modern industrial enterprise have changed dramatically in little over a decade, making possible for the first time in history the successful operation of concerns of the size and scope of an IBM or ITT. These companies manufacture many diverse products, operate in a large number of different countries, and employ hundreds of thousands of people.

Less than half a century ago, it was very difficult to operate a company with foreign-based manufacturing facilities. Alfred Sloan and his associates travelled by boat to Germany to consummate their first real overseas venture, the General Motors purchase of Adam Opel A.G. in March, 1929.[4] The round-trip crossing took approximately two weeks. In addition, they spent several weeks on the Continent. During this time communication was difficult, and limited largely to telegraphic cable. Absence of top management for such an extended period would have been unthinkable for most companies. Sloan, however, had successfully delegated most operating decisions to relatively autonomous divisions. Once management had returned to Detroit, control over Opel's operating decisions rested largely with the man in Germany, I. J. Reuter. It was significant that he was a "company man," known and trusted by Detroit management. Reports were long in transit, and it was difficult for head office staff to check and interpret data once received. Reaction time at the center was slow; however, with the the state of the art of management of the time, this was also true for other firms. It was not surprising that the few U.S. firms looking for other worlds to conquer turned their attention first to Canada. This neighboring country had the advantages of proximity, a common language, and similar cultural heritage.

Today's jet travel enables businessmen to cross the Atlantic and back simply to attend a single meeting. With improved telecommunications, large amounts of data can be quickly and inexpensively transmitted from overseas plant to head office. There they may be digested by digital computer and critical operating data channeled to the executives concerned.

---

[3] These and other statistics on foreign investment are given in N. William Hazen, "Overseas High Stakes of Multinational Firms," in Bernard A. Morin (ed.), *Marketing in a Changing World* (Chicago, Ill.: American Marketing Association, June, 1969), pp. 47–52.

[4] The events surrounding the Opel purchase are detailed in Alfred P. Sloan, Jr., *My Years with General Motors* (New York: Macfadden-Bartell Corp., 1963), chap. xviii.

The health of hundreds of operating subsidiaries may thus be continuously monitored, fed back to corporate management, and corrective steps taken quickly before events get out of control. This is simply the application of the feedback and control principles of cybernetics to management of the overall corporation.

Organizations such as the modern-day ITT would have been impossible to administer economically prior to these developments. The thousands of clerks, bushels of records, and untold quantities of management time that would have been necessary to manage such an enterprise were out of the question only 15 years ago. Today, the job is being performed largely by electronic equipment and related planning and information systems coupled with a cadre of highly paid management specialists. This system of hardware, software and people, unlike a primarily clerical operation, represents a large capital investment and high fixed costs of operation. Such systems not only make possible the management and control of large-scale operations, but they also constitute a powerful force *compelling* businesses to extend their scope to make efficient use of the system itself.

At ITT, for example, each subsidiary works on the basis of annual, two- and five-year plans designed in detail and reviewed at least annually with the top officers of the corporation. Reports flow daily in to ITT's European headquarters in Brussels from subsidiaries in vastly differing lines of business. Even a small operating unit must submit as many as 13 reports per month, plus a number of others on quarterly, semi-annual or annual bases. The reports are processed by computer and analyzed by a highly skilled staff of financial and general business analysts. Where operations diverge from the plan, inquiries follow by Telex. Where trouble persists, teams of specialists converge upon the subsidiary and work with it until it is back on plan. Meanwhile, staff product line managers oversee various groupings of products seeking opportunities for intra-company sales, product improvements, or other business opportunities.

The core of ITT's business is this highly sophisticated planning and control system and, even more important, the talented team of about 2,000 managers who make it work. One criterion constantly in the forefront in the analysis of potential acquisitions is the opportunity to improve management under ITT control; i.e., by applying the ITT system. The central nature of the system to ITT's operation is underlined by the fact that several years ago the company stopped considering the acquisition of companies with less than $10 million in sales. This was due in part to the fact that small companies could not support the costs and effort required by the ITT control system.

This indicated that top managers in such situations, instead of facing eventually increasing marginal costs of management, as in classical theory, are actually facing a management cost curve which for all practical purposes is constantly declining. *The economics of management have undergone a complete transformation,* and it is this which has really been both the cause and effect of the growth of large multinational firms. It is significant that the growth of conglomerates also began to take off at about the same time as the growth of multinational companies, and for many of the same reasons. A principal task of top management in such firms has become to manage managers.

These developments imply that for the large multinational firm, management is not only a key resource, it is *the* key resource both in terms of people and systems. Having developed a large, sophisticated, and well-organized group of managers skilled in acquisitions and in operating complex systems, this team must be operated at a high level of its capacity. Continuous attention must be focused on acquiring new businesses, and more operating units must be integrated into the elaborate and expensive system for monitoring operations. Growth begets growth; expansion begets expansion. As yet the end is not in sight.

SOME IMPLICATIONS

The implications are many and complex, and some are still obscure. These implications pose serious questions to business leaders, to national policy makers, and to teachers and researchers in economics and business administration.

Because of the growth of multinational corporations, world business is no longer primarily concerned with trade, but with direct investment. In 1967, world output from foreign-owned subsidiaries of international corporations was about $240 billion, while exports from the major nations totalled $130 billion. Sidney Rolfe, who developed these figures, has pointed out the following:

> It is therefore clear that for the whole developed world, international investment has bypassed exports as the major channel of international economic relations, and there has been a massive shift from the original extractive industry investments to manufacturing and trade, banking, services and a further shift from developing to developed countries.[5]

Unfortunately, neither national policies nor conventional wisdom at the universities have yet caught up with these changes. Much of the theory by which we attempt to understand and predict events in the world of international business is derived from international trade theory. This has largely been considered from the point of view of the nation as a whole; i.e., it has been macro in nature, a tradition that dates back to the mercantilists and Adam Smith. Its principal cornerstone has been the theory of comparative advantage, which attributes trade patterns to a country's relative advantages in the factors of production—land, labor, capital and, more recently, management. The theory's main concern has been with flows of goods and capital across national boundaries.

It is becoming increasingly evident that this traditional approach is

---

[5] Dr. Rolfe is so quoted in the Toronto *Globe and Mail* Report on Business, Friday, May 2, 1969, in a report on an international conference on trade held in Washington, D.C.

entirely inadequate for the 1970s. The theory does not explain real-world trade flows very well, and in concentrating on nation-to-nation flows the theory deals with phenomena that are becoming less significant. In looking at trade from the country's point of view, we have lost sight of the fact that, except in certain special cases, countries do not trade with each other, companies do. The statistics we gather are aggregates, representing the sum of many thousands of transactions made by business firms with other business firms. Many of these business firms' critical decisions involve decisions on reinvestment of earnings or raising funds in foreign countries, neither of which results in any flow across borders. The decision to export, usually seen as something quite separate from capital flows, is coming to be looked upon as inextricably interlinked with the decision to invest; to decide to export is a decision *not* to invest in plant, and vice-versa. Contrary to classical theory, such decisions are based more often on demand and competitive considerations than on seeking lowest cost production sites. Most of these points become clear only when trade and investment are perceived as part of the decision-making process of business managers.

If we wish to explain phenomena in the world of international economics, we must adopt a micro orientation, focusing on the decision processes of individual firms, both buyers and sellers. We should look more to the study of direct investment and less to the study of international flows of goods. Kindleberger and Vernon, for example, have carried us part of the way; however, much is yet to be covered.[6]

The skills of the international marketing man are crucial in direct investment. Traditional international trade theory has ignored marketing; it has assumed perfect knowledge and has overlooked the key importance of demand functions. What we are seeing in an early stage of its development is the creation of a new body of theory in international economic relations, in which demand analysis and imperfections in knowledge will play a central role. There is hope that such a body of theory will bridge the gap that has for too long existed between the fields of international economics and international marketing. One example, already being explored, lies in the tremendous potential contribution of diffusion theory to understanding and improving the processes of economic development.

CONCLUSION

The revolution that has taken place in the economics of business management in the last 15 years has been profound. It has resulted in an international environment in which the old rules, policies, and theories are no longer adequate. New theories are desperately needed to help explain past events and to help us predict future developments.

The author has suggested that more useful theory can only come if a

---

[6] Charles Kindleberger, *American Business Abroad, Six Lectures on Direct Foreign Investment* (New Haven and London: Yale University Press, 1969); and Raymond Vernon, "International Investment and International Trade in the Product Cycle," *Quarterly Journal of Economics*, Vol. 80 (May 1966), pp. 190–207.

completely new orientation is adopted. A start could be made by looking at the decision processes in individual business firms operating under conditions of imperfect information. In the development of new theory, demand considerations must play a much more important part than they have in the past, and here the potential contribution of marketing is great. Above all, it must be recognized that the old world of trade has been largely superseded by the multinational corporation and direct investment. This will be the central fact of international business in the decade that lies ahead.

The less developed countries represent important areas for profitable service by business. However, multinational firms must adjust marketing policies to reflect an understanding of each country's distinct market characteristics. Only then should management attempt to capitalize on these potentially profitable markets.

---

31. MARKETING POLICY DECISIONS FACING INTERNATIONAL MARKETERS IN THE LESS DEVELOPED COUNTRIES *

Harry A. Lipson † and Douglas F. Lamont ‡

Marketers ask the following questions in making policy decisions to create profitable returns for their firms: What are the market opportunities? What market goals can be set? What type of market organization can be established? What market resources are available? What are the possible market offerings? How can control over market performance be maintained? What type of market audits will show future profit-making possibilities?[1]

International marketers make these policy decisions within national market economies whose sectoral capabilities to produce high-level standards of living for a majority of the population range from highly developed,

* Reprinted from "Marketing Policy Decisions Facing International Marketers in the Less Developed Countries," *Journal of Marketing*, Vol. 33, No. 4 (October 1969), pp. 24–31.

† University of Alabama.

‡ University of Alabama.

[1] For a discussion of the responsibilities of administrators of business systems, see Harry A. Lipson and John R. Darling, Jr., *Introduction to Marketing Administration* (New York: John Wiley & Sons, Inc. 1971).

as in the United States, to very poorly developed, as in Nigeria. Marketing policies employed in a mass consumption economy cannot be transferred to less-developed economies without a great deal of change. As a consequence, international marketers face the difficult task of adapting marketing policies to fit the peculiar requirements of local national markets.

This article will show marketers how to make proper marketing decisions within the less-developed countries (LDCs) of the world. LDCs are those countries which have a per capita national income of less than $500 per year. Their middle class is small; the majority of the people are poor. Markets are highly fragmented in terms of income, social class, language and tribal differences, and other socioeconomic characteristics. The institutional structure needed to integrate these markets is organized on a very inefficient basis or is nonexistent.

Marketers have to deal with these conditions in setting policy decisions that will lead to profits. They are faced with impoverished economies whose governments seek change. National economic plans drawn up to formalize the desire for greater economic prosperity give marketers an indication as to how they can support the public goals of the country in which they are doing business, and at the same time find new avenues for marketing success. Examples of adaptations in marketing policies to fit local governmental and cultural circumstances are presented below from experiences actually encountered within the underdeveloped world. India, Nigeria, and Mexico were selected for presentation simply because they show that the marketing adaptation problem is not bound by geography, cultural differences, or stages of economic growth. The problem exists for markets in Asia, Africa, and Latin America.[2] These examples may be interpreted as a running account of the "game of marketing adaptation" in the three countries and are designed to give marketers some guidance as to how they might better carry out their jobs within the LDCs.[3]

ANALYSIS OF MARKET OPPORTUNITIES

In the LDCs, an analysis of possible market opportunities is a three-fold procedure. First, given the paucity of information and its relative unreliability, marketers are faced with the problems of estimating customer markets from gross data sources. Means are available to do so,[4] and esti-

---

[2] The results presented in this paper are a part of a research project carried out in the International Business Program of the Graduate School of Business at the University of Alabama. Two graduate students, John W. Roquemore and Richard H. Kenyon, were responsible for the basic findings on India and Nigeria.

[3] The "game of marketing adaptation" was first suggested in a paper presented by one of the authors, Douglas F. Lamont, at the 1968 Southern Marketing Association meetings held in Washington, D.C. It has been published under the title of "Opportunities for Marketing Growth in the Mexican Market," *Southern Journal of Business*, Vol. 4 (April 1969), pp. 272–78.

[4] Reed Moyer, "International Market Analysis," *Journal of Marketing Research*, Vol. 5, (November 1968), pp. 353–61.

mates of potential markets through production figures converted into apparent consumption figures provide a marketer with useful analytical information. The knowledge that 5% of India's 520 million population, or 26 million people, have incomes that give them the buying power of the average American should suggest to marketers that it is imperative for them to get in early in India's industrialization and market development. Such a market size in fact represents an affluent market that is just a little larger than the Canadian market. If marketers only had a knowledge of India's per capita national income, they more than likely would have overlooked this "well-to-do" potential consumer market within the sea of a traditional society.

Second, such national estimates must be tempered with a qualitative understanding of the real regional and cultural differences that exist within the LDCs. The boundaries of most Indian states were drawn to represent the local dominance of a particular subcultural language. Before the war between Nigeria and Biafra, Nigeria had been divided into four regional areas; although in each area one major tribe dominated the others, 200 different languages are still spoken among the 40 million people of Nigeria. In West Africa, language differences reflect such wide cultural differences that only a very few products can bridge the gap successfully. Such simple things as the print on cotton fabrics fail to gain sufficient consumer acceptance for economy-of-scale purposes, because there are so many ideas as to what is right and proper. Market size in Nigeria is so small that marketers develop a market at their own peril if they do not know beforehand the *real* size of their potential market.

English is used as the *lingua franca* along with Hindi in India and Hausa in Nigeria. Spanish has played the same role in Mexico, but now it is slowly coming into full time use among the remaining three or four million Mexicans who speak different Indian languages. Language, therefore, plays a different role in Mexico for marketers. Marketers can be sure that the areas in which the Indian languages predominate are for the most part outside the developing sectors of the Mexican market economy. These would be areas that marketers should leave until last when planning new marketing activity within an LDC.

The real opportunities for marketers lie in regional and cultural market segments rather than in thinking about a broad national market opportunity. For each market segment, marketers should determine available income, effective buying power, propensity to buy, economic awareness for consumption increases, and those other socioeconomic characteristics that will give them the size of their potential market within highly fragmented national economies.

Third, an analysis of market opportunities will be complete only when marketers take into consideration the current shifts in governmental attitude on import-substitution industries, incentives for new investment, taxes and social security payments, and the many other items that will markedly affect whether the business operates at a profit or at a loss. Marketers should pay careful attention to changes in the administrative rules governing market entry. For example, by reading India's Second Five Year Plan (1956–1961), marketers found that certain industries were to be the exclusive responsibility of the Indian government. (This group includes munitions, atomic energy, iron and steel, heavy engineering and heavy electrical plant, coal, oil, most mining, aircraft, air transport, railways, shipbuilding, communications, and electrical generation and distribution.) A second group was listed for gradual state ownership. (This group includes some mining, aluminum, machine tools, ferro-alloys and tool steels, heavy chemicals, essential drugs, fertilizers, synthetic rubber, and road and sea transport.)[5] All other industries were left to private-sector enterprises for competitive market behavior. As the plan was carried out, it became apparent that the Indian government's Hindustan antibiotics factory and Tata's, an Indian private-sector drug enterprise, could not meet the growing demand for drugs; Merck Sharpe and Dohme was given permission to enter a market that formerly had been closed to foreign private-sector enterprises.[6] A similar situation developed in the production and distribution of fertilizers. The demand for fertilizers increased as the need for Indian agriculture increased, and Armco was brought into the fertilizer business to service the growing demand.[7] These are only two examples of why marketers should carefully study the developmental plans and administrative rulings of the governments in the LDCs.

Nigeria's first developmental plan, published in 1964, did not present any involved schedules of industries that would become government owned. It simply defined the priorities for investment. If marketers wished to make investments in those industries that were on the top of the priority list, then they would be given special benefits by the Nigerian government. Knowledge about Mexico's plans for the improvement of irrigation, agriculture, public retail markets, and towns along the American border tells marketers about potential profit-making opportunities.[8] Many development plans such as those of INP (Peru's National Planning Institute) or CORFO (Chile's Development Corporation) simply state the objectives to be achieved through the government's support of specific private-sector enterprises. A few plans, such as those of CORDIPLAN (the national plan of the Central Planning Agency of Venezuela) and the regional development plan of its offspring CVG (the Guyana Development Corporation), detail how new industry and new services will be brought to the wilderness of

---

[5] John P. Lewis, *Quiet Crisis in India* (Washington, D.C.: Brookings Institution, 1962), p. 205.

[6] Ibid., p. 220.

[7] "The Role of Private Enterprise in Developing Indian Industry," *Foreign Trade*, Vol. 126 (October 1, 1966), pp. 11–12, at p. 12.

[8] Robert J. Shafer, *Mexico: Mutual Adjustment Planning* (National Planning Series, Vol. 4 [Syracuse, New York: Syracuse University Press, 1966]). Also see Miguel S. Wionczek, "Incomplete Formal Planning: Mexico," in *Planning Economic Development*, (ed.) Everett E. Hagen, (Homewood, Ill.: Richard D. Irwin, Inc., 1963), pp. 150–82.

the Guyana area of Venezuela. The reading of national economic plans and their implementing directives is part and parcel of how market opportunities should be analyzed in the LDCs.

MARKET GOALS

Using the analytical procedure outlined above, marketers are able to set goals for business institutions that can be realistically achieved. These range from an increase in sales volume, higher profitability, and greater return on investment to dominance of market position. Each goal is stated numerically as the result to be achieved at the end of the planning period under consideration. As long as these goals are predicated upon the reinvestment of earnings within the LDC, their achievement will lead to little resentment on the part of the local government. On the other hand, if these goals are predicated on the idea that earnings should be repatriated to the parent company on a long-term, continuing basis, then their achievement would be hindered and the company may open itself to a possible takeover by the local government.

There are no good rules of thumb about how much to reinvest and how much to repatriate. At the same time that the American government is insisting that U.S. firms overseas repatriate their profits as quickly as they can so that the American balance of payments position will be enhanced, serious study is being given in the LDCs to the notion that foreign businesses already have taken too much out of the economies of these countries. The petroleum and minerals extracting companies, which historically have paid only small amounts in taxes and have done little to increase the level of skills in the local work forces, have created a political environment in the LDCs that is highly suspicious of foreign direct investment. American marketers who insist on repatriation of profits because it will give them a payback period short enough to justify their higher assumed risks may find their markets taken over by German and Japanese marketers.

Local capital participation in joint venture arrangements plus Eurodollar financing can overcome some of these problems. However, such equity arrangements cannot overcome the basic unwillingness of American marketers to realize that the climate for their investments in the LDCs has changed. Consequently their goals concerning proper means for achieving market success in these countries must also change.

MARKET ORGANIZATIONS

India, Nigeria, and Mexico along with almost all LDCs have explicit policies encouraging business firms to employ only nationals in the local subsidiaries. Foreigners, whether they be former British civil servants turned commonwealth managers or American expatriate management, are restricted in number to less than 1% of the total number of people employed by the local subsidiary. That is, these governments would tolerate the president and perhaps another management officer not being a citizen, but beyond that the whole management structure and the entire work force have to be citizens of the country in which the subsidiary is located.

India, acting as if it already had a sufficient number of trained managers, would so delay the processing of work permits for foreigners that the foreign firm seeking entry into the Indian market would be driven in the end to utilizing local talent who were trained in a management environment that was based upon family and caste rather than on the basis of impersonal relations. It is only when a specific need for new technology is determined and no Indian can be found to provide this technology that the Indian government permits the local subsidiary to utilize foreigners in its organization. In these cases, too, the government encourages the "Indianization" of these positions as soon as Indians can be trained to carry them out.

Mexico's policy is similar, but it is not as strictly enforced. Many more management positions are held by foreigners, and their "Mexicanization" proceeds much more slowly. Where "Mexicanization" has been pushed, some firms have organized Latin American divisions with one subsidiary being the Mexican subsidiary. Although Mexicans are now in marketing positions in the Mexican subsidiary, the foreigners have become the managers of the Latin American division and in one firm, the latter effectively manage both the division and the subsidiary. This change in form will last only until the Mexican government enforces its laws on the employment of foreigners within its national territory.

Certain firms in India, Mexico, and Nigeria have developed sophisticated employee training programs. In Nigeria for example, Shell-British Petroleum owns its own trade school and sends some of its graduates away for engineering degrees.[9] American firms now operating in West Africa found that they have to do the same thing, for it is virtually impossible to get a sufficient number of Americans to live in that area of the world.

In most LDCs, the marketer is a scarce resource. Very few people in these types of countries know how to organize, administer, and risk resources for profit-making returns in highly fragmented markets. Few people can weld mass production to mass marketing for the overall improvement of a people's standard of living. When foreign marketers commit resources to an LDC, they commit themselves to training local people in the practice of marketing with the idea that local marketers will take over the marketing job in the not too distant future. Except for this requirement of local hiring whenever local talent is available, LDCs that are committed to the growth of a market economy rarely interfere in the internal management of private-sector enterprises.

---

[9] Alan Sokolski, *The Establishment of Manufacturing in Nigeria* (New York: Praeger Special Studies in International Economics and Development [Frederick A. Praeger, Publisher, 1965]), p. 75.

MARKET RESOURCES

There are several kinds of market resources needed by marketers for effective performance in the LDCs: foreign exchange; internal sources of supply; a transportation network; a wholesale-retail infrastructure; and internal sources for consumer credit.

Marketers who have planned to produce or at least assemble goods within an LDC using foreign raw materials or semi-finished goods will find that the availability of these foreign materials, whether they are coming from the parent corporation or from elsewhere, is *always* contingent upon the availability of foreign currency. The failure of the nation to sell all of their primary export commodities in the world market will reduce the quantity of foreign currency available for imports. Clear and precise choices as to which industry will receive scarce currency and which will not are often set forth in the development plan and supporting administrative documents. Marketers whose products are low on the priority list will be forced to adjust production runs and market commitments to lower levels until the foreign exchange situation eases. Marketers who rely on the importation of materials that could be made within the LDC will find that their permission to use foreign exchange for these items will not be forthcoming once their firms have sunk their investment dollar in fixed facilities.

In today's world, it is unreasonable for marketers to assume that governments of the LDCs will permit national markets to be supplied from foreign production sources. No marketer should include in his plans long-term dependence on foreign sources of supply. Within a year after Sears opened its Mexican retail operation, a severe currency crisis forced the Mexican government to forbid the importation of almost all goods from the United States. Up until that time, Sears had stocked its Mexican stores from United States sources of supply. Now it was forced to find local sources. The story of how Sears force-fed local manufacturers to produce quality items in standard qualities, sizes, and assortments, and how Sears established a distribution system to wholesale these locally manufactured items to its retail outlets is well known.[10] It has accomplished similar tasks in building up its own market resources in other countries of Latin America and is also carrying out these marketing activities in Spain.

Marketers who plan to produce goods in one region of an LDC and who want to market these goods throughout the national territory should carefully analyze the functional usefulness of existing transportation and distribution networks. Although they may exist on paper, their continued usefulness as market resources should not be accepted without question.

---

[10] Richardson Wood and Virginia Keyser, *United States Business Performance Abroad: The Case Study of Sears, Roebuck de Mexico, S. A.* (Washington, D.C.: National Planning Association, May 1953), pp. 3–45.

There are numerous examples of how marketers built facilities on the assumption of being able to service the national territory, only to find after the plant was built that the critical market infrastructure worked occasionally or not at all. For example, slides and washouts close the dirt and gravel sections of the Pan American Highway and other highways in most Central American countries during the rainy season. Guerrillas in Guatemala have in the past prevented Kerns, whose canning facilities are located between Guatemala City and Puerto Barrios, from shipping their canned products to the capital for resale there or for wholesale distribution throughout Guatemala.[11] The forcing of trucks with foreign registry to unload their goods at the border of each Central American country and then reload them on trucks with domestic registry incurs higher costs for these products.[12] Marketers who plan on using a "through" system of transportation and fail to judge correctly the kinds of market resources they have available to them may find their products spoiling in the short run and their plants operating at excess capacity levels in the long run. Such miscalculations breed losses rather than profits for marketers.

Consumer installment loans (or hire purchase agreements) are a function of the willingness of financial institutions to insure such installment payments. The availability of such loans assists mass production and mass distribution, and brings about rapid increases in the standard of living. Twenty years ago, Indians were able to make such agreements so that they could purchase durable goods. Today, a shortage of goods together with a lack of insured installment credit have eliminated this resource for marketers to use in raising India's standard of living.[13] In Nigeria, two West African trading companies, United African Company and John Holt, and several independent finance companies extended credit for such durable goods as automobiles, TV sets, refrigerators, and air conditioners.[14] Marketers depend upon such credit to support their own plans for market development, and its absence or potential diminution should be considered before risk capital is expended on an LDC.

In the LDCs, market resources are generally not available in sufficient quantities for efficient and effective business performance. Their unavailability limits the size of final customer markets by impeding marketers from servicing these markets. Thus for marketers operating in the LDCs it becomes a question of what resources they can do without and still service a market of sufficient size for profit-making returns.

If marketers can generate sufficient volume and keep the price high

---

[11] Douglas F. Lamont, "Possible Alternative Goals that Can Be Achieved in the Short Run by the Business and Industry Committee of the Alabama-Guatemala Partners of the Alliance" (report submitted to the Alabama-Guatemala Partners of the Alliance, July 4, 1968).

[12] Thomas J. Greer, "The Central American Common Market: Political Setting and Transportation Infrastructure," *Southern Journal of Business*, Vol. 4 (April 1969), pp. 261–68 at p. 265.

[13] S. Kesava Iyengar, *A Decade of Planned Economy: A Critical Examination of Indian Plans* (Mysore, India: The Indian Academy of Economics, 1961), pp. 218–19.

[14] Sokolski, *The Establishment of Manufacturing in Nigeria*, p. 142.

enough to cover higher distributive margins, then the problem for marketers is which market infrastructure activities are they willing to perform themselves in the short run, and which market infrastructure activities are they willing to develop by long-term marketing training of wholesale-retail distributors, warehousemen, and financial men.

MARKET OFFERINGS

The real market in Nigeria is not the country's 40 million people but its many market segments fragmented by regional, cultural, and language differences. Before the war between Nigeria and Biafra, the surplus production of one area was rarely moved to other areas of the country. Market offerings had to be fashioned to service so many multiple cultural norms that the economies which could have been gained from mass production and mass distribution were lost and the Nigerian standard of living remained in its traditional setting. One of the results of the war has been to speed up the "Nigerianization" of the tribes and language groups supporting the Federal Nigerian Government. This had permitted marketers to provide more uniform market offerings in the food, clothing, shelter, and munitions that are being utilized by the troops and the supporting populace in the war against Biafra. When the war is over, there is no doubt that marketers will find that new social patterns have developed, and that completely new market offerings will have to be made to service a more integrated Nigerian market.

Market offerings in the LDCs are designed on the familiar bases of product, terms of sale, communication, and distribution strategies; only the cultural nuances and governmental requirements are different. For example, in terms of product strategies, the product line for Mexican made automobiles has been reduced from 25 models to 12 models.[15] GM, Ford, and Chrysler are allowed three models each by the Mexican government. The remainder of the production quota is taken up by Volkswagen, Datsun, and the new wholly owned Mexican company, Borgward. The government forced certain automobile manufacturers out of business, and forced others to cut down on the number of models produced or sold in Mexico. It is an attempt by a government to provide some economies of scale for domestic production and thereby lower the price to the final customer.

The market offering will be conditioned also by the supplies available for packaging purposes. Some LDCs lack adequate supplies of wood and paper products. Marketers of milk and soap powders have had to shift their package offerings to clear plastic containers. This has meant that they have had to devise new means for storing these items at retail locations and new ways of labeling the packages themselves.

Brand names, as well as the advertisements used in communicating about and promoting the market offering, must reflect new language and cultural norms, but there are dangers here for marketers. In Africa, when

---

[15] Same reference as footnote 3, p. 277.

English or French language descriptions were given up in favor of local languages, many Africans refused to buy the products with the new labels for fear that they were getting inferior products. This problem is particularly acute for marketers in the food and beverage industries. Carelessness in handling items that require high levels of sanitation is commonplace in the LDCs. Even Cola drinks, such as Coke, can be carriers of sugar bacteria that can make consumers ill. Tuberculin cows pass their disease on to the unsuspecting human when care is not taken to protect consumers. Those who have money will select products they know are safe. Brand names from the United States and Western Europe tell the illiterate but relatively affluent consumers in the LDCs that these products will not endanger their health. To meet the requirements of these consumers plus the new laws of the LDCs, marketers put their market information on packages in both the recognized Western language and the locally required language.

How high should marketers set prices? It is the policy of governments in the LDCs to promote higher standards of living. One way to do this is to maintain low retail prices on the basic necessities of life. Carnation was forced to sell its canned milk to the Mexican government's limited-line retail supermarkets (CONASUPO) at prices lower than it charged the privately owned middle class supermarkets.[16] Naturally, Carnation offset its CONASUPO losses with higher prices to the middle class supermarkets. The Mexican government was able to utilize the price offering of a firm to redistribute some of the wealth of the country. The Indian government, however, has been unable to do the same thing. Its traditional wholesalers are the dominant economic units in the commodities that make up the basic necessities of Indian life. No amount of persuasion has made these wholesalers change their habits of speculation on the prices of these commodities, and retail markets must continue to provide the consumer with low-volume, high-priced necessities of life. Marketers will face continued pressure to price their products at some predetermined rate established by the government. It behooves them to know their costs, and to be willing to make their profits in market segments that are not under price control.

In summary, social behavior and impediments in inter-regional exchange are the givens for marketers in the LDCs. National market offerings are often a fruitless waste of resources; instead, market offerings carefully developed for local and regional markets will be both beneficial and profitable. Sales and advertising campaigns should be geared to local differences in taste and thought. Although the Esso tiger has been a phenomenal success as an advertising theme throughout the world, it is folly in many cases to import on a wholesale basis each and every piece of promotional material developed for the United States market. It is just as great a folly to import these campaigns from the capital city market to other areas within the LDC. Levels of literacy, economic sophistication, and local prejudices differ widely from one region to another in many of the LDCs. Thus, market offerings should be customized to fit into the local scene as well as possible.

---

[16] Same reference as footnote 3, pp. 275–76.

This means more than changing the language of the copy. It means putting additional clothes on female figures so as not to offend more conservative tastes. It means using dialect variations in so-called national languages rather than the phraseology considered proper in the capital city. Several authors have suggested that there is a place for standardized international advertising among the developed countries.[17] A case can be made for appealing to the market segment within the LDCs that relates more to international themes than national themes. Assuming this to be true, it would further strengthen the point that the tastes of the internationally oriented market segment within the capital city are not the tastes of the bulk of the national market within the LDC. And thus the folly of importing advertising themes from the capital city to the provinces is doubly compounded when this internationalized market segment is used as "the true national market consumer group." The care used by marketers in developing market offerings that match real market segments will go a long way toward insuring that international marketing is profitable.

CONTROL OVER MARKET PERFORMANCE

There are two aspects to market control—who are the legal owners and how is the responsibility for specific management functions divided up among the participating owners?

Each LDC has its own predilections as to how much equity foreigners should have in local subsidiaries. These run from 100% foreign ownership to some sort of joint venture arrangement in which the foreign firm can have either a majority or minority share in the local subsidiary. The Nigerians are willing to have the former; the Mexicans prefer the latter. Usually the Indian government prefers to have a foreign firm sell its production and marketing technology to an Indian firm. However, if this is not possible, the Indian government will permit a joint venture subsidiary to be established if the equity assets are "Indianized" through the sale of common stock as soon as possible.

The initial agreement for establishing a local subsidiary will outline which management functions will be controlled by the foreign parent and which areas will be controlled by the participating local businessman or governmental agency. The marketing area is usually reserved for the foreign parent until such time as there is a sufficient number of trained local marketers who know how to utilize the new marketing technology being brought into the country.

How can market performance be evaluated? It should not be judged on the same basis as performances are judged in other countries. Marketers must do two jobs in the LDCs rather than just one as in the parent com-

---

[17] John K. Ryans, Jr. and James H. Donnelly, Jr., "Standardized Global Advertising a Call as Yet Unanswered," *Journal of Marketing*, Vol. 33 (April 1969). See also Erik Elinder, "How International Can European Advertising Be?" *Journal of Marketing*, Vol. 29 (April 1965), pp. 7–11.

pany's country. First, they must translate parent demands for market performance into locally profitable market activities. As has been shown above, their analytic tools are cruder and less helpful in generating useful answers; their goals, organization, and resources must be in line with the conditions prevalent in the LDC; finally, their offerings must be adapted to such a variety of differences that many marketing concepts developed for a mass consumption market are of little value in the LDCs. Second, they must alter local cultural habits to meet the performance standards set up by the parent company and other participating groups. Such local changes in work attitudes, shelf-space rotation, timeliness of advertising copy, and similar marketing activities are the hidden iceberg upon which many marketing performances of good marketers have floundered. These tradition-encrusted habits can only be changed over long periods of time. It is folly to set performance standards that do not take these things into consideration.

On-the-spot inspections by a team of technicians from the international headquarters rather than periodic written reports have worked well for a number of international firms in evaluating market performance. Where local subsidiaries have been left to work out problems by themselves, control has lapsed. A few local subsidiaries, such as Pan American Sulphur in Mexico or International Petroleum Company (IPC) in Peru, have failed to adapt themselves sufficiently to new local conditions. Pan American Sulphur was "Mexicanized" by the forced selling of its Mexican mineral assets to a group of Mexican businessmen who were backed by the Nacional Financiera, the Mexican developmental bank.

IPC, Standard Oil of New Jersey's subsidiary in Peru, claimed ownership in fee simple of oil rights that it had been granted 50 years ago by a Peruvian government. Successive regimes, including the last democratically elected one, sought to convert this claim of ownership to sub-soil rights into a lease without any claim to ownership of the oil at all. Other American firms in Peru, such as Cerro, have sensed the desire of Peruvians to own and control their own natural resources, and have returned ownership rights to sub-soil minerals to the Peruvian government. (This put these companies in the correct position vis-à-vis the sub-soil minerals according to the traditional Roman-Hispanic law as to who owns what kinds of property in Civil Law countries; IPC's insistence on an ownership claim to its sub-soil petroleum holdings flew in the face of the common understanding of what is and what is not law in Peru. This was the same kind of refusal to recognize a different concept of law that led to the nationalization of Jersey Standard's assets in Mexico in 1937.) Instead of seeking an accommodation with the new military regime, IPC began destroying its geological documents and forcing all customers, even the Peruvian military, to pay for refined gasoline products in cash. Naturally, its assets were seized.[18] Per-

---

[18] "Peru Turns Tougher," *Business Week* (February 15, 1969), pp. 32–33.

haps if Jersey Standard had intervened in its subsidiary's continuing battle with successive Peruvian governments, it would still have refining and distribution capability in Peru. Clearly in today's world, parent companies that do not maintain proper control may have their assets expropriated or nationalized.

FUTURE MARKET PROSPECTS

A market audit, a firm's plan for establishing the validity of what it is presently doing and for deciding on the things it should be doing in the future, brings one back to a study of the conditions for economic development and the requirements of the development plan. Short-term changes in goals of the government can readily be adapted within the continuing market analysis. However, long-term shifts in both public goals and conditions of the market itself must be recognized as factors that will have a decisive impact upon the direction in which the businesses may pursue their own institutional goals. Thus, it behooves marketers to annually audit the market systems in which they operate, and to integrate into their plans for the future any and all changes that will significantly affect the profit-making potential of its local subsidiary. One example of what should be included in the audit would be an LDC's prospects for future integration within any of the emerging common markets. Marketers who failed to locate facilities in Guatemala or Salvador to service the emerging Central American Common Market have found for example that the choice locations were closed to them as this Common Market steadily progressed in creating a new market system. Those marketers who waited were consigned by the terms of the implementing treaty to locate in Honduras or Nicaragua. Their delay caused locational disadvantages in servicing the primary customer-market—that is, the zone running from Guatemala City west to Escuintla, Guatemala, and then turning south to and including the capital city of Salvador. Of course, their delay gave them small locational advantages over the original manufacturing facilities established in the Guatemalan capital city in servicing the San Jose, Costa Rica market. These trade-offs are not, however, equivalent, for the primary market in Central America remains in and around the Guatemalan-Salvadorian urban-rural agglomeration. This is the type of information that should be fed into the market audit so that marketers can plan ahead with greater care than they had in the past.

MARKETING ADAPTATION: A REVIEW

These seven business policies constitute a list of activities marketers need to perform to achieve business and public goals. Adaptations have been suggested using a particular national frame of reference. It would be a cardinal error to assume that because one LDC favored a particular form of adaptation others would favor the same or similar forms. Each country must be studied carefully. Its customs and prejudices need to be understood. Its internal differences must be known. When these things are accomplished, then and only then should marketers move to adapt their marketing technology to the local market.

Whatever adaptations are made should be those that fit together in a properly organized relationship. The business policies that come from those adaptations will form the basic pattern of marketing activity within a national market system. Unless marketers go into an LDC with the idea of totally adapting their marketing technology to local conditions they will fail. Unfortunately, in today's world a rash of marketing failures could turn an LDC away from a market economy to a centrally planned, state-oriented command economy.

This paper has suggested that marketers who do business in more than one country must make certain changes in their business activities. No two countries will react to the same stimuli. Moreover, no two environments will be the same. It is the job of marketers to find acceptable business policies that will produce profit-making returns for their firms and increased social welfare for their host countries.

Is marketing strategy a local problem and should it be different in heterogeneous national markets? If not, what are the obstacles and benefits to the application of common marketing policies in different countries? Which elements of the marketing mix can or should be standardized?

---

32. CAN YOU STANDARDIZE MULTINATIONAL MARKETING? *

Robert D. Buzzell †

FOREWORD

From the standpoint of the multinational marketer, the differences between nations overseas are great. In the past, these differences generally led a U.S. company to view its strategy in each country strictly as a local

* Reprinted from "Can You Standardize Multinational Marketing?" *Harvard Business Review*, Vol. 46, No. 6 (November–December 1968), pp. 102–13.

† Harvard University.

Author's note: I wish to acknowledge the valuable contributions of Richard Aylmer and Jean-Louis LeCocq, who conducted interviews with executives of multinational companies under my direction during 1967. This research was conducted under a joint project of the Harvard Business School and the European Institute of Business Administration (INSEAD), and was supported by research grants of The Ford Foundation.

problem. However, in recent years the situation has been changing, and the experiences of a growing number of multinational companies suggest that there are real *potential gains to consider in standardizing various elements of the marketing programs used in different areas.* These gains range from substantial *cost savings* and more consistent dealings with customers to *better planning, control, and exploitation of ideas with universal appeal.*

Mr. Buzzell is Professor of Business Administration at the Harvard Business School. He has directed research on the marketing programs of multinational companies; also, he has taught at the Institut Européen d'Administration des Affaires in Fontainebleau, France. He is the author of numerous books and articles on various aspects of marketing.

One of the most widely discussed developments of the past decade has been the emergence of *multinational* companies as important competitors in an ever-growing number of industries. As the trade barriers in Western Europe and elsewhere have diminished, more and more companies have found attractive opportunities for expansion in countries other than their traditional home markets. For some of these companies, operations abroad have become so extensive and so complex as to require significant changes in organization and operating methods. The problems confronting management in a truly multinational company are clearly different in degree, if not in kind, from those of traditional firms.

WHAT ABOUT MARKETING?

The growing importance of multinational companies has stimulated a flood of comment and advice. Conferences, seminars, and surveys have probed the distinctive financial, legal, accounting, organizational, and personnel problems of this new breed of enterprise. In all of this discussion, however, relatively little has been said about marketing.

To be sure, some advertising men have advocated the adoption of uniform advertising approaches, on the grounds that fundamental consumer motives are essentially the same everywhere. This proposition often has a partisan tone, however, especially when it is put forward by executives of large advertising agencies with international networks of subsidiary and affiliate offices. More importantly, the question of advertising approaches cannot be considered realistically in isolation from other elements of a company's marketing "mix" in each market, including its product line, packaging, pricing, distribution system, sales force, and other methods of promotion.

Is it practical to consider the development of a marketing strategy, in terms of *all* of its elements, on a multinational scale? The conventional wisdom suggests that a multinational approach is *not* realistic, because of the great differences that still exist—and probably always will exist—

among nations. For example, George Weissman, President of Philip Morris, Inc., has concluded that "until we achieve One World there is no such thing as international marketing, only local marketing around the world." [1] Apparently most other marketing executives agree with this view. Thus, Millard H. Pryor, Jr., Director of Corporate Planning for Singer Company, writes:

> Marketing is conspicuous by its absence from the functions which can be planned at the corporate headquarters level. . . . The operating experience of many "international firms appears to confirm the desirability of assigning long-range planning of marketing activities to local manager.[2]

The prevailing view, then, is that marketing strategy is a local problem. The best strategy for a company will differ from country to country, and the design of the strategy should be left to local management in each country.

Two-sided case

But is the answer this simple? The experiences of leading U.S.-based companies in recent years suggest that there may indeed be something to be said in favor of a multinational marketing strategy. This article is intended to outline some of the possibilities—and limitations—of an integrated approach to multinational marketing. My thesis is that although there are many obstacles to the application of common marketing policies in different countries, there are also some very tangible potential benefits. The relative importance of the pros and cons will, of course, vary from industry to industry and from company to company. But the benefits are sufficiently universal and sufficiently important to merit careful analysis by management in virtually any multinational company. Management should not automatically dismiss the idea of standardizing some parts of the marketing strategy, at least within major regions of the world.

BENEFITS OF STANDARDIZATION

As a practical matter, standardization is not a clear-cut issue. In a literal sense, multinational standardization would mean the offering of *identical* product lines at identical prices through identical distribution systems, supported by identical promotional programs, in several different countries. At the other extreme, completely "localized" marketing strategies would contain *no* common elements whatsoever. Obviously, neither of these extremes is often feasible or desirable.

---

[1] "International Expansion," in *Plotting Marketing Strategy, A New Orientation,* ed. by Lee Adler (New York: Simon & Schuster, 1967), p. 229.

[2] "Planning in a Worldwide Business," *Harvard Business Review* (January–February 1965), p. 137.

The practical question is: Which *elements* of the marketing strategy can or should be standardized, and to what degree? Currently, most multinational companies employ strategies that are much closer to the "localized" end of the spectrum than to the opposite pole. If there are potential benefits of increased standardization, then they would be achieved by incorporating *more* common elements in a multinational strategy. Each marketing aspect of policy should be considered, first, in its own right, and second, in relation to the other elements of the "mix."

Let us examine the most important potential benefits of standardization in multinational marketing strategy.

Significant cost savings

Differences in national income levels, tastes, and other factors have traditionally dictated the need for local products and corresponding local marketing programs. The annals of international business provide countless examples, even for such apparently similar countries as the United States and Canada. Philip Morris, Inc., for example, tried unsuccessfully to convert Canadian smokers to one of its popular American cigarette brands. The Canadians apparently would rather fight; they preserved their traditional preference for so-called "Virginia-type" tobacco blends. Examples of this kind suggest that to attain maximum sales in each country, a company should offer products, as well as packages, advertisements, and other marketing elements, which are tailored to that country's distinctive needs and desires.

However, maximizing sales is not the only goal in designing a marketing strategy. Profitability depends ultimately both on sales *and* costs, and there are significant opportunities for cost reduction via standardization. The most obvious, and usually the most important, area for cost savings is product design. By offering the same basic product in several markets with some possible variations in functional and/or design features, a manufacturer can frequently achieve longer production runs, spread research and development costs over a greater volume, and thus reduce total unit costs.

The "Italian invasion." The lesson of mass production economies through standardization, first demonstrated by Henry Ford I, has been dramatically retaught during the 1960s by the Italian household appliance industry.[3]

In the mid-1950s, total combined Italian production of refrigerators and washing machines was less than 300,000 units; there were no strong Italian appliance manufacturers. In 1955, only 3% of Italian households owned refrigerators and around 1% owned washing machines.

---

[3] See, for example, Philip Siekman, "The Battle for the Kitchen," *Fortune*, (January 1964).

Starting in the late 1950s, several companies began aggressive programs of product development and marketing. Ironically, some of the Italian entrepreneurs were simply applying lessons learned from America. One member of the Fumagalli family, owners of the appliance firm, Candy, had been a prisoner of war in the United States and brought back the idea of "a washing machine in every home."

The Italian appliance firms installed modern, highly automated equipment, reinvested profits, and produced relatively simple, *standardized* products in great numbers. By 1965, refrigerator output was estimated at 2.6 million units, and washing machine output at 1.5 million units. Much of this volume was sold in Italy; home ownership of the two appliances rose 50% and 23%, respectively. But the Italian companies were aggressive in export marketing, too; by 1965 Italian-made refrigerators accounted for 32% of the total French market and for 40% to 50% of the Benelux market. Even in Germany, the home market of such electrical giants as AEG, Bosch, and Siemens, the Italian products attained a 12% market share. The export pattern of washing machines has followed that of refrigerators; by 1965 Italian exports had accounted for 10% to 15% of market sales in most other Western European countries.[4]

The success of the Italian appliance industry has been a painful experience for the traditional leaders—American, British, and German—as well as for the smaller French companies that had previously had tariff protection. Whirlpool Corporation, which acquired a French refrigerator plant in 1962, subsequently leased the facility to a French competitor. Even Frigidaire decided, in mid-1967, to close down its refrigerator production in France.

In competition with other European appliance makers, the Italian companies have benefited from some natural advantages in terms of lower wage rates and government export incentives. But mass production of simple, standardized products has been at least equally important. And, according to *Fortune,* "refrigerators have begun to look more and more alike as national tastes in product design give way to an international 'sheer-line' style."

Turnabout at Hoover. To compete with this "Italian invasion" in appliances, some of the established manufacturers have tried new approaches. An interesting example is the recent introduction of a new line of automatic washing machines by Hoover Ltd., the market leader in the United Kingdom. Hoover's previous automatics, introduced in 1961, were designed primarily for the British market. The company's new "Keymatic" models featured:

[4] The estimates of production, exports, and so forth, cited here are given by Carlo Castellano, *L'Industria Degli Elettrodomestici in Italia,* Universita Degli Studi di Genova (Torino, 1965), or are drawn from *Marketing in Europe* (October 1966 and September 1967).

An exclusive "pulsator" washing action.

A tilted, enamelled steel drum.

Hot water provided by the home's central hot-water heater.

In contrast, most European manufacturers, including the Italian producers, offered front-loading, tumble-action washers with stainless steel drums and self-contained water heaters. Either because these features were better suited to continental needs, or because so many sellers promoted them, or perhaps both, Hoover saw its position in the major continental markets gradually decline.

When the Hoover management set out to design a new product line, beginning in 1965, it decided to look for a *single* basic design that would meet the needs of housewives in France, Germany, and Scandinavia as well as in the United Kingdom. A committee including representatives of the continental subsidiaries and of the parent company, Hoover Worldwide Corporation (New York), spent many weeks finding mutually acceptable specifications for the new line.

The result, which went on sale in the spring of 1967, was a front-loading, tumble-action machine, closer in concept to the "continental" design than Hoover's previous washers, but with provisions for "hot water fill" and enamelled steel drums on models to be sold in the United Kingdom. By standardizing most of the key design elements in the new machine, Hoover was able to make substantial savings in development costs, tooling, and unit production costs.

Other economies. The potential economies of standardization are not confined solely to product design decisions. In some industries, packaging costs represent a significant part of total costs. Here, too, standardization may offer the possibility of savings. Charles R. Williams cites the case of a food processor selling prepared soups throughout Europe in 11 different packages. He observes, "The company believes it could achieve a significant savings in cost and at the same time reduce consumer confusion by standardizing the packaging."[5]

Still another area for cost savings is that of advertising. For some of the major package goods manufacturers, the production of art work, films, and other advertising materials costs millions of dollars annually. Although differences in language limit the degree of standardization that can be imposed, *some* common elements can often be used. To illustrate, Pepsi-Cola is bottled in 465 plants and sold in 110 countries outside the United States. Part of its foreign advertising is done by films. According to one of the company's top marketing executives. "We have found that it is possible . . . to produce commercial films overseas in one market, if planned properly, for use in most (but not all) of our international markets." Ac-

---

[5] "Regional Management Overseas," *Harvard Business Review* (January–February 1967), p. 89.

cording to company estimates, the added cost of producing separate films for each market would be $8 million per year.[6]

All of these examples illustrate the same basic point: standardization of product design, packaging, and promotional materials *can* offer important economies to the multinational marketer. Even if these cost savings are attained at the expense of lower sales in some markets, the net effect on profits may be positive.

Consistency with customers

Quite apart from the possibilities of cost reduction, some multinational companies are moving toward standardization in order to achieve consistency in their dealings with customers. Executives of these companies believe that consistency in product style, in sales and customer service, in brand names and packages, and generally in the "image" projected to customers, is a powerful means of increasing sales.

If all customers lived incommunicado behind their respective national frontiers, there would be no point in worrying about this matter; only diplomatic couriers and border-crossing guards would ever notice any inconsistencies in products, services or promotion. But in reality, of course, this is not the case. The most visible type of cross-border flow is international travel by tourists and businessmen. Especially in Europe, with its relatively high income levels and short distances, the number of people visiting other countries has reached flood proportions in the 1960s, and shows no sign of abating. If the German tourist in Spain sees his accustomed brands in the store, he is likely to buy them during his visit. More important, his reexposure to the products and their advertising may strengthen his loyalty back home or, at least, protect him from the temptation to change his allegiance to a competitor.

Then there is the flow of communications across boundaries. Magazines, newspapers, radio and television broadcasts—all including advertising—reach international audiences. For example, according to estimates by Young & Rubicam International:

German television broadcasts are received by 40% of Dutch homes with TV sets.

Paris Match has a circulation of 85,000 in Belgium, 26,000 in Switzerland, and substantial readership in Luxemburg, Germany, Italy, and Holland.

On an average day, over 4 million French housewives tune to Radio Luxemburg; the same broadcast reaches 620,000 Belgian housewives, 30,000 in Switzerland, and 100,000 in Holland.[7]

---

[6] See Norman Heller, "How Pepsi-Cola Does It in 110 Countries," in *New Ideas for Successful Marketing*, ed. by John S. Wright and Jac L. Goldstucker (Chicago: American Marketing Association, 1966), p. 700.

[7] *When Is a Frontier Not a Frontier* (pamphlet) (Brussels: May 1966).

The possibility of reaching multimarket audiences with common advertising messages, and the risk of confusion that may result from reaching such audiences with different brand names and promotional appeals, has led some of the major consumer goods producers to explore ways and means of standardizing at least the basic elements of their European campaigns. For instance, the Nestlé Company, Inc. and Unilever Ltd., probably the most experienced multinational consumer goods firms, have both moved in the direction of more "unified" European advertising during the 1960s. When Nestlé launched "New Nescafé" in 1961–62, for example, the same basic theme ("fresh-ground aroma") and very similar creative treatments were used not only throughout Europe, but also in other markets such as Australia. The value of this approach is, perhaps, reflected in the fact that several years ago Nescafé was the leading brand of instant coffee in every European country.

Pressures from customers. During the 1960s an additional argument for consistency in marketing strategy has emerged—the needs of the multinational *customer.* Increasingly, both consumer and industrial goods manufacturers find themselves selling to companies which themselves operate on a multinational scale. Industrial users, retail chains, and wholesalers with operations in several countries may buy centrally; even if they do not, personnel in one country often have experience in other countries, or communicate with their counterparts in these countries. In either case, there is a strong pressure on the seller to offer similar products, prices, and services in each market. Thus, IBM has standardized the services provided to customers, the duties and training of sales and service personnel, and even the organization of branch offices, on a worldwide basis. A major reason for this policy is the need to provide the same level of service to major customers, such as international banks, in each of the several countries where they do business with IBM.

In some industries, multinational customers virtually force suppliers to standardize products, prices, and terms of sale. If a better deal is available in one country than another, the customer may find it worthwhile to transship goods and will do so.

In certain industries, trade and professional associations exert a pressure toward standardization similar to that exerted by multinational customers. Engineers, chemists, doctors, computer programmers—these groups and many others hold conferences, publish journals, and exchange ideas on an international basis. One result is that companies selling products to professional and technical groups find it advantageous to standardize their offerings. This factor may even affect consumer goods; the marketing director of a major food-processing company told us that dietetic products must be sold on the same basis everywhere because "science and teaching are international anyway."

Improved planning and control

Flows of people and information across national boundaries may affect multinational marketing strategy in still another way. Consider the following situation: Philips Gloeilampenfabrieken, one of the world's largest producers of electrical products, found that prices of some of its appliances in Holland were being undercut by as much as 30% by the company's own German subsidiary! How did this come to pass? The German subsidiary had lower costs than the Dutch plant, and sold at lower prices to meet the more intensive competition of the German appliance market. Wholesalers buying from Philips in Germany had a further incentive to sell to outside customers on account of a 7% export subsidy given by the German government. To complete the circle, a European Economic Community antitrust ruling prohibited manufacturers from interfering with the rights of independent distributors to export freely within the Common Market. Consequently, there was little that Philips could do except to "equalize" prices in the two countries or live with the new sourcing arrangements.[8]

Philips' experience illustrates the difficulty of orderly planning and control by top management if a subsidiary or distributor in country A is subject to the risk of unpredictable competition from his counterparts in nearby countries, B, C, and D.

The feasibility of transshipments among markets obviously varies from one industry to another, depending on the value/weight ratio of the products. Thus, transshipping is common for such items as scientific instruments, cameras, and precision equipment, but relatively rare for major electrical appliances. Even in the food trade, however, cross-border sales have increased in volume considerably during the 1960s.

Effective control of transshipping requires harmonization of pricing policies in the multinational company. This does not necessarily mean *equalizing* prices at either the wholesale or retail levels, for if a company's prices to dealers and/or distributors are the same in all countries, then the incentive for transshipping will be eliminated. Rather, it means some adjustments and compromises for the sake of consistency in pricing at the retail and wholesale levels.

Exploiting good ideas

A fourth argument for standardization is that good marketing ideas and people are hard to find, and should therefore be used as widely as possible. Moreover, good ideas tend to have a universal appeal. This point of view is held especially strongly with regard to the "creative" aspects of advertising and promotional programs. Arthur C. Fatt, chairman of the board and chief executive officer of Grey Advertising, Inc., states:

---

[8] Reported in *Business Europe* (August 23, 1967), p. 1.

A growing school of thought holds that even different peoples are *basically* the same, and that an international advertising campaign with a truly universal appeal can be effective in any market. . . . If an advertiser has a significant advertising idea at work in one country, not only may it be wasteful but often 'suicidal' to change this idea just for the sake of change.[9]

The key word in this statement is "significant." It is the scarcity of really good or significant ideas that encourages standardization. It may be easy to find creative concepts of average quality in each of many different national markets, but really new or unique approaches are not so easily matched.

During the 1960s there have been several widely discussed examples of successful application of common advertising themes.

Esso's "Put a Tiger in Your Tank" campaign, with very minor changes in art and wording has been used from Southeast Asia to Switzerland. The tiger is, of course, an internationally recognized symbol for power. Avis Rent-A-Car has used minor variations on its "We Try Harder" theme throughout Europe as well as in the United States. Magazine advertisements for Playtex brassieres in many different countries feature the same "stop-action" photographic demonstration of the product's strength and dependability. Although attitudes toward undergarments vary from country to country, Young & Rubicam, Inc. (the Playtex agency) believes that there is a *segment* in each market for which this appeal is effective.

But even the most ardent proponents of the theory that "good ideas are universal" recognize the need to apply the concept with care. Approaches shown to be effective in one market are *likely* to be effective elsewhere, but they do not necessarily apply across the board.

Balanced appraisal needed

To summarize, then, many companies have found real benefits in a multinational approach to marketing strategy. The gains have included greater effectiveness in marketing, reduced costs, and improved planning and control. Moreover, especially in Western Europe but also in some other parts of the world, social and economic trends are working in favor of more, rather than less, standardization in marketing policies. Tourism, international communication, increased numbers of multinational customers, and other forces are all tending toward greater unification of multinational markets.

But this is just one side of the story. It would be a mistake to assume, as at least a few companies have done, that the marketing programs can be transferred from one market to another without careful consideration of the *differences* which still exist. Let us turn next to that side of the picture.

---

[9] "The Danger of 'Local' International Advertising," *Journal of Marketing* (January 1967), pp. 61–62.

COMMON BARRIERS

Despite the potential benefits of standardization, the great majority of companies still operate on the premise that each national market is different and must therefore be provided with its own, distinctive marketing program. For instance, after a careful study of the marketing policies of U.S. appliance and photographic manufacturers in Europe, Richard Aylmer concluded: "In over 85% of the cases observed, advertising and promotion decisions were based on *local* product marketing objectives." [10]

Why is diversity still the rule of the day in multinational marketing? In many cases, differences simply reflect *customary* ways of doing business which have evolved in an earlier period when national boundaries were more formidable barriers than they are today. But even if tradition did not play a role, it must be recognized that there are and will continue to be some important obstacles to standardization.

A comprehensive list of these obstacles would fill many pages, and would include many factors that affect only one or two industries. The most important and generally applicable factors are summarized in Exhibit 1. The rows of this exhibit represent the major *classes* of factors which limit standardization in multinational marketing strategies. The columns correspond to different elements of a marketing program, and the "cells" in the table illustrate the ways in which the various factors affect each program element. In effect, each cell represents a condition or characteristic which *may* differ sufficiently among countries, and *may* require variations in marketing strategies. As we shall see presently, the experiences of multinational companies afford numerous examples of these barriers to standardization that are listed in Exhibit 1.

Market characteristics

Perhaps the most *permanent* differences among national markets are those arising from the physical environment—climate, topography, and resources (see the top left of Exhibit 1). Climate has an obvious effect on the sales potential for many products, and may also require differences in packaging. Topography influences the density of population, and this in turn may have a strong influence on the distribution system available to a manufacturer.

The cell in Exhibit 1 labeled "Product use conditions" includes a wide variety of environmental factors affecting marketing strategies. Differences in the size and configuration of homes, for example, have an important bearing on product design for appliances and home furnishings. European kitchens are typically small by U.S. standards, and there is seldom any

---

[10] "Marketing Decision Making in the Multinational Firm," unpublished doctoral thesis. Harvard Business School, 1968.

EXHIBIT 1. Obstacles to standardization in international marketing strategies

	Elements of marketing program				
Factors limiting standardization	Product design	Pricing	Distribution	Sales force	Advertising and promotion; branding and packaging
Market characteristics Physical environment	Climate Product use conditions		Customer mobility	Dispersion of customers	Access to media Climate
Stage of economic and industrial development	Income levels Labor costs in relation to capital costs	Income levels	Consumer shopping patterns	Wage levels, availability of manpower	Needs for convenience rather than economy Purchase quantities
Cultural factors	"Custom and tradition," Attitudes toward foreign goods	Attitudes toward bargaining	Consumer shopping patterns	Attitudes toward selling	Language, literacy Symbolism
Industry conditions Stage of product life cycle in each market	Extent of product differentiation	Elasticity of demand	Availability of outlets Desirability of private brands	Need for missionary sales effort	Awareness, experience with products
Competition	Quality levels	Local costs Prices of substitutes	Competitors' control of outlets	Competitors' sales forces	Competitive expenditures, messages
Marketing institutions Distributive system	Availability of outlets	Prevailing margins	Number and variety of outlets available	Number, size, dispersion of outlets	Extent of self-service
Advertising media and agencies			Ability to "force" distribution	Effectiveness of advertising, need for substitutes	Media availability, costs, overlaps
Legal restrictions	Product standards Patent laws Tariffs & taxes	Tariffs & taxes Antitrust laws Resale price maintenance	Restrictions on product lines Resale price maintenance	General employment restrictions Specific restrictions on selling	Specific restrictions on messages, costs Trademark laws

basement space available to apartment dwellers for laundry facilities. As a result, there is a great emphasis on compactness of design in automatic washers, for they must somehow be fitted into a small and already crowded area. As noted in the example of Hoover Ltd., given earlier, washing machines must also be equipped with self-contained water heating systems to compensate for the lack of central hot-water heaters in most continental homes.

Industrial goods manufacturers also frequently encounter differences in product use conditions. A U.S. producer of farm equipment found that one of his pieces of machinery could not be moved through the narrow, crooked streets of French and Belgian farm villages. Concluding that there is more dissimilarity than similarity in industrial markets in Europe, a chemical industry marketing researcher writes: "[A factor] which would severely affect the market for surface coatings is the fact that materials used in building construction are vastly different in various parts of Europe. Brick, mortar, and tile are used predominantly in Southern Europe, whereas this is not the case in Northern Germany and in Benelux." [11] Many similar examples could be cited of differences in the environment which call for variations in product design and other aspects of marketing policy.

Development stage. Differences among countries in stages of economic and industrial development (second item under "Market characteristics" in Exhibit 1) also have a profound influence on marketing strategies. Because of the wide gaps in per capita income levels, many products or models which are regarded as inexpensive staples in the United States or Western Europe must be marketed as "luxuries" elsewhere. Even among the industrialized countries income differences are substantial: appliance manufacturers such as Philco-Ford Corporation and Kelvinator of Canada, Ltd. find themselves with little choice but to position their products as deluxe, relatively high-priced items. This, in turn, implies a very different marketing strategy from that used in the United States.

For industrial products, differences in economic development are reflected in variations in relative costs of capital and labor. Thus General Electric Company and other companies have sold numerical controls for machine tools to U.S. factories primarily on the basis of labor cost savings. The same approach may be suitable in Germany, where there is a critical shortage of labor. But in most other countries it would be far more difficult to justify numerical controls on the basis of labor substitution.

Differences in income levels may suggest the desirability of systematic price variations. As explained earlier, many companies do charge different prices in different countries, but these variations are seldom, if ever, based solely on incomes.

Consumer shopping patterns and purchase quantities, too, tend to vary

---

[11] William Gerunsky, "International Marketing Research," in *Chemical Marketing Research*, ed. by N. H. Giragosian (New York: Reinhold Publishing Corp., 1967), p. 258.

with stages of economic development. In underdeveloped countries, there typically are many small retail stores and many consumers who buy in smaller quantities than do those in highly developed nations. For instance, cigarettes and razor blades are bought one at a time in some countries. Even in England, according to one international marketing executive, "the smallest size of detergent available in U.S. supermarkets is the largest size available in the United Kingdom."

Finally, variations in wage levels may affect choices between personal selling and other forms of promotional effort. One relatively small Italian food processor has a sales force as large as that of General Foods Corporation in the United States. Presumably salesmen's salaries are proportionately less!

Cultural factors. This category is a convenient catchall for the many differences in market structure and behavior that cannot readily be explained in terms of more tangible factors. Consider, for example, the figures in Exhibit 2, which are taken from a recent survey made by the European

EXHIBIT 2

Average household consumption of beverages, 1963–1964

Country	Milk	Wine	Beer
France	103	116	28
Germany	100	7	46
Holland	153	2	11
Italy	87	95	2

Source: *Le Monde*, weekly overseas edition, February 15–21, 1968, p. 7.

Economic Community's Statistical Office. Why do French households consume more than 50 times as much wine as Dutch households, but only two thirds as much milk? No doubt these differences could be explained historically in terms of variations in water, soil, and so on. But for practical purposes, it is usually sufficient and certainly more efficient simply to take differences in consumption patterns and attitudes *as given*, and to adjust to them.

There are many examples of cultural differences that have affected marketing success or failure. One cultural factor is the attitude of consumers toward "foreign" goods. To illustrate, Princess Housewares, Inc., a large U.S. appliance manufacturer, introduced a line of electric housewares in the German market. The company's brand name was well known and highly regarded in the United States, but relatively unknown in Germany; and the brand had a definitely "American" sound. The company discovered that the American association was a real drawback among German consumers. According to a survey, fewer than 40% of German individuals felt "confident" about electrical products made in the United States, compared with 91% who were "confident" of German-made products.

Lack of brand awareness, coupled with suspicion of the quality of "American" products, required the company to adopt a very different marketing strategy in Germany than that employed in the United States, where both awareness and a quality image were taken for granted.

Industry conditions

A convenient framework for comparing industry and competitive conditions in different national markets is that of the "product life cycle." The histories of many different products in the United States suggest that most of them pass through several distinct *stages* over a period of years, and that marketing strategies typically change from stage to stage.

Some products are in different stages of their life cycles in different national markets. Vacuum cleaners are owned by over 75% of the households in Great Britain, Germany, and Switzerland, for example, but by only 10% of the households in Italy and 45% in France. Even more marked contrasts exist for some newer types of products, such as electric toothbrushes and electric carving knives, which are widely owned in the United States but virtually unknown in most other countries. Such differences in life cycle stages usually call for adaptations of "home country" marketing approaches, if not for completely separate strategies. For example, in late 1965 the Polaroid Corporation introduced the "Swinger" Polaroid Land camera in the United States. The Swinger, with a retail list price of $19.95, was Polaroid's first camera selling for less than $50. The introductory promotion for the new model in the United States placed very heavy emphasis on price; there was no need to explain the basic concept of "instant photography," since millions of Polaroid Land cameras had already been sold over a 17-year period. Surveys indicated that over 80% of U.S. consumers were aware of the name "Polaroid" and of the company's basic product features.

The Swinger was introduced in Europe during 1966. Prior to that time, Polaroid cameras had been extremely high-priced, owing in part to high tariffs, and the company's sales had been at a very low level. Distribution of Polaroid cameras and film was spotty. Most important, fewer than 10% of consumers were aware of the Polaroid instant photography concept.

Under these circumstances, a very different marketing strategy was needed for the Swinger in Europe. Polaroid advertising had to be designed to do a more basic educational job, since awareness of the instant picture principle could not be taken for granted. The promotional program also had to be aimed at building retail distribution, which was also taken for granted in the United States.

If products are in different stages of their life cycles in different countries, then it is tempting to conclude that marketing strategies used in the past in the more "advanced" countries should be used in other "follower" nations. There is some evidence to support this conclusion. For instance, as described earlier, the Italian appliance manufacturers have successfully employed strategies similar to those of Henry Ford in the early 1900s; similarly, Polaroid in the 1960s in Europe can profitably use many of the same approaches that it employed in America in the early 1950s. However, history does not repeat itself exactly, and past marketing strategies cannot be reapplied without some modifications.

Competitive practices.   Another important industry condition, partly but not entirely related to the product life cycle, is the extent of competition in each national market. Differences in products, costs, prices, and promotional levels may permit or even require differences in the strategies used by a multinational company in various markets. Even within the European Common Market, there are still substantial variations in prices of many products, reflecting in part traditional differences in the degree of competition. A survey made in 1967 by the European Economic Community's Statistical Office showed that price variations are still substantial even within the Common Market. Typical prices were compared for some 125 different consumer products by country; on the average, the difference between prices in the countries with the highest and lowest prices was 58%. Even the price of a staple item such as aspirin varied from a high of 38¢ in Germany to a low of 22¢ in Holland.

The growth of multinational companies in itself has tended to reduce traditional differences in competitive practices. For example, advertising expenditures have traditionally been lower in France than in the United States and other European countries; on a per capita basis, total French advertising outlays are around one eighth those of the United States and one third those of Germany. However, according to M. Andre Bouhebent, a top French advertising agency executive, the entry of foreign competitors is changing the situation: "When German advertisers sell in France, they have the habit of spending at the same rate (as at home), which is three times that of their French competitors . . . ." [12] As an example, *Advertising Age* noted that the German Triumph bra and girdle company spends three to four times as much as a French undergarment company to promote its products.

Marketing institutions

The multinational company's opportunities in each market depend critically on the marketing institutions available in each country—including retail and wholesale outlets and advertising media and agencies. Some of

---

[12] Quoted in *Advertising Age*, August 29, 1966, p. 218.

the most drastic revisions in strategy made by U.S.-based companies over-seas have been imposed by the lack of adequate supermarkets, retail chains, and commercial television. Differences in the number, size, and dispersion of distributive outlets call for differences in promotional methods; and dif-ferences in prevailing wholesale and/or retail margins may require vastly different price and discount structures. Some of these variations in insti-tutional systems are related to legal regulations, especially in the area of resale price maintenance.

As in the case of competitive practices, traditional disparities in market-ing institutions have narrowed considerably since 1945. For instance, one element of the "Americanization" of Europe is the spread of chains, super-markets, and other U.S.-style institutions of distribution. In "borrowing" these methods from the United States, the Europeans add their own modifi-cations; their supermarkets are not as large, they rely on walk-in neighbor-hood trade rather than on vast parking lots, their average transactions are smaller, and there are other adaptations. But there is a clear trend toward similarity in distributive systems.

The combination of continued differences in marketing institutions *now* with the prospect of greater similarities in the *future* creates some difficult problems for multinational marketers. One such problem may be timing. The experience of Princess Housewares in Germany, previously mentioned, is a case in point: When Princess Housewares went into the German mar-ket, the company had a basic choice to make regarding channels of distri-bution. In the early 1960s, the predominant system of appliance distribution was independent wholesalers selling to retail stores. Small specialty retailers still dominated the market. However, department stores, mail-order firms, and discounters were growing in importance. Most of these large retailers were able to obtain *grosshandler* (wholesaler) discounts from manufactur-ers, and many of them sold at substantial discounts from "suggested" retail prices. The suggested prices, in turn, were often set at artificially high levels (so-called "moon" prices) to permit the appearance of large price cuts at retail. At the same time, because of public confusion and discontent over artificial list prices and equally artificial discounts, the resale price mainte-nance law was under increasing attack.

Princess Housewares, as a relatively unknown brand, felt that its first task was to obtain distribution. To do this, the company decided to estab-lish maintained prices and enforce them, so that small retailers' margins would be protected. But this put the company at a disadvantage in selling to the large discounters. It also meant that the company had to sell direct to retailers, since wholesalers could not be relied on to enforce resale prices.

In some ways, the Princess Housewares case boils down to a choice be-tween a traditional distributive system, similar to that used in the United States in the early 1950s, and an emerging but still undeveloped system. U.S. experience suggests that the emerging system will become the domi-nant one. But can a manufacturer afford to be ahead of the trend?

Legal restrictions

Different countries require or permit very different practices in the areas of product design, competitive practices, pricing, employment, and advertising. They also impose differing taxes and tariffs, and multinational companies often follow devious paths in the attempt to minimize the total cost effects of these levies. Obviously, such practices can be stumbling blocks for the would-be standardizer.

Some product standards, though ostensibly designed for purposes of safety, are used by governments as a device for protecting home industries. A notable case in point was the imposition of new regulations for electrical appliances by France in 1967, along with delays in issuing approvals. This was generally regarded as a deliberate move to slow down the onslaught of competition by the Italian companies and thus give the domestic industry a breathing space.

But other legal restrictions are established for more legitimate purposes. The use of a 220-volt electrical system in Europe, for example, has led to a stringent set of safety standards for such products as irons—more stringent than U.S. standards. Cord connections must be stronger, and shielding against radio interference is necessary. These requirements, in turn, dictate modifications in product design.

Resale price maintenance and other laws designed to protect small retailers still have a strong influence on distribution policies in many countries. The trend has been away from restrictions of this kind, however, and some nations, such as the United Kingdom, have virtually abolished price maintenance.

Custom and legislative regulation combine to discourage some types of advertising and promotion. Goodyear Tire & Rubber Company, for instance, demonstrated the strength of its "3T" tire cord in the United States by showing a steel chain breaking. In Germany, this visualization was not permitted because it was regarded as disparaging to the steel chain manufacturers.[13] Such exaggerated sensitivity may be amusing, but it cannot be ignored in planning advertising campaigns.

CONCLUSION

Traditionally, marketing strategy has been regarded as a strictly local problem in each national market. Differences in customer needs and preferences, in competition, in institutional systems, and in legal regulations have seemed to require basically different marketing programs. Any similarity between countries has been seen as purely coincidental.

There is no doubt that differences among nations are still great, and that these differences should be recognized in marketing planning. But the

---

[13] *Advertising Age* (May 9, 1966), p. 75.

experiences of a growing number of multinational companies suggest that there are also some real potential gains in an integrated approach to marketing strategy. Standardization of products, packages, and promotional approaches may permit substantial cost savings, as well as greater consistency in dealings with customers. The harmonization of price policies often facilitates better internal planning and control. Finally, if good ideas are scarce, and if some of them have universal appeal, they should be used as widely as possible.

All of this adds up to the conclusion that both the pros *and* the cons of standardization in multinational marketing programs should be considered, and that a company's decisions should be based on estimated overall revenues and costs. Obviously, each case must be considered on its own merits —slogans and formulas are not very helpful guides to intelligent planning.

If marketing strategy is to be designed with a multinational perspective, then the firm's organization must make provision for line and staff marketing positions at appropriate levels. Space does not permit a full discussion of the organizational issues here, but it may be noted that there is a clear trend among leading companies toward establishment of marketing coordinators, international committees, and other mechanisms for at least partial centralization of marketing management. Hoover, Singer, General Electric, Eastman Kodak, and many other companies have recently made changes in this direction.

Finding the right balance between local autonomy and central coordination is not an easy task, any more than is balancing the gains of standardized marketing strategy against the needs of heterogeneous national markets. But it is an important task, with high potential profit rewards for management. Finding the best solutions to these problems should be high on the priority list for every multinational company.

International and multinational firms face a critical decision area not faced by firms selling only in domestic markets. These firms encounter decisions related to the problem of transferring to foreign environments a product and communications mix that is appropriate for local markets. This article outlines strategic alternatives and discusses how the most effective strategy for any particular product-company-market mix can be achieved.

33. MULTINATIONAL PRODUCT PLANNING: STRATEGIC ALTERNATIVES*

Warren J. Keegan †

Inadequate product planning is a major factor inhibiting growth and profitability in international business operations today. The purpose of this article is to identify five strategic alternatives available to international marketers, and to identify the factors which determine the strategy which a company should use. Table 1 summarizes the proposed strategic alternatives.

STRATEGY ONE: ONE PRODUCT, ONE MESSAGE, WORLDWIDE

When PepsiCo extends its operations internationally, it employs the easiest and in many cases the most profitable marketing strategy—that of product extension. In every country in which it operates, PepsiCo sells exactly the same product, and does it with the same advertising and promotional themes and appeals that is uses in the United States. PepsiCo's outstanding international performance is perhaps the most eloquent and persuasive justification of this practice.

Unfortunately, PepsiCo's approach does not work for all products. When Campbell soup tried to sell its U.S. tomato soup formulation to the British, it discovered, after considerable losses, that the English prefer a more bitter taste. Another U.S. company spent several million dollars in an unsuccessful effort to capture the British cake mix market with U.S.-style fancy frosting and cake mixes only to discover that Britons consume their cake at tea time, and that the cake they prefer is dry, spongy, and suitable to being picked up with the left hand while the right manages a cup of tea. Another U.S. company that asked a panel of British housewives to bake their favorite cakes discovered this important fact and has since acquired a major share of the British cake mix market with a dry, spongy cake mix.

Closer to home, Philip Morris attempted to take advantage of U.S. television advertising campaigns which have a sizable Canadian audience in border areas. The Canadian cigarette market is a Virginia or straight tobacco market in contrast to the U.S. market, which is a blended tobacco market. Philip Morris officials decided to ignore market research evidence

* Reprinted from "Multinational Product Planning: Strategic Alternatives," *Journal of Marketing*, Vol. 33, No. 1 (January 1969), pp. 58–62.
† Columbia University.

TABLE 1

Multinational product-communications mix: Strategic alternatives

Strategy	Product function or need satisfied	Conditions of product use	Ability to buy product	Recommended product strategy	Recommended communications strategy	Relative cost of adjustments	Product examples
1	Same	Same	Yes	Extension	Extension	1	Soft drinks
2	Different	Same	Yes	Extension	Adaptation	2	Bicycles, motor-scooters
3	Same	Different	Yes	Adaptation	Extension	3	Gasoline, detergents
4	Different	Different	Yes	Adaptation	Adaptation	4	Clothing, greeting cards
5	Same	. . . .	No	Invention	Develop new communications	5	Hand-powered washing machine

which indicated that Canadians would not accept a blended cigarette, and went ahead with programs which achieved retail distribution of U.S.-blended brands in the Canadian border areas served by U.S. television. Unfortunately, the Canadian preference for the straight cigarette remained unchanged. American-style cigarettes sold right up to the border but no further. Philip Morris had to withdraw its U.S. brands.

The unfortunate experience of discovering consumer preferences that do not favor a product is not confined to U.S. products in foreign markets. Corn Products Company discovered this in an abortive attempt to popularize Knorr dry soups in the United States. Dry soups dominate the soup market in Europe, and Corn Products tried to transfer some of this success to the United States. Corn Products based its decision to push ahead with Knorr on reports of taste panel comparisons of Knorr dry soups with popular liquid soups. The results of these panel tests strongly favored the Knorr product. Unfortunately these taste panel tests did not simulate the actual market environment for soup which includes not only eating but also preparation. Dry soups require 15 to 20 minutes cooking, whereas liquid soups are ready to serve as soon as heated. This difference is apparently a critical factor in the soup buyer's choice, and it was the reason for another failure of the extension strategy.

The product-communications extension strategy has an enormous appeal to most multinational companies because of the cost savings associated with this approach. Two sources of savings, manufacturing economies of scale and elimination of product R and D costs, are well known and understood. Less well known, but still important, are the substantial economies associated with the standardization of marketing communications. For a company with worldwide operations, the cost of preparing separate print and TV-cinema films for each market would be enormous. PepsiCo international marketers have estimated, for example, that production costs for specially prepared advertising for foreign markets would cost them $8 million per annum, which is considerably more than the amounts now spent by PepsiCo International for advertising production in these markets. Although these cost savings are important, they should not distract executives from the more important objective of maximum profit performance, which may require the use of an adjustment or invention strategy. As shown above, product extension in spite of its immediate cost savings may in fact prove to be a financially disastrous undertaking.

STRATEGY TWO: PRODUCT EXTENSION—COMMUNICATIONS ADAPTATION

When a product fills a different need or serves a different function under use conditions identical or similar to those in the domestic market, the only adjustment required is in marketing communications. Bicycles and motorscooters are illustrations of products in this category. They satisfy needs mainly for recreation in the United States but provide basic transportation in many foreign countries. Outboard motors are sold primarily to a recreation market in the United States, while the same motors in many foreign countries are sold mainly to fishing and transportation fleets.

In effect, when this approach is pursued (or, as is often the case, when it is stumbled upon quite by accident), a product transformation occurs. The same physical product ends up serving a different function or use than that for which it was originally designed. An actual example of a very successful transformation is provided by a U.S. farm machinery company which decided to market its U.S. line of suburban lawn and garden power equipment as agricultural implements in less-developed countries. The company's line of garden equipment was ideally suited to the farming task in many less developed countries, and, most importantly, it was priced at almost a third less than competing equipment especially designed for small acreage farming offered by various foreign manufacturers.

There are many examples of food product transformation. Many dry soup powders, for example, are sold mainly as soups in Europe but as sauces or cocktail dips in the United States. The products are identical; the only change is in marketing communications. In this case, the main communications adjustment is in the labeling of the powder. In Europe, the label illustrates and describes how to make soup out of the powder. In the United States, the label illustrates and describes how to make sauce and dip as well as soup.

The appeal of the product extension communications adaptation strategy is its relatively low cost of implementation. Since the product in this strategy in unchanged, R and D, tooling, manufacturing setup, and inventory costs associated with additions to the product line are avoided. The only costs of this approach are in identifying different product functions and reformulating marketing communications (advertising, sales promotion, point-of-sale material, and so on) around the newly identified function.

STRATEGY THREE: PRODUCT ADAPTATION—COMMUNICATIONS EXTENSION

A third approach to international product planning is to extend without change the basic communications strategy developed for the U.S. or home market, but to adapt the U.S. or home product to local use conditions. The product adaptation-communications extension strategy assumes that the product will serve the same function in foreign markets under different use conditions.

Esso followed this approach when it adapted its gasoline formulations to meet the weather conditions prevailing in foreign market areas, but employed without change its basic communications appeal, "Put a Tiger in Your Tank." There are many other examples of products that have been adjusted to perform the same function internationally under different environmental conditions. International soap and detergent manufacturers have adjusted their product formulations to meet local water conditions and the characteristics of washing equipment with no change in their basic communications approach. Agricultural chemicals have been adjusted to meet different soil conditions as well as different types and levels of insect resistance. Household appliances have been scaled to sizes appropriate to different use environments, and clothing has been adapted to meet fashion criteria.

STRATEGY FOUR: DUAL ADAPTATION

Market conditions indicate a strategy of adaptation of both the product and communications when differences exist in environmental conditions of use and in the function which a product serves. In essence, this is a combination of the market conditions of strategies two and three. U.S. greeting card manufacturers have faced these circumstances in Europe where the conditions under which greeting cards are purchased are different than in the United States. In Europe, the function of a greeting card is to provide a space for the sender to write his own message in contrast to the U.S. card, which contains a prepared message or what is known in the greeting card industry as "sentiment." European greeting cards are cellophane wrapped, necessitating a product alteration by American greeting card manufacturers selling in the European market. American manufacturers pursuing an adjustment strategy have changed both their product and their marketing communications in response to this set of environmental differences.

STRATEGY FIVE: PRODUCT INVENTION

The adaptation and adjustment strategies are effective approaches to international marketing when potential customers have the ability, or purchasing power, to buy the product. When potential customers cannot afford a product, the strategy indicated is invention or the development of an entirely new product designed to satisfy the identified need or function at a price within reach of the potential customer. This is a demanding but, if product development costs are not excessive, a potentially rewarding product strategy for the mass markets in the middle and less developed countries of the world.

Although potential opportunities for the utilization of the invention strategy in international marketing are legion, the number of instances where companies have responded is disappointingly small. For example, there are an estimated 600 million women in the world who still scrub their clothes by hand. These women have been served by multinational soap and detergent companies for decades, yet until this year not one of these companies had attempted to develop an inexpensive manual washing device.

Robert Young, vice president of marketing-worldwide of Colgate-Palmolive, has shown what can be done when product development efforts are focused upon market needs. He asked the leading inventor of modern mechanical washing processes to consider "inventing backwards"—to apply his knowledge not to a better mechanical washing device, but to a much better manual device. The device developed by the inventor is an inexpensive (under $10), all-plastic, hand-powered washer that has the tumbling action of a modern automatic machine. The response to this washer in a Mexican test market is reported to be enthusiastic.

HOW TO CHOOSE A STRATEGY

The best product strategy is one which optimizes company profits over the long term, or, stated more precisely, it is one which maximizes the present value of cash flows associated with business operations. Which strategy for international markets best achieves this goal? There is, unfortunately, no general answer to this question. Rather, the answer depends upon the specific product-market-company mix.

Some products demand adaptation, others lend themselves to adaptation, and others are best left unchanged. The same is true of markets. Some are so similar to the U.S. markets as to require little adaptation. No country's markets, however, are exactly like the U.S., Canada's included. Indeed, even within the United States, for some products regional and ethnic differences are sufficiently important to require product adaptation. Other markets are moderately different and lend themselves to adaptation, and still others are so different as to require adaptation of the majority of products. Finally, companies differ not only in their manufacturing costs, but also in their capability to identify and produce profitable product adaptations.

PRODUCT-MARKET ANALYSIS

The first step in formulating international product policy is to apply the systems analysis technique to each product in question. How is the product used? Does it require power sources, linkage to other systems, maintenance, preparation, style matching, and so on? Examples of almost mandatory adaptation situations are products designed for 60-cycle power going into 50-cycle markets, products calibrated in inches going to metric markets, products which require maintenance going into markets where maintenance standards and practices differ from the original design market, and products which might be used under different conditions than those for which they were originally designed. Renault discovered this latter factor too late with the ill-fated Dauphine which acquired a notorious reputation for breakdown frequency in the United States. Renault executives attribute the frequent mechanical failure of the Dauphine in the United States to the high-speed turnpike driving and relatively infrequent U.S. maintenance. These turned out to be critical differences for the product, which was designed for the roads of France and the almost daily maintenance which a Frenchman lavishes upon his car.

Even more difficult are the product adaptations which are clearly not mandatory, but which are of critical importance in determining whether the product will appeal to a narrow market segment rather than a broad mass market. The most frequent offender in this category is price. Too often, U.S. companies believe they have adequately adapted their international product offering by making adaptations to the physical features of products (for example, converting 120 volts to 220 volts), but they extend U.S. prices. The effect of such practice in most markets of the world where average incomes are lower than those in the United States is to put the U.S. product in a specialty market for the relatively wealthy consumers rather than in the mass market. An extreme case of this occurs when the product for the foreign market is exported from the United States and undergoes the often substantial price escalation that occurs when products are sold via multilayer export channel and exposed to import duties. When price constraints are considered in international marketing, the result can range from margin reduction and feature elimination to the "inventing backwards" approach used by Colgate.

Company analysis

Even if product-market analysis indicates an adaptation opportunity, each company must examine its own product/communication development and manufacturing costs. Clearly, any product or communication adaptation strategy must survive the test of profit effectiveness. The often-repeated exhortation that in international marketing a company should always adapt its products' advertising and promotion is clearly superficial, for it does not take into account the cost of adjusting or adapting products and communications programs.

What are adaptation costs?

They fall under two broad categories—development and production. Development costs will vary depending on the cost effectiveness of product/communications development groups within the company. The range in costs from company to company and product to product is great. Often, the company with international product development facilities has a strategic cost advantage. The vice president of a leading U.S. machinery company told recently of an example of this kind of advantage:

We have a machinery development group both here in the States and also in Europe. I tried to get our U.S. group to develop a machine for making the elliptical cigars that dominate the European market. At first they said "who would want an elliptical cigar machine?" Then they gradually admitted that they could produce such a machine for $500,000. I went to our Italian product development group with the same proposal, and they developed the machine I wanted for $50,000. The differences were partly relative wage costs but very importantly they were psychological. The Europeans see elliptical cigars every day, and they do not find the elliptical cigar unusual. Our American engineers were negative on elliptical cigars at the outset and I think this affected their overall response.

Analysis of a company's manufacturing costs is essentially a matter of identifying potential opportunity losses. If a company is reaping economies of scale from large-scale production of a single product, then any shift to variations of the single product will raise manufacturing costs. In general, the more decentralized a company's manufacturing setup, the smaller the manufacturing cost of producing different versions of the basic product. Indeed, in the company with local manufacturing facilities for each international market, the additional *manufacturing* cost of producing an adapted product for each market is zero.

A more fundamental form of company analysis occurs when a firm is considering in general whether or not to pursue explicitly a strategy of product adaptation. At this level, analysis must focus not only on the manufacturing cost structure of the firm, but also on the basic capability of the firm to identify product adaptation opportunities and to convert these perceptions into profitable products. The ability to identify preferences will depend to an important degree on the creativity of people in the organization and the effectiveness of information systems in this organization. The latter capability is as important as the former. For example, the existence of salesmen who are creative in identifying profitable product adaptation opportunities is no assurance that their ideas will be translated into reality by the organization. Information, in the form of their ideas and perceptions, must move through the organization to those who are involved in the product development decision-making process; and this movement, as any student of information systems in organizations will attest, is not automatic. Companies which lack perceptual and information system capabilities are not well equipped to pursue a product adaptation strategy, and should either concentrate on products which can be extended or should develop these capabilities before turning to a product adaptation strategy.

SUMMARY

The choice of product and communications strategy in international marketing is a function of three key factors: (1) the product itself defined in terms of the function or need it serves; (2) the market defined in terms of the conditions under which the product is used, including the preferences of potential customers and the ability to buy the products in question; and (3) the costs of adaptation and manufacture to the company considering these product-communications approaches. Only after analysis of the product-market fit and of company capabilities and costs can executives choose the most profitable international strategy.

Bibliography

A. INFORMATION SYSTEMS

ALBAUM, GERALD. "Information Flow and Decentralized Decision Making in Marketing," *California Management Review*, Vol. 9, No. 4, Summer 1967, pp. 59–71.

ALDER, LEE. "Symbiotic Marketing," *Harvard Business Review*, Vol. 44, No. 6, November–December 1966, pp. 59–71.

AMSTUTZ, ARNOLD E. "Marketing-Oriented Management Systems: The Current Status," *Journal of Marketing Research*, Vol. 6, No. 4, November 1969, pp. 481–96.

BERENSON, CONRAD. "Marketing Information Systems," *Journal of Marketing*, Vol. 33, No. 4, October 1969, pp. 16–23.

BRIEN, RICHARD H., AND STAFFORD, JAMES E. "Marketing Information Systems: A New Dimension for Marketing Research," *Journal of Marketing*, Vol. 32, No. 3, July 1968, pp. 19–23.

COX, DONALD F., AND GOOD, ROBERT E. "How to Build a Marketing Information System," *Harvard Business Review*, Vol. 45, No. 3, May–June 1967, pp. 145–54.

KOTLER, PHILIP. "Corporate Models: Better Marketing Plans," *Harvard Business Review*, Vol. 48, No. 4, July–August 1970, pp. 135–49.

MURDICK, ROBERT G. "MIS Development Procedures," *Journal of Systems Management*, Vol. 21, No. 12, December 1970, pp. 22–6.

SCHIFF, J. S. AND SCHIFF, MICHAEL. "New Sales Management Tool: ROAM," *Harvard Business Review*, Vol. 45, No. 4, July–August 1967, pp. 59–66.

STAATS, ELMER B. "Information Systems in an Era of Change," *Financial Executive*, Vol. 35, No. 12, December 1967, pp. 37–41.

B. MARKETING OPPORTUNITY ASSESSMENT

HUMMEL, FRANCIS E. *Market and Sales Potentials.* New York: The Ronald Press Company, 1961.

KELLEY, EUGENE J., AND LAZER, WILLIAM, eds. "Innovation—A Central Task of Management Consultant," *Managerial Marketing: Perspectives and Viewpoints*. Homewood, Ill.: Richard D. Irwin, Inc., 1967.

KOTLER, PHILIP. *Marketing Management.* Englewood Cliffs, N.J.: Prentice-Hall, Inc., 1972.

LEVITT, THEODORE. "Exploit the Product Life Cycle," *Harvard Business Review*, Vol. 43, No. 6, November–December 1965, pp. 81–94.

LEVITT, THEODORE. *Innovation in Marketing.* New York: McGraw-Hill Book Company, Inc., 1962.

LEVITT, THEODORE. "The New Markets—Think Before You Leap," *Harvard Business Review,* Vol. 47, No. 3, May–June 1969, pp. 53–67.

REYNOLDS, WILLIAM H. *Products and Markets.* New York: Appleton, Century, Crofts, 1969.

C. PLANNING AND PROGRAMMING MARKETING ACTIVITY

ALDERSON, WROE, AND GREEN, PAUL E. *Planning and Problem Solving in Marketing.* Homewood, Ill.: Richard D. Irwin, Inc., 1964.

ANSOFF, IGOR. "Planning as a Practical Management Tool," *Financial Executive,* Vol. 32, No. 6, June 1964, pp. 34–37.

CLARK, WILLIAM A., AND SEXTON, DONALD E. *Marketing and Management Science: A Synergism.* Homewood, Ill.: Richard D. Irwin, Inc., 1970.

DARDEN, WILLIAM R., AND LAMONE, RUDOLPH P. *Marketing Management and the Decision Sciences: Theory and Applications.* Boston, Mass.: Allyn and Bacon, Inc., 1971.

DAY, RALPH L., AND PARSONS, LEONARD J. *Marketing Models: Quantitative Applications.* Scranton, Pa.: Intext Educational Publishers, 1971.

DRUCKER, PETER F. "Long-Range Planning," *Management Science,* Vol. 5, No. 8, April 1959, pp. 238–49.

KELLEY, EUGENE J. *Marketing Planning and Competitive Strategy.* Englewood Cliffs, N.J.: Prentice-Hall, Inc., 1972.

KING, WILLIAM R. *Quantitative Analysis for Marketing Management.* New York: McGraw-Hill Book Company, 1967.

LAZER, WILLIAM. *Marketing Management: A Systems Perspective.* New York: John Wiley and Sons, Inc., 1971.

MAGEE, JOHN F. *Physical-Distribution Systems.* New York: McGraw-Hill Book Company, 1967.

MURDICK, ROBERT G. *Mathematical Models in Marketing.* Scranton, Pa.: Intext Educational Publishers, 1971.

PESSEMIER, EDGAR A. *New Product Decisions: An Analytical Approach.* New York: McGraw-Hill Book Company, 1966.

SMITH, WENDELL R. "Long-Range Planning and Research and Development," *Managerial Marketing: Perspectives and Viewpoints.* Eugene J. Kelley and William Lazer, eds. Homewood, Ill.: Richard D. Irwin, Inc., 1967.

STERN, MARK E. *Marketing Planning: A Systems Approach.* New York: McGraw-Hill Book Co., 1966.

STURDIVANT, FREDERICK D.; STERN, LOUIS W.; GRABNER, JOHN R.; ROBERTSON, THOMAS S.; MYERS, JAMES H.; KERNAN, JEROME B.; LEVY, SIDNEY J.; ALPERT, MARK I.; BUCKLIN, LOUIS P.; AND STASCH, STANLEY F. *Managerial Analysis in Marketing.* Denview, Ill.: Scott, Foresman and Co., 1970.

WASSON, CHESTER R. *Product Management: Product Life Cycles and Competitive Marketing Strategy.* St. Charles, Ill.: Challenge Books, 1971.

D. MARKETING ORGANIZATION AND LEADERSHIP

AMES, B. C. "Payoff of Product Management," *Harvard Business Review*, Vol. 41, No. 6, November–December 1963, pp. 141–52.

BENNIS, WARREN G.; BENNE, KENNETH D.; AND CHIN, ROBERT. *The Planning of Change*. New York: Holt, Rinehart and Winston, 1969.

BOARD CONFERENCE. *The Product Manager System*. New York: National Industrial Conference Board, 1965.

CASCINO, ANTHONY E. "Organizational Implications of the Marketing Concept," *Managerial Marketing: Perspectives and Viewpoints*. Eugene J. Kelley and William Lazer, eds., Homewood, Ill.: Richard D. Irwin, Inc., 1967.

COLLIER, R. B. "The Product Management Concept in Marketing," *The Marketing Concept in Action*. R. Kaplan, ed. Chicago: American Marketing Association, June 1964, p. 55.

DRUCKER, PETER F. *Managing for Results*. New York: Harper & Row, Publishers, 1964.

LAWRENCE, P. R., AND LORSCH, J. W. "The New Management Job: The Integrator," *Harvard Business Review*, Vol. 45, No. 6, November–December 1967, pp. 142–51.

LUCK, DAVID J. "Interfaces of Product Managers," *Journal of Marketing*, Vol. 33, No. 4, October 1969, pp. 32–36.

E. CONTROLLING MARKET PERFORMANCE

MONTGOMERY, DAVID B., AND URBAN, GLEN, L. *Applications of Management Science in Marketing*. Englewood Cliffs, N.J.: Prentice-Hall, Inc., 1970.

SEVIN, CHARLES H. *Marketing Productivity Analysis*. New York: McGraw-Hill Book Company, 1965.

SHUCHMAN, ABE. "The Marketing Audit: Its Nature, Purposes and Problems," *Analyzing and Improving Marketing Performance*, American Management Association Report No. 32, p. 31.

SMITH, SAMUEL V.; BRIEN, RICHARD H.; AND STAFFORD, JAMES E. *Reading in Marketing Information Systems*. Boston, Mass.: Houghton Mifflin Company, 1968.

STANTON, WILLIAM J. "Evaluating Marketing Effort," *Managerial Marketing: Perspectives and Viewpoints*. Eugene J. Kelley and William Lazer, eds. Homewood, Ill.: Richard D. Irwin, Inc., 1967.

STASCH, STANLEY F. *Systems Analysis for Marketing Planning and Control*. Glenview, Ill.: Scott, Foresman and Company, 1972.

UHL, KENNETH P., AND SCHONER, BERTRAM. *Marketing Research*. New York: John Wiley and Sons, 1969.

F. MULTINATIONAL MARKETING

CATEORA, P. R., AND HESS, J. M. *International Marketing*. Rev. ed. Homewood, Ill.: Richard D. Irwin, Inc. 1971.

FAYERWEATHER, JOHN. *International Marketing.* Englewood Cliffs, N.J.: Prentice-Hall, Inc., 1965.

KEEGAN, WARREN J. "A Conceptual Framework for Multinational Marketing," *Columbia Journal of World Business,* Vol. 7, No. 6, November–December 1972, pp. 67–76.

LEIGHTON, DAVID S. R. *International Marketing.* New York: McGraw-Hill, 1966.

LIANDER, BERTIL. *Comparative Analysis for International Marketing.* Boston, Mass.: Allyn and Bacon, Inc., 1967.

ROOT, FRANKLIN R. *Strategic Planning for Export Marketing.* Scranton, Pa.: International Textbook Company, 1966.

RYANS, JOHN K., AND BAKER, JAMES C. *World Marketing.* New York: John Wiley and Sons, Inc., 1967.

TERPSTRA, VERN. *International Marketing,* New York: Holt, Rinehart and Winston, Inc., 1972.

VERNON, RAYMOND. *Manager in the International Economy.* Englewood Cliffs, N.J.: Prentice-Hall, Inc., 1969.

4 MANAGING THE MARKETING MIX

COMPETITIVE PRESSURE requires that marketing executives design and manage the total market offering of the firm to meet the demands of the marketplace. The environment in which this takes place is extremely complex and continually changing. The marketing manager is faced with a wide variety of variables which are the determining factors of success. The marketing mix is generally considered to include the systematic organization and control of those variables over which the firm has influence. Each variable must be evaluated singularly and then integrated and coordinated with every other variable, in order for a unified course of action with the success of the entire organization as a common goal to be the result.

In developing the marketing mix, the marketing manager must initially consider the needs of the consumer. His success and that of the entire firm depends on the allocation of a limited amount of resources in a manner which will continually satisfy consumer wants and needs.

Essentially all of the variables which concern the marketing manager can be placed in at least one of the components of the marketing mix. These are the product and service mix, the distribution mix, and the communications mix. The product and service mix has control over the elements that are directly related to the product. While each of these elements is normally considered separately, they must eventually be integrated with one another to provide the most suitable product offering. Included in the wide variety of elements in this mix are the composition of the product line(s), pricing, packaging, labeling, product planning and development, guarantees, and servicing of the product.

The distribution mix is divided into two components: channels of distribution and physical distribution. The former includes those institutions employed by the company to promote and/or sell their products to members of the trade, or in some cases to the ultimate consumer. Some of the possible "middlemen" which a company may use in the channel of distribution are representatives, wholesalers, and distributors. The physical distribution system is concerned with the logistical problems of moving and storing the product during the period from the time the product is completed by the manufacturer until it is available to the ultimate consumer. Warehousing, modes of transportation, level of inventories, and distribution centers are some of the areas involved with this physical flow of goods.

Advertising, promotions, and personal selling are the activities which the marketing manager employs in managing the communications mix. These three areas are of prime importance to the firm since they provide the major link between the consuming public and the manufacturer.

Every element of the marketing mix is dependent upon the other variables within the mix. Every decision made must be evaluated in terms of the combined effect on the various marketing objectives of the firm. This interdependency requires the marketing manager to plan, evaluate, and coordinate the functions of the marketing mix as a set of mutually dependent variables.

The goal of the marketing manager is to devise an overall marketing mix that can optimize system performance. Considering the infinite number of possible combinations, the only way to approach optimal performance is through a well-coordinated and executed marketing plan. However, even after a well-planned mix has been developed, its execution must contain provisions for readjustment as market conditions dictate. Irrespective of the quality of the initial marketing plan, it is unreasonable to expect that it will continue to meet expectations over a long period of time. It is therefore necessary to incorporate into the marketing plan a system to: (1) monitor results and changing conditions in the product environment, (2) evaluate alternative courses of action, and (3) make any necessary changes in the marketing plan to accommodate these changes.

a.

The product and
services mix

THE PRODUCT or service is the key variable in the corporate marketing operation—it is the firm's source of income and the consumer's source of satisfaction. The firm's long-term success is a function of management's ability to satisfy both of these needs.

Products and services are continually subject to the uncertainty and changes that are characteristic of the marketplace. Demand shifts, alterations in consumer preference, pricing, and new product introductions are just a few of the variables which concern the marketing manager. Because of this, the marketing decisions involved with the product mix require a continuous effort. These decisions require an aggressive and creative approach that must also be integrated with the goals, objectives, and policies of the entire firm.

In the first article, Smallwood discusses the measuring and contribution of the product life cycle in sales forecasting, advertising, pricing, and market planning. Next, Luck discusses the problems of the product manager and his role within and outside the firm. The final article by Oxenfeldt emphasizes the pricing of a product in relation to the rest of the firm's product line and in relation to competitive products.

A thorough understanding of the product life cycle can provide the marketing manager with insights into many marketing problems such as programming an appropriate marketing mix. The author, an experienced marketing executive, describes the four-phase product life cycle concept as one way of "translating information into profits." Several relevant concepts and perspectives are presented that can aid decisions involving the product-service mix.

---

34. THE PRODUCT LIFE CYCLE: A KEY TO STRATEGIC MARKETING PLANNING*

John E. Smallwood †

VALUE OF THE PRODUCT LIFE CYCLE CONCEPT

Modern marketing management is increasingly supported by marketing information services of growing sophistication and improving accuracy. Yet the task remains for the marketing manager to translate information into insights, insights into ideas, ideas into plans, and plans into reality and satisfactory programs and profits. There is a growing realization among marketing managers of the need for concepts, perspectives, and constructs that are useful in translating information into profits. While information flow can be mechanized and the screening of ideas routinized, no alternative to managerial creativity has yet been found to generate valuable marketing ideas upon which whole marketing programs are based. The product life cycle is one concept that has been extremely useful in focusing this creative process.

In many ways, the product life cycle concept may be considered as the marketing equivalent of the periodic table of the elements in the physical sciences. Like the periodic table, it provides a framework for grouping products into families for easier predictions of reactions to various stimuli. With chemicals, it's a question of oxidation temperature and melting point; with products, it's marketing channel acceptance and advertising budgets. Like chemicals react in similar ways and so do like products. The product life cycle helps to group these products into homogeneous families. Thus the similarity to the periodic table of elements.

The PLC can be the key to successful and profitable product management, from new product introduction through profitable disposal of obsolescent products.

PRODUCT LIFE CYCLE—A CONCEPT OF GROWTH AND DECLINE

Figure 1 illustrates the fundamental concept of the product life cycle.

---

* Source: Reprinted from "The Product Life Cycle: A Key to Strategic Marketing Planning," Business Topics, Vol. 21, No. 1, (Winter, 1973), pp. 29–35.
† Director of economic and marketing research, Whirlpool Corporation.

FIGURE 1

Life cycle stages of various products

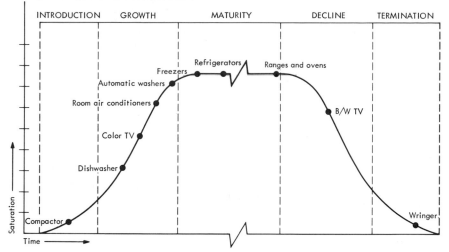

In application, the vertical scale is often measured in saturation of the product (percent of market units using) while the horizontal scale is calibrated to represent the passage of time. Months or years are usually the units of time used in calibration, although theoretically, an application of much shorter or longer durations (milliseconds in physical sciences, millennia in archaeology) might be found. In Figure 1 the breakdown in the time scale is given by stages in the maturity of product life.

The saturation scale, however, is a guide only and must be used accordingly. When comparing one product with another, it is sometimes best treated in qualitative terms, left without units. It is important to the user of the PLC that this limitation be recognized and conceptual provisions made to handle it.

For example, if the basic marketing unit chosen is occupied U.S. households, one can never expect a product such as room air conditioners to attain 100% saturation. The reasons are that many households have already been fitted with central air conditioning; thus, the saturation attainment falls well short of 100 percent of the marketing measurement chosen.

To overcome this difficulty, marketing managers have two basic options. They can choose a more restrictive, specific marketing unit such as all occupied U.S. households that do not have forced air heating and thus are not candidates for central air conditioning. They can then anticipate that room air conditioners will saturate not only *that* market by almost 100 percent but portions of other markets as well. On the other hand, management can conclude, on the basis of informed judgment, just what the *potential* saturation of total households might be, and then convert our PLC growth scale to a measure representing the degree of attainment of poten-

FIGURE 2
Product life cycle

Marketing	Introduction	Growth	Maturity	Decline	Termination
Customers.	Innovative/ high income	High income/ mass market	Mass market	Laggards/ special	Few
Channels.	Few	Many	Many	Few	Few
Approach	Product	Label	Label	Specialized	Availability
Advertising	Awareness	Label superiority	Lowest price	Psychographic	Sparse
Competitors.	Few	Many	Many	Few	Few

Pricing

Price	High	Lower	Lowest	Rising	High
Gross margins	High	Lower	Lowest	Low	Low
Cost reductions	Few	Many	Slower	None	None
Incentives	Channel	Channel/consumer	Consumer/channel	Channel	Channel

Product

Configuration.	Basic	Second generation	Segmented/sophisticated	Basic	Stripped
Quality.	Poor	Good	Superior	Spotty	Minimal
Capacity.	Over	Under	Optimum	Over	Over

tial saturation of U.S. households. The latter approach is the one the author has found to be most useful. By this device automatic washers are considered at 100 percent saturation when at their full potential of an arbitrarily chosen 80 percent.

Consider Figure 1, where various products are positioned by life cycle stages. The potential saturations permit the grouping of products into like stages of the life cycle even when their actual saturations are vastly different.

Note that in Figure 1 automatic washers (58 percent saturation) and room a/c (30 percent) are positioned in the same growth stage. Freezers (29 percent) and refrigerators (99 percent), on the other hand, are in the maturity stage. This occurs because, *in our judgment*, freezers have a potential of only about one third of occupied households and thus have attained almost 90 percent of that market. Automatic clothes washers, however, have a potential of about four fifths of occupied households and so are only at about 70 percent of their potential and still show some of the characteristics of the growth stage of the PLC.

Note also how the general characteristics of the products and their markets are summarized in Figure 2.

This illustrates the PLC as a convenient scheme of product classification. The PLC permits management to assign given products to the appropriate stages of acceptance by a given market: introduction, growth, maturity, decline, and termination. The actual classification of products by appropriate stages, however, is more art than science. The whole process is quite imprecise. But unsatisfactory as this may be, a useful classification can be achieved with management benefits that are clearly of value. This can be illustrated by examining the contribution of the PLC concept in the following marketing activities: sales forecasting, advertising, pricing, and marketing planning.

APPLICATIONS OF THE PLC TO SALES FORECASTING

One of the most dramatic uses of the PLC in sales forecasting was its application in explaining the violent decline in color TV sales during the credit crunch recession of 1969–1970. This occurred after the experience of the 1966–1967 mini-recession which had almost no effect on color TV sales that could be discerned through the usual "noise" of the available product flow data. A similar apparent insensitivity was demonstrated in 1958, 1961, and again in 1966–1967, with sales of portable dishwashers. But it too was followed by a quite noticeable sales reduction in the 1969–1971 period. This is shown in Figure 3.

In early 1972 both products show a positive response to an improving economic climate. The question is, why did both products become vulnerable to economic contractions after having shown a great degree of

FIGURE 3

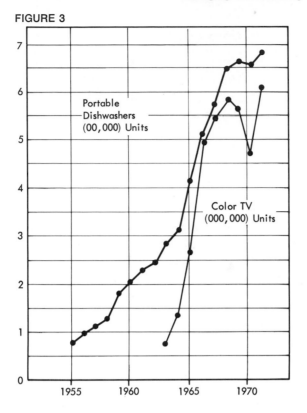

independence of the business cycle during prior years? The answer seems to lie in their stage in the product life cycle. Comparing the saturation as shown in Figure 4 of color TV and dishwashers we see an interesting phenomenon.

Consider the case of the color TV.

We can ascertain that as late as 1966 saturation was only around 8 percent. By late 1969, however, saturation had increased swiftly to almost 40 percent. The same observation for dishwashers is true, which has only been a mass market appliance since 1965. This is the key to explain both situations.

At the early, introductory stages of their life cycles, both appliances were making large sales gains as a result of being adopted by high income consuming units. Later, when sales growth depended more upon adoption by the less affluent members of the mass market—whose spending plans are modified by general economic conditions—the product sales began to correlate markedly to the general economic conditions.

It appears that products tend to saturate as a function of income—even more than age. This is dramatically illustrated by the data displayed in

FIGURE 4

Saturation levels of various appliances, 1950–1980 (percent of U.S. households)

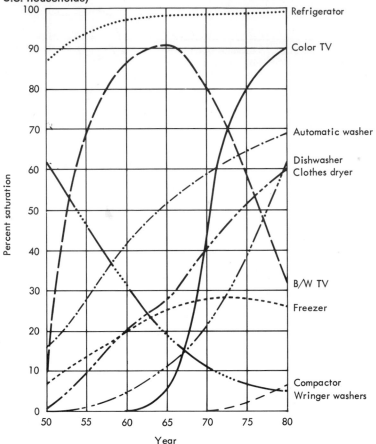

Figure 5. Here the reader will note the clear-cut relationship—across the four products—of the economic status of their most important customers and the position noted in the product life cycle, Figure 2.

Accordingly, one can anticipate the day when the compactor, along with the microwave oven, and even nondurables such as good quality wines, will some day be included in the middle-income consumption patterns, and thereby become much more coincident with ordinary economic cycles.

PRODUCT LIFE STAGES AND ADVERTISING

The concept of a new product filtering through income classes, combined with long-respected precepts of advertising, can result in new per-

FIGURE 5

Purchase patterns (by age and income of households)

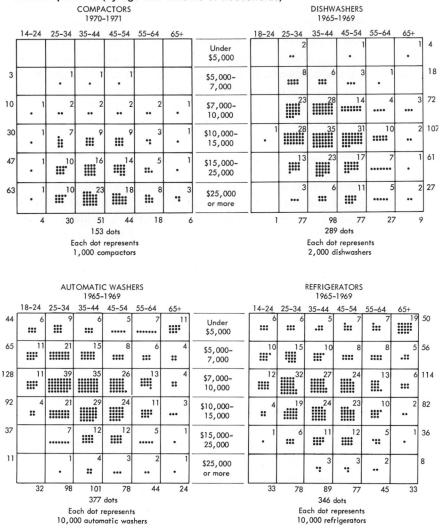

COMPACTORS
1970-1971

	14-24	25-34	35-44	45-54	55-64	65+	
							Under $5,000
3		1	1	1			$5,000–7,000
10	1	2	2	2	2	1	$7,000–10,000
30	1	7	9	9	3	1	$10,000–15,000
47	1	10	16	14	5	1	$15,000–25,000
63	1	10	23	18	8	3	$25,000 or more
	4	30	51	44	18	6	

153 dots
Each dot represents
1,000 compactors

DISHWASHERS
1965-1969

18-24	25-34	35-44	45-54	55-64	65+	
	2		1		1	4
	8	6	3	1		18
	23	28	14	4	3	72
1	28	35	31	10	2	107
	13	23	17	7	1	61
	3	6	11	5	2	27
1	77	98	77	27	9	

289 dots
Each dot represents
2,000 dishwashers

AUTOMATIC WASHERS
1965-1969

	18-24	25-34	35-44	45-54	55-64	65+	
44	6	9	6	5	7	11	Under $5,000
65	11	21	15	8	6	4	$5,000–7,000
128	11	39	35	26	13	4	$7,000–10,000
92	4	21	29	24	11	3	$10,000–15,000
37		7	12	12	5	1	$15,000–25,000
11		1	4	3	2	1	$25,000 or more
	32	98	101	78	44	24	

377 dots
Each dot represents
10,000 automatic washers

REFRIGERATORS
1965-1969

14-24	25-34	35-44	45-54	55-64	65+	
6	6	5	7	7	19	50
10	15	10	8	8	5	56
12	32	27	24	13	6	114
4	19	24	23	10	2	82
1	6	11	12	5	1	36
		3	3	2		8
33	78	89	77	45	33	

346 dots
Each dot represents
10,000 refrigerators

spectives for marketing managers. The resulting observations are both strategic and tactical. New advertising objectives and new insights for copy points and media selection may be realized. Consider the advertising tasks by stages:

Phase I: *Introduction*
The objective is to make the best customer prospects aware that the new product or service is now available, what it does,

what the customer's benefits are to be, why claims are to be believed, and what the conditions of consumption will be.

Phase II: *Growth*

The objective now is to saturate the mass market with the same idea of further product registration as in Phase I. In addition, it is to gain recognition that a particular brand of the product is clearly superior to other "inferior" substitutes while, at the same time, providing a rationalization that this purchase is not merely a wasteful, luxury-indulging activity but makes the consumer a better *something*—husband, mother, accountant, driver, etc.

Phase III: *Maturity*

In this phase besides intensifying the brand superiority ("don't buy substitutes; get the real XYZ original, which incidentally, is *new* and *improved....*") and dropping to a great extent the *product* registration, a new rationalization is added: *respectability*. Respectability is a prerequisite of the American lower class, which in this phase is the economic stratum containing the most important opportunities for sales gains. But companies do not abandon higher income customers. Rather, they now match advertising to a variety of market segments instead of concentrating on only one theme for the market. Several distinct advertising programs are used. All elements of the marketing mix—product, price, advertising, personal selling, channels and promotion—are focused on specific market segments.

Phase IV: *Decline*

Superior substitutes for a product will generally be adopted first by those people who first adopted the product in consideration. They are usually the upper economic and social classes. Advertising themes reflect this when they concentrate on special market segments like the West Coast families or "consumption societies" such as beer drinkers.

PRODUCT LIFE STAGES AND PRICING

As a product works its way through all five stages of the life cycle shown in Figure 1, the price elasticity can be expected to undergo dramatic changes. Generally speaking, price elasticity of a relatively simple product will be low at first. Thus, while customers comprise higher income classes, demand is relatively inelastic. Later, when most customers are in the lower income categories, greater price elasticity will exist.

Of course, increased price elasticity will not automatically lower prices during the growth stage of the PLC. For in this phase costs are not tightly controlled. In this growth stage, however, per unit costs *are* most dramatically reduced. Here the learning curve has been at work in engineering, production, and marketing. This is because rising volume and more importantly, the *forecasts* of higher volume, justify increased capital investments and higher fixed costs. But these are spread over a larger number of units, thereby reducing unit costs markedly. Profits also increase dramatically in this stage and so new competitors surface with great rapidity.

Pricing in the mature stage of the PLC is usually found to be unsatisfactory. None of the producers are as profitable as they were. Price competition is keener in spite of the fact that a relatively small price difference for the consumer does not really seem to be very significant to them at this stage.

PRODUCT PLANNING AND THE PLC

Curiously enough, the very configuration of the product takes on a classical pattern of evolution as it advances through the PLC. At first, the new device is designed for function alone—the initial design is sometimes crude by standards that will be applied in the future. As the process continues, performance sophistication increases. Eventually the product develops to the point that competitors are hard-pressed to make meaningful differences which are perceptible to consumers.

As the product progresses through the PLC, these modifications tend to describe a pattern of metamorphosis from "the ugly box" to a number of options. The adjustment cycle includes:

Part of house: The "built-in" look and function. Light fixtures, cooking stoves, wall safes, furnaces, are examples.

Furniture: A blending of the product into the home decor. Included are television, hi-fi consoles, radios, clocks, musical instruments, game tables, etc.

Portable: A provision for increased *presence* of the product through provisions for easier movement (rollers or compactness), or multiple unit ownership (wall clocks, radios, even refrigerators), or miniaturization for portability until it achieves the ultimate. Portability and *personalization,* such as the pocket knife and the wrist watch can occur.

System: A combination of components into one unit that has compatible uses and/or common parts for increased convenience, lower cost, or less space. Home entertainment centers including TV, radio, hi-fi capabilities, refrigerator-freezers, combination clothes washer-dryers, clock radios, pocket knife-can-and-bottle openers are illustrative.

Similar changes can also be observed in the distribution channel. Products often progress from specialty outlets in the introductory stage to mass distribution outlets such as discount houses and contract buyers during the mature and decline phases of the PLC. Interestingly enough the process eventually is reversed. Buggy whips can still be found in some specialty stores and premium prices are paid for replicas of very old products.

CONCLUSION

The product life cycle is a useful concept. It is the equivalent of the periodic table of elements in the physical sciences. The maturation of production technology and product configuration along with marketing programs proceed in an orderly, somewhat predictable, course over time with the merchandising nature and marketing environment noticeably similar between products that are in the same stage of their life cycle. Its use as a concept in forecasting, pricing, advertising, product planning, and other aspects of marketing management can make it a valuable tool for marketing management, although considerable amounts of judgment must be used in its application.

The product manager is, among other things, a source of information, a planner, a coordinator, and the focal point of all activity concerning his product. His effectiveness is determined by the success of his many interfaces within and outside the organization. The product management concept reflects a departure from the traditional management vertical organizational structure to a cross functional structure. The author maintains that the product manager position promotes efficient marketing planning in the spirit of the marketing concept.

35. INTERFACES OF A PRODUCT MANAGER *

David J. Luck †

The position of product manager was established over 40 years ago in a prominent marketing organization, that of Procter and Gamble. Despite this long history, scholarly research and writing have seemingly ignored the product management organization. Literature specifically treating

* Reprinted from "Interfaces of a Product Manager," *Journal of Marketing*, Vol. 33, No. 4 (October 1969), pp. 32–36.

† Southern Illinois University.

product management organization is confined to perhaps three or four monographs or thin volumes which are largely descriptive.[1]

Does this obscurity imply that the product manager is a rare or unimportant functionary in modern business? Evidence points to the contrary. This writer's experience and that of other observers indicates that most large multiproduct companies have initiated the product management plan of organization.

Product managers operate on a horizontal plane, in contrast to the primarily vertical orientation of most marketing personnel. Their specialization is cross functional with primary focus on a specific product line or brand. They have numerous titles such as brand manager, product planning manager, or product marketing manager. These titles frequently denote varying emphases, but do not alter their basic responsibilities. The position of "product manager" is a radical departure in management that is not easily slotted into and absorbed by the existing organization. Consequently, it is not readily defined, staffed, and implemented.

OBJECTIVES OF THE PRODUCT MANAGER

Enthusiasts for product management have envisioned this position to be the answer to the needs of large enterprises to create true profit centers within the organization. This vision has proved generally impracticable.[2] Product managers are seriously hampered by ambiguity of authority in the execution of their plans and decisions, in addition to the problems of a new type of position asserting its intended role. Undefined authority precludes clear-cut, enforceable responsibility. Despite such problems, the main purposes of product managers are seemingly being accomplished. They are:

1. Creation and conceptualization of strategies for improving and marketing the assigned product line or brands.
2. Projection and determination of financial and operating plans for such products.
3. Monitoring execution and results of plans, with possible adaptation of tactics to evolving conditions.

An underlying role of the product manager is that of becoming the information center on the assigned products.

Product management provides integrated planning which is intimately related to the market needs and opportunities of specific products. This contrasts with decisions that formerly were diffused among functional specialists who could not bring to bear comprehensive knowledge and

---

[1] The more thorough analyses of product manager's work are in: Gordon H. Evans, *The Product Manager's Job* (New York: American Management Association, 1964) and Gordon Medcalf, *Marketing and the Brand Manager* (London, England: Pergamon Press, Ltd., 1967).

[2] David J. Luck and Theodore Nowak, "Product Management: Vision Unfilled," *Harvard Business Review*, Vol. 43 (May 1965), pp. 143–50.

analysis of factors peculiar to a product. The establishment of interfaces between product manager and these functional specialists is necessary in order to insure acquisition of the variety of information which these specialists can contribute. Simultaneously, the product manager needs to maintain interfaces with the functional personnel who execute the strategies and plans that he originates.

This leads us to the product managers as vital organizational loci for the focus of marketing interfaces. The subject of these interfaces and the means whereby they may be efficiently realized thus merits our serious concern.

INTERFACES VITAL TO PRODUCT MANAGERS

Research information obtained during studies of 17 product managers in the course of an advertising decision study[3] and during a current study of eight product managers for pharmaceutical manufacturers indicates that the interfaces which are important to a product manager's work are perhaps the most numerous and varied of any in middle management. They may be placed in the following six categories.

The buying public

In ultimate significance to marketing strategy and planning, the buyers and users of the particular product line overshadow all other interfaces. The man who is to conceive product and promotion strategies and prepare competitively viable plans can hardly be too well apprised of how, when, and for what purposes the product is bought and used. Market segments with unique needs may be identified and are often the clue to very effective strategies. Brand images, brand loyalties, consumer profiles, and the reception of advertising and sales promotion campaigns are further examples of the vast information the experienced product manager acquires and studies as he appraises the past and explores future possibilities.

Distributors

Wholesalers and retailers play major roles in the market success of products which they distribute. Relatively small shifts in shelf facings, out-of-stocks, displays, and other dealer support may produce favorable or dangerous trends. A significant portion of the product distribution strategy may be aimed at the distributors themselves to stimulate and maintain their interests through special programs, sales aids, and other trade promotion. Often the product manager's concern includes monitoring the inventories in the pipelines in order to control production rates.

---

[3] This study under sponsorship of the Marketing Science Institute contributed to the volume: P. J. Robinson and D. J. Luck, *Promotional Decision Making* (New York: McGraw-Hill Book Co., 1964).

Sales force

The salesman is a necessary ally of the product manager, although often a very independent one. For most industrial products and for some consumer products, personal selling is the principal force in promoting the product. Since the salesman is frequently selling many products of the firm, product managers often compete with one another in seeking the salesman's support. Product managers are most concerned with the development of selling methods, sales aids, and applications literature. For industrial products, the products manager often makes sales calls with the salesman, particularly where technical expertise is needed.

Advertising agencies

The degree of involvement with advertising agencies varies widely among product managers. For most industrial products it is of less concern than the sales force. In some consumer goods organizations, product managers are limited by policy to working with the agencies only to the extent of developing advertising strategies, with all other liaison conducted through advertising departments. At the other extreme, there are companies which place virtually all collaborations with the agencies in the hands of product managers. Typically a consumer goods product manager works intimately and continuously with his counterparts in the agency—a relationship that has received some criticism where inexperienced product managers have been troublesome to agencies.[4] Regardless of such views, agency account men tend to work as a team with product managers of major advertisers in developing advertising campaigns and in providing market information and merchandising ideas to the client.

Product development

The product manager's involvement with new product development is dependent on the firm's organizational structure, the nature of the product itself, and the background of the manager. Where there is a separately designated manager for new products, the managers of current products are usually confined to planning modifications in existing products and packaging. With new products that can be designed relatively quickly, the product manager may maintain a close relationship with all stages of their development; in cases requiring prolonged research and development, product managers tend to have little contact with the emerging products until a market testing stage approaches. Another factor is that, typi-

---

[4] In *Management and Advertising Problems* (New York: Association of National Advertisers, 1965), this problem is discussed on page 53. The study reported in this volume, however, later affirmed the continuous growth of product management, but in more effective relationships with advertising agencies (p. 92).

cally, industrial products managers are technically trained and oriented, while the contrary is true in consumer goods. The former naturally have more frequent interface with research and development.

Marketing research

In their roles of originating and formulating marketing plans and of monitoring the progress and obstacles of products, product managers require substantial marketing research information. Typically, they depend heavily on marketing research personnel to obtain and process this information. Within the enterprise, a marketing researcher may be the closest collaborator with a product manager.

Other marketing and corporate personnel

The product manager's superior within the organization represents the interface most critical to the manager's personal career. Regardless of the superior's title, which will vary from firm to firm, this superior will usually bear the responsibility for marketing planning of a division or corporation. Very commonly these men are themselves former product managers and a high level of empathy tends to exist between these men, as the superior strives to develop the analytical and decision powers of his product managers.

When a product manager interprets his position broadly, he may have many intra-firm interfaces. For example, Scott Paper Company's diagram of its product manager relationships depicts up to 17 interfaces with other departments in the company and its advertising agency, not including the higher management line of responsibility.

SIGNIFICANCE OF PRODUCT MANAGEMENT INTERFACES

One may assert that product managers' interfaces are exceedingly important to effective marketing, at the same time acknowledging the value of involving other corporate personnel. The much more numerous confrontations of salesmen with buyers might be considered of primary importance; yet these are relatively routine and remote from marketing strategy and policy. High-echelon marketing executives' interfaces, both internal and external, are quite important since the more comprehensive and far-reaching decisions on goals, allocations, and programs are reached at that level. Regardless, product managers' interfaces are of high importance from each of three viewpoints.

Product manager viewpoint

Position descriptions for product managers are aptly couched in terms of "formulating" or "originating" product plans and strategies, or "centralizing" information about assigned products. A man placed in a conceptual and informational hub of the organization must personally be an intelligence headquarters. To maintain competitive position and profit of his products, with his performance starkly exposed to higher management, he must strive to be the best informed man about any aspect substantially affecting their future. He must arrange and nurture a number of information interfaces to achieve his functions.

The verb "coordinate" is often and aptly used to describe how a product manager should execute his "responsibilities." His interfaces are used to enthuse others about his plans and to obtain their concurrence and action. To a substantial degree, his success depends upon his effectiveness in motivating others to implement his plans without direct organizational authority.

The firm's viewpoint

The properly functioning product manager is the firm's main intelligence center for its product lines. Much more than a repository, he is an action center at which all strategy and plans for his product lines converge. A large company cannot rely on higher executives, functional middle managers, or committees to become sufficiently informed about the situation and opportunities facing an individual product line. Higher executives and committees should be well briefed in order to integrate various product managers' recommendations and make allocations fairly to each program; however, they cannot possess the depth of understanding and analysis of each product manager.

A general marketing viewpoint

The marketing institution viewpoint and the consumer or user viewpoint, taken broadly, should coincide in seeking what Paul Mazur considered marketing's goal to deliver a standard of living. This can be accomplished only when marketing interfaces with its buying publics as fully and intelligently as possible. The potential for effectively realizing this goal is enhanced when the information focus and the marketing strategy focus are centered within one position in the firm. This position ideally is that of a product manager who can devote all his powers and attention to his assigned product area. The man who serves as a gatekeeper in the firm at the spot where market needs and opportunities meet the firm's capabilities, objectives, and strategies, is most critical from a socially-aware marketing viewpoint.

OBSTACLES

While the number of interfaces realized by product managers may be adequate, the quality of these relationships tends to fall seriously short of the ideal. Product managers should be of gregarious nature, ready and anxious to meet others, and typically they are. Establishing a wide network of contacts is thus not overly difficult. The deficiency tends to arise from the failure of the product manager to develop the most productive associations in depth. Causes underlying this failure might include the following:

1. *Preoccupation with trivial and distracting tasks.* Many product managers find their time burdened with correspondence with salesmen and customers about minor problems and adjustments. Many allow themselves to become expediters of deliveries, and of the production and distribution of promotional literature.

2. *Lack of assistance.* This tends to prevent a product manager from allocating time to the interfaces which are most important. Most product managers have no help beyond a secretary (and some share secretaries). Some have trainees who are only temporary help before being elevated into full production managerships. More companies are providing assistant product managers, but there has not been general recognition of the need.

3. *Lack of cooperation with functional departments.* This may result in the functional department either passing along to the product manager tasks that the functional department should assume, or conversely, encroaching on the decision sphere of a product manager by making decisions that are rightly his. At the extreme, a functional department may actually balk at cooperating in carrying out product plans.

4. *Lack of well-conceived formal position descriptions.* Where they exist, such descriptions either tend to assign the product manager too broad a responsibility, or list his duties in unrealistic detail. The interfaces implied for the manager may be too many and too unsystematic to be efficient. Sometimes the number of products and brands assigned a manager are excessive. In one case, for example, the author found a product manager responsible for 17 distinct nationally advertised products.

5. *Restriction of the product manager to a single brand or type of a product* with no supplemental participation regarding new products serving the same needs. While specific brand managers are needed where a single brand sells in enormous volume, product managers should not be excluded from the dynamics of product improvement and innovation.

6. *Inadequate scheduling of available time.* A specific set of priorities should be established and periodically reviewed, particularly for the novice product manager.

7. *Inadequate training of product managers.* Because the demands of the position are more varied than those of most other middle-management jobs, training of product managers is relatively more important. Unfortunately, many product managers learn under loose supervision or by trial and error. If each product manager kept explicit records of his planning and decision analyses and of the ensuing results, others could

profit from this store of experience. This training technique, however, is often overlooked.

8. *Short job tenure.* The median in consumer products is about two years. The period is usually somewhat longer for industrial products managers. One product line, aggregating over $20,000,000 annual sales, was observed to have had three product managers in four years. In addition, new product managers appear to have little communication with their predecessors, although they are still working in the company.

9. Last, but very important, is *the excessive number of interfaces that most product managers attempt, particularly intra-company.* The product manager should be selective in the interfaces he establishes. This positions him to concentrate on decoding and analyzing the inputs he receives from these especially strategic linkages, and where necessary, to direct his communications skills toward them.

SOME RECOMMENDATIONS

There appears to be a gradual shift in the positioning, functioning, and training of product managers as firms which utilize this approach gain experience. The writer has identified four dimensions of development which may promote effective interfacing by product managers.

1. Realignment of product managers' assignments toward a market orientation. The typical assignment is in terms of a particular product or products, and the concentration is on promoting their sales. The result can be a myopic vision of the market in terms of the given product. A more balanced and progressive view is likely when this manager is assigned a specific market or product-use area, in which he works to improve market penetration through innovation while simultaneously formulating the optimal strategy and marketing mix to increase the profitability of his existing products. This should result in a systematic market/product development while also accentuating the entirety of the market interface. Further, involvement with a homogeneous market may be less confusing for the product manager than a strict product alignment which often involves dealing with the heterogeneous uses and markets that a single product may serve.

2. Provision of an improved atmosphere for the serious study by product managers of markets and alternative strategies in product, pricing, promotion, and distribution. Some companies do provide sufficient privacy and, on a smaller scale, some seek to limit the many tasks and other distractions in order to provide product management with adequate time for marketing planning.

3. Restrictions of the interfaces attempted by product managers to the few that are most productive. This avoids the superficial contacts and fragmentary communications that are much too common. It is suggested that a

consumer goods product manager restrict himself within the interfaces shown in Figure 1 and concentrate on those itemized below:

Marketing research	Sales management
Advertising agency	Advertising management
The market (dealers and buyers)	Product development

His relationship should be conducted primarily through one liaison in the four named departments and the advertising agency. This is increasingly common with the market research interface, the chief and constant aid of many product managers. It is further suggested that the time saved by reducing intra-company communication be devoted to more personal interface with markets.

FIGURE 1

Interfaces of a product manager

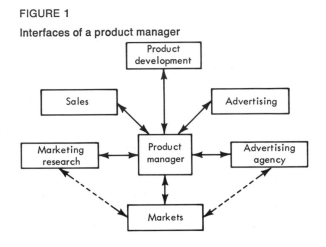

4. Development of complete and realistic job descriptions accompanied by more specific performance evaluation criteria. In addition to removing much of the vagueness that contributes to inefficient product manager work, this would relieve personal frustration and direct the manager's efforts, including those related to interfacing within and outside the firm. In providing a solid basis for extensive job training and manpower development, this procedure can make a long-range contribution to the product manager concept.

CONCLUSION

Product managers are surely here to stay, for it appears that no other organizational arrangement so well promotes efficient marketing planning in the spirit of the marketing concept. Clear recognition of the fundamental role that effective interfaces play, both within the firm and with the external publics who shape the firm's destiny, will be a long first step to realization of the profit potential of the product manager system.

The marketing executive must be aware of what the author calls "sales-linked product pricing." This refers to the demand interdependence that occurs within the firm's own product line. The complications involved in pricing competitive and complementary products are discussed.

36. PRODUCT LINE PRICING *

Alfred R. Oxenfeldt †

Product line pricing decisions confront marketing executives with a major challenge. They get very little help in meeting it from the available literature on pricing, however. Economists treat product line pricing only indirectly and then only in terms of what they call "demand interdependence." Moreover, they consider demand interdependence only as it occurs among the competing products of rival companies; they neglect it as it occurs among competing items *within* the individual company's product line — what I call "sales-linked product pricing." Managerial economists and marketing specialists, on the other hand, do discuss sales-linked product pricing, but they do so only sketchily, leaving a very wide gap between their broad *dicta* and specific decision. The purpose of this article is to narrow that gap.

In the first part I will discuss mainly the considerations that do—or should—operate in setting price differentials between items within the same product class. Next, I will look at the implications of adding items at either end, or of changing the prices of end items already in the line. Finally, I will discuss the considerations that do and should determine the pricing of complementary items in a product mix.

SALES-LINKED PRODUCTS

Three classes of sales-tied or interlinked items can be readily distinguished in concept:

1. Many buyers are prepared to substitute certain items for others; these products are called *competitive* (or substitute) because when a person buys one of them, he usually purchases less of another item.

2. In contrast, *complementary* items are those whose sale boosts the sales of other products.

---

* Reprinted from "Product Line Pricing," *Harvard Business Review*, Vol. 44, No. 4 (July–August 1966), pp. 137–44.
 † Columbia University.

3. If, however, the existence of an item has absolutely no effect on the sales of other products, we speak of it as *neutral,* and say that its demand is not interlinked with the demand for any other product.

In all probability, no product falls exclusively into one of these three classes. Quite possibly, items that are substitutes for some buyers are complementary products for others.

Marketing relationships

Let us now consider sales-linked items in the product line of an individual company and see how such relationships among products occur.

Interlinkage is likely to arise whenever a company offers more than one item. Most marketing executives with multiple product offerings are literally in active competition with themselves, and this relationship is usually quite clear. If a company takes measures designed to increase its sales of, say, beef, it may reduce its sales of lamb and ham; if a company promotes the sale of one model of refrigerator, it may be depressing the sale of some other models.

On the other hand, by adding new items or reducing certain prices, companies may actually increase the dollar sales of products already in their line because they become a preferred source of supply; this relationship, however, is usually far less clear and direct. And certain items that may have no effect on the sales of others in the line may deserve inclusion because they add more to revenue than to cost.

Interlinkage does not usually "just happen" by accident. An aggressive marketing manager will consciously seek out items just because of a desired sales-linked relationship. One would therefore expect most items in a multiproduct company's line to have some effect on the sales of some other items in its line. That is, one would expect few items in a product line to be completely neutral in regard to their effect on sales of other items in the *same* product line.

In other words, it is likely that the demands for products carried by a company are interrelated, since marketing managers often try to offer items that will increase the sales of the other products they offer. But, in an effort to give customers some variety from which to choose, they usually offer directly competitive items as well. We must conclude that planned interlinkage is the rule rather than the exception.

Demand-price connection

Marketing executives who offer sales-linked products would be unwise to ignore the possible effects of interlinkage when making their price-setting decisions. In general terms, they should establish prices that will (*a*) expand their sales of highly profitable items and (*b*) contract the sales of relatively unprofitable products within the same product line.

The reason they would be unwise to ignore interlinkage is that differences in the price of individual products in a line will ordinarily influence strongly the proportions in which they are sold. Especially among competing items in a company's line, the sensitivity to differentials in price probably is quite high.

Similarly, but far less obviously, when products in a line are complementary, the price of one item will often affect the sales of complementary products. We may thus view product line pricing as a conscious effort to exploit opportunities held out by sales-linked items and to avoid the perils such products may create.

I shall consider two aspects of sales-linked items associated with the product lines of an individual company. First, in the next section, we will look at price setting under conditions of *competitive* interlinkage. Then, in the following section, we will examine price setting where products are *complementary*.

"COMPETITIVE" PRICING

How can a marketing executive determine whether, in what way, and to what extent the existence of one item in a line affects the sales of other products offered by his company? How would a change in the price of one product in a line affect the sale of other items in the line?

Market segmentation

Marketing managers selling competitive items may gain by conceptualizing their pricing problem in terms of market segmentation. They may find that only certain types of customers are interested in any one of their product offerings and are not potential customers for their other offerings. In such cases, the different items they sell are not directly or intensely competitive. Conversely, if the customers who buy the different items that they offer are highly similar, these products probably are directly competitive —that is, the cross-elasticity of demand is likely to be quite high. (Cross-elasticity of demand is a quantitative measure of the degree of competition between two specific items. It is based on the percentage change in one item's unit *sales* resulting from a given percentage change in the *price* of the other item. The higher this proportion, the greater the intensity of price competition between the two products.)

The logic underlying these generalizations is quite simple: if customer-types are divided up among an individual company's offerings, they must be deriving different values and benefits. Or, at least, they are seeking and perceiving different things in the company's separate offerings. Accordingly, under those circumstances, each item has the characteristics of a separate product that appeals to a separate market.

Ordinarily, the sales gain as a result of including a directly competitive item in the line is likely to be minimal from the company's present customers. However, if it is a particularly attractive product, it may divert new customers away from competitive companies.

Managers will usually want to segment their markets and to develop special offerings for each target segment for several reasons. First, they should be able to serve each class of customers better. In so doing, marketing executives may gain the loyalty of such customers, and they may also be able to charge prices that yield a greater-than-average margin. In addition, they may increase their sales patronage by attracting new customers. Finally, by meeting each class of customers' wishes fully, they often can reduce their sales costs.

To take account of market segments in designing a product line and in setting a price, a seller is obliged to—

. . . identify the groups of customers that not only are sufficiently numerous to warrant separate attention but seek special benefits from the products;

. . . explore different ways of serving the various segments by designing special offerings for every type of customer;

. . . set a price for each offering—one that is consistent with cost, competitive offerings, and the price of other items in that line—and determine the benefits each product offers to the particular class of customers for which it is designed;

. . . estimate the cost and revenue effects of treating each segment separately, and particularly the effects of adding and/or combining segments;

. . . decide what number of segments the company should cultivate separately, in terms of the relevant costs, revenues, investment, and risk of each alternative considered to be feasible and potentially attractive.

Substitution research

In a specific case, what might a marketing specialist do to determine the potential loss of sales that might follow the addition of some item or a change in the price of an item already in the line?

It is all very well to say, "Conduct market research," but unless the manager knows what information to collect, and how to obtain it with considerable accuracy and at feasible cost, the advice will not help much. Moreover, a seller's need is to determine the *degree* of the danger, rather than its mere presence.

To discover the extent and nature of substitution interlinkage, a marketing executive requires data that include:

1. The number and nature of persons who would buy the added product and the company's other offerings if the new item were added to its line, as well as the quantity these customers would purchase.
2. The quantity of each specific item the company would be able to sell if the prospective item were not added.
3. The number of people who would buy the new item *soon*, instead of buying an older item in the same line at a *later* date.

4. The number of units of the new item that would be sold to persons who, if it were not added to the line, would not have bought a similar product from any other supplier.
5. The number of potential customers for the item who would otherwise patronize another vendor.

The informational requirements on substitute items are difficult to meet in most cases and usually involve heavy cost. Nevertheless, the five factors listed above indicate the kinds of issues that marketing executives must consider—and the things they must measure—if they are to detect and measure competitive interlinkage. In many cases they can only guess at their magnitude. Even so, they would be far less likely to err in guessing than if they ignored the issues altogether, or if they measured precisely those things that were irrelevant. Clearly, the data required for product line pricing decisions include more than mere estimates of the number of persons who will buy the *new* item and how *soon* they will buy it.

Special factors

Much has been written about new product pricing, skimming prices, penetration pricing, "stay-out" pricing, and the like. These approaches presumably apply whether an item is a company's only offering or an addition to a large line. I shall *not* discuss these various methods of pricing because my concern is with the special factors to be considered when an item is a substitute in a product line. What factors should determine the size of price differentials among substitute items in a line?

Establishing differentials. Economic theory is concerned with only one type of price differential—the kind that results from price discrimination and is made possible by markets that are "separate." This helps very little even in conceptualizing the task of selecting differentials among items in a product line, for separate markets do not exist in the same sense at all, as will be explained.

It is a safe generalization that buyers of any product consider the purchase of closely related items offered by the same seller. If they buy his line of micrometers, his refrigerators, his neckties, or his cigars, they will examine several—and the most closely related—items in his line. Buyers will ordinarily compare several items; in fact, the seller will often couch his sales messages in terms that suggest a comparison of his different offerings from the standpoint of what is best for his customers. In this way, the seller will try to establish price relationships that "make sense" to his customers and contribute to his own self-interest.

Buyers have no legal right to require logical explanations for price differences; moreover, they recognize that sellers are motivated by pecuniary gain. Nevertheless, a vendor whose prices show no logic beyond naked self-interest is likely to taint his relations with customers. Buyers and sellers ordinarily develop relationships that are more than strictly legal and commercial; they contain a sizable personal ingredient. Affection, trust, consideration, and respect all seem to matter in the conduct and distribution of business. The vendor wants the customer to give him special privileges at times—as in permitting him to meet the lower price offers that the customer receives from other suppliers. For this reason, price relationships should possess a modicum of reason and apparent equity.

What contributes toward the impression of equitable and reasonable prices? For the overwhelming majority of buyers, it is some rough relationship between price and cost differences. They apparently believe that price should vary with cost—so long as other circumstances related to the product are the same. On the other hand, if the new item offers unique features, most buyers apparently accept the fact that the seller must "cover his investment" in the new features and be compensated for his risks of failure. They generally agree that the seller is entitled to something extra while the item is new and before his competitors copy it. These general guides usually give the vendor leeway so that demand considerations can be allowed to affect his price decision, but they militate against his simply maximizing profit in the short run.

Beyond establishing differentials that make sense to the buyer, a seller must ordinarily price a new item in his line at a level which permits him to sell at least some minimum quantity to make the venture worthwhile. He must balance the gains in higher profit margin—from higher price but also possibly with high costs—against gains from higher sales. Customers will purchase relatively large amounts of the old product if the price of the new one is set high. Therefore, higher profit margins usually restrict unit sales for a new item, and usually minimize the unfavorable effect of the new item on sales of other products in the line. While the arithmetic of this relationship is fairly straightforward, the best price that takes it into full effect usually is difficult to discover in any specific case.

Moreover, in establishing differentials, a company adding a product to its line must consider the offerings of competing companies as well as the items in its own line. Here again, sellers must balance conflicting factors: the higher the price, the greater the probability of losing business to competitors; the lower the margin, the greater the amount of business that can be taken away from rivals.

In specific cases, however, these generalizations require strong qualification. For example, a seller may not be able to communicate to customers the detailed information required in order to appraise the many individual items in his line; in such cases, sales and price differentials of individual products will not be greatly affected by the prices charged by rivals. (These and previous remarks on the subject refer to close substitutes—different sizes, styles, and versions. The same generalizations may also apply to different but related product classes—such as radio, stereo, and TV.)

Pricing of end items.   It is helpful to distinguish between "end" and "in-between" items in a product line. Up to this point, I have discussed mainly the considerations that do or should operate in setting differentials between items *within* the same product class—such as different refrigerators or lamps or shoes, and so forth—in a company's line of products. I have not yet discussed the implications of adding items at either end— or of changing the prices of end items already in the line.

The lowest-priced item in a product line ordinarily affects the total sales of the *line* far more than does the price of any other product in the line, even though the actual sales of the lowest-priced *item* may be but a tiny proportion of the total. It appears that the lowest price for an item in a line usually is the most frequently remembered and "perceived" price, and many customers will compare it with the lowest price charged by rivals.

Customers could hardly be expected to use and remember all prices in a line in making such comparisons, so they probably select the most visible items. The lowest-priced item ordinarily influences *marginal* buyers to consider a purchase. (Marginal buyers are persons who are doubtful about the wisdom of making a purchase; they are hovering on the brink of buying the item.) Low price helps to overcome such doubts more than any other factor for the average marginal buyer of most products. Consequently, the lowest-priced item in a line is a "traffic builder." More than any other product in a line, it attracts customers to the place of purchase or induces prospects to make inquiries of sellers.

For these two reasons, and possibly there are others, reductions in the price of the lowest-priced item in a company's line are likely to have a highly stimulating effect on sales. Similarly, increases in that price are likely to reduce sales far more than would increases in the price of in-between items.

The highest-priced item in a line is also relatively visible, but usually far less so than the lowest-priced product. Interestingly enough, increases in the price of the most expensive item in the line sometimes have a stimulating effect on sales. Just as it seems to be a distinct advantage to offer the lowest-priced item in the market—even though it may possess few attractive features, or may be small in size and actually high in cost on a per-ounce basis—so too it appears to be an advantage to make the highest-priced item available. An indeterminate proportion of potential customers apparently assume that the most expensive is also the highest in quality (if clear evidence to the contrary is lacking). And some customers want "the very best."

These generalizations cannot carry one very far, unfortunately. A seller must select a *specific* price for his top end item. His decision must take into account the fact that his competitors, as well as his customers, are highly sensitive to changes in the price of end items. Any action that he takes which is highly effective in his favor will probably evoke retaliatory action of some kind. Consequently, his gains from certain price actions may prove to be small and fleeting, and may ultimately create an unfavorable pricing situation for all sellers.

Pricing in-between items. Sellers are wise to consider the following dimensions when pricing their in-between products: (*a*) the gap or differential between adjacent items, (*b*) the possible presence of "blank spaces" in their lines, and (*c*) the existence of "step-up" features that justify established price differentials. These are highly complex subjects, and only a few propositions will be advanced here:

Offerings that are extremely close in price do not present clear and distinct alternatives to customers, and therefore seem to confuse and alienate many potential customers. If the pain of choice is great, customers may not make any purchase. Accordingly, some minimum difference in price among offerings is usually indicated. If the differences between alternative items are too small to justify a minimum price difference, ordinarily it is preferable to make the items equal in price. As with other marketing generalizations, however, exceptions can be found to this one.

The price gaps between offerings tend to grow as the items offer more features, and as they approach the high end of the line. For example, whereas a difference of $15 or $20 may separate low-end appliances, sums twice as large may separate the high-end items.

Sales tend to concentrate at several points in a product line—for reasons that are rarely clear. A company must ensure that it has offerings at these "price points," and know what these points are. Price points, which are not necessarily the same as "psychological prices," seem to change with some frequency—possibly over a few years in the case of appliance and clothing items.

Most sellers must guard against large price gaps in their line lest they lose a disproportionate amount of business to competitive companies. Large price gaps also tend sometimes to create an impression of a limited line of offerings.

COMPLEMENTARY PRICING

Let us now turn to the second type of sales-linked product that is found in most product lines. In this section we will examine price setting where the items are complementary.

Demand-link sources

A sales-linked product relationship between complementary items in a company's product line can stem from many sources. A seller would be wise to distinguish them carefully, since they may require quite different forms of price treatment. The eight most important sources of complementary demand will be listed briefly, without discussion of their implications for a company's pricing decisions.

1. *"One-stop shopping."* Most customers—both household consumers and business enterprises—purchase a number of related products; the buyers can save time and even money by purchasing many items from a single source. This phenomenon is well known. Accordingly, the greater the number of items in a line regularly purchased by the same individual or organization, the greater the probability that the same individual or

organization will be attracted to that seller by increases in his offerings of the things they need, and the larger the number of items they will buy from him.

2. *"Impulse buying."* Whenever people are exposed to products for sale, the possibility of a purchase exists. However, the probability that a purchase will take place varies with the "match" between the item, the kinds of customers to whom it is exposed, and the conditions of exposure—that is, how, when, and where it is offered to the customer. A vendor knows the kinds of patrons he is serving and can estimate their reactions to the other kinds of merchandise he might offer them when they are inspecting his offerings or being called on by his salesmen. The items in a line explained by one-stop shopping and impulse buying are similar in that they need have no relationship at all to other products *in use*.

3. *Broader assortment.* The addition of items to a line will increase the breadth of choice that a seller offers his customers. This action offers customer benefits in itself; in addition, it adds prestige to the manufacturer's reputation. The availability of a broader assortment also reduces the number of unproductive shopping trips made by customers. Companies that offer wide assortments thus develop a favorable, and often unconscious, association in the minds of potential customers; the buyers will tend to patronize those companies regularly.

4. *Related use.* Complementary demand results usually when a company adds to its line an item that is used directly in conjunction with its current products. The classical example of this is the purchase of tennis balls when one is buying a new tennis racket or having an old racket restrung. Such situations are characterized by the high probability that some customers will desire to purchase more than one item at a time. Since the items will be used at the same time, customers will be particularly aware of their needs for the related products and therefore relatively inclined to buy them.

5. *Enhanced value.* This category results from offering items that either enhance the value of related items in the product line or reduce the cost—in terms of money or inconvenience—of related items. For example, added telephone extensions in a home reduce the effort required to place calls. Consequently, sales of extensions do tend to increase the sale of calls—both local and long distance. What is special about related items is that they often have no direct use in themselves, but are designed to increase the customer's satisfaction with the vendor's main product or service—and presumably will increase their purchases of it. This type of interlinkage is growing. Often these kinds of product additions come to be incorporated within the original item itself or are sold together with the original. Examples of such products are special cases for carrying or storing items, remote-control devices for TV sets, defrosters for refrigerators, thermostatic controls and timing devices for air conditioners, and the like.

6. *"Prestige builders."* The presence of an item which enhances the reputation of the manufacturer and his total line of offerings gives rise to this

source of complementary demand. It may consist of an elaborate, expensive, and prestigious version of the product, which conveys the impression that the manufacturer makes items of the highest quality, or it may contain real or claimed technological advances that make the company appear to be in the forefront of the industry's technology. Manufacturers whose offerings are questioned by customers on such grounds have strong reasons to add items for the sake of "building prestige."

7. *"Image effects."* The addition of items that are "traffic builders," "attention getters," or "image builders" is another source of complementarity. Although very little of these items may be bought, they may nevertheless attract the attention of many customers. Items of advanced design or technology are useful for this purpose, even if they are not the kind of thing that most people want to own. For example, some high-style women's clothing manufacturers will consciously design a fashion item or two that is "way out" in styling in the hope that it will appear on the cover of some magazine which features style developments. The interest generated in the brand and "image effects" of such exposure will facilitate the sale of the company's more conservative offerings.

8. *Quality supplements.* The final important source of complementary demand arises when one item in the line is designed for the repair, maintenance, care, or beautification of another item. For example, manufacturers offer "special" lubricants for delicate engines; others sell special devices to sharpen or adjust their cutting tools. In such cases, buyers seem anxious to obtain supplementary items of high quality in order to maintain their expensive pieces of equipment. (Some evidence suggests strongly that they will avoid low-priced items on this score, even when such items are high in quality. André Gabor and Clive Granger have cited two interesting examples of this. One was an auto wax which sold much better at $1.69 than at $0.69; the other, a fountain pen ink which sold better at $0.25 than at $0.15.[1])

Sales-tied items

Complementary demand takes many forms, as we have seen. The fundamental character of these situations from the price setter's standpoint is made clear by analysis of an extreme form of complementary demand. In certain cases the purchase of one product virtually requires customers to obtain other items from the same supplier because only his supplies fit the original equipment. Under these circumstances the seller can afford to offer strong price incentives to have the buyer obtain the original item. He may subsidize its sale while demanding high margins on the supplemental items used in conjunction with it. This is in contrast to a situation

---

[1] See "The Pricing of New Products," *Scientific Business,* August 1965, p. 141.

where the original item (say, razors) could be used with a number of other manufacturers' supply items (razor blades), and where the vendor would have little incentive to sacrifice profits to spur sales of his original item.

The concept of treating the entire line as a unit, and subsidizing the sale of some items to increase sales of the others, is the key to pricing complementary products; but it does not fit every door, and at best it can open doors to the right price only a small part of the way.

Where complementarity takes the form of adding items of possible interest to the customer in order to help him economize his time and effort in the purchase process, the seller usually is wise to take his gains primarily in the form of increased volume, rather than in higher profit margins. Of course, the seller must be sure that the items he includes in his line have a mix of margins that is profitable for the entire operation.

If complementary demand takes the form of offering products which, when used in combination, yield greater satisfaction to the customer (e.g., telephone extensions and their usage), then the vendor has the opportunity of obtaining a higher price. For example, if the vendor is the only provider of the service, or can provide some item of equipment which facilities the use of the service (such as the delivery of recorded messages to callers during the absence of the persons called), then he has two options: (1) he can raise the price of the service, since it renders more satisfaction; or (2) he can charge large profit margins for the piece of equipment, since it makes the service more valuable than before.

Complementarity in the form of an improved image for the total line, at least theoretically, permits a seller to charge higher prices on all items in the line. That is, if the addition of one or more items to a company's offerings leads prospective buyers to value all products in that line more than before, presumably the vendor could charge more for everything he sells. But even greater gains might be realized by keeping prices at the same level and enjoying greater sales volume. The choice of policy, however, must depend on the particular circumstances. In some cases a higher price would be required in order to sustain the image of superior quality.

CONCLUSION

We really know very little about product line pricing, even though almost all companies offer a line of products and the fact that they do is relevant to most pricing decisions. Economic theory and managerial economics do no more than distinguish among three broad classes of total product demand: substitutes, complementary items, and neutral products. In most specific cases it appears that any product may be a substitute for some customers and a complementary item for others. It is dangerous to rely solely on common sense to estimate the net effect of these offsetting relationships in specific cases. It is even more dangerous to place individual

items in a single class on the basis of introspection or general impression.
Research can help to indicate the number and kinds of customers who treat
an item as a substitute.

When one deals with sales-linked products among the individual offerings of an individual company—the usual situation created by product
lines—many problems arise that are not treated at all in economic theory.
The managerial economist himself has left this domain largely in a descriptive state and advises price setters to treat a product line as a single unit,
emphasizing that the pricer's objective is maximum profit on the total *line*
rather than on any individual *item* in the line.

EXHIBIT 1

Level of interlinkage

	Among products	Among companies	Among product lines	Among items in a product line
Mainly substitute				A
Mainly complementary				B
Fairly even blend of substitute and complementary				
Neutral				

A simple matrix (see Exhibit 1) may help to sort out the different kinds
of relationships that are—or could be—covered under the heading of
sales-linked products. This matrix distinguishes four *levels* of interlinkage:
(1) among products; (2) among companies; (3) among different product
lines offered by the same company; and (4) among different products
within a single line carried by an individual company.

Four *types* of relationships can also be distinguished: competitive or
substitute; complementary; a blend of substitute and complementary (this
must be included for the sake of realism and comprehensiveness); and
complete neutrality. Not all of the cells in this matrix are of interest to
price setters, but marketing managers would be wise to consider the relevance and possible importance of each one.

This article has dealt largely with the cells marked A and B. However,
a price setter must also take into account the interlinkage with his other
product lines, and with other items sold by competing companies.

Many generalizations were offered here for the guidance of marketing
executives who must take sales-linked items in a line into account in their
pricing decisions. While no important purpose would be served by sum-
marizing them, some reflections on the character of those generalizations
should help to illuminate the nature of marketing as a field of study.

Marketing draws heavily on economic theory, particularly on managerial economics. However, these other fields carry a price setter only a
small part of the way toward a specific decision in concrete cases. The gap

between theory and specific decision often is much wider than necessary; and marketing specialists aim to narrow this gap.

As for marketing analysis, it does advance many rough empirical generalizations. These are not offered as universal, applicable, or eternal. They can't be. Moreover, the basis for these generalizations is rarely made explicit, and if they are based on specific evidence, that evidence is rarely indicated. One must admit that casualness is commonplace in stating generalizations that allegedly have—or that could have—a sound empirical base. The reader seldom is given the information that he needs to assess the validity of these generalizations. Usually the author himself does not know how generally it does apply.

Much of what appears in the marketing literature (and admittedly it contains much that is extremely helpful) is either a consensus of informed business opinion, or represents some speculation which business practitioners would be wise to regard as only a hypothesis to be tested for its applicability to their specific needs. *The foregoing remarks apply fully to the factual statements and distinctions contained in this article.*

Finally, the marketing literature does—and can do—even more. It identifies, catalogs, and evaluates alternative strategies and policies. Although such writings cannot be applied to derive correct solutions to specific business problems, they can nevertheless be highly illuminating to marketing managers. After all, the practitioner has little opportunity and, in many cases, little appetite for reflection, hypothesis formulation, and model building. The fact remains that he should find such explorations helpful, even if they provide no cook-book recipes guaranteed to make a chef out of every would-be cook.

b.

The distribution mix

THE DISTRIBUTION process includes all those activities that are related to the product from the time the product is considered complete until it reaches the ultimate consumer. Without proper and careful consideration of this key variable, the best laid plans for a product or service cannot be fully realized. The selection of the most appropriate methods and channels of distribution can be the competitive edge that enables a firm to place the product or service within easy reach of the customer at the right time and place and in the condition demanded by the customer.

A wide variety of activities are included in the distribution process. Their coordination and integration into a unified system and with the overall decision-making process of the firm is required to attain optimal planning effectiveness.

The following articles discuss some of the major segments of the distribution mix. The first article, by Matthews, describes how the channel of distribution is affected by product growth and changes in the marketing environment. The basic systems approach to the planning of the distribution mix is discussed by Lazer. The next article, by Davidson, points out some of the possible problems and changes that have occurred or will be occurring in the distribution area. Finally, emphasis is given to retail aspects of distribution channels in an article on the retailing mix by Lazer and Kelley.

Even with the increased emphasis on market planning, marketing managers have given little attention to evaluating and planning for changes in the channel of distribution. In this excerpt from a research study, the author considers how the structure of the industrial marketing channel relates to the stages of product growth and to changes occurring in the marketplace.

37. CHALLENGE FOR INDUSTRIAL MARKETERS: CHANGING CHANNELS OF DISTRIBUTION *

William E. Matthews †

A manufacturer of industrial goods is not operating in a static system, but in a changing environment. From time to time, top management receives signals that "all is not well" with its channels of distribution and that it ought to evaluate possible changes. The role of any marketing or product manager, who is concerned with the distribution of one or more products or product lines, should be able (*a*) to recognize the pressures for channel changes as quickly as possible, (*b*) to implement policies that lead to an effective evaluation of alternative responses to such pressures, and (*c*) to take appropriate action by following through with the necessary channel change.

TYPES OF CHANNEL CHANGE

Given that a channel of distribution consists of a number of channel members performing certain functions in the movement of the product from the manufacturer to the customer, a manufacturer can then implement four types of channel change—namely, in the *nature* of the channel, *composition* of the channel, *role* of the channel, and in the *relationship* between the channel and the manufacturer.

1. Nature of the channel

Theoretically, a manufacturing company selecting the channel of distribution through which to market its products has a number of alterna-

* Reprinted from Marketing Science Institute Working Paper (August 1972).

† William E. Matthews, research associate, International Institute of Management, West Berlin.

tives. For example, it can utilize an "internal" channel (its own sales force), or one of a wide variety of "external" channels (distributors, representatives, agents, brokers). In reality, however, not all channel alternatives are available to the manufacturer at the time the channel decision has to be made. Thus, the manufacturer chooses among *available* channels. This decision may later prove to be nonoptimal and lead to growing pressure for a change in the channel of distribution.

More important, the industrial goods' manufacturer operates in a changing environment. Not only does the nature of the manufacturing operation itself change through the addition or deletion of products, but actions by competitors affect the manufacturer's position in the marketplace. These and other changes in the marketing environment create pressures for change in the channel of distribution so that the manufacturer can remain competitive.

At the extreme, the manufacturer may completely discontinue the use of one channel of distribution and replace it by another distinctly separate channel. For example, a manufacturer with a nationwide network of distributors might decide to sell only through the company's own sales force. In most situations, however, the manufacturer can neither justify the complete discontinuance of a channel, nor is such a channel change appropriate. In this case, a manufacturer selling through distributors may develop so many large customers in one geographic area that they could justifiably be handled on a direct basis. In other areas, however, the number of large customers might be insufficient to justify direct sales. Under these circumstances, the manufacturer might replace only a part of the channel of distribution for the product. Such a change can be classified as a *channel shift*.

A second distinct type of channel shift involves the establishment of a new channel of distribution to handle an existing product. Let us say that a manufacturer decides to sell a product in a new market segment not previously covered by the existing channel of distribution. The existing channel continues to handle the product so there is no shift in terms of the channel itself. However, a shift does occur in terms of the product since it is now handled by a second channel.

2. Composition of the channel

While a channel shift affects distribution as a whole, a more common and numerous form of change affects individual members of the channel, as in the case where members are replaced without reference to other channel members. This type of channel change can be characterized as a *channel alteration*.

A manufacturer using an internal channel normally expects a turnover in personnel as a result of either promotion, transfer, or dismissal. On the one hand, a manufacturer utilizing an external channel may force a turnover in individual members either due to dissatisfaction with the marketing performance (insufficient sales effort, ineffective technical assistance to customers, and so on), or because management has an opportunity to upgrade its representation by adding a competitive channel member. On the other hand, a channel alteration may also be forced on the manufacturer should the channel member become dissatisfied with its relationship with the manufacturer and choose to carry the products of another manufacturer.

3. Role of the channel

In the channel of distribution, each member performs specific marketing tasks for the manufacturer. The role of the channel can be changed, however, in two major respects by the nature of the market served, and by the services provided.

Market served. The channel of distribution represents the manufacturer's sales effort within a geographic area and, over a period of time, develops a specific set of customers. In the event that a new market segment develops within that geographic area, the manufacturer has the options of (*a*) utilizing a separate channel of distribution for the new market segment, (*b*) making a channel alteration, or (*c*) modifying the role of the existing channel member.

In view of the fact that I have already discussed the first two alternatives, let us look at the manufacturer's third option: a *channel role modification*. This is more easily implemented when an internal channel is being used since an external member may be unable or unwilling to make such a change. An example of this type of channel role modification might be sales by a manufacturer through distributors to maintenance and repair customers but not to original equipment manufacturers. If the company wishes to expand into the latter market, it is faced with either a modification in terms of its existing members, a channel alteration, or a channel shift.

Similarly, the manufacturer can limit the number of customers to which the channel members sell, thus effectively changing the role of the channel member. Though it is illegal to reserve customers,[1] it is legal to follow pricing policies which de facto limit the customers to which the external channel sells.

For example, a volume discount for an extremely large volume purchase may be attractive only to large user-customers. If the volume is above the level which a channel member could justifiably purchase and warehouse, the channel member's role may be limited to smaller customers. This limita-

---

[1] In the past, a company could legally reserve certain customers for the internal channel, and external members were not allowed to sell to these reserved customers. In 1965, the Supreme Court, in *United States* v. *Arnold Schwinn Co.*, interpreted such practices as illegal under Section 1 of the Sherman Act.

tion of customers can be also obtained by formal contracts between the manufacturer and user-customer. Such a contract may be for the user-customer's total requirements of a product or product line, or for a guaranteed purchase volume.

Services provided. While the channel performs a specific set of functions, there is always the possibility that the manufacturer will respond to the changing market environment by a channel role modification. Such a modification can represent either the addition of new functions to the channel's role or the removal of existing functions. Thus, a manufacturer may decide that a product requires extensive technical assistance, and may provide a technical sales force to support the channel members. As the product matures, technical assistance may become less important and the manufacturer may delegate this function to the independent channel members.

4. Relationship between the manufacturer and the channel

While the manufacturer and the channel are both concerned with profitability, each is concerned with its own profitability, not that of the overall system. Therefore, the goals and strategies of the two parties do not necessarily coincide. The manufacturing company can alter its relationship with the channel either by modifying its rewards to the channel or by exerting pressure on the channel.

The modification of the rewards to the channel normally involves a change in the commission or discount allowed the external member, or in the salary and/or commission paid to the internal channel member. The value of the commission or discount can be varied depending upon the manufacturer's objectives. For example, the manufacturer may introduce a reward system designed to encourage the channel to handle a specific product, to encourage pioneering effort of a highly technical nature, and so forth. Variations in the rewards are of major concern to the channel and are often a source of conflict between the channel member and the manufacturer. Intense dissatisfaction on the part of the member may force a channel alteration.

In addition to changes in the financial rewards, a manufacturer can affect the relationship with channel members in ways which have indirect financial implications. Thus, the manufacturer may assist the channel member in financing its inventory, in developing and financing an advertising program, and so on.

At the other end of the spectrum is the pressure that the manufacturer can exert on the channel. However, such pressure is relatively limited in scope. While, in the case of the internal channel, the manufacturer can tie remuneration to performance by the establishment of goals and quotas, similar pressure is considerably more difficult to apply to the independent external channel.

PRESSURES LEADING TO CHANNEL CHANGES

Possibly the best way to consider any pressure for channel change is to view it as a metamorphosis model. William H. Starbuck describes metamorphosis models as those which "take the view that growth is not a smooth, continuous process, but is marked by abrupt and discrete changes in the conditions for organizational persistence and in the structures appropriate to these conditions."[2] Among the most useful of the numerous metamorphosis models are the two of D. G. Moore[3] and Alan C. Filley and R. T. House,[4] both of which envisage three stages of growth.

These two models form the basis for the model that I propose. However, unlike Moore's model, which implies that an organization passes through stages from disorganized creativity to organized professionalism, my model suggests that there are a series of channel changes (associated with a specific stage in the organization's growth) which are appropriate to a well run company.

My proposed model can be characterized in terms of the four phases—establishment, takeoff, growth, and maturity.

Phase 1: Establishment

The newly formed company normally has a single product or product line and, characteristically, severely limited financial and personal resources. The company's concern is often focused on the manufacturing processes and, more generally, on the solution of day-to-day operating problems. The major task facing the company is that of communicating with its potential customers. This process of communication, education, and persuasion can be a lengthy one often complicated not only by the number of persons involved in the purchasing decision but also by the need to test new products under operating conditions.

The first channel of distribution decision faced by the company, therefore, is whether (a) to attempt this communication process internally by utilizing management's own time and efforts, or (b) to rely on an external sales organization. The critical factors in this decision appear to be the company's financial status, its personnel resources, the number of potential customers, the nature of the selling task, the skills of different types of channel members, and the availability of suitable members.

If the *financial status* is relatively weak, then it is likely that the company will be unable to afford a direct sales effort and will have to rely on an ex-

---

[2] James G. Marsh, ed., "Organizational Growth and Development," *Handbook of Organizations* (Chicago: Rand McNally, 1968), chap. II.

[3] W. L. Warner and N. H. Martini, eds., "Managerial Strategies," *Industrial Man* (New York: Harper, 1959), pp. 220–22.

[4] *"Managerial Process and Organizational Behavior"* (Glenview, Ill.: Scott, Foresman and Company, 1969), pp. 443–51.

ternal sales effort. Similarly, a company with limited *personnel resources* is likely to rely initially on an external channel. The number of *potential customers* affects the channel decision since the larger the number of potential customers—the wider their geographic distribution—the more expensive a direct sales effort becomes. Management, however, may be able to identify a number of companies with high sales potential, and may wish to concentrate its own sales effort on those prospects while utilizing an external channel for the remainder of the effort.

The *nature of the selling task* also has a major impact on the channel decision. If it is highly technical, requiring extensive interaction between the seller and the customer, then the manufacturer may choose to perform the task on a direct basis; a less technical selling task, however, may be adequately handled by the external channel. If the task is expected to be a lengthy one, it is likely that management will rely on the external channel to reduce costs, especially if it is largely that of maintaining continuing contact until the sale is consumated.

Finally, the *skills of different types of channel members* in the newly formed organization's industry and the *availability of suitable members* are critical. The manufacturer does not choose a specific channel because it has the correct name but because it provides certain critical skills at an acceptable cost. However, as mentioned earlier, not all channels of distribution are open to the manufacturer at the time the decision is made, and thus the company is forced to select its channel members from among those that are available.

As a broad generalization, newly formed companies tend to rely initially on an external marketing organization, often utilizing manufacturer's representatives which provide sales effort plus some technical expertise. There is, however, no automatic selection rule. It depends very much on the various influencing factors mentioned above. Thus, an electronics component manufacturer with a highly sophisticated product might first utilize distributors who possess engineering and sales staffs with the specialized training, knowledge, and contacts to do the necessary "door opening" work and to gain acceptance of the product.

However, unless the product requires a highly sophisticated sales force, the initial decision is normally to utilize manufacturer's representatives. The manufacturing company usually supports its sales representatives with technical assistance provided by its own skilled personnel. The company's advantage in utilizing representatives is that they have at least some technical skill and they are motivated by the commissions on actual sales. The sales coverage may, however, be fairly limited, and the length and extent of the sales effort may be less than the manufacturer might desire.

Therefore, the first pressure for channel change may result from the performance of one or more of the representatives. If a representative does not perform up to the manufacturer's standard, then there is an inevitable pressure for a channel alteration—that is, the replacement of the representative by another in the same geographic area.

Phase 2: Takeoff

Whereas the problem facing the manufacturer in Phase 1 is deciding which channel alternative to select given a number of important constraints, Phase 2 sees the development of pressures for channel change. These pressures stem from the very success of the manufacturer in the education of potential customers, the acceptance of the product, and the growth of sales.

Let us return to the previous example of the manufacturer selling through representatives. Once the representative's primary function of sales generation has been achieved, the focus shifts to satisfying the need of the customer which the manufacturer's representative cannot normally satisfy. Namely, it is rapid service through the existence of a local stock. In addition, in many cases, the manufacturer's representative is not interested in providing long-term technical assistance with less certain rewards than the generation of new sales.

The pressure developing in this situation is for the replacement of the existing channel by a local channel better able to satisfy the customer's need. This pressure is further supported by the fact that as potential customers become more aware of the product they begin to contact both the manufacturer *and* the local distributor with whom they normally do business. The local distributor then becomes interested in carrying the product since there is now a demand for it.

The replacement of manufacturers' representatives by distributors presupposes the existence of suitable distributors. If the product is new and has demonstrable advantages, the manufacturer may have little difficulty in obtaining new distributors. In many instances, however, the manufacturer will find that the leading local distributors already represent other industrial companies and are thus unwilling to carry the potentially competitive line. As a result, the manufacturer will be forced to utilize smaller and possibly less effective distributors. Sometimes the manufacturer may find that adequate distributors are obtainable in certain geographic areas and not in others. In the case of the latter, the company is forced to continue to sell through manufacturers' representatives.

The replacement of manufacturers' representatives by distributors also presupposes that the manufacturer's personnel are capable of administering a distributor network. The absence of such in-house capability may force the manufacturer to continue to use representatives to assist in administrating and controlling the distributor network.

Obviously, the control of the distributor network by manufacturers' representatives contains the seeds of a further channel change. First, there is the danger of discord between the two organizations. The manufacturer's representatives and distributors may have conflicting motivations and objectives. Second, pressure may result from the economics of the two-step control of the channel. External pricing systems (by manufacturers who sell either through their own sales organization or directly through distributors) may force the company to change its channel of distribution in order to be competitive.

Phase 2, therefore, is primarily concerned with channel shift. The pressures for channel alteration are relatively limited during this phase since the manufacturer may still have only a minor position in the industry and thus may not be in a position to attract new members to replace the existing channel. Channel role modification and relationship modifications are possible during this phase, but they are not likely to be implemented.

Since the company's position vis-à-vis the channel members is still extremely weak, it is in no position to implement changes either in the role of the channel member or in the interrelationship. In fact, it is conceivable that the channel members will be in a sufficiently strong position to force changes on the manufacturer.

In Phase 2, the manufacturer tends to be primarily concerned with the general functioning of the channel rather than with specific problems associated with the performance of the members.

Phase 3: Growth

The growth phase sees a broadening of the pressures for channel change. Not only does further growth result in additional pressures for change, but there are also pressures generated by changes in the product itself and by changes in the nature of the user-customer.

Expanded product sales. As a result of the distributor's sales effort, certain large user-customers begin to emerge and a small number of them begin to account for a high percentage of the manufacturer's sales. As a result, the manufacturer begins to focus increasing attention on these customers and to spend more time in direct contact with them.

Pressure develops, therefore, to bypass the distributor in favor of direct sales to these customers. The subsequent channel shift reflects not so much the company's dissatisfaction with the former channel's performance but, rather, a change in the economic balance of the relationship between the manufacturer and the customer. The volume of business generated now makes direct sales more economical and enables the company to offer the new channel volume discounts which would not have been a feasible arrangement with the old channel.

Product maturation. If a product at the time of its introduction involves (a) new technology or new applications, (b) extensive education of the user-customer, or (c) a long testing period (and hence a long-term relationship between the manufacturer and the user-customer), then the manufacturer may utilize a specific channel of distribution. Once the educational task is complete, however, that channel may no longer be attractive or desirable. Other channels may now be in a better position to provide the manufacturer's needed services. Thus, as the product matures from its initial introductory state to that of a commodity (when a number of competitors offer a product basically indistinguishable from that of the original manufacturer), there is increasing pressure for either a channel shift or a channel relationship modification.

A channel shift is relatively unlikely to occur unless the product is the only one sold through the specific channel. More likely, the product will be one unit in a product line sold through the channel. Under these circumstances, the manufacturer might choose to modify the channel's relationship through, say, a reduction in the channel's margins, thus attempting to put the emphasis on other products. If the manufacturer originally sold the product through a primary channel with back-up support from a secondary channel, then as the product matures the manufacturer might implement a channel change involving the reduction of the role of the secondary channel (a) by limiting the back-up sales effort to major customers, or (b) by eliminating company-owned inventory points and requiring that adequate inventory be carried by the primary channel.

Product line expansion. The introduction of a new product may have little direct impact on the existing channel if it is either the addition of a product only slightly different from existing products, or a new product so dissimilar that it requires a separate channel of distribution. An example of the latter would be the addition of a high-priced product to an otherwise low-priced line selling to a different market. (From a managerial viewpoint, modification of the existing channel is conceptually simpler than the establishment of a new channel. For this reason, the manufacturer will tend to incorporate the new product into the existing channel. This in itself contains the seeds of pressure for channel change. The situation is basically unstable if the channel selected does not satisfy the needs and requirements of the product for which it was established.)

In certain circumstances, however, the broadening of the product line may have a major impact on the channel of distribution. For example, a company may have been restricted to a specific channel because of its limited line. The addition of new products may give the manufacturer a full line, and thus enable him to shift to a new channel. Similarly, as a result of broadening the product line, total sales of *all* products in a specific area may become sufficiently large to justify a direct sales effort. Thus, there may be pressure for a channel shift to take advantage of the changed economics associated with sales to that geographic area.

The addition of a new product to an existing product line may also result in pressure for a channel relationship modification. For example, a manufacturer may introduce a new product which provides a certain level of profitability and has a certain long-range sales potential. The channel, however, may neither perceive the potential for this product nor be impressed by the anticipated rewards, and thus may make little effort to sell the new product. The manufacturer may therefore be forced to alter the margins on existing products to generate the desired sales effort.

Customer changes.   Even when the product remains unchanged, both the nature of the customer and his purchasing behavior can and do change. A channel of distribution, established to satisfy the requirements of one set of customers, may be unable to satisfy a second set. If either the customer's nature or his requirements change, then there is likely to be pressure for a channel change.

Consider first the *nature of the customer.* Over a period of time, the number of customers may change through an increase or decrease in the *total* number. If the expansion in the number of customers occurs in the same industry, then the manufacturer is faced with the need to expand the coverage of the existing channel or to implement a channel shift to cover certain segments of the market. For example, a company marketing through an internal channel to a small number of customers might be faced with the emergence of a large number of extremely small customers. Under these circumstances, expansion of the internal channel might be uneconomical, and thus a channel shift would be necessary to serve this growing segment of the market.

The nature of the customer can change in ways other than an increase or decrease in number. For example, the growth or decline of *one* segment of the market can result in pressure for either a channel shift or alteration. As we have seen, the initial channel decision is implemented because the chosen channel is best suited to meet the objectives of the manufacturer and the needs of a specific set of customers. Yet the market for the product may shift to one not served by the original channel. The exact nature of the change would depend upon the magnitude of the differences between the customer characteristics in each industry.

In some cases, a channel alteration in which individual members in the channel are replaced by new units with a different orientation might be sufficient. In many instances, however, it may be extremely difficult to find channel members capable of serving effectively both the old *and* new segments of the marketplace. Under these circumstances, management must decide among three alternative courses of action:

1. To ignore the emerging market segment completely.
2. To focus on the older market segment, and market to the new segment only where convenient.
3. To implement a channel shift designed to enable the company to add an additional channel to handle the emerging new markets.

Another way in which the nature of the customer can change is on a geographic basis. This normally represents a broadening of the area in which potential customers are located. For example, in the early stages of an industry's development, potential customers cluster in those geographic areas with optimal economics. As the industry develops, however, technological innovations and improvements in transportation, power supply, and so on enable industry members to expand into new areas. The channel of distribution, established to satisfy the initial geographic distribution of the customer, is unlikely to be able to satisfy the expanded market, and thus there will be a growing pressure either for an expansion of the existing channel or the addition of a second channel.

The second major change is in terms of the customer's *purchasing behavior*. In recent years, many larger companies have turned their attention to the economies associated with optimal purchasing such as annual buy contracts. These changes in purchasing behavior have resulted in growing pressures for channel change. For example, an external channel which has regularly serviced a specific account may find itself unable to compete should the customer, who previously purchased on a plant basis, decide to purchase his nationwide requirements on a bid basis. Under these circumstances, the channel may no longer be able to compete effectively since regular pricing schedules may offer inadequate margins to obtain the business.

Management is then faced with three alternative courses of action:

1. To maintain the existing channel structure and face the loss of this particular type of business.
2. To implement a channel shift by establishing a new channel capable of competing for the business.
3. To implement a channel relationship modification to enable the existing channel to compete by offering additional volume price discounts, reduced selling prices, and similar measures.

Phase 4: Maturity

This phase reflects the situation in which (a) the organization is firmly established, (b) the product no longer involves high technological inputs, and (c) the nature of the customers has reached a position of relative stability.

The organization, however, still experiences a wide variety of pressures for channel change during the maturity phase. In fact, certain pressures become extremely important for the first time.

Maturity is often characterized by increased competition leading to reduced selling prices and margins. With limited flexibility in pricing, management normally experiences a profit squeeze as labor and material costs increase. There is, therefore, pressure for any type of channel change which will lower selling costs. Thus, there is growing pressure for a channel shift in order to utilize a less expensive channel.

Management action, however, may be difficult because (a) the existing channel underwent changes during the earlier phases and is now best adapted to fit the marketplace, (b) there is a high level of involvement with and commitment to the existing channel, (c) the existing channel accounts for a large volume of sales, and management is reluctant to disturb the status quo, and (d) the existing channel has considerable power vis-à-vis the manufacturer and will resist any change.

During the maturity phase, a normal channel shift is relatively rare.

However, management may consider a special type of channel shift—namely, the acquisition of channel members so that in effect they become a direct sales effort. By taking over the profitability of the distribution function, management attempts to restore the overall profitability of the operation.

An alternative means of improving the profitability is to increase the volume of sales (assuming that there are production economies of scale). One way of doing this is to replace weaker channel members by others which are more aggressive and effective. In those situations where the manufacturer utilizes an internal channel, the continual upgrading of the channel is feasible (through both normal attrition and transfer of weak members). In the case of the external channel, however, the upgrading process has generally continued throughout the first three phases and thus, to a very large extent, the weaker members have already been weeded out. Those channel members that remain represent the best available to the manufacturer, and to some extent the company is locked into the existing channel. For this reason, channel alterations are much less common during this fourth phase.

The two most important and common types of channel change during the maturity phase are channel role and channel relationship modification. Channel role modification becomes important because the manufacturer is primarily concerned with obtaining a competitive edge relative to the competition. If a price advantage cannot be achieved, the manufacturer is forced to fall back on other means of satisfying the customer's needs and requirements.

For this reason, the manufacturing company looks more closely at the roles played by its own organization and by the channel of distribution. For example, the manufacturer may be able to gain a competitive edge by providing extensive warehouse stocks, direct credit, drop shipments, and other inducements to the user-customers.

Equally important during the maturity phase is the channel relationship modification through changes in the margins and discounts offered to the members. In theory, this is a relatively simple type of channel change to implement. However, in reality it can prove to be extremely difficult. The manufacturer treads a narrow path between gaining increased profitability and losing the support of the channel of distribution. By the maturity phase, the channel is not only aware of its power position in the system but it also tends to represent an important position in the manufacturer's sales effort.

Therefore, the manufacturer may face extensive resistance to any relationship modification; in fact, the company may find that it has very limited flexibility. This is particularly true in those situations where the manufacturer has encouraged the channel to take on additional responsibility for part of the "manufacturing" process (finishing, cutting to size, and so forth).

During this fourth phase, pressures for both channel role and channel relationship modification may result from the channel itself as it exerts the

	Ranking		
	Phase 2 takeoff	Phase 3 growth	Phase 4 maturity
Channel shift	1	1	3
Channel alteration	2	3	4
Channel role modification	—	4	1
Channel relationship modification	—	2	2

power of its position. The channel may feel that it is not competitive with the members representing other manufacturers and may thus request further assistance which requires a channel change by the manufacturer.

As stated earlier, certain types of channel change appear to be both more common and more appropriate at different phases of an organization's growth. The accompanying table suggests a ranking of the importance of different types of channel change.

The advent of management science and management's acceptance of the marketing concept have fostered an increased awareness of the significance of physical distribution. This article considers the benefits of integrating and coordinating physical distribution and its two major subsystems —transportation and warehousing—through the systems concept of marketing management.

---

38. THE DISTRIBUTION MIX— A SYSTEMS APPROACH *

William Lazer †

INTRODUCTION

The past 15 years have witnessed dramatic changes in the management of business enterprise. Some of these changes are reflected in new organi-

---

* Commissioned contribution. For a discussion of the importance of coordination and administration in manufacturer-dealer systems, see Valentine F. Ridgeway, "Administration of Manufacturer-Dealer Systems," *Administrative Science Quarterly*, Vol. 1, No. 4 (March 1957), pp. 464–83.

† Michigan State University.

zational patterns such as the breaking out of new line and staff activities, or the development of new centers of authority, i.e., physical distribution. Others are embodied in the applications of mathematical techniques and computer technology to solve business problems. In distribution for example, linear programming, waiting-line theory, and simulation techniques have been employed successfully to improve business policies and to arrive at optimal solutions to problems.

A dramatic management shift has occurred in the marketing domain. It stems from management's recognition of the increasingly important and pervasive role of marketing in the business system. It culminates in the acceptance by management of the marketing concept of business operations. This change fosters a new perspective for distribution activities and an increased understanding of the significant role of distribution in company operations.

Corporate management today functions in an economy of abundance. In such a business environment, marketing problems in general, and distribution problems in particular, receive increasing emphasis. The task of matching the technical excellence of mass production with parallel progress in mass distribution becomes as crucial as any confronting management. Customers and consumers cannot enjoy the benefits of mass production without efficient distribution systems. This is as true in Russia as it is in the United States. An automated economy produces only filled warehouses and clogged supply pipelines unless great progress is made in distribution.

Our economic climate places heavy burdens on marketing activities. Continuous production is accompanied with increasing market responsibilities. Yet, marketing is constantly criticized for high costs, wastes, and inefficiencies. The significant progress that has been made in increasing marketing effectiveness is often unrecognized. Distribution is one area of marketing that has evidenced considerable progress in increasing efficiency and in reducing costs. It is the purpose of this article to discuss the relationship between distribution and the marketing mix.

DISTRIBUTION AND MARKETING STRATEGY

The distribution mix essentially is comprised of two sub-mixes. One centers on the selection of distribution channels and the determination of channel strategy. The other is concerned with physical distribution. The latter will receive the major focus in our discussion. However, the physical distribution task can only be perceived properly in terms of its relationship to the various mixes and to overall marketing strategy.

Chart 1 illustrates the key role of physical distribution in marketing strategy. It also relates the distribution mix to the other elements in marketing programs which are directed at achieving such corporate goals as profit, volume, market share, image and reputation.

CHART 1

Distribution and marketing strategy

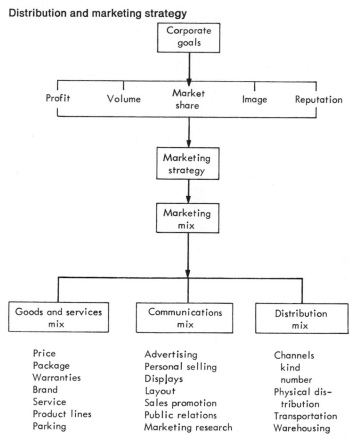

DISTRIBUTION STRATEGIES

Distribution strategies are concerned with overcoming forces of space, costs, time and competition. Distribution adds value to goods by meeting such barriers. In so doing it creates time, place, possession and information utilities. As a result of distribution activities consumers and customers are able to obtain goods and services at the time and place they desire them, possession is greatly facilitated, and more pertinent information is made available.

Distribution has been termed the dark continent of our economy.[1] Increasing attention must be paid to distribution problems in the future. To achieve the proper perspective and fully understand distribution problems they must be perceived in a marketing setting. Distribution strategies are part of the overall marketing strategy. They have a great impact on

[1] See Peter F. Drucker, "The Economy's Dark Continent," *Fortune* (April 1962), pp. 103 and 270.

marketing operations and vice versa. They establish certain parameters within which marketing policies are determined and marketing decisions are implemented. Yet, in reality, it is market forces which govern distribution operations.

In essence, marketing distinguishes business organization from other forms of organization. Marketing is the vital part of any business enterprise. Marketing factors are the fundamental considerations in establishing corporate policies and strategies and programming effective systems of action. In a very real sense questions of distribution policy and strategy (like those of other business areas) cannot be separated from dominant marketing influences.

Distribution strategies are more likely to be successful when two essential elements are combined. First there must be management understanding of the concept of marketing as a philosophy of business action. This involves the recognition of the significance of environmental forces which shape market opportunity. It emphasizes an understanding which must be reflected in distribution policies. It establishes the fact that distribution decisions must be brought into line with market wants, needs and opportunities. The consumer then becomes the ultimate force in distribution activities.

The second ingredient of effective distribution strategies is that of translating marketing perspectives into an operational distribution program. This results in the choice of effective distribution channels and the efficient distribution of products.

The relationship of distribution strategy to marketing strategy is portrayed in the bottom half of Chart 1. It indicates that distribution managers are increasingly concerned with the planning and strategy aspects of their jobs. To a large extent, planning and the development of effective distribution strategies depend upon the utilization of market information to design an effective total marketing mix.

THE PHYSICAL DISTRIBUTION SYSTEM

The physical distribution system is comprised of two major sub-systems. The first is a transportation system. The second is a warehousing system. These are illustrated in Charts 2 and 3. The transportation system in turn is comprised of two major components: transportation carriers and transportation agencies. The carriers consist of rail, air, truck, pipeline and water. The agencies consist of such institutions as freight forwarders, railway express, parcel post, air express, and shippers' associations. In contructing a transportation system, transportation carriers and agencies are linked and integrated to form economic units that are more efficient from the user's point of view. As a result, an integrated and coordinated transportation system is developed which leads to the establishment of new types of carriers, services, and methods of movement and handling, such as piggyback and trailer ship.

CHART 2

Transportation system

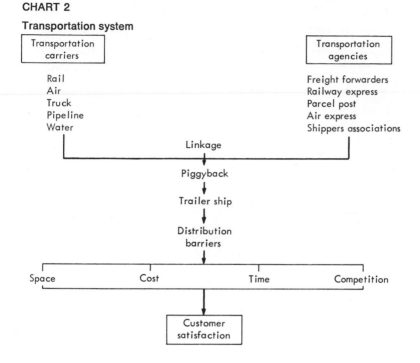

The transportation system is designed to overcome the barriers separating a company from its customers and consumers. These barriers include time, place, cost and competitive elements. The integration of separate transportation institutions and activities into a transportation system is resulting in new economies of movement and more adequate servicing of market wants, needs, and opportunities.

The second subsystem in the physical distribution complex is the warehousing system. It is comprised of two types of activities: storage and handling activities, and merchandising activities. These two groups of activities are linked together to achieve an integrated distribution center.

Storage and handling include layout, warehousing, receiving, consolidation, breaking bulk, packing, order processing, shipping, delivery and receiving. The merchandising services include packaging, grading, financing, displaying, selling and credit. Both the storage and handling and merchandising activities must be coordinated, sequenced and linked to form a distribution center that moves goods effectively rather than merely storing them.

When the transportation system is linked with the warehousing system, we achieve an integrated physical distribution system. This system is able to overcome barriers that separate the company from the market place thereby rendering services to customers and consumers and achieving

CHART 3

Warehousing system

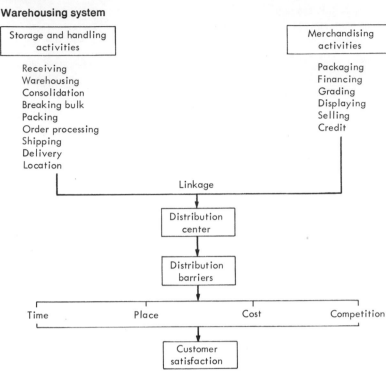

better market posture for the firm. The physical distribution system is portrayed in Chart 4.

The physical distribution system operates within a larger marketing setting. It is one part of the marketing mix. It pertains directly to the distribution mix and must be designed to support and coordinate the activities that occur in distribution channels. Moreover, it must be in line with both the goods and service mix and the communications mix. As a result, physical distribution activities and policies can only be properly perceived in their marketing framework. Marketing activities, problems, policies and decisions must be linked to physical distribution factors.

SYSTEMS THINKING

Such widely hailed marketing developments as the physical distribution concept, the marketing philosophy, and the marketing mix, which we have been describing, are merely manifestations of a more fundamental and significant management development that has occurred. In essence management has adopted a new perspective of distribution operations. They are embracing the systems viewpoint of distribution.

The characteristic which differentiates a system from a jumble of parts and pieces is that the elements form a coherent group. Systems thinking,

CHART 4

Physical distribution system

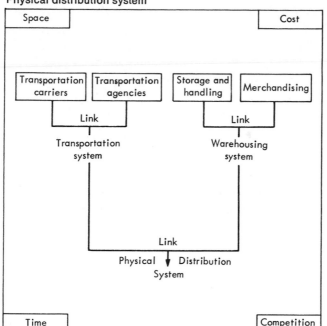

therefore, is based on the integration and coordination of business activity. Under the systems concept distribution agencies and operations are viewed as complex, large-scale, dynamic action systems.

Distribution managers have the major responsibility of recognizing the relationships existing among the elements of the distribution system, comprehending their potential combinations, and coordinating and integrating business factors so that goals are achieved effectively. This implies that the master model for distribution activity is the systems model.

The marketing management concept, which is a signal breakthrough in the management thinking, by its very nature, implies a systems approach to the management of marketing effort. It requires a recognition of the interrelationships and interconnections between marketing and other business elements. It involves the integration of all the components of the marketing program into a coordinated marketing mix. It demands the establishment of a communications network and linkages between the various functionaries and activities necessary for the accomplishment of marketing missions. It is concerned with the flow of information and resources through a firm to the market place. The very implementation of the marketing concept requires that marketing activities be grouped under the authority of a top-level executive.

Physical distribution is a systems concept. It is concerned with the coordination and linkage of various institutions and activities related to storing, handling, and moving goods. It is dependent upon the adoption of a systems perspective by distribution managers.

Among the concrete benefits of applying systems thinking to distribution are: (1) A business is seen as an integrated production system including both the physical production of products and their distribution, to serve areas of marketing opportunity in the most profitable manner consistent with company objectives. The dichotomy between production and distribution is eliminated and the fact that each of these activities find meaning in the other is stressed. This approach gives distribution forces the increased stature they deserve as an integral part of the business decision making framework. (2) A more realistic viewpoint is gained in the role of distribution in the management of an enterprise. Distribution activities are grouped under the direction of a top-level executive. Changes in organizational structures have resulted to adapt business enterprise more effectively to changing market needs. (3) Systems thinking fosters the coordination of related distribution activities to develop a total system of distribution action. It does not splinter distribution management into a number of distinct specialized operations such as storing, handling and transportation. (4) The application of the systems concept to distribution has resulted in savings in cost, time, and spoilage, and increased distribution effectiveness. The entire distribution process from start to finish is viewed and engineered as a total system, and savings are gained in total costs of physical handling and distributing goods rather than in any one cost center.

The marked increase in vertical marketing systems and a willingness of consumers to alter buying habits have caused rapid changes in the structure of the distribution system. Exploitation of market opportunities in the future will necessitate adaptation to and anticipation of changes in the distribution process at a faster pace than in the past.

---

39. CHANGES IN DISTRIBUTIVE INSTITUTIONS*

William R. Davidson †

The purpose of this article is to indicate briefly the major changes to be expected in the distribution industries during the first half of the 1970s.

* Reprinted from "Changes in Distributive Institutions," *Journal of Marketing*, Vol. 34, No. 1 (January 1970), pp. 7–10.
† Ohio State University.

Some of the major implications of these changes from the standpoint of business strategy and research will be identified. The distributive structure of the economy is defined to include retailing, service, and wholesaling establishments, plus the distribution activities of manufacturers and other form-utility producers as well as the product-acquisition activities of consumers. It is important to consider both the manufacturer and the consumer as active participants in the distribution process, in an era characterized by increasing vertical integration and enlarged willingness to shift marketing functions among or between the traditional channel of distribution levels.

CHANGES IN THE DISTRIBUTIVE STRUCTURE

It is not possible to deal with all anticipated changes in a comprehensive manner or to support points of view with documentation within the scope of this article. Consequently, attention is focused upon a few major interrelated institutional changes. The discussion will be somewhat oversimplified for purposes of emphasizing the major thrusts within a complex and dynamic distribution environment. Moreover, attention is restricted primarily to the distributive structure for consumer goods, although many of the changes here discussed have a counterpart in industrial marketing.

The following changes were selected for discussion:

1. Rapid growth of vertical marketing systems.
2. Intensification of intertype competition.
3. Increasing polarity of retail trade.
4. Acceleration of institutional life cycles.
5. The emergence of the "free-form" corporation as a major competitive reality in distribution.
6. The expansion of nonstore retailing.

Each of these changes represents a trend the direction of which is already evident. These trends are expected to accelerate and intensify in the early 1970s. The major impact of these trends will be upon the range of strategies which can be successfully implemented by firms within the distributive structure.

GROWTH OF VERTICAL MARKETING SYSTEMS

Conventional marketing systems are being rapidly displaced by *vertically organized marketing systems* as the dominant distribution mechanism in the economy. Conventional channels are those fragmented networks in which loosely aligned and relatively autonomous manufacturers, wholesalers, and retailers have customarily bargained aggressively with each other, established trade relationships on an individual transaction basis, severed business relationships arbitrarily with impunity, and otherwise behaved independently.

Vertical marketing systems, by way of contrast, consist of networks of horizontally coordinated and vertically aligned establishments which are managed as a system. Establishments at each level operate at an optimum scale so that marketing functions within the system are performed at the most advantageous level or position.

The recent rapid and expected continued growth of vertical marketing systems is evident by the performance of three major types of distributive systems with high vertical programming potential—corporate, contractual, and administered systems.

Corporate systems may be regarded as roughly synonymous with integrated chain store systems, although the impetus for vertical programming may come from companies primarily regarded as retailers (e.g., Sears, Roebuck & Company), or manufacturers (e.g., company-owned stores in the self supply network of Firestone Tire & Rubber Company), or wholesalers, some of whom have company-owned stores and are integrated into manufacturing. Chains of 11 or more store units, which accounted for a relatively stable one-fifth of total retail sales between 1929 and 1958, exhibited a renaissance of growth in the 1960s and now account for some 30% of all retailing, with a continuously accelerating growth rate evident.

Contractual systems include three sub-types—wholesaler-sponsored voluntary chains, retailer-cooperative organizations, and franchising organizations. Each sub-type involves voluntary but contractual integration of retail store or service units with other supply units at an antecedent channel level. There are no official data on the aggregate importance of such systems. A recent trade-by-trade analysis by the author and his associates suggests that 35 to 40% of all retail trade is accounted for by some form of voluntary chain, cooperative, or franchising organization. This includes old organizational forms such as automobile dealer franchises and the I.G.A. type of food store voluntary, and very new organizations such as Ethan Allen furniture franchise stores of the Baumritter Corporation. Other new forms are the various convenience food stores and fast-food franchise operations.

Contractual systems, like chain store organizations, are not new. However, their recent and expected future rapid growth rate *plus* the increasing sophistication of vertical programming are of major interest. Once characterized primarily by goals of economy in the form of buying power and low operating expense ratios, such operations have moved into an era of complete management systems, achieving high market impact through the rationalization and clarification of the total firm product-service offer.

The third type of vertical system, *administered,* pertains to a line or classification of merchandise rather than to a complete store operation. While historically many examples of close store-vendor relationships existed, there is current intensification of such relationships by means of vendor-developed *comprehensive programs* for distribution through the entire channel. Of interest are retail merchandising programs developed by O. M. Scott and Sons Company in lawn products, by Villager in young women's apparel, by Magnavox Company in the home entertainment field, and by Kraftco Corp. in the supermarket dairy case. There are no data of any overall significance for administered systems of this type. However, proprietary studies conducted by the author and his associates for a group of leading firms in the general merchandising field clearly indicate that such vertically coordinated programs are growing rapidly.

INTENSIFICATION OF INTERTYPE COMPETITION

All channel levels are characterized by increasing competition of an intertype character. A phenomenon known in the early 1950s as *scrambled merchandising* has surpassed all early expectations predicted for it. Owing to increased fragmentation or segmentation of the consumer market, a wide variety of establishment types find it increasingly feasible to abandon "line of trade" conventions and to offer a variety of products that may be purchased by consumers to which that type of firm has market access. It is estimated that as many as 450,000 retail establishments (about one-fourth of all retail stores) are involved to some degree in selling tires, batteries, or other automotive parts, supplies, or accessories. As many as 200,000 outlets are believed to be involved to some degree in marketing housewares.

This accelerated trend means that wholesale distributors and manufacturers who wish to achieve a significant total market share will find it increasingly necessary to develop multiple marketing programs designed to meet the economic goals and operating characteristics of specific outlet types. It also demonstrates the diminishing analytical significance of conventional Census of Business classifications (e.g., drugstores, hardware stores, and jewelry stores).

INCREASED POLARITY OF RETAIL TRADE

Retail trade is becoming increasingly polarized at two extremes. On the one hand are mass-merchandising operations that have successfully implemented supermarket approaches. This group includes the general merchandise types of discount or promotional department stores, and also the more specialized establishments with a large mass appeal. Examples are the 70,000-square-foot stores of Central Hardware Company of St. Louis, the home modernization stores of the Wickes Corporation and Lowe's Companies, Inc., and the large mass appeal drug store such as Super X, a relatively new division of The Kroger Company. Super X has developed into the third largest U.S. drug chain since its first store opening in 1961. At the other pole are highly specialized boutique types of stores which carry a deep assortment of a very specialized line, often limited to a concept or a "look," as opposed to commodity types. Illustrative examples are Villager specialty shops which feature only a well-coordinated assortment of classic sportswear items, and the Ethan Allen stores of Baumritter which sell only Early American style furniture and coordinated furnishings. Such shops tend to be strong on services and are often distinguished by the provision of consumption advice as opposed to conventional selling approaches.

At both poles, establishments tend to be organized into vertical marketing systems upon the achievement of scale. Between the poles are conventional and often nonprogrammed single-line stores of the family apparel, hardware, drug, and jewelry types. For these stores and their supply systems, the polarization is suggestive of increased obsolescence and profit difficulties in the 1970s.

ACCELERATION OF INSTITUTIONAL LIFE CYCLES

Institutions, like products, may be regarded as having life cycles which consist of stages such as inception, rapid early growth, maturity, and decline. The time required to reach a mature stage is constantly diminishing. Conventional department stores, as an institutional type, achieved a mature position over the span of about three-quarters of a century. The more standardized variety store reached maturity within half a century. Supermarkets achieved the same within little more than a quarter of a century. Fast-food service chains and franchising organizations will have achieved maturity in little more than one decade.

Further acceleration of institutional life cycles is to be expected. There will be an attendant massive impact upon existing institutional forms. The reasons include a variety of total vertical marketing systems models, a growing number of entrepreneurs and managers with interorganizational administrative skills, and a stock market that will instantly fund on a large scale any promising new concept.

THE "FREE-FORM" CORPORATION IN DISTRIBUTION

Distribution industries, once characterized by institutions which specialized by channel level and by kind of business classifications, are feeling the accelerated impact of the emergence of the free-form distribution corporation as a major competitive reality. Free-form corporations are in part a response to other changes previously discussed, especially intertype competition and the polarity of trade, and in part a perceived opportunity to redefine business purpose so as to better utilize corporate resources and distinctive competences.

The J. C. Penney Company, Inc., is now an example of a free-form corporation. Ten to fifteen years ago, Penney's was a chain of small-town, limited service, general merchandise stores. It has now evolved to an aggressive free-form operation consisting of full-scale urban Penney department stores, Penney auto and truck service centers, Treasure Island discount stores, the Thrifty Drug Company chain, a large catalog sales division, a financial subsidiary for accounts receivable funding, a life insurance marketing program, and European stores through an equity interest in Sarma S.A., a Belgian company with 100 stores and 270 franchised units. Another outstanding and prophetic example is the Dayton-Hudson Corporation formed in 1969 by the merger of two of the best known department store companies (Dayton's of Minneapolis and Hudson's of Detroit). This corporation also operates Diamonds department stores (Phoenix); Lipman's department stores (Portland, Ore.); Target Stores, Inc., a prominent general merchandise discount chain; Lechmere's, a Boston area hard lines mass merchandiser; two chains of specialty book stores; several jewelry store operations; and real estate subsidiaries engaged in shopping centers and other land development activities.

The number of corporations with a newfound willingness to go anywhere and do anything in distribution will have increasing competitive impact. This development is likely to enlarge markedly concentration ratios at all levels of distribution. Moreover, such corporate approaches are often perceived as strategic ways of avoiding the decline phase of the institutional life cycle.

GROWTH OF NONSTORE RETAILING

In an increasingly affluent society which is ever more oriented to education, leisure, and recreation, it may be expected that functions performed by consumers in the product acquisition process will be somewhat reshuffled with important benefits accruing to various forms of nonstore retailing and the distribution networks that supply nonstore operations. Many housewives will have a lower relative preference for "shopping," especially for routine categories of consumption, than for other demands upon or optional uses of time.

This trend is expected to benefit at-home selling, illustrated by the growth of Avon Products, Inc., with 1968 sales of $558.6 million, an increase of 59% since 1965. Catalog selling is also expected to expand. Penney's adventuresome entry into this field and the expanded use of seasonal catalogs by all manner of regular store retailers illustrate the growth of catalog selling. Marketing through the mail is presumably increasing as illustrated by single-item and short catalog promotions. Examples are product selling promotions by major oil companies and banks to credit card customers, credit card companies, magazines, and other firms not basically in the business of operating stores. The consumer's desire for time and place utility is increasing the range of products available through vending machines as well as the number and types of vending locations. The development of electronic devices is making new approaches possible to at-home shopping for staples which can be supplied by routinized order processing and delivery from central distribution warehouses.

Many new concepts involving nonconventional forms are expected to emerge partly as the contribution of entrepreneurs and also as a new dimension of the mature corporation which has been reprogrammed for project management approaches under the free-form pattern.

RESEARCH IMPLICATIONS

None of the major trends selected for emphasis in the preceding sections is readily traceable through Census of Business benchmark data, other conventional wholesale trade series, or annual statistical series of trade associations. Hence, one research problem of considerable magnitude is merely one of measurement. Beyond that, there are reseach challenges of managerial significance to ascertain improved methods of managing interorganizational relationships, to devise sophisticated management systems which will provide information that will help managers understand and optimize total system relationships, and to explore ways in which product life cycle concepts can be better applied to institutions. In the realm of social concern, it is essential to study more comprehensively the impact of these developments upon consumer choice, the state of competition, and the need for modifications in public policy, especially antitrust.

Among the methodologies that are expected to receive major emphasis in the pursuit of these research objectives are (1) empirical economic studies of competitive conditions and market performance; (2) computer simulation models to evaluate total systems performance under varying conditions; (3) behaviorial analyses of concepts of power and conflict in channel relationships; and (4) the utilization of laboratory methods in the refinement of such behavioral concepts, with a view to better understanding their utilization in total system marketing.

Retail managers are faced with the challenge of planning and developing an effective retailing mix to adjust profitably to changing market conditions. Sound planning is the basis for developing coordinated and goal-directed retailing strategy. The retailing mix, like the marketing mix, is comprised of three submixes: a product and service mix, a communications mix, and a distribution mix. Consumer satisfaction is achieved through optimal blending of these three elements. These elements are considered in the following article.

---

40. THE RETAILING MIX: PLANNING AND MANAGEMENT *

William Lazer† and Eugene J. Kelley‡

Some retail managers have been observing the rapid growth of the marketing management concept in manufacturing firms with considerable interest. This concept of marketing is resulting in the acceptance of a new perspective for business activities in which marketing is viewed as the basis of an integrated system of business action. Adaptation of the marketing management approach has significance for retail managers concerned with designing a total retail capability to achieve realistic and attainable objectives.

The marketing management concept in retailing is characterized by:

1. *Planning.* An emphasis on planning to achieve clearly defined retailing targets is the key concept. It stresses that retailing objectives can be identified and that an integrated program of action be designed to achieve these objectives through orderly retail planning.

2. *Customer orientation.* The customer orientation is adopted as the focus for retail decision making. A philosophy of customer orientation is more important than any body of retailing techniques, personnel policies, or organizational arrangements. It ensures that retail decisions are viewed through the consumer's eyes.

3. *Systems approach.* The systems perspective of retailing action is used. In this approach, a retail organization is viewed as a total system of retail action. The interaction between the components of the retailing system is stressed as in the functioning and structure of the whole organization. This approach focuses on the integrated use of all retail resources to satisfy current market needs and future opportunities.

4. *Change.* Change is recognized as the "constant" in planning, organizing, and controlling retailing activity. The prime managerial responsibility is seen as that of adapting retailing organizations creatively to conditions of accelerating change. Retailing leadership's charge becomes that of planning for the management of change.

5. *Innovation.* There is a new emphasis on research and innovation. Innovation is seen as the basis for retailing action. The important fact is that innovation is becoming programmed and a basic part of the retail management process. In short, research, a system of commercial intelligence, and

* Reprinted from "The Retailing Mix: Planning and Management," *Journal of Retailing,* Vol. 37, No. 1 (Spring 1961), pp. 34–41.
† Michigan State University.
‡ Pennsylvania State University.

innovation are becoming standard factors in modern retail action. This is resulting in the application of findings from the behavioral and quantitative sciences to retailing. The effect is new techniques of retail control, better management of inventories, improved communications, and a greater awareness of the usefulness of theory in understanding and solving retailing problems.

The crucial factor for retail management to recognize is that socio-economic developments are operating so as to stimulate the emergence of more accurate and intelligent planning on the part of retail executives. Retailing executives are operating in an economy which is characterized by rapid change and explosive cultural and economic developments. The increasing degree of competition from both downtown and suburban areas, the impact of population shifts, trends in income and expenditures, the degree of innovation in both areas of products and services, the availability and utilization of more information about customers and markets, are examples of forces which require retail management to accept change as a normal way of life and to assign high priorities to developing creative adaptations to change. It is in such a climate that the marketing management movement, with prime emphasis on planning, has made its greatest headway.

To manage retailing effort effectively in such an environment requires planning. Yet retail planning is more than just a tool of growth. It is a rational means of achieving continuing profitable adjustment of the retail system to current and future marketing conditions.

Retailing planning, in its broadest terms, may be thought of as the utilization of analysis and foresight to increase the effectiveness of retail action. Planning retailing effort, therefore, is necessarily concerned with the objectives and goals that the retailing organization seeks to attain, the development of retailing systems, the operating system, through which retail management is attempting to achieve these goals, the availability of capacity and resources within the firm and existing facilitating agencies to exert the quantity and quality of effort necessary for their achievement. The planning process in retail management is portrayed in Chart 1. Although this chart is necessarily a simplification, it does indicate the requisite arrangements of various factors in retail planning.

Retail plans must be conceived as functioning within an external framework determined by various forces beyond the control of the management of a given retail enterprise. This is one reason why it is becoming increasingly important in retail planning to consider environmental business factors as well as to identify the many retailing inputs, their interactions, and expected outputs.

The retail planning process involves at the first level three actions on the part of executives: analysis, evaluation, and prediction. The analysis of available information, and an evaluation of trends and relationships will give retail management the frame of reference from which to perceive

CHART 1

The planning process in retail management

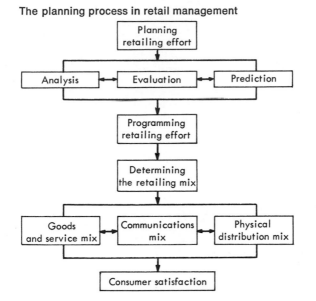

current and future problems. It will afford executives a perspective of the future. Past data is useful to management mainly as it helps predict the future.

RETAILING MIX

The analysis and evaluation of data and the predictions made place executives in a position of being able to program total retailing effort. Retail programming is achieved through determination of a retail store's retailing mix. Such a mix becomes the total package of goods and services that a store offers for sale to the public. The retailing mix, then, is the composite of all effort which was programmed by management and which embodies the adjustment of the retail store to its market environment.

The retailing mix, as such, is comprised of three submixes: a goods and service mix, a communications mix, and a distribution mix. Consumer satisfaction is achieved through optimal submix blending. It is through the achievement of a high customer satisfaction that a store prospers and grows. Some of the components of each of these submixes are depicted in Chart 2.

In Chart 2 the consumer is presented as the focus for all market planning and programming. The retail program is designed specifically to bring the offerings of a retail organization into line with the wants and needs of its customers and the natural market areas. The established program, therefore, sets the tone for all retailing activity.

CHART 2

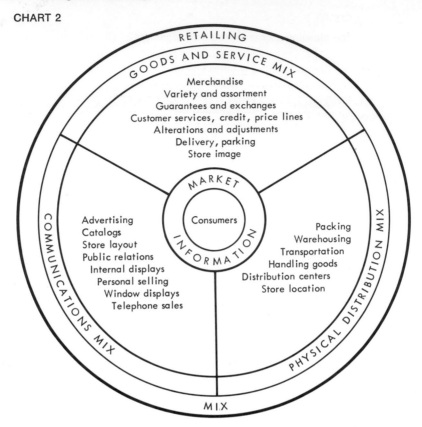

The submix that is most apparent in retailing is the *Goods and Service Mix.* Retailers are often well aware of the impact of the variety and assortment of goods offered for sale and the customer services that are extended. Other components of the goods and service mix are various credit plans that are offered, the price lines that a store will adhere to, the guarantees that are made and exchanges, alterations and adjustments, the image of the store and the goods it offers for sale, delivery, sales service, and parking facilities. The total goods and service mix should be so integrated that it will tie in with the store's own marketing goals. For example, if the image of the store is one of high quality, then the customer lines offered, the price lines offered, and the types of service offered should be such that they will blend with this concept, rather than clash with it.

The *Physical Distribution Mix* essentially has two components: a channels of distribution component and a physical distribution component. The channels of distribution component is concerned with the number and type of retail outlets that comprise the total retailing complex. For example, the number and type of branch stores are part of the retail enterprise, and the types of suburban stores that are members of the organization, are part of the mix. The physical distribution part of the distribution mix is concerned with integrating the warehousing, handling, and transporting of goods. It is evident, therefore, that the distribution mix is concerned with such factors as store location, the establishment of distribution centers, breaking bulk, warehousing, transporting, physically handling of goods, and packing them. This group of activities has been traditionally grouped under the authority of an operations manager or a store operations manager.

The *Communications Mix* is the third submix. The retailer is separated in time and space from the ultimate consumer. He attempts to overcome these barriers by obtaining information about the market and by communicating information to it. The provision of information about the retail store and the goods and services available for sale constitute the crux of the communication mix. The retailer has a variety of tools for communicating with the market place. Included among these tools are personal selling, advertising, window displays, internal displays, public relations efforts, store layouts, catalogs, and telephone sales.

The communications mix is extremely important in adjusting the goods and services that are offered for sale to consumer demand. It can convince consumers that the retail store's program is primarily satisfactory to the consumer. The communications mix should be such that it ties in with the image and the reputation of the store and the goods that are offered for sale.

It should be noted that the consumer is separated in Chart 2 from the retail program. A gap exists that must be bridged by the total retailing mix. Here marketing research helps management to adjust the mix and become aware of future trends in order to plan and make rational decisions. As retail organizations grow larger, develop more branches, and become more decentralized, the existing gap between top retail management and consumers becomes wider. Therefore, more pertinent and readily available marketing information becomes a requisite for proper programming and control of retailing effort.

THE RETAIL MANAGEMENT SYSTEM

Planning an optimal retailing mix involves viewing a retailing operation as an integrated action system affected by both internal and external forces. The success of a retail system depends not only on proper selection of each element and submix but on the interaction between them.

The retail management system can be perceived as an input-output system. All of the ingredients of the retailing mix may be viewed as the inputs which flow through the retail organization and attain the outputs realized by the retailing organization. Hopefully, the outputs achieved match the accepted objectives of the organization. The response of consumers in the market place ultimately determines whether or not the store actually achieves its objectives, or the outputs planned by the programmer. In this sense, consumers hold veto power over the entire retail system.

The retail management system, as an organization, has been studied in various books and research studies. It is composed of various levels of "departmental" managers. In Chart 3, five levels are depicted from the

CHART 3

The retail management system

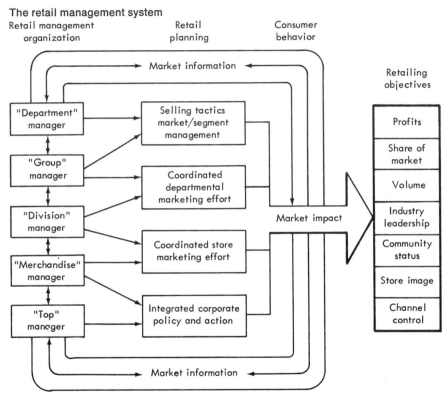

actual selling department to top management. The department manager is concerned with management and cultivation of a particular market area. He is immediately concerned with selling and sales tactics. The group manager coordinates the departmental marketing effort of several departments. Therefore, his is an integrative function to alleviate dysfunctioning between the departments. The division manager has a higher-level integrative point of view and is concerned with coordinating the store's marketing effort with the marketing effort of a number of departments. The merchandise manager is more concerned with integrated corporate policy and action as it relates to the total marketing effort within the store. Top management, of course, is concerned with the broader corporate issues including store adjustment to noncontrollable environmental forces.

The consumer reactions to the retailing mix determine the profits that are achieved by the organization, its volume, its share of markets, its image as an industry leader, its status in the community, and the degree of channel control that retail management earns. If the proper planning has taken place, the outputs that are achieved through consumer behavior will be in line with the retailing objectives originally planned by management. If this alignment does not occur, then retail management has three alternatives:

1. Alter the objectives of the retail organization.
2. Adjust the retailing mix.
3. Combine the two.

The systems view also has implications for manufacturers who are concerned with developing a retailing-customer orientation. The systems view of retail planning and management is more likely to foster a genuine customer-retailer orientation by manufacturers than the product or process orientation typical of many manufacturers selling through retailers today.

CONCLUSION

The marketing management approach assigns high importance to planning. This philosophy of business, when applied to retail operations, requires that retail managements place heavy emphasis on planning and developing a total retailing strategy. Only then will they program a retailing mix which achieves predetermined objectives.

Sound retail planning, in other words, becomes the basis for developing coordinated and goal-directed systems of retail action. Fundamentally the main functions of retailing leadership are similar to those of other business areas. Retail management must plan, organize, actuate, and control market and customer-related factors to achieve clearly defined market and organization objectives. They must view their retailing operations as a total system of action comprised of the goods and services, communication and distribution mixes, geared to the satisfaction of consumers' wants and needs, and be willing to adjust quickly to the demands of market change. Only through such enlargement of perspective can the profit thrust of a retail organization be maximized.

C.

Communications mix

THE THIRD MAJOR ELEMENT in the marketing mix is marketing communications. Nearly all the information a consumer receives concerning a product or service is channeled in some way through the communication mix. Because of this link, the producer must place heavy emphasis on effective communications. In general, this mix is divided into three segments: advertising, personal selling, and sales promotion.

Although each component of the communications mix can be viewed as having a distinct and separate character, they must be integrated into a marketing program so that they interact with and reinforce each other in maximizing the specific objectives of a communications process. Since the firm is constrained by limited resources, the marketing manager is faced with the problem of allocating his funds among the components of this mix.

The communication process must be fully coordinated and integrated with the other functions in the marketing mix. Once a product or service is available to the consumer, he must know it exists and know why he should purchase this product as opposed to any others that may be offered. The quality, quantity, and timing of the communication mix all influence the degree of success the product or service will attain.

The application of the systems concept to the communications mix has provided managers with ample evidence that an integrated approach to the process of management is a workable and efficient means in achieving the objectives of the firm.

The articles that follow deal with several of the major facets of the communication mix. The first article, by Crissy, compares the two key factors in the communication mix—advertising and selling. The next article, by Cash and Crissy, examines the differences and similarities between advertising and personal selling. Efficiency of the communication mix and an approach to this objective is discussed in the following article by Lee and Mason. Webster's article steps out of the traditional area of consumer communication into the area of industrial market communication to consider the applicability of communications theory to the industrial market. The last selection, by Miracle, discusses the appropriateness of using standardized international advertising.

The author believes the salesman will become much more sophisticated and will eventually be the "marketing tactician" of the firm. One reason is that changing values and expectations in the business community will have a significant impact on the personal selling function of the firm. An innovative and creative approach is necessary to redesign the personal selling effort to accommodate such changes.

---

41. SELLING IN THE SEVENTIES—CHANGE, CHALLENGE, OPPORTUNITY *

W. J. E. Crissy †

It is a moot question whether competitive enterprise is more a change agent or a means of accommodation to change. In any case the individual firm must plan its marketing strategy in a way that its market members see the value of its offerings. Selling, the personal force in marketing, is the key means which most firms use to personalize and customize their offerings to individual market members.

To appreciate the pending changes in selling we must first examine the changing values and expectations of those comprising markets. The American way of tomorrow most certainly will be significantly different from the American way of yesterday. These are some of the specific factors with which firms must cope in their marketing efforts.

1. *Antimaterialism.* This is evident in the dress of the teenager, in the appearance of the unshorn, unshaved, unshod, unsoaped hippie, and in the lessened symbolism of the new car.

---

* Commissioned contribution.
† Michigan State University.

2. *Anti-big business.* The corporation, symbolizing the establishment, has shifted its role from that of hero to that of villian in the eyes of many young people. Politicians are making hay out of consumerism as a key platform issue. There appears to be a pervasive repudiation of conspicuous consumption.

3. *Social conscience.* The combination of formal benevolent organizations and mass media have stirred the American conscience in an unprecedented fashion. Causes proliferate and multiply almost like binary fissions. The public sector is growing apace like a giant Santa Claus with presents for all. The voluntary sector of the economy is also expanding at an unprecedented rate, complementing government agencies in coping with social needs.

4. *Ecological concerns.* At long last the nation is facing up to the need for preserving natural resources and protecting the environment. Illustratively, antipollution goods and services now comprise a substantial industry in their own right. Much remains to be done and the magnitude of the effort is likely to stimulate the evolution of new forms of enterprise to cope with the problems.

5. *Use versus possession.* Pride of ownership is disappearing as a key value in both the consumer and industrial sector. Evidence of this is all around us—the family vacationing in a rental car at a seaside motel; the business enterprise operating in rental quarters with leased equipment.

6. *"Fashionableness" of debt.* The Protestant ethic of toil and thrift is being replaced by a neohedonism in which it is considered a virtue to satisfy needs and wants with a minimum of discomfort and effort. "Buy now, pay later" has replaced the goal of saving for years to celebrate a particular wedding anniversary. The cashless society is just around the corner.

7. *Disenchantment with growth.* This is evident in changed attitudes toward population control, the exploitation of natural resources, and the expanded responsibilities of firms beyond the achievement of mere economic objectives.

These changes in values, attitudes, and life styles are likely to be accompanied by these changes in marketing:

1. *Expansion of marketing information systems.* To compete effectively each firm needs a broader data and information base for its marketing plans, decisions, and actions. The information dealt with must include economic, psychological, social, and political considerations along with the conventional fiscal and marketing data.

Accelerated changes in values along with burgeoning ecological developments will require the firm to analyze *indirect* as well as *direct* competition in its various markets.

2. *Selectivity in market definition.* Aided by improved market research and marketing intelligence, the firm must use greater care in defining just which opportunities are likely to be profitable and enduring in the face of keen competition and in a likely curtailment of growth. One aspect of this

calls for more effective use of intermediaries in reaching smaller users and in providing necessary coverage of after-markets in the case of industrial firms.

3. *Increased services.* The repudiation of conspicuous consumption and the attendant decrease in planned obsolescence as a marketing strategy is likely to require more posttransactional services in connection with the firm's product/service mix. There is likely to be a greater emphasis in the posttransaction phase of marketing in insuring the customer's satisfaction. This, like (2) above, suggests a more effective use of intermediaries to accomplish this objective.

4. *Profit centering.* Keen competition, rising costs, and expanded social responsibilities combine to make diagnostic and analytical cost/revenue accounting a necessity in the management of the firm's marketing effort. Profit-centered accounting is likely to be commonplace. One outcome of this will be that the incentive ingredient of income for members of the marketing staff will be related directly to profit contribution.

5. *Alternatives to purchase and the extension of credit.* The lessened importance of ownership and the virtual disappearance of the Protestant ethic require that firms provide an option of short-term and long-term rentals on hard goods and extended credit on most if not all purchases. This trend is likely in both the consumer and industrial sectors. It is likely to change markedly the firm's capital requirements and to stimulate the evolution of new enterprises specializing in handling rental and credit.

6. *Marketing career tracts.* Firms compete not only for markets but for mind power as well. To attract the high-level talent needed to manage the firm's marketing effort there are likely to be many changes and innovations in marketing organizations. Associated with these will be an evolution of new career tracts for those engaged in marketing. These are some likely changes in organization: increased decentralization associated with profit centering, task group structures for handling product development and management, market analysis, and customer relations. Provisions will be made for both lateral and vertical movement of talent in order to provide the necessary versatility required to handle the complexities of the firm's competitive efforts.

What will the above developments do to the personal selling function? It is obvious that the selling job in the firm must be radically redefined with a view to making the salesman more of a marketing tactician and a prime member of the firm's marketing intelligence core. Further, with the increased emphasis on the posttransactional side of marketing, the salesman will need to mediate, not only customer relations, but relations between the firm and its indirect representatives in the various channels.

These specific changes are anticipated:

1. *Increased systems selling.* In almost any market where big-ticket items are sold, the purchaser seeks to optimize either a *machine system* or a *man-machine system.* Consumer examples include: furniture purchases which round out the total decor and home environment; appliances provid-

ing complementary fulfillment of needs associated with food preparation, garbage disposal, and laundering. In the industrial sector: the selection of machinery and equipment designed to combine into *machine* and *man-machine systems* with specific missions. An example would be the road-building contractor who considers the impact on his entire fleet of shovels, loaders, scrapers, and trucks in making purchases.

2. *Team selling.* The increasing complexity of products and the diversity of uses and of the varied technologies associated with them combine to make selling more and more a team effort. Tomorrow's salesman will need to know what today's does not now need to know, and he will need the authority to commit supportive personnel in providing necessary expertise and advice to both prospects and customers. The tempo at which business is done will require such staff support to be deployed near action points within the various markets.

3. *Value analysis.* Both value analysis and value engineering have been commonplace in many parts of the industrial sector. There is an accelerated trend toward applying this same kind of thinking to consumer markets. There are many sources of information assessing the worth of various products and services. This means that the salesman must be value-oriented and capable of demonstrating explicitly the worth of the firm's total offering—*product, service, people,* and *source.* One aspect of this is that the salesman must be able to show that his expertise and that of supportive personnel comprise a *value added* from the buyer's standpoint.

4. *Contract purchasing.* Firms applying value analysis to their purchasing attempt to optimize inventories. This leads to buying goods and services which meet recurring needs through annual contracts. Salesmen offering such items must be as sophisticated as the purchasing executive is with respect to this. It is his task to show that his firm's total offering vis-à-vis "make or buy" alternatives is the best possible value. Related to contract purchasing is the position taken by many purchasers of an annual efficiency improvement factor which they expect vendors to meet through improved technology, reduced costs, better distribution. This requires the salesman to coordinate his proposals with his firm's production facilities.

5. *Rental vs. leasing.* With the focus shifting to use rather than possession, the salesman must be equipped to recognize when rental or leasing is a better solution to the prospect's needs than an outright purchase. This will require the salesman to have a much higher level of financial sophistication than he needed when conventional transactions granted no such options to the purchaser.

6. *Increased ancillary activities.* As the salesman becomes more and more the marketing tactician of the firm, he is likely to have not only a wider spectrum of "nonselling" activities to perform, he must also have a much more sophisticated knowledge of marketing in all its facets. This will be needed, first, to appreciate his expanded role, and, secondly, to provide value added as a marketing consultant to intermediaries in his territory.

The salesman's marketing intelligence role deserves special mention. The salesman is truly the eyes and ears of the firm in the marketplace. He is likely to be called upon to generate more marketing information than ever before as well as to provide entree to those engaged in marketing research.

7. *Professional representation.* The salesman will continue to be the firm's image in the flesh. Historically, the salesman has been the butt of humor directed toward business. . . . With the disenchantment being shown toward business, the salesman has a positive role to play in "showing it as it is" in his own conduct on and off the job.

If the firms are to raise their talent requirements for marketing generally, there is bound to be an upgrading in the field sales organization. This will be in terms of character as well as talent. The salesmen will be able to contribute considerably toward establishing the professional nature of marketing and sales. An aspect of this internally will be the clearer demarcation of career tracts for the salesmen, including meaningful and differential levels of cempetency to be achieved by those pursuing lifetime careers in field sales.

Advertising focuses primarily on the pre-transactional phase of the purchase cycle in the cultivation of demand; it also has an important but lesser role in the post-transactional phase. On the other hand, personal selling's major importance lies in the transactional phase. The differences and similarities between these two basic marketing activities are presented. Specific suggestions for the effective and integrated use of advertising and personal selling are presented.

42. COMPARISON OF ADVERTISING AND SELLING *

Harold C. Cash † and W. J. E. Crissy ‡

Advertising, like selling, plays a major role in the total marketing effort of the firm. The degree to which each is important depends upon the nature of the goods and the market being cultivated. In the industrial

* Reprinted from "Comparison of Advertising and Selling," *The Salesman's Role in Marketing, The Psychology of Selling,* Vol. 12 (1965), pp. 56–75.
† Personnel Development Associates.
‡ Michigan State University.

product field, personal selling is generally the major force. Here the nature of the goods often requires specific application information that is best presented in person by the salesman. The dollar value of the order generally makes it economically feasible to finance this more effective and expensive method of presentation. Comparable effort to sell a box of soap powder to the housewife would be a ridiculous extravagance. On the other hand, it is likely that personal selling will be used to get this consumer product into the channels of distribution—through the wholesaler or chain store buying organization.

The person-to-person two-way communication of personal selling makes it a superior means of selling every time. Advertising by contrast is only a one-way communication system and is necessarily generalized to fit the needs of many people. Where the unit value of the sale is small, however, advertising is more economical. For example, a full page advertisement in an issue of *Life* magazine, which costs upwards of $30,000 will deliver the message at a rate of less than ½ cent per copy. And since, on an average, about 4 persons read each copy, message exposure per reader is in the neighborhood of ⅛ cent per copy-reader. A full-color page advertisement provides exposure for about ⅙ cent per copy-reader. Of course, not every reader is likely to see a particular advertisement but even if only 25 percent of the exposures capture attention, the cost is minute. Comparable costs of message delivery apply to radio, T.V. and other mass media. Recent figures indicate a total of $31.31 as the cost of a typical sales call when all expenses are considered.

The worth of the sales call and an advertising impression is not likely to be equal. If the prospect is serious and has sincere interest in the proposal, the sales call is definitely worthwhile. If, on the other hand, the prospect is not nearly ready to place an order, a reminder of the existence of the product or services in the form of an advertisement would have been more economical.

Generally speaking, advertising needs additional support, either through personal selling or through promotional activities, to effect the sale. In most cases, its basic function is in the demand-cultivation area. Hence it is more significant in the pretransactional phase of marketing. There are, of course, instances where advertising alone makes the sale, as in the case of mail-order selling. This channel, however, represents only a very small volume of total sales in any year. To a lesser extent, advertising can help in the posttransactional area of demand-fulfillment by providing a rationalization to the purchaser after the buying decision has been made.

Advertising can be thought of in many ways. Perhaps, however, the most useful perspective to take is in terms of primary objectives. Most advertising is aimed at inducing purchase of a particular brand of product. Sometimes this is referred to as preselling since the aim is to lead the person to the transactional stage, even though the transaction itself is not accomplished. This type of advertising is essentially competitive.

There are many things that can be accomplished through advertising. Perhaps the most obvious is to create an awareness of, an interest in, or demand for a product. When fluoride was added to toothpaste, large-scale advertising was conducted to let customers know that the product was available. Concurrently, the sales organization obtained distribution in retail outlets so that customers could acquire the product. It is doubtful that many sales could be accomplished without the advertising program. The alternative to advertising would be to have retail store personnel personally sell the toothpaste to customers. This is not feasible because the unit sale is too low to support the salary and expense of a sales person. In this sense, advertising paves the way for the salesman because, without the promise of a huge advertising and promotion campaign, retailers would not cooperate in finding display space. It has been said "Salesmen put products on shelves and advertising takes them off."

Less frequently, advertising is used to introduce an entirely new idea. The educational effort may be underwritten by a single company or, where there are a number of producers in the field, it may be the cooperative effort of the industry. Here the advertising is designed to win for the industry a share of the consumer's dollar. Again it is a preselling activity. Such advertising is often called "pioneering" as contrasted with "competitive" advertising.

Many advertisements are aimed at reinforcing the product name or brand in the minds of the buying public This may be considered as reminder advertising. It is normally used when a product has a dominant share of the market and cannot expect to attain any marked increase in volume within the economic limits of the extra promotional cost.

Some advertisements are primarily designed to convey a favorable image of the company as a good firm with which to do business. This institutional or public relations advertising is used by public utilities and major corporations which have an important stake in gaining a favorable public acceptance.

It is not unusual for a single advertisement to attempt to achieve a combination of these objectives.

As was noted before, generally speaking, advertising plays a more significant role in the marketing of consumer goods than it does in the case of industrial products. This is particularly true with respect to contact with the end users. However, even consumer goods depend to a significant extent on personal selling to move them through the channels.

When the item represents a substantial outlay and when there are complexities to be explained to the prospect, obviously, personal contact is both practical and necessary. Advertising for such goods, however, is often used in specialized media for the purpose of generating leads for the field sales force.

When goods flow through indirect channels, advertising grows in complexity. It may be used to cultivate demand on the part of the ultimate users through nationally distributed media. It may also be used in selected specialized media to encourage the various intermediaries to stock the merchandise.

When advertising is used with industrial products, it has different functions. As mentioned above, one function is to generate leads for salesmen. It is common for the advertisement to carry a coupon. When the coupon is received at the home office, it is relayed to the salesman covering that territory, who then makes a sales call.

A second function of the advertising of industrial products is to keep the name of the company and product before the customers between sales calls. Good advertising also reassures a customer that he is buying from a good supplier. The advertising adds prestige to the product, the company, and the salesman, especially when it equals or excels that of competitors.

When a company has a substantial advertising program, salesmen can use tear sheets of the advertisments to good advantage. These can appropriately be shown to both prospects and customers. With prospects, consideration should be given to leaving copies of the advertisements as they create a feeling of stability and solidity with regard to the supplier. When prospects see advertisements, normally in the trade press, this paves the way for salesmen.

In a well-organized and disciplined industrial sales force, there will be a similarity between the content of the advertisement and the sales presentation. Thus the advertisement and the sales call reinforce each other.

Many products must be used in a certain way to produce the desired results. Complaints arise when the product does not fulfill the salesman's claims. Advertising can carry instructions on using the product. This will help to insure satisfactory performance. If the product has already been used inappropriately, the advertising may cause the customer to understand the poor performance and give it another chance. In this way, it holds customers that might otherwise be lost.

SIMILARITIES AND DIFFERENCES BETWEEN ADVERTISING AND SELLING

From the viewpoint of communications, advertising and selling have much in common. Both must meet four criteria. They need to be *understandable, interesting, believable,* and *persuasive* if they are to achieve their purpose. There are, however, some noteworthy differences. Communication through advertising is one-way. In contrast, selling is uniquely two-way. There is an inherent weakness in advertising—*"noise."* This is likely to be present in greater amounts in advertising than in the case of the sales interview where misunderstandings can be cleared up on the spot. Whatever the medium being used, advertising must compete with other messages. For example, in a magazine the ad competes with surrounding editorial copy. The message conveyed by the salesman does not compete with other messages, at least at the time of the presentation.

Advertising may be used to generate either primary or selective demand; for example, an industry group may collaborate on its advertising with a view to enlarging the total market. In contrast, selling is aimed invariably at selective demand, that is, preference for the products and services being sold by the particular company over those available from competitors.

From the standpoint of persuasion, a sales message is far more flexible, personal, and powerful than an advertisement. An advertisement is normally prepared by persons having minimal personal contact with customers. The message is designed to appeal to a large number of persons. By contrast, the message in a good sales presentation is not determined in advance. The salesman has a tremendous store of knowledge about his product or service and selects appropriate items as the interview progresses. Thus the salesman can adapt his message to the thinking and needs of the customer or prospect *at the time of the sales call*. Furthermore, as objections arise and are voiced by the buyer, the salesman can treat the objections in an appropriate manner. This is not possible in advertising.

Company control over the advertising message is more complete than over a sales presentation. When an advertisement is prepared, it is submitted for the approval of all interested executives before it is released to the media. Thus there is little likelihood of any discrepancy between company policy and the content of the advertisement. In theory, salesmen receive training so that they understand the product or service and company policy. With the best possible training program, there are two possible sources of error or bases for deviation from company doctrine. One is loss of memory. Salesmen just cannot remember everything they are told. Also, they may meet situations that are unforeseen, and their reaction may not be identical with what the company management would specify if the problem were referred to them.

There is little a prospect can do to avoid a well-planned advertising campaign. With the number of media available, he is almost certain to be exposed to one or more advertising messages. Buyers can refuse to see salesmen. When the salesman arrives at the premises of the buyer's company, he is subject to the will of the buyer as to whether he enjoys an interview. Thus, over a period of time, advertising will bring the product to the attention of persons who would be missed by salesmen.

Perceptual similarities and differences

In terms of perceptual process, there are also similarities. Both must penetrate the sensory mechanisms of the customer or prospect if they are to be effective. With both, careful selection of the stimuli to be presented is important. However, significant differences do exist from the standpoint of perception.

In selling, it may be possible to enlist not only the senses of vision and audition, but taste, smell, and the tactual senses as well. Time and space restraints on advertising limit the number and array of stimuli that can be presented. In selling, it is possible to vary the stimuli and to apply them as the salesman deems appropriate. Actual time duration of an ad generally limits the opportunity to summate and reinforce the message. In contrast, during the sales interview, frequent repetition and reinforcement are possible. In most instances, advertising commands less full attention than does selling. This limits the number of concepts that can be conveyed and places a high premium on careful construction of the ad copy and selection of the illustrations. In the case of the "commercial" on radio or television, few opportunities for reinforcement are possible within the ad itself. The salesman, too, must have a well-planned presentation. However, it can be varied and adjusted as the sales interview progresses. Further, the salesman on the spot is able to re-arrest attention when he detects it is waning. This is not possible with an advertisement.

Cognitive similarities and differences

In terms of cognitive process, both advertising and selling are designed to induce favorable thoughts toward the company, its products and services, and its people. Both are aimed at conveying an image of *different* and *better* vis-à-vis competition. Advertising is far more limited than selling in influencing thought process. A relatively small number of ideas can be conveyed by an ad. There is no way to check on understanding. In the sales interview, the ideas and concepts can be tailored to the under-standing of the prospect or customer. Because advertising employs mass media, the message must often be geared to the less sophisticated segment of the readership or audience. In contrast, the salesman who is effective gears his message to the sophistication of the person with whom he is conversing. Only to a limited extent can advertising carry the person exposed to the message through a reasoning process about the product or service. Instead, suggestion must be utilized.

In contrast, the salesman is able to employ suggestion or reasoning as the sales interview progresses, depending upon the perception of his message on the part of the customer or prospect. In the case of relatively complex products and services, the most that can be hoped for from advertising is a whetting of the prospect's appetite for more information. Questions can be raised but relatively few answers can be provided. In the case of those same goods and services, the salesman is able to cope with problems and questions at first hand. In fact, in some instances he plays an important role as a problem-solver for the prospective customer.

Feeling state similarities and differences

Advertising and selling both try to induce favorable feelings. In the case of selling the salesman himself becomes an important determiner of the customer's feeling state by the manner in which he conducts himself while he is with him. In advertising, too, it is important to induce a favorable feeling state or mood in order to provide more favorable receptivity to the message itself. This may be attempted directly within the ad by means of pleasant illustrations, anticipatory enjoyment attending the use of the product, emotional words, phrases, analogies and comparisons. This is accomplished less directly, where the medium permits it, by the entertainment bonus preceding and following the ad, as in the case of a television show or a radio program. In the case of printed media, the surrounding editorial copy may be employed to set the mood. Even with these direct and indirect efforts, it is unlikely that any advertisement meets the objective of emotional reinforcement with all those who are exposed to the message. In fact, what may please one person may annoy another. Paradoxically, there is some research evidence from the radio field that if an add doesn't please the person it is next best to have it annoy him rather than to leave him in a neutral feeling state.

Selling, in contrast, has a tremendous advantage in the domain of feelings. The salesman in the first few seconds of face-to-face contact gauges the mood of the other person and adjusts his own behavior accordingly. Further, if he detects an unfavorable feeling state he may provide the other individual the opportunity to vent his feelings, or he may, in an extreme case, decide to withdraw and call on a more favorable occasion. This option is not open to the advertiser.

Advertising permits the firm far less control over the ultimate buying decision than does selling. The person exposed to the ad may turn the page or spin the dial, or walk out of the room. In contrast, once a salesman has gained entry, if he is effective, he is likely to be able to make a reasonably full presentation of the sales message.

Transactional similarities and differences

If the market is viewed as having the three phases . . . , *pretransactional,* *transactional,* and *posttransactional,* it is evident that advertising fits mainly in the pretransactional phase as a market cultivating force. It may also enter into the posttransactional phase by providing a rationalization to the purchaser. Only in rare instances does it accomplish the transaction itself. In contrast, selling is of importance in all three phases. (Figure 1.)

Advertising may be viewed as readying the market for the salesman's personal efforts. Even with carefully selected media and well-conceived

FIGURE 1

Relative importance of advertising and selling (market phase)

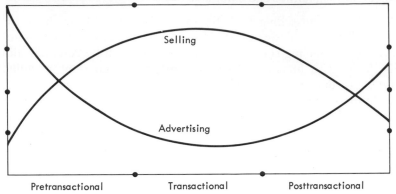

| Pretransactional | Transactional | Posttransactional |

advertising, the strategy employed must be relatively general. In the case of selling, not only can strategy be formulated for each account and each decision maker in the account, but tactical adjustments can be made on the spot in order to influence those accounts.

SALESMAN'S USE OF ADVERTISING

Even though the salesman may not be directly involved in planning and formulating the advertising campaign of his firm, he certainly must be aware of the company's advertising plans, the media in which the advertisements are appearing, and the objectives that are being sought. If this information is not being furnished to him, it is legitimate for the salesman to request it. It can be very embarrassing to have a customer or prospect refer to an ad of which the salesman is unaware. The astute salesman is not only aware of his own company's ads, but he is also observant of the advertising done by competitors. The latter is often an important input for his own selling strategy. . . .

Certainly if the demand cultivation of the company is to be coordinated, there must be a congruency between the content of the advertising and the salesman's presentations to customers and prospects. . . . Temporally, the exposure to the advertisements plus the periodic sales calls combine to reinforce the message. From a spatial summation standpoint the ads plus the sales messages bring to bear a varied array of stimuli on the customer and prospect.

Many companies accomplish this mutual reinforcement of advertising and selling by furnishing the sales force with selling aids, reprints and tear sheets of advertisements from printed media. If this is done, the salesman has a direct means of reinforcing his oral presentation with advertising copy. Further, he is able to leave copies of ads as reminders to the persons called on.

When such ads are taken from prestige media they contribute to the building of a favorable image of the salesman's company. Sometimes local spot advertisements on radio and television make specific references such as "advertised in *Life* (or *Time*, or some other medium)" as an attempt to build up the prestige of the product and the company. The salesman accomplishes the same result with effective use of reprints and tear sheets.

The salesman is in a prime position to gauge the effectiveness of advertising. He is able to determine by inquiry how many of his customers and prospects have actually seen or heard the ad. By judicious questioning he also can learn of their reactions to the ads. This provides management useful feedback. He also may be able to suggest changes that will render the advertising more effective.

If suggestions are to be meaningful to management and the personnel who work on the advertising program, they must be in sufficient detail so that they can understand the reasoning of the salesman who submits them. They should include the following kinds of information:

1. Specific reasons why the campaign was not maximally successful. This should be supported by comments or behavior of customers and other interested parties, not merely an opinion of the salesman.
2. Sales figures which are directly related to the advertising campaign. If advertising mats are supplied, a comparison of the relative use of mats with those of other campaigns may be appropriate.
3. Comparisons can be made with competitive advertisers in the local area. In this case, samples of the competitive advertising should be submitted along with comments.

The foregoing observations should relate primarily to large-scale print or broadcast media. In the case of dealer aids and point-of-purchase materials, the salesman is in an even stronger position to offer sound criticism. He can give first-hand reports of the ease with which display stands could be erected. He can report dealers' reactions to the materials and, even better, tally the actual use of the materials. When the materials have not been well received, he can inquire into the reasons for the poor reception and pass the information through the proper channels. It is perfectly proper for a salesman to state his opinion as well as the data he has collected but to preserve his intellectual honesty and make his ideas more useful to management and advertising personnel, he should indicate which ideas are his own and which are opinions or behavior of dealers and customers.

Salesmen who wish to have their ideas considered should find out when advertising campaigns are in a formative stage and submit their ideas so that they can be considered before the final ideas have been selected for development.

Lead generators

Advertising containing a coupon or a request to write to a box number or to phone may be a useful lead-generating device for the salesmen. An important caution: Such leads must be carefully screened before an appreciable investment of time and effort is made. A recent study of leads generated through reader service cards in a trade magazine indicated that only ten to twelve percent were bona fide prospects for the goods offered. The remainder were curiosity seekers, literature collectors, and high school students.

In some sales situations, an added value expected by the reseller is assistance from the salesman with his own advertising. In such instances the salesman must be knowledgeable on the actual principles, methods and techniques of advertising. Usually, however, if this is a job duty, his firm furnishes instructional materials and specimen ads for use directly or with some modification. To the extent that the salesman can convince the customer of the worthwhileness of advertising, he is likely to generate increased profitable business for himself. Some firms encourage their intermediaries to advertise by sharing the costs. When this is the policy, it becomes even more imperative for the salesman to be astute in his recommendations. He is investing his company's money in the suggestions he makes. Ideas expected of him may range from choice of media, size of advertisement, frequency of insert, optimum time, to coordination of the advertising with other promotional efforts.

Where indirect channels are employed, the salesman may be able to use his firm's national advertising program as a potent force in his sales presentation. He can demonstrate as a *value-added* that his company is applying a powerful, demand generating force on the ultimate user which will develop increased business for all intermediaries. This is the "push-pull" effect. In this connection, if the salesman has information concerning an impending campaign, this can become a means of creating increased business in anticipation of likely demand. Inadequate inventory or "stock-out" can be translated into a loss of profit for the reseller as well as an attendant loss of good-will by not having the merchandise available when the customer wants it.

SALESMEN'S ATTITUDES TOWARD ADVERTISING

A company's emphasis on advertising will vary depending on the nature of the product, the price, and the distribution of its customers. Salesmen's attitudes will vary with the relative importance of selling and advertising in the promotional mix. One common finding, however, is that salesmen tend to become critical of their own company's advertising.

In some instances, salesmen, especially those handling industrial goods, feel too much money is spent on advertising. There is no point in discussing this problem, except in a specific instance. It can be pointed out that a salesman in his territory seldom has all the facts necessary to decide on the proper ratio of advertising and selling. It may be that he is entitled to more facts but that is an internal management decision, not one for outsiders. The best assumption for a salesman to make is that his company has established sound marketing objectives and has selected the right tools to achieve them. If the salesman feels differently, he should offer constructive criticism or, in the extreme case, consider seeking other employment. (Few salesmen have any idea of the cost of advertising per prospect. While the figures cited earlier in this chapter apply to consumer mass media, the cost per reader of industrial media is not too much greater.)

The content of advertising messages is often criticized by salesmen. As salesmen are face to face with customers and prospects every day, they are in a good position to gauge the impact of the firm's advertising. This does not mean they should compose the advertising because, as in the case of the amount of advertising, the company may have some objectives not known to the salesmen. It may wish to use part of the budget to promote what the salesmen feel is a minor rather than a major product in the line. This could very well happen if the salesmen are not informed on the profitability of each item in the line. In any event, each salesman should back up the company advertising because, however little immediate value he sees in it, he is in a stronger position supporting the advertising than opposing it.

Another area of possible disagreement between salesmen and management may be the media used. When the number of available advertising and promotional media is considered (T.V., radio, magazines [general and trade], newspapers, direct mail, transportation [car cards], outdoor, point of purchase, and sampling), it is not surprising that there may be disagreement. Indeed, there have probably been prolonged and exhaustive discussions within the management group before the media decision was reached. There are specialists in advertising agencies to help in selecting appropriate media. The likelihood of salesmen making constructive suggestions in this area of advertising is minimal except for some local conditions which may not have come to the attention of those making the final decision.

SUMMARY

Advertising and selling play major roles in the total marketing effort of the firm. Advertising, however, focuses mainly on market cultivation, though it sometimes plays a part in the actual transaction, and with some frequency, in the posttransactional aspect of the marketing program. The most useful way for the salesman to view advertising is in terms of its three key objectives—to induce an intention to purchase, to keep the product or brand in conscious awareness in the market place, and to project a favorable image of the firm. Similarities and differences between advertising and selling are discussed in terms of communication, perception, thought-process, feelings, and degree of control. Specific suggestions are made for effective use of advertising by the salesman, as well as ways and means the salesman can employ for apprising his management of the impact of the company's advertising efforts and for suggesting ways of improving them.

Modern advertising requires a highly complex, thoroughly integrated communication system, which extends from the initiating firm to the consumer and back to the initiating firm. A model that simulates a communications network in a generalized advertising situation is presented in this excerpt.

---

43. ADVERTISING OBJECTIVES, CONTROL, AND THE MEASUREMENT CONTROVERSY *

Charles E. Lee † and Jarvis Wolverton Mason ‡

. . . Advertising is generally regarded as a form of communication the purpose of which is to convey concepts about companies, goods, and services by means of words, pictures, diagrams, sounds, music, color, shapes, and symbols on two levels of significance—the rational and the emotional. Rarely, however, is this definition followed through in the application of available measurement techniques or in the search for new ones. Apparently a desire for results in terms of sales and sales only all too frequently intervenes and, of course, the most effective communication may be negatively correlated with sales or profits.[1]

THE COMMUNICATIONS SYSTEM

Modern advertising requires the services of a highly complex and thoroughly integrated communications system stretching from the initiating firm to the consumer or other intended receptor of the message. The

---

* Reprinted from "Advertising Objectives, Control, and the Measurement Controversy," *Business Topics*, Vol. 12, No. 4 (Autumn 1964), pp. 37–42.
† University of Connecticut.
‡ Consultant.
[1] C. K. Raymond, "Profitable Advertising is Everybody's Business," speech to the Marketing Association of Canada, May 14, 1963.

functions performed, however, fit a very simple pattern: the source or instigating firm, the encoder—the advertising agency that puts the ideas into symbols of some kind, the connector (media) required to convey the information (the signal), the decoder (reader of the ad) and the reactor (usually the same reader) who carries out the *objective* or purpose of the communication. Each stage, of course, is a potential source of measurement data. The accompanying model (Diagram 1) portrays the essential features of this process as a generalized advertising situation.

DIAGRAM 1

The process of communication

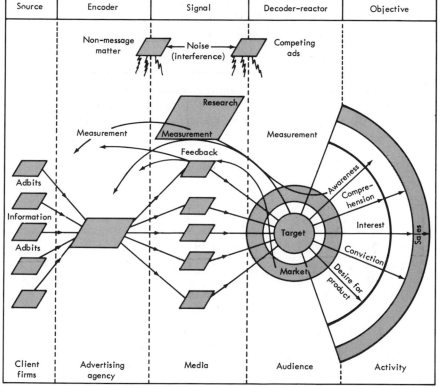

While this model simulates the network through which information[2] flows, it is incomplete without a consideration of its purpose. This undoubtedly includes the exchange of intelligence between at least two minds, one of which is informed and motivated to communicate, the other capable of understanding, and willing to receive, the message. The connection must, of course, be adequate and complete; the message should be

[2] See Francis Bello, "The Information Theory," *Fortune* (December 1953).

suited to the situation; it must have a definite purpose and the desired sales response should be readily and rapidly realized.

In advertising, many who receive the communication (signal) fail to enter the market. This may be because the message does not adequately relate, stimulate, or persuade; it may be improperly encoded or decoded, the connection may be faulty or associated with the wrong receptor, the timing may be bad, the environment unfavorable, and the response delayed or impossible to carry out. And, of course, it may be that the message has been confused with non-message matter, offset by competing ads and other interferences, or possibly the purpose of the ad itself has been incorrectly conceived. Obviously, research (feedback) is needed at every stage of the operation to decide which, if any, of these hypotheses is responsible for the apparent difficulty. . . .

The application of communication theory to industrial markets holds profitable potential for marketing efforts. The author identifies several pertinent variables that when properly understood will provide a new guide to industrial marketing communications.

---

44. ON THE APPLICABILITY OF COMMUNICATION THEORY TO INDUSTRIAL MARKETS*

Frederick E. Webster, Jr.†

Patterns of influence within a given buying organization and among the various companies in an industry make industrial markets complex targets for marketing effort. Efficient marketing strategies build on these patterns of influence or, at least, do not seriously challenge these established relationships. It is therefore surprising that marketing literature has few studies of influence processes in industrial markets. With appropriate modifications, a broadly defined communication theory may help to identify, to structure, and to analyze patterns of influence in industrial markets. This article considers ways communication theory can be made more applicable to industrial markets.

* Reprinted from "On the Applicability of Communication Theory to Industrial Markets," *Journal of Marketing Research,* Vol. 5, No. 4 (November 1968), pp. 426–28.
† Dartmouth College.

COMMUNICATION THEORY

There are at least three central notions in communication theory that overlap in important ways. The first notion is Schramm's source-message-receiver model and elaborations on it. This model has been applied primarily to the study of mass communications and, in marketing, specifically to advertising in mass media. A second notion is represented in the study of interpersonal interaction and, specifically, two-person or dyadic interaction. Concepts of interpersonal interaction have had only limited application to marketing management, principally in Evan's investigation of personal selling. Tosi has summarized and tested the important developments in this area. The third notion in communication theory involves the study of other people's influences on the individual's response to communication. The best known study of group influences is the examination of the diffusion of a new pharmaceutical among physicians.

One major conceptual problem in studying industrial markets is whether to consider the firm or the individual buyer or manager as the decision-making unit. Though some authors contend that one or the other is the proper viewpoint, both firm and individual variables must be considered. It is often helpful to view the firm's objectives, policies, procedures, and past experiences as constraints upon the individual buying-decision maker who is also influenced by his predispositions.

THE ECONOMIST'S CONTRIBUTION

Economists have been concerned with the decision by industrial firms to adopt a new product or process and, with its diffusion through an industry. Economists have studied characteristics of firms—such as size, liquidity, and growth rate—and of innovations—such as amount of investment required, and divisibility—that influence rates of intrafirm adoption and interfirm diffusion.

The several studies reported by Mansfield, the theory's principal investigator, have yielded interesting but sometimes conflicting evidence about the influence of such variables as size of firm and liquidity. For example, it appears that larger firms are more likely to be among the first to adopt a new product or process if the innovation requires substantial investment. However, small firms are more likely to adopt a new product or process when the innovation makes existing plant or technology obsolete. Smaller firms move through the adoption process more quickly, once initial positive interest has been stimulated.

However, the economist's contribution to our understanding of industrial buying behavior is limited because he overlooks the influence process by which firms become aware of and evaluate new products. On the other hand, the communication theorist is so concerned with the influence process that his analysis of the hard economic facts of industrial buying decisions is perfunctory or nonexistent. His concern for the effects of norms, values, peer group influence, etc., overshadows the possible influence of customer needs and market demand, competition, profitability, required investment and capital availability, or similar variables. A proper under-standing of industrial markets will require a careful look at both influence processes and economic problem-solving behavior.

WHAT THEN?

Evidence from research dealing specifically with communication in in-dustrial markets is limited but interesting. For example, Levitt's research showed that communication theory has some applicability to industrial markets. But more research aimed at testing particular concepts, such as opinion leadership, the adoption process, and reference group for their validity in the industrial market is needed. Further research resulting in elaboration and modification of such concepts is necessary for applying communication theory to industrial marketing.

At this stage, one can only speculate about a mature theory of commu-nication in industrial markets. Such a theory must recognize, for example, that industrial buying decisions are motivated by a search for relative ad-vantage, defined as the incremental profit to be realized from the chosen course of action, compared with alternatives and the *status quo*. To the buying firm, incremental profit estimated or predicted from increased rev-enues or decreased cost is the basis for the buying decision. Therefore, the various kinds and sources of information available in industrial markets can be evaluated in terms of their ability to help the decision maker make estimates of incremental profit.

Specifically for new products, sellers' attempts to identify innovators and early adopters in industrial markets could be aided by the identification of firm characteristics generally associated with innovativeness. It is probable that a firm is motivated to innovate by changes in such variables as profit-ability and market share. Thus a specific mechanism can be hypothesized that will revise a firm's goals upward or downward, in response to its recent success and failure experience, as measured by variables such as changes in profitability and market share. Consideration of such variables can help to explain differences among firms in their responses to communication.

The adoption of an innovation involves risk because the outcome is un-certain; some outcomes might be negative in an opportunity loss sense. The amount of risk in an adoption decision is a function of uncertainty about possible outcomes and the loss attached to such outcomes.

Firms differ in their ability to tolerate risk. Ability to tolerate risk is posi-tively related to such objective factors as (a) size (e.g., assets, sales, employ-ees, etc.), (b) liquidity, (c) diversification (number of products), and (d) profitability. Ability to tolerate risk may also be related to subjective fac-tors, such as management's optimism and aggressiveness which undoubtedly will be related to rate of growth in sales, market share and profits. The notion of self-confidence in consumer motivation is analogous. These variables suggest appropriate industrial dimensions to predispositions which will likely influence response to communication in industrial markets. The selective processes of communication (e.g., attention, perception, retention) will more than likely be found in industrial buying as they are in consumer behavior.

The *amount* of information available to a prospective adopter is a function of the total promotional effort allocated to the innovation by the selling firm, the extent to which the selling firm has directed promotion toward the adopter's market segment, and the length of time since the innovation was introduced. The longer the innovation has been on the market, the more information is available from all sources including the supplier, earlier adopters, and news media.

For a prospective adopter the *quality* of information available can be defined by how well it reduces uncertainty and provides convincing evidence of the innovation's ability to meet his needs, i.e., provides relative advantage. The quality of information is thus related to its accuracy, its thoroughness, and the credibility of its source. To be convincing the information must come from a trustworthy and expert source.

Besides the amount and quality of available information, the adoption decision will be facilitated by the *relative advantage to be derived from the information itself*. In industrial marketing especially, sellers may provide information in the form of technical assistance, training, and other services, which also influences the buyer's revenues or costs—this information is probably more valuable for smaller firms. Technical information offers more relative advantage for smaller firms because it helps them to compete with the greater in-house technical capability of larger competitors. Other things being equal, this may lead the smaller firm to adopt earlier than the larger firm. It also may result in a faster adoption decision (ie., from initial awareness to full-scale use) by the smaller firm. The smaller firm may be willing to base decisions on the seller's information whereas the larger firm, which has the capability, will insist on developing evidence from its laboratories and pilot plants. Evaluation and trial probably take longer in larger firms. Any theory of communication in industrial markets must recognize differences in the value of supplier-provided information to various buyers.

Again considering the use of information in the buying decision, information can be evaluated in terms of its ability to reduce uncertainty, which is a function of the amount of bias the receiver attributes to the information source. Bias in information can be defined as a consistent difference between the true parameter value (e.g., the profitability of the supplier's offering) and the value estimated by the source. Receivers tend to discount particular information sources based on estimates of their bias. For example, salesmen are often described as being naturally biased.

Because of estimates of bias, commercial sources of information are often discounted. Though commercial sources are usually more valuable for creating awareness, noncommercial sources tend to be more convincing. Information from another firm about the use of an innovation is probably the most convincing type of information. Even if this information is provided by the selling company's representatives, it may have high credibility because the validity of the information may be confirmed by checking directly with the user.

There is little information on the use of noncommercial sources of information by industrial buyers. For example, what is the role of professional purchasing, engineering, and other associations in the dissemination of information about products? What factors influence word-of-mouth advertising among buyers in different companies? There is huge research potential here.

These comments suggest the specific variables that must be examined in research on industrial buyers' communication behavior and a possible framework for interpreting results. In summary we need an integrated research attack to determine those characteristics of sources, messages, and receivers that influence response to industrial marketing communications.

Is the key issue of international advertising whether advertising themes and advertisements should be uniform or developed specifically for individual national markets? The author believes that the real issue is when can advertising materials and ideas developed in one country be useful in another country, and when not? Universal communications principles are discussed and generalizations are stated for the factors which influence the appropriateness of standardized international advertising.

45. INTERNATIONAL ADVERTISING PRINCIPLES AND STRATEGIES *

Gordon E. Miracle †

Traditionally many international advertising men have maintained that the nature of the advertising task varies from market to market. In

* Reprinted from "International Advertising Principles and Strategies," *MSU Business Topics,* Vol. 16, No. 4, (Autumn 1968), pp. 29–36.

† Michigan State University.

recent years the arguments have shifted and it has been fashionable to debate whether advertising themes and advertisements should be uniform or developed specifically for individual national markets. Although some are still debating this question at a fairly general level of argument, it is recognized increasingly that the issue is a phantom. The issue is not whether advertising messages and media strategy should be uniform from market to market. The real issue has to do with uniformity of procedures and criteria: when can advertising materials and ideas developed in one country be useful—or adapted for use—in another country, and when not?

It is the thesis of this article that the advertising task is essentially the same at home or abroad—namely, to communicate information and persuasive appeals effectively. The requirements of effective communication are fixed, and cannot vary with time, place, or form of communication; therefore, the same approach to communication, that is, the same *approach* to the preparation of messages and selection of media, can be used in every country. It is only specific advertising messages and media strategy that sometimes must be changed from country to country. In international marketing and advertising as well as in domestic advertising, the communicator must learn about his audience, define market segments as precisely as possible, and study backgrounds and motivational influences in detail before he begins preparing an advertising campaign. In recent years advertising men in the United States and in other countries have discussed widely the degree to which ideas and advertising materials created in one country can be used in another. Eric Elinder, head of a Swedish advertising agency, has said: "Why should three artists in three different countries sit drawing the same electric iron and three copywriters write about what after all is largely the same copy for the same iron?"[1] Mr. Elinder believes consumer differences are diminishing from nation to nation and he would prefer to put top specialists to work devising a strong international campaign, which could then be presented "with insignificant national modifications rendered necessary by changes in language."[2]

Mr. Elinder and those who hold his point of view argue that sometimes the appeals, illustrations, or other features of advertisements need not be changed from market to market. They have rightly observed that in many respects, consumers in diverse markets are similar and that human nature is basically the same in most societies. Men everywhere require satisfaction of physiological and psychological needs.

However, on the other side it can be argued that a communicator should rightly take cognizance of the differences between consumers in his own

---

[1] Eric Elinder, "International Advertisers Must Devise Universal Ads, Dump Separate National Ones, Swedish Adman Avers," *Advertising Age*, November 27, 1961, p. 91. See also Erik Elinder, "How International Can European Advertising Be?" *Journal of Marketing*, April 1965, pp. 7–11, and Erik Elinder, "How International Can Advertising Be?" in S. Watson Dunn, *International Handbook of Advertising* (New York: McGraw-Hill Book Co., 1964), pp. 59–71.

[2] Ibid.

country and those in other countries. They not only speak another tongue, but they adhere to other religions, philosophies, and traditions; they differ with regard to family patterns, childhood training, and the role of members in the family. The occupational hierarchy varies among nations; climate and geography and other aspects of consumers' physical environment are diverse; consumers engage in a wide variety of sports, hobbies, and other forms of amusement and entertainment. These environmental differences play an important part in shaping the demand for specific types of goods and services and in determining what promotional appeals are best. Thus while human nature and the motives of men are more or less universal, the ways in which men satisfy their needs are not. The nature of need satisfaction is determined by cultural and socio-economic conditions. Since such conditions are not the same in all countries, it may be argued that products, or the appeals, illustrations, and other advertising features used to sell them, often must differ from market to market.

The obstacles to effective communication are of the same type in both domestic and international markets, but they are magnified because of the relative heterogeneity of buyers in diverse markets. Thus the tasks of identifying and assessing the aggregate characteristics of markets, and of analyzing the individual characteristics and behavior of buyers, are more complex for world markets than for a single domestic market.

Communication with buyers in foreign markets may not be effective for a number of reasons. Of particular importance to international marketing communication are the following:

The message may not get through to the intended recipient. Either the medium may not reach the recipient, or the message may not be perceived for some reason—perhaps because the person is uninterested in the message at the moment, or other matters are more important, or other distractions may take the intended recipient's attention away from the message. Such difficulties may be due to the advertiser's lack of knowledge about which media are appropriate to reach foreign target audiences, and lack of knowledge about when to reach them (scheduling difficulties, for example).

The message may not be understood in the way intended by the sender. Because of the advertiser's lack of knowledge of the factors which influence how persons from different cultures will interpret messages, it is possible for him to prepare messages which will not be interpreted correctly—or as the advertiser intended.

The message may not induce the recipient to take the action desired by the sender. Although a message may be perceived correctly, lack of knowledge about foreign cultural factors which influence attitude formation, purchasing behavior, and so forth may cause communication to fail in producing the desired effect. Such failure may be due to the advertiser's lack of knowledge on such matters as consumer motives, reference group influence, or consumers' economic circumstances.

SYMBOLS

The successful communicator depends upon symbols as a means of establishing empathy with another person. Thus the advertiser must choose with care the symbols used in advertisements for a market.

Advertising symbols may be either: (1) verbal, such as the words in advertising copy, or (2) visual, such as the illustrations in an advertisement or television commercial. Color is one type of visual symbol. Today, in the United States, there is a continued effort to establish the effect of colors and various shades of colors on consumer behavior. It may be well for the advertiser to remember that in other cultures, colors may not have the same significance. In China, for example, light and bright colors are chosen by the young people, and plainer and deeper colors by their elders. Yellow has always been the imperial color; originally its use by the masses was prohibited, and it is still not used extensively save for religious purposes; it suggests grandeur and mystery.[3]

Because of the differences in traditions, customs, religions, and related cultural features of a foreign society, an advertiser must exercise care in selecting symbols that can convey the intended message and that do not offend the sensibilities of the audience. For example, comparing people to animals, or utilizing animals in cartoon advertisements to portray human beings may be quite unacceptable to Buddhists, who believe in reincarnation. An advertisement comparing people to animals also runs the risk of being offensive to an Arab. ("A beast is a beast and a man is a man. Allah says so.") Thus the use of animals as symbols to illustrate human behavior may not be attractive, even though understandable.

APPEALS

Appeals must be in accordance with consumer tastes, wants, and attitudes—in short, in harmony with the prevailing mentality of the market. In some countries, the use of a certain brand of lipstick or toothpaste by a well-known fashion model will enhance the product's appeal in the eyes of a working girl. But, "In Belgium (for example) it doesn't. Models are scarce and their trade is hardly considered honorable." [4]

The health appeal varies in effectiveness from country to country. Belgians are hard-working, earn a good living, and spend freely. They appreciate the good things in life. They desire comfort in clothing, heating, and home facilities. They are fun-loving and appreciate radio, television, beer, wine, and other products which add to the enjoyment of life. One observer believes that "the Belgian will hardly be found ready to buy something

---

[3] For additional examples, see Elma Kelly, "Use Symbols with Sense to Earn More Dollars," *Export Trade*, May 12, 1959, p. 15.

[4] Dan E. G. Rosseels, "Consumer Habits and Consumer Advertising in the Benelux Countries," *Export Trade and Shipper*, January 28, 1957, p. 17.

because it is good for him. He will buy if the taste pleases him, even if it is bad for his health." [5] Likewise, in France, the suggestion that the use of a certain toothpaste will help prevent dental caries is likely to be less effective than the same appeal in the United States, since Frenchmen are not as inclined as Americans to be concerned about the numbers of cavities in their teeth. In nearby Holland, health attitudes are quite different from those in Belgium or France. The Dutch show greater concern about their health. To the Dutch, the vitamin content and energy value of some foods are more important than taste.

For products that are identical physically but which are used differently from one market to the next—for example, cornstarch, cake mixes, instant coffee, margarine, and many other food products—the advertising message often has to be adapted for each market segment. Campbell Soup, however, in order to convey the idea of active people on the move around the world and at the same time underscore the universal appeal of Campbell Soup, commissioned the filming of a sixty-second film spot which includes a high-speed train in Japan, a market scene in Singapore, and a children's playground in Puerto Rico. It was dubbed into a number of languages, including Cantonese, Spanish, and Creole for cinema presentation in twenty countries.[6]

The list of companies that are trying to locate universal appeals for their products, which can serve as the basis for preparing prototype campaigns, is increasing. Revlon, a large manufacturer of cosmetics, is one of the best examples. "Revlon is particularly concerned that their international advertising . . . contribute to the over-all Revlon image. Latitude is granted field managers in revising individual ads or budgets; but even these must be cleared first with headquarters." [7]

J. W. Rintelin, vice president of the Coca-Cola Export Corporation, says that his company aims for world-wide advertising uniformity, even in such exotic tongues as Swahili, Urdu, Yoruba, Ga, Twi, Ibo, Sesuto, and others. Coca-Cola has a universal thirst-quenching appeal, and "the statement that 'Coca-Cola refreshes you best' has universal significance that transcends all sectional barriers. . . . Therefore Coca-Cola strives to achieve a similarity of messages, visual appearance, good taste, and major media selection. . . ." [8] The theme, "things go better with coke" is used in Germany as follows: *"Besser geht's mit Coca-Cola."*

Union Carbide markets a line of car-care products—polishes, waxes, additives for oil and gasoline, antifreeze—under its Prestone brand in European markets.[9] Before moving into Europe, however, the company

[5] Ibid.

[6] "Soup Around the Globe," *Advertising Age*, November 28, 1966, p. 56.

[7] *Grey Matter*, January 1966, p. 4.

[8] "Languages, Goals Are International Advertisement Pitfalls: Garcia," *Advertising Age*, July 16, 1962, p. 8.

[9] The following information on Union Carbide's venture into Europe was adapted from "Shining Up to a European Market," *Business Week*, May 14, 1966, pp. 190–94.

and its advertising agency, Young & Rubicam, surveyed more than fifty dealers, as well as a sample of consumers, in eleven countries. They studied buying habits and patterns, retail distributor practices, and many other factors in order to provide the base for a successful marketing program, including the content and nature of advertisements. As a result, they concluded that certain ideas and techniques applied previously in the United States should be appropriate for Europe. For example, in one advertisement selling car polish, run in seven languages in as many countries, Union Carbide told what salt could do to a car and offered the customer his money back if he was not satisfied with its product. Carbide and Young & Rubicam were told that European consumers would be suspicious of any product for which the maker had to offer money back if they were not satisfied. Anyway, the gloom-sayers insisted, thousands of people would buy the polish, use it, and then send back the empty can. However, the research proved correct, and the gloomy predictions were not fulfilled. The advertisement was successful in Europe just as similar advertisements have been successful in the United States. The key, of course, to ascertaining what was likely to happen in Europe was careful consumer research.

One of the most widely-heralded international themes is Esso's "Put a a tiger in your tank." After considerable success in the United States, the company decided to test the slogan in Europe and Asia. Minor modifications in wording had to be made; for example, in France the word tank is *reservoir* which in the context of the phrase could be risqué, so the word *moteur* was substituted. Consumer research showed the campaign was highly successful in European countries. The theme was also appropriate in some countries in southeast Asia where the tiger is a symbol of power and luck.[10] However, in Thailand, the tiger is not a symbol of strength, and the campaign was not understood.[11]

The infusion of U.S. methods into the German "soap war" starting in 1963 has caused considerable excitement.[12] Although there are 65 producers of laundry products in Germany, three companies manufacture 90 percent of the all-purpose and delicate detergents: (1) Henkel & Cie, GmbH, an old established German company, with *Persil*, (2) Sunlicht GmbH, a subsidiary of Unilever, with *Sunil* and *Omo*, and (3) Procter and Gamble, with *Dash*. Dash rose to a position of eminence—15 percent share of market—in two short years by using an assortment of techniques that are standard in the United States: trial samples, repetitive and motivation-oriented advertising spots replete with bright, hard-to-forget jingles. Sunlicht and Henkel adopted similar tactics quickly; nevertheless, their brands lost share of market. Generally speaking, the customary appeals of price and quality were replaced by amorphous claims of "whiter than

---

[10] "Put a Tiger in Your Tank," *Marketing Insights,* November 28, 1966, p. 11.

[11] Margaret Carson, "Admen in Thailand, Singapore, Find Unusual Problems, Novel Solutions," *Advertising Age,* November 27, 1967, p.50.

[12] The following information is adapted from "P & G Adds a Bit of Dash to German Marketing," *German American Trade News,* May, 1966, pp. 10 ff.

white," "the best ever," and "the most sparkling white of my life." Price comparisons were difficult because P & G introduced "odd" sizes, forcing competitive activities more heavily into the realm of package design, display, and advertising.

ILLUSTRATIONS AND LAYOUT

Illustrations and layout are perhaps more likely to be universal than other features of advertisements. Certain types of illustrations are being used with increasing frequency in several nations. For example, advertisements for Canadian Pacific Airlines which were created in Mexico City have appeared not only in U.S. and Canadian publications but also in newspapers in such faraway places as Tokyo and Hong Kong. The advertisements originally were planned for people in cities along the company's Latin American routes, but the airline found much of the work suitable for world-wide use as well. A company spokesman said: "It's one of the best campaigns we've got going. It's too good to limit it to Latin America. A slight change in copy, and we find it does the job as well for us in Vancouver or Hong Kong." [13]

The campaign to which the Canadian Pacific Airline spokesman referred had several features which may account, at least in part, for its wide suitability. The advertisements displayed large attention-getting photographs, usually with no more than 20 percent of the space used for copy. For example, a picture of a Canada goose, a symbol of the airline, is captioned, "He knows the best routes south, so does Canadian Pacific." [14] Short and simple copy with the same message, of course, can be written for other routes.

Perhaps some forms of art work are understood universally, and hence the same illustrations sometimes may be appropriate in different markets. Revlon, to take another example, has been a leader in the production of television commercials designed for use in several nations, using Parisian models and settings. In 1962 when Filmex, Incorporated, opened its new commercial production facilities in France, Revlon International moved in as its first client. The production, representing eight days of shooting, included a series of four one-minute color commercials, earmarked for fall showing in theaters and on television in markets outside the United States. The commercials, in English and Spanish, promote lipsticks and nail enamel, face make-up, eye make-up, and facial beauty-care products. It may be surprising to find English and Spanish advertisements produced in a French-speaking country, but there are several good reasons for doing so. For one thing, the French have considerable experience and reputation as producers and users of cosmetics. Furthermore, French commercials,

---

[13] *Advertising Age*, August 6, 1962, p. 70.
[14] Ibid.

filmed in Parisian settings, are often more elaborate than those produced in other countries; usually the French spend much greater time and effort on each commercial than could be spent in the United States. Finally, there are economies involved in foreign production which reduce the total cost below costs in the United States.

On the other hand, cultural influences may dictate that illustrations for the same product must differ from country to country. In German magazines an advertisement for cheese might show a large foaming glass of beer with the cheese, which would whet the appetite of a Bavarian. But in France an advertisement for cheese would more appropriately substitute a glass of red wine for the beer.

COPY

There is considerable diversity of opinion with regard to the translation of copy from one language to another. On the one side are those who warn against translations. They point out that while mistakes can be made in any language, even by local copywriters, it is more likely that they will be made if advertisements are prepared in one country, translated, and inserted in international or foreign media without review by competent local linguists. One writer has listed several "famous goofs," for example:

Copywriters for General Motors found out that "body by Fisher" came out "corpse by Fisher" in Flemish. "Schweppes tonic water" was speedily dehydrated to "Schweppes Tonica" in Italy, where "il water" idiomatically indicates a bathroom.[15]

Many advertising personnel in the French-speaking regions of Canada feel strongly that separate copy must be written for advertisements designed to appeal effectively to French-speaking people. Some advertising people feel that commercials which were originally in English and subsequently French-dubbed are passé, and that the few of these still being shown only give the commercials with copy created especially for a French-Canadian audience more atmosphere and more selling power.

On the other hand, a spokesman for a company selling in South America says that English copy can be translated into Spanish if it is done by a person who has: (1) good literary knowledge and command of the technical terminology of both languages, (2) a good understanding of the technical aspects of the products, and (3) copywriting ability which can recreate the persuasive tone of English copy.[16] Therefore, it appears that there is a need for a creative, not just a routine word-for-word, translation.

---

[15] Edward M. Mazze, "How to Push a Body Abroad Without Making It a Corpse," *Business Abroad and Export Trade*, August 10, 1964, p. 15.

[16] Emmet P. Langen, "How to Write Spanish Copy—Without a Yankee Accent," *Industrial Marketing*, July 1959, p. 49.

The effects of dubbing and adapting television commercials have been studied by a commercial research organization, the Schwerin Research Corporation.[17] In one study, Schwerin tested thirty-one commercials shown in Canada. English versions were tested in Toronto and French-dubbed versions were tested in Montreal. The Schwerin competitive preference scores were used to compare the impact of the advertisements. There were two instances in which the dubbed version did even better than its English counterpart; there were eight cases in which considerable declines in effectiveness resulted. The remaining cases showed no significant difference between the effectiveness of the English and French versions of the same commercial. The losses in effectiveness occurred mainly among commercials which were very strong in English, whereas the French versions which duplicated the results of the original commercials were largely confined to examples that were not outstanding in English. It should be noted that the dubbed commercials were essentially literal translations. However, when fifteen of the same commercials were *adapted* [18] rather than translated literally, it was found that six registered a significant gain in effectiveness, nine showed no significant change, and *none* showed a significant decline. The report concluded that it is possible for television commercials originally designed for one particular market to obtain comparable results in a market where a different language is spoken; it also seems clear that adaptation of the commercial is preferable to literal translations.

With regard to whether or not to prepare new copy for a foreign market or to translate the English copy, it seems reasonable to conclude that an advertiser must consider whether the translated message can be received and comprehended by the foreign audience to which it is directed. Anyone with a knowledge of foreign languages realizes that it is usually necessary to be able to think in a language in order to communicate accurately. One must understand the connotations of words, phrases, and sentence structures, as well as their translated meaning, in order to be fully aware of whether or not the message will be received and how it will be understood. The same principle applies to advertising—perhaps to an even greater degree. Difficulty of communication in advertising is compounded, because it is essentially one-way communication, with no provision for immediate feedback. The most effective appeals, including organization of ideas and the specific use of language—especially colloquialisms and idioms—are those developed by a copywriter who thinks in the language and understands the consumer to whom the advertisement is directed. Thinking in a foreign language involves thinking in terms of the foreigner's habits, tastes, abilities, and prejudices; one assimilates words, customs, and beliefs.

---

[17] "The Effects of Dubbing and Adapting Television Commercials for Foreign Markets," *Schwerin Research Corporation Technical and Analytical Review*, No. 9, (Summer 1961).
[18] The word "adapted" was not defined in the report.

COMPLETE ADVERTISEMENTS

Professor S. Watson Dunn of the University of Illinois has reported [19] on the results of a series of field tests to determine the extent to which the language of advertising is international, specifically, that is, to find out under what conditions an entire American advertisement would be successful in a foreign market. Five products, all low-priced convenience items which were widely used internationally, were chosen. They had all been advertised in at least one American magazine, and the appeals featured in the advertisements violated no cultural or other taboos in France and Egypt, the countries in which the test was run.

Three variations of the illustrative material and two of the headlines and copy—all of them consistent with the original creative platform— were used. One of the illustrations was the original as used in the American magazine, one was replaced with French models, and another with Egyptian models. One version of the copy and headlines consisted of an idiomatic translation into French and Arabic. The other was composed from the original by a professional copywriter of each country. The audiences consisted of a sample of middle and upper middle class consumers in the largest city in each country. Three measures of effectiveness were used for each advertisement.

The results showed surprisingly little difference in the effectiveness of the various versions. There was little evidence to support the idea that in a case such as this it is necessary to show a local model in the advertisement, or that one must attribute the message to a local (as compared with a foreign) source. There was only limited evidence that the message which is started from scratch in a foreign country is any more effective than a good, refined translation from the U.S. original.

The flow of ideas and creative materials is not all one way.[20] Foote Cone & Belding GmbH, the German subsidiary of the U.S. advertising agency with that name, acquired the Silly Putty account when the product was being considered for introduction in Germany. Silly Putty can be molded into any form; left alone it flows slowly, like molasses; it can be stretched or with a sudden jerk it can be broken; it bounces higher than a rubber ball; it lifts pictures, print, and drawings from a newspaper. For sixteen years it has been sold in the United States in small, egg-shaped containers.

FCB Frankfurt started from scratch to prepare German advertising for Silly Putty; only the product came from the United States. The "European" package was prepared in nine languages. The product was introduced to retailers at the Nuremburg Toy Fair, where it proved to be a major attrac-

---

[19] S. Watson Dunn, "The International Language of Advertising (a talk presented at the East Central Region Annual Meeting of the American Association of Advertising Agencies, Detroit, November 16–17, 1966).

[20] The following is adapted from information in "Commercial for German TV Now Used in U.S. Campaign," Effective Solutions to German Marketing Problems, Case History No. 9, German American Trade News, December 1966, p. 14.

tion. Consumer advertising was concentrated on cinema and television. A film was designed so that it could be used in all European markets, altering only the sound track. The famous German stage and film comedian George Thomalla presented the product. He showed how Silly Putty can be stretched, how it bounces, and how it picks up photos from paper. Then a trick camera made Thomalla act out one of the qualities of Silly Putty. His face stretched and suddenly broke into two halves. Sales of Silly Putty rose rapidly in Europe. The TV spot was so successful that it was subsequently shown on U.S. television, with sound dubbed into English.

On the other hand, there are, of course, numerous examples of advertisements that are appropriate in one country but not in another. For example, an advertisement in some of India's leading newspapers showed an attractive and apparently nude young woman dousing herself liberally with talcum powder while partly hidden behind a black strip that read "Don't go wild—just enough is all you need of Binoca talc." Irate readers condemned the paper for carrying "indecent" advertising offensive to traditional standards of Indian morality.[21] The article went on to report:

> The controversy reflects the sweeping changes that have taken place in the Indian advertising industry within the last few years.
>
> Until recently, Indian advertising has been generally cautious and conservative. As one advertising man put it, "Just three years ago we probably would have sold talcum powder with a picture of the box and a bit of copy which began 'known for 75 years as the queen of talcums. . . .' "[22]

SOME GENERALIZATIONS

Generally speaking, most advertising men would agree that it is unlikely that Mr. Elinder's recommendations for "uniform advertising" can be successful for all products, for all companies, in all markets. Thus the critical questions are *when* will Mr. Elinder's approach be successful and *when not?* And, *what criteria* can be used to make a selective judgment?

The factors which influence the appropriateness of "uniform advertising" for various market segments (whether national or international) are:

1. *The type of product.* When there are certain universal selling points for some products—for example, razor blades, electric irons, automobile tires, ball point pens—products are sold primarily on the basis of objective physical characteristics. These objective characteristics are likely to be considered by consumers to be identical, regardless of market differences, suggesting that the same appeals will be effective in all markets.

2. *The homogeneity or heterogeneity of markets.* When aggregate characteristics such as income, education, and occupation are alike, individual consumer characteristics such as needs, attitudes, and customs may also be alike, thus suggesting that the advertiser use the same selling points.

---

[21] "Nude in Talc Ad Offends in India," *The New York Times*, April 29, 1967, p. 36.
[22] Ibid., pp. 36, 55.

3. *The characteristics and availability of media.* If certain media are available in one country but not in another, certain messages and materials may not be usable.

4. *The types of advertising agency service available in each market segment.* If in some markets only poor agency service is available, a firm may be forced to rely on centralized control of advertising, with necessary uniformities in messages and media strategy.

5. *Government restrictions on the nature of advertising.* Some governments prohibit certain types of messages, thereby making certain appeals or copy unlawful.

6. *Government tariffs on art work or printed matter.* Such expenses may offset a cost advantage achieved by centralization of the art and production functions.

7. *Trade codes, ethical practices, and industry agreements.* In some countries there may be a "gentlemen's agreement" among competitors: they will refrain from using certain media, such as television, an expensive medium, which in a limited market might only increase "competitive advertising."

8. *Corporate organization of the advertiser.* If a company is organized to conduct business on a multinational basis, and if personnel are available, uniform advertising may be feasible—for example, if a company has "controlled" subsidiaries it can often control advertising better than companies that use independent licensees to produce and market their brands abroad.

People the world over have the same needs, such as food, safety, and love. But people sometimes differ in the ways in which they satisfy their needs. Just as it is important to provide physical variations in products to meet the varying demands of diverse market segments, it is also important to tailor advertisements to meet the requirements of each market segment. But it is the demands of the market segements which are diverse, not the approach to planning and preparing marketing programs. The principles underlying communication by advertising are the same in all nations. It is only the specific methods, techniques, and symbols which sometimes must be varied to take account of diverse environmental conditions. Therefore U.S. advertisers may be well advised to export their approach to planning and preparing international advertising, but before making final decisions on copy or media they should be sure to consult personnel who know the foreign market intimately.

Bibliography

A. PRODUCT AND SERVICE MIX

ALEXANDER, R. W. "The Death and Burial of 'Sick' Products," *Journal of Marketing*, Vol. 28, April 1964, pp. 1–7.

BECKMAN, THEODORE N. *Credits and Collections: Management and Theory.* 7th ed. New York: McGraw-Hill Book Co., Inc., 1962.

KLINE, CHARLES H. "The Strategy of Product Policy," *Harvard Business Review*, Vol. 33, No. 4, July–August 1955, pp. 91–100.

LEVITT, THEODORE. "Innovative Imitation," *Harvard Business Review*, September–October 1966, pp. 63–70.

WASSON, CHESTER R. "What is New about a New Product?" *Journal of Marketing*, Vol. 25, No. 1, July 1960, pp. 52–56.

B. DISTRIBUTION MIX

BARGER, HAROLD. *Distribution's Place in the American Economy since 1896.* Princeton, N.J.: Princeton University Press, 1955.

CLEWETT, RICHARD M., ed. *Marketing Channels.* Homewood, Ill.: Richard D. Irwin, Inc., 1954.

COX, REAVIS; GOODMAN, CHARLES S.; AND FICHANDLER, THOMAS C. *Distribution in a High-Level Economy.* Englewood Cliffs, N.J.: Prentice-Hall, Inc., 1965.

DUNCAN, DELBERT J.; PHILLIPS, CHARLES F.; AND HOLLANDER, STANLEY C. *Modern Retailing Management.* 8th ed. Homewood, Ill.: Richard D. Irwin, Inc., 1972.

GOLDSTUCKER, JAC L. "The Influence of Culture on Channels of Distribution," pp. 468–73.

REVZAN, DAVID A. *Wholesaling in Marketing Organizations.* New York: John Wiley & Sons, Inc., 1961.

SMYKAY, EDWARD W.; BOWERSOX, DONALD J.; AND MOSSMAN, FRANK H. *Physical Distribution Management.* New York: The MacMillan Co., 1961.

WEIGAND, ROBERT A. "The Management of Physical Distribution: A Dilemma," *Business Topics*, Vol. 10, No. 3, Summer 1962, pp. 67–72.

C. COMMUNICATIONS MIX

BERLO, DAVID K. *The Process of Communication.* New York: Holt, Rinehart & Winston, Inc., 1960.

CRANE, EDGAR.   *Marketing Communications: A Behavioral Approach to Men, Messages, and Media.* New York: John Wiley & Sons, Inc., 1965.

ENGEL, JAMES F.; KEGERREIS, ROBERT J.; AND BLACKWELL, ROGER D.   "Word-of-mouth Communication by the Innovator," *Journal of Marketing,* July 1969, pp. 15–19.

GENSCH, DENNIS H.   "Computer Models in Advertising Media Selection," *Journal of Marketing Research,* Vol. 5, November 1968, pp. 414–24.

HALL, EDWARD T.   *The Silent Language.* Greenwich, Conn.: Fawcett Publications, Inc., 1959.

KATZ, ELIHU, AND LAZERSFELD, PAUL F.   *Personal Influence: The Part Played by People in the Flow of Mass Communications.* Glencoe, Ill.: Free Press, Inc., 1957.

LEVITT, THEODORE.   "Communications and Industrial Selling," *Journal of Marketing,* April 1967, pp. 15–21.

MIRACLE, GORDON E.   "International Advertising Principles and Strategies," *MSU Business Topics,* Autumn 1968, pp. 29–36.

MORRILL, JOHN E.   "Industrial Advertising Pays Off," *Harvard Business Review,* March–April 1970, pp. 4–14, 159–69.

WEBSTER, FREDERICK E., JR.   "On the Applicability of Communication Theory to Industrial Markets," *Journal of Marketing Research,* November 1968, pp. 426–28.

WHITNEY, JOHN O.   "Better Results from Retail Advertising," *Harvard Business Review,* May–June 1970, pp. 111–20.

Editorial postscript:
Horizons of marketing
management and education

THE GOALS of higher education in marketing include the development of a disciplined approach to dynamic marketing problems, a capacity for analysis, and, most important, the motivation and ability for continuing intellectual growth in marketing and related fields. To assist readers in the achievement of these goals, a conceptual framework for the analysis of marketing management problems has been presented in this book. This analytical framework and the future orientation of these articles are designed to stimulate readers to think independently and creatively about current and emerging marketing problems and developments.

Two ideas which underlie the need for continuing professional development by all who aspire to understand marketing are emphasized: (1) the accelerating rate of knowledge accumulation and (2) the interdisciplinary approach to the solution of marketing problems. Several selections in this book emphasize that marketing managers and scholars are confronted by rapidly changing environmental forces and an explosive development of usable knowledge. These forces and others—such as changing societal priorities, changing business needs and goals, the growing complexities of business, more rigorous competition, and increasing emphasis on research and innovation—influence both the practice and study of marketing.

The rate of knowledge accumulation in business administration, marketing, and the supporting fields will accelerate. Some believe that meeting the challenge of this change involves the solution of intellectual problems comparable in difficulty to those confronting education in the pure and applied sciences. The further research goes in trying to understand all phases of marketing, especially consumer behavior, the more complex the field becomes and the need for further knowledge becomes even greater.

Closer ties will develop between marketing and some nonmarketing subjects, as well as among the functional fields of business administration. Marketing managers will find it increasingly difficult to clearly distinguish between marketing and nonmarketing, between business and nonbusiness activities. The result of this interdisciplinary focus will be a better understanding of societal environments. The very foundations of business strategy are shaped by the environmental forces discussed in this book.

This accelerating rate of change means that it is easy for well-educated marketing students to become professionally obsolete in a few short years. The best insurance against obsolescence is individual commitment to the need for continuing study and professional growth. Indeed, to a greater degree than ever before, this commitment will be a prerequisite for success in the dynamic marketing environment of the future.

Any marketing curriculum provides only the foundation from which to continue self-education and development. Tomorrow's manager must continue to educate himself, and those with whom he works, if capabilities are to keep pace with the demands and opportunities of marketing.

The basic thrust of this book is influenced by systems theory. The systems approach is presented as an organizational orientation—as a way of studying marketing management problems. Systems analysis will continue to affect the development of the marketing management philosophy and the marketing concept. Both are, in fact, systems concepts. They emphasize the coordination and linkage of marketing elements to achieve a total system of business action. Thus, the systems approach—with its emphasis on adjustment, survival, and growth—and the study of marketing as an input-output system reinforce the environmental perspective.

Several of the concepts and ideas presented in this book have been restated and extended in summary form in this last chapter. The student or manager who has leadership as a goal must continue to study these themes and seek their integration. Each serious marketing student should develop an operational framework within which he can appraise and place marketing developments and opportunities as they relate to his special sphere of interests.

MANAGERIAL MARKETING: A CONCEPTUAL FRAMEWORK

In the past it would have been generally appropriate to define the boundaries of managerial marketing as being confined only to internal managerial dimensions, the emphasis being placed on the policy, strategy, and decision-making aspects of marketing planning. However, present trends are changing the emphasis of marketing in a new direction. Environmental issues are expanding marketing development into the new area of social marketing. The changing societal priorities as well as general environmental changes necessitate that such change be not only accepted, but also anticipated. From this view develops the obvious, that the firm match its own resources with the potential opportunities arising from such changes in order to maintain survival and growth.

Time is of the essence in adapting to change. Management must monitor the environment for evolving change and then without unnecessary delay capitalize on the opportunities created. It must also be remembered that, in marketing planning because of the influence of the passing of time, the focal point of the firm becomes the future and not the past.

The development of marketing thought has advanced through various stages. This is reflected by the role marketing has played in an advancing industrial economy. From its initial role of performing a disposal function for the nation's production output, marketing thought has passed through a sales orientation period, a consumer orientation period, a marketing control orientation period, and now marketing thought is entering a social orientation period. With each advancing stage marketing's emphasis has changed. However, the past has always been incorporated into the succeeding stage, but on a modified level. Thus, as the economy progresses there develops a broader concept of marketing.

The present volume has taken a micromarketing systems view, emphasizing the marketing management function of the firm. The companion volume on social marketing has concentrated on the macromarketing system perspective. The two volumes together have defined the present and the evolving state of marketing thought.

The present volume has stressed the importance of (1) the managerial approach to marketing, (2) utilization of the marketing concept as the directive force in marketing planning and development, and (3) the coordination and integration of the elements of the marketing mix.

CONSUMER BEHAVIOR MODELS AND THEORIES

The marketing concept emphasizes the consumer as the pivotal axis around which marketing development, planning, research, and the emerging dimension of social responsibility all revolve and depend. The dynamic and continually changing characteristics of consumer expectations requires the same of the field of marketing. The concern is not only for the present existing characteristics of the consumer, but also for the developing trends that shall define the future. The projections made will enable the marketer to avoid dying markets, enter new markets, and overcome the constraint of time. Anticipation and expectancy, and not surprise, should define the future of the marketplace.

Dynamic marketing is concerned with understanding the consumer and the changing consumer demographics. It is concerned with the understanding of the restructuring of the consumer's "psychological field," especially with reference to attitudes and values. In addition, dynamic marketing concentrates on the influence of change and how it affects aspects such as time and place convenience, motivations and needs, the self-concept, social interaction, lifestyles, and the physical versus the psychological dimensions of a product. There is also the challenge of pictorially modelling the total complexities of consumer behavior in order to understand the consumer even more than ever thought possible. To date, this challenge has only partially, yet significantly, been met. However, with further research new frontiers will be achieved.

In total, then, what is required is the adoption and utilization of a "consumer orientation" concept. In essence, this is the marketing concept —a concept that places the focus of the marketing planner on consumer needs and satisfactions first, and then on marketing mix elements and the broader aspects of marketing policy. Market and competitive pressures make the consumer orientation vital to the survival and growth of the firm. Therefore, marketing managers must be environmentalists, anticipators of change, and creative innovators in order to meet market problems and opportunities.

MARKETING MANAGEMENT ACTIVITIES

The primary construct that guides the marketing management activities of the firm is the systems approach. The marketing division of a firm is only one of the functional units of the organization. This unit, like all other units, finds itself interacting not only with other units, but also interacting within its own division between various departments. Thus, marketing management must remember that the activities it carries out will be viewed from various perspectives.

The major activities of the marketing management group involve: decision making, marketing opportunity assessment, planning and programming, marketing organization, and leadership dimensions and control. The group may also be involved in multinational marketing activities.

The task of marketing decision making involves confronting environmental uncertainties in a systematic and logical way. It also seeks the goal of achieving effective utilization of the marketing mix variables under the firm's command. In the attempt to attain the level of accomplishment sought by marketing decisions, the management group utilizes both models and information systems. These tools provide the firm with a continuous monitoring system.

The assessment of marketing opportunity requires the organization of resources in a creative and innovative way in order to take advantage of developing opportunities. Programmed product innovation, anticipation and adaptation to change, utilization of R & D, and sales forecasting are all critical elements to a firm seeking survival.

Marketing planning incorporates an objective achievement orientation in the development of marketing strategies. The formulation of these marketing strategies involves objective definition, target setting, and the selection of the appropriate marketing mix. To aid in the development of marketing plans, the firm can utilize various quantitative models. However, it must be remembered that such models are tools and not a panacea for marketing planners.

One of the most important aspects in the area of marketing organization and leadership is the fact that the achievement of the corporate goals can only become a reality if a total organization systems perspective is taken not only by the marketing department, but also by the other functional units within the firm. Furthermore, participation and cooperation are required by all marketing personnel if total support of their ideas and the attainment of corporate goals are to be achieved.

The control of the marketing system can be greatly facilitated by the adoption of an integrated systems approach that leads to the understanding of the interdependency of the various areas of the firm. To aid in the achievement of the described level of control, the firm has at its disposal such tools as computer simulation and various other quantitative techniques.

Finally, the task of firms involved in international markets is to uncover possible marketing universals, as well as to decide to what extent their present organization and marketing mix have to be modified or even totally changed to meet foreign requirements.

Thus, the marketing management activities of the firm are numerous, complex, and vital to the proper functioning of the firm.

MANAGING THE MARKETING MIX

The attainment of an optimum marketing mix is through creatively coordinating the various elements of the mix through the use of the systems approach. A sensitivity to environmental changes is also essential.

The uncertainty of the marketplace directly affects the product/service mix decisions of the firm since in order to achieve and maintain growth and survival both successful revenue generation and customer satisfaction must be attained. Uncertainty hinders such success. Furthermore, in determining the product/service mix, an understanding is required of the product life cycle, the many interfaces of the product manager, changing distribution channels, and the internal and external influence product line pricing generates.

In analyzing the distribution mix segment of the marketing mix, primary concern is with the transportation and warehousing of the product. Decision making in this area involves balancing the cost and time dimensions (as they relate to customer satisfaction) involved in moving the product through the channels of distribution. The various functionaries within the channel (from manufacturers to retailers) have a tendency to change their roles over time and thereby abandon traditional means of distribution. It takes an alert marketer to be able to anticipate and adapt to such changes as they evolve.

The final element of the marketing mix, the communications mix, involves areas such as personal selling, advertising, and promotions. Through the systems approach the communication mix is integrated with the other two marketing mix elements to achieve a balanced marketing program. In the past, communications theory was applied mainly to the consumer market, but marketers now realize the relevance and importance of communications in the area of industrial marketing. Finally, for firms advertising in international markets interest lies in whether or not effective communication universals exist.

Thus, the firm's marketing mix reflects the many complex and highly important dimensions that are involved in marketing planning.

EDUCATION FOR MARKETING

The area of marketing education should be considered in any future-oriented discussion of marketing. Marketing as a discipline involves intellectual problems of a high order of educational and social importance. Because of its social significance, marketing is an area of major importance in the modern institution of higher learning. University courses and curricula should reflect and lend direction to the changing needs of society. The modern university is the laboratory of society, and modern education should have its focus in the world of reality. Students in all areas of specialization should be familiar with marketing as a social process. Graduates of professional schools are concerned with intellect, values, ethics, esthetics, and important ideas of the times. Business administration courses, including those in the marketing sector, can be as broadly intellectual, educational, and challenging as those of any other discipline.

Our society is not faced with the question of whether there should or should not be university education in marketing. Such a question evades the realistic issues. We shall have marketing education on both the undergraduate and graduate levels. Moreover, the numbers educated will continue to expand. The real questions confronting executives and teachers are what forms marketing education of the future *should* take and what forms it *will* take.

Marketing's role in society, as it has been portrayed in this book, is a more formative factor than university curricula now reflect. Marketing is a dynamic social process of direct relevance to many other university curricula. It is a major and distinguishing characteristic of American business. Marketing knowledge and technology are being studied and adapted on a global basis within the context of various economic systems. An understanding of marketing is, in fact, essential to develop a thorough comprehension of our economic system, our way of business life, and our very lifestyles.

The marketing discipline itself is in a state of flux. It is not a mature discipline with a well-established body of information, theories, and principles that have been shaped and structured and institutionalized through centuries of university affiliation. Rather, marketing is a discipline and phenomenon of our century and of the American culture. As a field of study it is very young.

The marketing curriculum or approach of any one school either now or in the future will not be superior to all others. Although desirable goals in marketing education have been identified rather clearly, the means of achieving them will vary. It is unrealistic to expect all business schools to offer the same marketing curriculum. No one superior model exists, and educational strength is rooted in diversity.

Marketing education need not produce narrow, specialized, uneducated graduates. True professionalism requires both specialization and breadth in education. Marketing as a professional area must have educational objectives that are broader than job requirements. This requires striking a delicate and rather difficult balance between general education and professional competence, between broad preparation for life and more specialized professional education. Knowledge gained from the liberal arts and the sciences is valuable for marketing students. Yet it is not a substitute for education in marketing. General education furnishes a broad base on which marketing can build. However, the converse is also true. Knowledge of marketing is of great value to students in various scientific areas. As of now this is not widely recognized nor accepted.

The discipline of marketing may be entering a new stage of development. There has been a clear trend away from the study of current practice to emphasis on the sciences underlying marketing, away from primary concern with immediate considerations to greater attention to the scientific, theoretical, intellectual, and social content of marketing. This trend is likely to continue and will probably result in new incentives and opportunity for the extension of marketing's frontiers and for the relating of marketing to other disciplines. It now seems likely that marketing is on the verge of significant breakthroughs along a number of fronts. It is also likely that advances in marketing education and practice will add significant knowledge to other disciplines.

AUTHOR INDEX

SUBJECT INDEX

This book has been set in 10 and 9 point Caledonia, leaded 2 points. Chapter numbers and section letters are in 48 point Baskerville, and chapter and section titles are in 24 point Baskerville. Reading number and titles are in 14 point Baskerville. The size of the type page is 27 × 46½ picas.